CAMBRIDGE STUDIES
IN ENGLISH LEGAL HISTORY
Edited by
HAROLD DEXTER HAZELTINE, LITT.D., F.B.A.
Of the Inner Temple, Barrister-at-Law;
Downing Professor of the Laws of England in
the University of Cambridge

IOANNIS SELDENI
Ad Fletam Dissertatio

IOANNIS SELDENI
Ad Fletam Dissertatio

REPRINTED FROM THE EDITION OF
1647 WITH PARALLEL TRANSLATION
INTRODUCTION AND NOTES BY

DAVID OGG

Fellow and Tutor of
New College Oxford

CAMBRIDGE
AT THE UNIVERSITY PRESS
1925

CAMBRIDGE UNIVERSITY PRESS
Cambridge, New York, Melbourne, Madrid, Cape Town,
Singapore, São Paulo, Delhi, Mexico City

Cambridge University Press
The Edinburgh Building, Cambridge CB2 8RU, UK

Published in the United States of America by Cambridge University Press, New York

www.cambridge.org
Information on this title: www.cambridge.org/9781107682115

© Cambridge University Press 1925

This publication is in copyright. Subject to statutory exception
and to the provisions of relevant collective licensing agreements,
no reproduction of any part may take place without the written
permission of Cambridge University Press.

First published 1925
First paperback edition 2013

A catalogue record for this publication is available from the British Library

ISBN 978-1-107-68211-5 Paperback

Cambridge University Press has no responsibility for the persistence or
accuracy of URLs for external or third-party internet websites referred to in
this publication, and does not guarantee that any content on such websites is,
or will remain, accurate or appropriate.

TO
MY WIFE

CONTENTS

	PAGES
GENERAL PREFACE BY H. D. HAZELTINE . .	ix–xvi
PREFACE	xvii, xviii
INTRODUCTION	xix–lxvi
AD FLETAM DISSERTATIO WITH PARALLEL TRANSLATION AND NOTES . . .	2–197
INDEX	199–204

THE HISTORICAL BACKGROUND OF SELDEN'S *DISSERTATIO AD FLETAM*

To many persons of our time John Selden is known only by their perusal of the *Table Talk*; and in that little classic of our literature, wherein fragments of Selden's learned and familiar discourse were preserved for posterity by his Boswell-like friend, Richard Milward, they gain the picture of a shrewd man of the world who struck with equal force, and not seldom in a spirit of satire and jest, at the frailties of all parties and all creeds. Other persons have knowledge of Selden as the great jurist who replied, in his *Mare Clausum*, to the *Mare Liberum* of his famous contemporary, Hugo Grotius; while there are those who think of him either as an orientalist of distinction or as a prominent public man speaking in Parliament on the great issues of his age or arguing cases of constitutional import in the Courts. With the increase of interest in institutional and legal development, the historians of our time are coming to look upon Selden in still a different light. To them he stands as the representative of a group of antiquaries and lawyers who, in the first half of the seventeenth century, turned their attention to a study of ancient records and to the writing of books on the history of the laws and constitutional institutions of the realm. Of all the members of that brilliant company of scholars, which included men like Cotton, Camden, Spelman, and Hale, it was Selden who possessed, in the judgment of the good critics of his and our day, the deepest learning and the broadest historical vision.

No one of Selden's contributions to legal history, not even the *Titles of Honour* or the *History of Tithes*, presents his learning and historical vision to better advantage than the *Dissertatio ad Fletam*. In this essay, which first appeared as an introduction to the edition of *Fleta* in 1647, Selden gives an historical account

of the English medieval law-books and the influence of Roman and Canon laws on Continental and English legal development. Although regarded from Selden's day to our own as one of the valuable writings upon these subjects, the *Dissertatio ad Fletam* has never appeared in a satisfactory edition. The first printed text contains mistakes; and the later editions of 1685 and 1726 are also far from faultless. Students of law and history will consider it, therefore, as a fortunate circumstance that Mr Ogg has chosen to devote much painstaking and scholarly labour to the preparation of a new and critical edition and to the writing of an Introduction which carries us, in a pleasureful and profitable manner, into the atmosphere of the historical problems which Selden endeavoured to solve. Mr Ogg's studies, both in this country and abroad, had well fitted him for his task. Through the writing of his *Cardinal de Retz* he was brought, moreover, into close touch with Selden's age; and although the subject of this book is somewhat limited, due to the fact that the Cardinal had little to offer to the biographer and historian except his human frailties, his literary genius, and his sense of humour, yet the preparatory studies which Mr Ogg pursued awakened in him a live interest in the seventeenth century. That early interest has already borne fruit in the volume entitled *Europe in the Seventeenth Century*, a recent study of Continental history in which the author prepares us, in more than one direction, for the reading of his edition of the *Dissertatio ad Fletam*; for Selden's essay is one of the characteristic products of European scholarship in the seventeenth century and closely allied, both in subject-matter and in method of treatment, to many Continental legal writings of the time.

It is peculiarly fitting that a Fellow of New College, Oxford, should be the editor of the *Dissertatio ad Fletam*. Selden received his University education at Oxford, where he was a member of Hart Hall, now Hertford College; and, moreover, he was indebted for part of his early training, as Mr Ogg's recent researches have revealed, to three New College men. In Lincoln's Inn Library Mr Ogg has examined the original MS. of an autobiographical fragment written by Selden in Latin in

his own hand[1]; while he has also transcribed, in the Bodleian, a later version of the fragment written in a late seventeenth or early eighteenth-century hand[2]. This fragment of Selden's autobiography, no further parts of which can be traced, appears to have been unknown to all of Selden's biographers and to all the editors of his writings, including Wilkins and Kelham; and, so far as can be ascertained, no previous reference has ever been made to it in print[3]. Mr Ogg decided not to make use of the fragment in the writing of his Introduction to the *Dissertatio ad Fletam*; and he has allowed me to use his transcript in the present place.

The important fact disclosed by the fragment is that Selden not only studied at Chichester Grammar School under Hugh Barker, the master, a distinguished New College man, but that while at Oxford he also came under the 'tutela' of two junior fellows of New College, Anthony Barker, who was Hugh Barker's brother, and John Yonge. One would like to have precise knowledge in regard to the influence wielded by these three New College men on the formation of the great jurist's character and tastes in scholarship; but the fragment, which is our only source of information, is provokingly silent on these points. It gives, however, one hint. Selden's reference to Hugh Barker, if that reference be interpreted liberally, could easily lead one to the conclusion that it may have been this Oxford civilian and canonist, Doctor of Civil Law and Dean of the Arches, who, in the last years of the sixteenth century, when Selden was under his instruction at Chichester, first interested the future jurist in the study of the two Romanic laws, the history of which, both on the Continent and in England, he traces at some length in the *Dissertatio ad Fletam*.

Selden's essay was written at a time when the sixteenth century, the age of transition from medieval to modern times, was already a matter of history. Renaissance, Reformation, and Nationalism, three of the main forces of that transforming century, had already stamped themselves indelibly upon the

---

[1] Hale MSS. XIII, No. 42.   [2] Smith MS. 103, f. 33.
[3] The sole exception is in the article on Selden in the *D.N.B.*, where it is mentioned among the authorities.

laws and jurisprudential thought as well as upon the social, religious, and political ideas and institutions of Europe. Moreover, before Selden wrote his *Dissertatio ad Fletam* the Reception of the foreign laws by Germany had already overwhelmed, in a revolutionary manner, the native laws and customs of that country; and in many of the other regions of Europe the political and legal ideas of the Bartolist jurists had been adopted, in greater or lesser degree, as a means of strengthening the machinery of national territorial states and of furthering the tendency towards absolutism. When, therefore, we study Selden's essay, we should hold these historical facts in mind. They help us to understand Selden's views as to the course of legal development on the Continent and in England; and they also present to us the environment in which the jurist's treatise was written.

To students of the *Dissertatio ad Fletam* the history of the Renaissance, and more particularly the history of the legal humanism of that epoch, is of special importance. In their protest against the medievalism of the Bartolist jurists, who dominated the theory and practice of the law, and in their endeavour to reconstruct the pure Roman Law of the classical jurists, undefiled by Byzantine and Bolognese jurisprudence, the humanists had brought to their aid the auxiliary sciences of philology, literature, and history. In developing their own method of legal study, the *mos Gallicus*, as opposed to the *mos Italicus* of the Bartolists, the humanists laid special emphasis upon the importance of historical investigation; and such studies were, indeed, an essential part of their effort to go 'back to the sources.' The Italian legal humanists of the fifteenth century had already drawn attention to the need of viewing the law from an historical standpoint; and it was, in fact, Valla's pupil, Pomponius Leto, who first attempted to reconstruct Roman legal history. In the sixteenth century, however, the French school of legal humanism, represented by Alciati, Cujas, Douaren, Doneau, Baudouin, and Hotman, brought the historical study of the Roman Law into the forefront of their programme of juristic reform; and in some respects the main

GENERAL PREFACE xiii

purpose of the school was summarised by Baudouin's famous remark, *sine historia caecam esse jurisprudentiam*. Nor were the historical investigations of the Renaissance jurists confined to the Roman Law; for, while Cujas and other scholars in France and elsewhere were reconstructing Roman legal history, Antonio Agostino, the great Spanish civilian and canonist of the sixteenth century, a humanist of the highest distinction, was founding also the historical study of the Canon Law.

The humanist civilians and canonists of the Renaissance were, in truth, the creators of legal history as a branch of juristic study; and as early as the sixteenth century itself their example was followed by the 'national jurists.' In all, or nearly all, the countries of Europe jurists, many of them trained in the Civil and Canon Law, turned their attention to the study of the native legal materials. They re-edited the medieval law-books and sources; and they wrote historical and systematic treatises upon the native and customary law. By their pioneer work they founded indeed the historical study of the several national legal systems of Europe; and, for this reason, they are to be revered as the predecessors of those great legal historians of our own day who have set themselves to the task of writing the history of the laws of Europe.

The influence of legal humanism upon the establishment of studies in English legal history is one of the cardinal facts which every reader of Selden's essay should bear in mind. In England, no less than in other countries, investigations in the history of the national law had their beginning in the sixteenth century, under the inspiration of the ideas and methods of the humanists; and, in the early seventeenth century, in Selden's time, a scientific school of English legal history was definitely founded. The work of that school, of which Selden was one of the leaders, was largely shaped by humanism. Humanism, indeed, helped to mould Selden, as it helped to mould his predecessors and his contemporaries; and this influence is illustrated in a striking manner by the *Dissertatio ad Fletam*. Particularly in those portions of the essay which deal with the history of the Roman and Canon laws on the Continent Selden's reliance

upon Alciati, Cujas, and other legal writers of the Renaissance, is marked. Not only do the humanists furnish Selden with historical facts; they shape many of his own views, as, for example, his view of the value of ancient legal writings and of the loss to scholarship caused by Tribonian in preserving in the Digest only fragments of the classical jurists. Selden's own attitude towards the schools of humanism and natural law is reflected in the *Table Talk*, where, in speaking of 'Learning,' he remarks: 'The Jesuites and the lawyers of France, and the low-country men, have engrossed all learning. The rest of the world make nothing but homilies.'

The reader of Selden's essay has need, therefore, to acquaint himself with the juristic and legal history of the age of the Renaissance; for only by this means can he properly understand the jurist's historical materials and methods, and form a true estimate of the place which his essay holds in the literature of legal history. If, however, our knowledge of the juristic and legal history of Europe be even more extensive, if it include not only the transitional epoch of the Renaissance, but also the centuries which preceded and followed it, we are the better prepared to appreciate the broader aspects of that long evolution which Selden partly presents to us. What we need, in fact, is a vision of the vast historical background of twenty centuries in the East and in the West. Grasping the whole of the Christian era with our mind's eye, we can see the action and reaction of the forces of history, we can behold both the rise and the decline of great movements in the past and also the present state of other great movements that are still in the ascendency. The struggle of two of these dominant movements in European history, the conflict caused by the spread and development of Romanic and of non-Romanic laws, is of vital interest to the reader of Selden's essay. Only certain aspects of that ceaseless strife come to the surface in Selden's pages: but, looking back on a longer range of history than the one which Selden surveyed, we of the twentieth century can see clearly that the Romanism which dominated the legal life of the later middle age has suffered a decline and that the significant note of the

GENERAL PREFACE

modern history of the civil laws of Europe has been the rise and progress of those elements that are Germanic, native, national, non-Romanic.

Students of English law and history will be particularly interested in Selden's account of the influence of Roman and Canon laws on the Common Law: nor will they have less interest in Mr Ogg's paragraphs upon this subject. His conclusion on one important point should be noticed. 'On the whole,' he remarks, 'Selden's contention is right: at no other period of our legal history are the commonplaces of Roman Law doctrine so frequently cited in court as in the reign of Edward II.' Mr Ogg adds, however, that the citing of maxims is, in itself, 'no evidence of any real Roman Law influence'; and yet, 'it must be admitted that the legal maxims have played some part in the development of our law.' To our learned editor's account of this matter one further instructive instance of the use of maxims may be appended. In *Anon.* v. *Page*[1], a case already mentioned by Mr Plucknett in dealing with Romanic influence on the early Year Books[2], Spigurnel, counsel for the plaintiff, remarked that 'he that pledges his oath to his adversary makes his adversary his judge.' Mr Bolland, commenting on this passage, says that 'it looks as if Spigurnel misquoted a Romanist maxim originally applied to the quite different case of tendering a decisory oath to the adversary, which does not occur in the Common Law.'

To Mr Ogg's learned Introduction another point may be added. In support of his view that Roman Law had become unknown in the common law courts in the reign of Edward III, Selden cites the Year Book case of the Abbot of Torre[3]. Sir Frederick Pollock, in his valued notes to Maine's *Ancient Law*[4], has pointed out, however, that Selden, with all his learning, misunderstood the case, and thereby misled Blackstone at a later time. There is nothing in the case, Sir Frederick Pollock

---

[1] Y.BB., Eyre of Kent, 6 & 7 Edward II, 1313-4, vol. II (edited by Mr Bolland for the Selden Society), p. 54.
[2] See *Statutes and their Interpretation in the First Half of the Fourteenth Century* (Cambridge Studies in English Legal History), pp. 36-38.
[3] Mich. 22 Ed. III, f. 14, ed. 1561; see pp. 157-161, *infra*.
[4] Pp. 117, 118.

concludes, which 'shows very gross ignorance, although the language might not satisfy a learned civilian; the Court, so far from treating Roman words of art as nonsense, professed to understand them quite enough for the purpose in hand.... [Selden's] general thesis that knowledge of Roman Law in England, except among professed canonists, declined rapidly after the reign of Edward II, is doubtless correct. But there was no question of hostility. Not the fourteenth or thirteenth, but the sixteenth century was the time of recrimination between common lawyers and civilians, and perhaps of some real danger to the Common Law.'

Although interest in Romanic influence on English Law was awakened in the sixteenth century, and although some of the legal writings of that main century of the Renaissance deal with aspects of Romanism in England, the earliest of the works that have survived as classics come to us from the middle of the seventeenth century. Selden's *Dissertatio ad Fletam* appeared in 1647; six years later Duck's *De Usu et Authoritate Juris Civilis* was first published. While recognizing the great value of Duck's long eighth chapter on the history of Roman Law in England, scholars will always assign to Selden's essay a special place in our literature as the first important investigation of this subject. Many writings on Roman legal influence in England have appeared since the days of Selden and Duck; and among them the essays of Güterbock, Stubbs, Maitland, Lord Justice Scrutton, and Sir Paul Vinogradoff, as well as the historical treatises of Pollock and Maitland and of Dr Holdsworth, have brought to light many facts unknown to the pioneers of the seventeenth century. The present edition of the *Dissertatio ad Fletam* places Selden's text in the setting of this wealth of later scholarship. The results of Mr Ogg's research prove to us that in the main Selden's essay has stood the test of time, and that even in the critical atmosphere of our age it is still worthy of careful study as one of the leading contributions to English legal history.

H. D. H.

PREFACE

THERE exist three distinct editions of the *Ad Fletam Dissertatio*—that of 1647, that of 1685, and the text published by Wilkins in his complete *Opera* of Selden (1726). The texts of 1647 and 1685 appeared as appendices to the reprints of *Fleta*: in Wilkins' edition, the *Dissertatio* was printed with the other works of Selden. Of these three texts, the first has numerous mistakes, some of which were corrected in a short list of *corrigenda* printed at the end of the volume; the 1685 edition incorporated these corrections, but repeated the uncorrected mistakes (with additional misprints): for the third edition, that of 1726, Selden's editor simply repeated the text of 1647, copying even the most obvious printers' errors, omitting to make any use of the 1647 *corrigenda* and perpetuating a fresh crop of misprints. Accordingly the text reprinted here, together with Selden's notes, is that of 1647, with the misprints corrected. The MS. of the *Dissertatio* does not appear to have survived Selden's lifetime: no trace of it nor reference to it has been found by the present writer.

A verbose and inaccurate translation of the *Dissertatio* by the eighteenth-century lawyer and antiquarian, Robert Kelham, was published in 1771, an edition which made no attempt to deal with the questions raised by the text. For whatever reason, this is now a very rare book. Since its appearance, no work of Selden's has been reprinted, except the *Table Talk* collected by his amanuensis the Rev. Richard Milward and first published in 1689. Its convenient size and the general interest of its subject are the main reasons why the *Ad Fletam Dissertatio* has been chosen to represent Selden in this series. The circumlocutions of seventeenth-century Latin generally warrant a freer translation than would be permissible with a classical text, but actual abridgments in my translation are specially indicated. Selden's style is so diffuse and involved that, from a literary point of view, he has little to lose by translation; on the other hand I have aimed always at interpreting his meaning accurately. The notes

AUTHOR'S PREFACE

added to the translation have been restricted to as small number as possible and are intended to facilitate reference to Selden's authorities as well as to indicate the results of modern research on the chief topics discussed. The references in these notes and in the introduction to MSS. are to the MSS. in the British Museum, except where otherwise stated.

In taking leave of this task, I wish that its performance were more worthy of the subject and of the very generous assistance afforded me. Its inception is due mainly to the inspiring teaching of Sir Paul Vinogradoff, whose services to the allied studies of law and history are second only to those of Selden himself. The general editor of the series, Professor Hazeltine, aided me with the introduction by making several helpful suggestions and criticisms: Dr de Zulueta, Regius Professor of Civil Law in the University of Oxford, assisted me with practical counsel and saved me from several blunders. To the Rev. H. E. Salter, Fellow of Magdalen College, Oxford, to Dr W. C. Bolland, of the Inner Temple, and to Mr G. R. Y. Radcliffe, Fellow and Bursar of New College, Oxford, I am indebted for guidance on specific points submitted to them. Mr H. L. Henderson, Fellow and Tutor of New College, corrected many misprints in the 1647 edition and gave both skilful and unstinted help with the translation: had this generous help not been available, it would not have been possible for me to complete this work. For mistakes, however, whether in the introduction, the notes or the translation, the present writer is solely responsible.

In conclusion, I wish to thank the Syndics of the Cambridge University Press for undertaking to publish a book which may, it is hoped, do a little to encourage a revived study of Selden in English-speaking lands.

DAVID OGG

March 1925

INTRODUCTION

THE *Ad Fletam Dissertatio* was written when Selden was in his sixty-third year, after he had attained to full maturity of his great intellectual powers, and its subject—the reception of Roman Law in mediaeval Europe—was eminently fitted for a display of the unique store of erudition accumulated by the most learned person who ever left Oxford without taking a degree. At the time when the debt of modern civilisation to the mediaeval and ancient past is being more eagerly investigated and more accurately gauged, Selden's *Dissertatio* still has its value both as a pioneer contribution to a great subject and the starting-point for all estimates of Roman Law influence on the ideas and institutions of later times.

It is with this short work of Selden's, originally printed as an explanatory essay to the first printed edition of the anonymous *Fleta*, that the present introduction is concerned.

This edition[1] of *Fleta* was based on the unique MS. (in Selden's custody), but in the *Dissertatio* appended thereto, Selden disclaimed all responsibility for the numerous mistakes in the printed text of *Fleta*, explaining that he wrote his essay only at the earnest request of the publishers, who desired their edition to be accompanied by some kind of explanatory treatise dealing with the questions raised by the publication of this anonymous fourteenth-century MS. The first chapter of Selden's Dissertation is devoted to a brief exposition of the historical value of legal writings which, from the practitioner's point of view, have been rendered obsolete by subsequent legal changes. In his second chapter Selden considers the relationship of Bracton's *De Legibus* to its epitomes, such as *Fleta*, *Britton* and the *Summa* of Thornton: he suggests that the compilation known as *Britton* was not, as was commonly supposed, the work of a bishop of Hereford named Britton, but was a working summary of Bracton, or rather Bratton[2], and received its title from a corruption of that

---

[1] 1647.
[2] For the name and some new biographical details, see Komar, 'De Origine Vitaque Brattonis Varia' in *Illinois Law Review*, vol. XVI (1922), pp. 516–522, 586–608.

name. This chapter contains an account of Selden's MS. of Thornton's *Summa*. A disquisition on the Lex Regia and Bracton's interpretation of it provides material for the third[1] chapter: the fourth[2] deals with the use of imperial law in England during the Roman occupation and contains a conjecture that not only Papinian but also Ulpian and Paul may have practised in this country. In the fifth[3] chapter Selden studies the Theodosian Code, correcting a widespread error in regard to the date of its promulgation: the use made by the Church of the so-called Donation of Constantine he condemns in scathing terms. In the sixth[4] chapter he attributes to the monks Ivo and Gratian the enterprise of combining elements from the Codes with the Canons in order that they might cheat secular rulers and subjects: the same chapter gives an account of the legal revival at Bologna associated with the name of Irnerius. In chapter VII[5] the subject of Roman Law influence in England is resumed: here Selden describes William of Malmesbury's well-known MS. containing the Alarician Breviary, and gives an account of Vacarius and the teaching of Roman Law in the England of Stephen's reign. Chapter VIII[6] illustrates the use of imperial jurisprudence during the period from Henry III to Edward III, after which, according to our authority, it ceased to be of force in English courts other than in certain exceptional or local jurisdictions. The reasons for English aversion from the use of civil law principles in our government are considered in the ninth chapter[7], where tribute is paid to English reverence for the common law. In the tenth[8] and last chapter Selden returns to *Fleta*, conjecturing that it was compiled in the Fleet prison, in the reign of Edward I, by a prisoner, possibly one of the legal functionaries deposed for malpractices by the judicial inquisition of 1288. A remarkable passage in *Fleta* concerning royal alienations gives him a final occasion for displaying his erudition, as well as an opportunity for a parting thrust at the clergy. Selden had never forgotten the clerical attacks on his *History of Tithes*.

[1] *Infra*, pp. 21–41.
[2] *Infra*, pp. 43–55.
[3] *Infra*, pp. 55–83.
[4] *Infra*, pp. 83–103.
[5] *Infra*, pp. 103–133.
[6] *Infra*, pp. 133–161.
[7] *Infra*, pp. 161–177.
[8] *Infra*, pp. 177–197.

INTRODUCTION

Such, in brief outline, are the most noteworthy contents of the *Dissertatio*. Its author wrote at a time when serious historical research was becoming possible, when the parliamentary lawyers were ransacking the national records for precedents and arguments, when the great wealth of mediaeval literature—despised throughout the Renaissance—was beginning to be appreciated, and when, owing to the intelligent munificence of collectors like Sir Robert Cotton and Sir Symonds d'Ewes, important manuscripts were, for the first time, becoming accessible to scholars. It was the age of Coke, Spelman, Lambarde and Prynne, a period of attempts to define the system labelled Feudalism and to illustrate its principles by the reprinting of old texts. In this burst of antiquarian enthusiasm it is not surprising that many mistakes were made: the *Dissertatio* provides ample evidence of the merits and demerits of a scholarship which, while robust, was not always discriminating, for the material at its disposal had not yet been fully sifted and examined. Selden made good use of his resources. He cited from his own manuscripts, many of them unique. He had access to the collection of Sir Robert Cotton, afterwards the nucleus of the great store of manuscripts in the British Museum. He was an assiduous researcher in the Exchequer archives. The mediaeval chronicles familiar to modern readers in the *Rolls Series*, the *Patrologia Latina* and the *Monumenta Germaniae Historica*, were, in many cases, known to him in MS. or in the sixteenth-century printed versions. A classical scholar and Orientalist, he was also a pioneer in those studies which the publications of the modern Selden Society have done so much to encourage. In none of his contemporaries was the historical sense[1] so highly developed, and probably none of his successors can claim to rival him in sheer weight of learning.

The first obvious characteristic of the *Dissertatio* is the great wealth of its sources. Of the MSS. referred to, the most important are the *Thornton*[2], the *Fleta*[3], the Collections of William[4] of

---

[1] See the two articles by Prof. Hazeltine in *Harvard Law Review*, XXIV, 105, 205, and in *Festschrift H. Brunner*, p. 579, on the subject of Selden as a historian.
[2] *Infra*, pp. 15-19.
[3] *Infra*, p. 3 and n. 1.
[4] *Infra*, p. 107 and n. 1.

xxii INTRODUCTION

Malmesbury containing the Alarician Breviary, and, lastly, the Inner Temple MS. of the Year Books[1]. Of these the second and third still survive, the one in the British Museum, the other in the Bodleian: the first and fourth are not now known to exist. The *Thornton* and the MS. of William of Malmesbury were the private property of Selden. Each MS. calls for special reference here.

(a) The *Thornton* was one of the MSS. which, on the dispersal[2] of Selden's library, went neither to the Bodleian nor to Lincoln's Inn, but was probably in one of the eight chests of his literary property destroyed by fire at the Inner Temple in January, 1679[3]. On that occasion, in order to prevent the flames spreading further, a small library was exploded with such violence as to cause injury to several spectators. Two years earlier the Inner Temple had suffered some damage from fire: in 1666 it had shared in the disaster of the Great Fire of London: it is not unlikely therefore that the MS. of Thornton was lost in one of these conflagrations. It is possible also that the Inner Temple MS. of the Year Books shared the same fate. Selden's descriptions are the only authentic evidence we possess regarding these two MSS. These however are only two of the sources used by Selden for his *Dissertatio* and no longer traceable: reference to the following pages[4] will show how extensive is the loss incurred by posterity in this respect.

Recently a distinguished American scholar[5] has adduced a considerable weight of evidence to show that one of the Selden MSS. in Lincoln's Inn Library, catalogued as a *Bracton*, is really a *Thornton*. This he proves mainly from internal evidence: it corresponds, in several important respects, to the description given in the *Dissertatio*, and it contains special reference to a law-suit in which Thornton was known to be interested. It does not have the frontispiece illumination described by Selden and the arrangement of chapters is different. The inscription of Selden's motto in his handwriting shows that it was one of

---

[1] *Infra*, pp. 149–53 and 151, n. 2.
[2] For the distribution of Selden's library after his death, see Macrae, *Annals of the Bodleian*, 2nd ed., 110–120.
[3] *Calendar of Inner Temple Records* (1901), vol. III. xxx–xxxi.
[4] *E.g.* p. 11, n. 1; p. 13, n. 7; p. 31, n. 2; p. 35, n. 5; p. 147, n. 3; p. 149, n. 5.
[5] Dr Woodbine in *Law Quarterly Review*, XXV, 44.

his MSS., and for this reason it must be considered to have come into Selden's possession after 1647, the date of the *Dissertatio*: alternatively, it may have been mistaken by Selden himself for a *Bracton*, though this hypothesis is unlikely. On the whole, it seems reasonable to conclude that Lincoln's Inn Hale MS. CXXXV is the only surviving MS. of Thornton's *Summa* and that it was not described by Selden either because he mistook it for *Bracton* or because he acquired it after 1647.

(*b*) The problems which puzzled Selden in *Fleta* still perplex his successors. 'Tractatus iste...merito Fleta poterit appellari, quia in Fleta de jure Anglicano conscriptus est[1]': this is the sum of our knowledge regarding the authorship of the treatise. The records of the Fleet do not go beyond the seventeenth century, so we do not know the names of those who were consigned to this prison in the reign of Edward I. It is possible that the author was one of the lawyers deposed and imprisoned by the great judicial investigation of 1288: his book shows that he had used Bracton, that he had read Walter of Henley's treatise on Husbandry and that he was familiar with the internal administration of the royal household[2]. Beyond that we can only conjecture. Investigation at the British Museum and Record Office has failed to produce any clue regarding the authorship of this treatise. It would be tempting to make out a case for Hengham, but this could be supported only by the facts that Hengham was one of the imprisoned judges and that he was given to the composition of legal compendiums. The prisoner of the Fleet has been successful in maintaining his anonymity.

(*c*) The MS. of William of Malmesbury's historical and legal collections has been the subject of considerable investigation[3]. In 1885 Stubbs suggested[4] that it was written about the year 1130 by William of Malmesbury himself, who, however, is not likely to have been the original compiler. What Selden thought to be the Theodosian Code has proved, in reality, to be the Alarician Breviary: nevertheless this part of the MS. has been

---

[1] *Infra*, p. 186.
[2] See F. M. Nicholl's edition of *Britton* (2 vols., 1865), I, xxv.
[3] *Infra*, p. 107, n. 1.
[4] In a letter bound up with MS. Bodley Seld. Arch. B. 16.

xxiv INTRODUCTION

found of considerable value to nineteenth-century editors like Haenel[1] and Mommsen[2]. Its special interest for Selden was that, compared with the older MSS., it revealed a more advanced degree of daring in the process by which the Donation of Constantine came to be regarded as an integral part of the Theodosian Code, for the sanction addressed to Ablavius, hitherto added cautiously as an appendix, now figures unashamed in the second title of Book XVI[3]. Considering the later use made of it, the MS. may be regarded as the most valuable of all in Selden's possession.

(d) Maitland did not regard the Inner Temple MS. of the Year Books as definitely lost, but his own failure to find it suggests that, like the illuminated Thornton, it may have disappeared in one of the seventeenth-century conflagrations at the Inner Temple. On the other hand, however, there is no proof that it perished in this way and it is a notorious fact that in the past libraries were careless in lending MSS. Not a few valuable literary treasures have been inherited by their present 'owners' from ancestors who purposely or negligently failed to return such borrowed property. The Inner Temple MS. of the Year Books may have passed, in this way, into private ownership; the same process is known to have happened to other MSS. of the Year Books. Selden supposed that the Inner Temple MS. was a transcription from an original by Richard of Winchedon, and he cites what appear to be different comments by compiler and copyist: but it has been conjectured by Maitland that this hypothesis is wrong and that compiler and copyist were one and the same person—namely, Richard[4] of Winchedon. The interest of the MS. is that it contains not merely conventional citations from civil law Regulae Juris, but attempts to illustrate an English case from what was thought to be civil law doctrine.

The secondary authorities used in the *Dissertatio* will be seen to consist mainly of the French and to a less extent the German,

[1] *Novellae Constitutiones* (part VI of Corpus Juris Antejustiniani, 1844), XII–XIV. Haenel believed that the MS. is a late twelfth-century copy and that its original compiler used a mutilated Breviary and a canon law source. The original compiler was almost certainly not William of Malmesbury.
[2] See Mommsen and Meyer's edition of the Theodosian Code (Berlin, 1905), LXV–LXVII.
[3] *Infra*, p. 77, n. 3.   [4] *Infra*, p. 151, n. 2.

INTRODUCTION xxv

Italian and Spanish juristic writings of the sixteenth century. Without the great revival of Roman Law studies during the Renaissance, the *Dissertatio* would have been impossible. The leader of that revival was Alciati (1492–1550), who taught Roman Law at Avignon, Bourges, Pavia, Bologna and Ferrara: by his critical and to some extent philological treatment of the texts, Alciati trained up a great school of jurists, including Muretus and Panzirol, a tradition carried on by Cujas, Baudouin, Rebuffy, Hotman and the brothers Peter and Francis Pithou. The papal interdict on Roman Law studies in Paris, promulgated in 1219, was not removed until 1679: hence it was at universities such as those of Bourges, Orléans and Toulouse that these studies flourished. The work of the new schools was mainly editorial. Throughout the greater part of the sixteenth century, the old glossed editions were still being printed, but they gradually gave way to texts unencumbered by mediaeval comment; until in 1575 Haloander published at Antwerp the first unglossed edition of the Digests. Peter Pithou published texts of the Theodosian Novels and the post-Theodosian Novels[1], as well as the *Codex Canonum Vetus Ecclesiae Romanae*; his brother Francis edited texts of the *Leges Barbarorum* and the *Epitome* of Julian. In 1549 Jean du Tillet produced a part of the *Liber Singularis Regularum* of Ulpian and in 1550 the sixteen books of the Theodosian Code. Of these editorial restorers, the greatest was Cujas (1522–1590), whose textual labours served to give to the Corpus Juris something like its definitive form. Nor were the scholars of Germany, Italy and the Low Countries far behind in this work of producing unglossed and critical texts. The Ingoldstadt John Sichard (1499–1552) published a complete text of the Theodosian Code and the Alarician Breviary at Basle in 1528: in 1553 an edition of the *Basilica* came from Viglius of Zuichem; in 1558, Scrimgeour, at Geneva, edited the first edition of the Greek Novels of Justinian. The Florentine edition of the Digests appeared in 1553 by the enterprise of the Torelli brothers: the legislation of Lombard and Carolingian kings was made accessible in Lindenbrog's *Codex Legum Antiquarum*, published in 1613:

[1] 1571.

xxvi   INTRODUCTION

Goldast's compilation of imperial rescripts from Charlemagne to Charles V appeared at Frankfort in 1607. As a result of this scholarly activity, jurisprudence parted company with dialectic to join forces with history and philology: 'sine historia, caecam esse jurisprudentiam' was the aphorism in which Baudouin defined the new ideals. By the end of the sixteenth century material for jurists like Selden had been classified and printed; the clear waters of judicial editorship had swept away the cloudy 'absinth of Accursius.'

The magnitude of this material can be inferred even from a glance at the vast library of printed books owned and read by Selden[1]. It would have been superhuman to have avoided errors in utilising this profuse literary wealth: consequently there are certain mistakes in the *Dissertatio*, inevitable perhaps in a work of its period. The most obvious of these can be easily pointed out. Thus *Fleta*, Thornton, Hengham, *Britton* and even Andrew Horn are all grouped together with Bracton as if they formed a homogeneous class, and in this way an injustice is done to the characteristic and original work of Bracton. It seems strange that a man of Selden's learning should not have detected the gross fabrications in Horn's *Mirror of Magistrates*, and it is a remarkable fact that all his contemporaries took quite seriously the strange medley of 'horn and ivory[2]' which the London fishmonger passed off on an unsuspecting public. It was Reeves[3] who first cast suspicion on a book which Selden actually placed in the same category as the *De Legibus*. Nor does Selden appear to have suspected the debt of Bracton to Azo, though he was deeply versed in both; not till the nineteenth century was the debt revealed[4]: it remained for Maitland[5] and Vinogradoff[6] to show that Bracton's borrowings are not, as Sir Henry Maine assumed[7], mere plagiarisms, but discriminating and generally

---

[1] About 8000 volumes; now in the 'Selden end' of the Bodleian Library.
[2] See Maitland's preface to the Selden Society edition of *The Mirror of Magistrates*.
[3] *History of English Law* (1787), II, 359, quoted by Maitland, *op. cit.*
[4] By Güterbock, in his *Henricus de Bracton und Sein Verhältnis zum Römischen Rechte* (1862).
[5] In *Bracton and Azo* (Selden Society).
[6] See, for instance, *The Roman elements in Bracton's treatise* (*Yale Law Journal*, June 1923).
[7] *Ancient Law*, ch. IV.

INTRODUCTION xxvii

intelligent selections of material which might be utilised for the illustration of native legal rules.

But the most serious mistake made by Selden is his confusion regarding Vacarius, the first teacher of Roman Law in Britain. It was common in the sixteenth and seventeenth centuries to confuse the jurists Roger and Roffred: Selden went a step further when, relying on an imperfect text of the chronicle of Robert of Torigny, he identified Vacarius with Roger, abbot of Bec, whom, in turn, he confused with the jurist Roger. From these initial assumptions, Selden was led into a series of startling consequences. His first deduction was that as Roger of Bec had won fame by devoting himself (*vacare*) to law teaching, he came to be called Vacarius. On his return to Bec, Roger (*i.e.* Vacarius) resumed his ecclesiastical duties and was afterwards elected to the archbishopric of Canterbury, vacant by the murder of Thomas à Becket. From the assumption that abbot and jurist were identical, it followed that Vacarius was the author of a number of treatises in addition to the *Summa Pauperum*, which Selden knew of but had never seen[1]. Not even serious chronological difficulties could convince Selden that he was working not on one false hypothesis but on several, and so, in his hands, Vacarius assumes a variety of aliases that would have done justice to the most hardened criminal. From Vacarius he is transformed into Roger, then Froger, then Freger, then Frederick: we are not altogether unprepared when he makes his final appearance as Robert[2]. There is a glimpse of the real Vacarius in pope Alexander III's rescript to the abbot of Fountains, but Selden has already so transformed his hero that he does not recognise him in his natural garb, and thinks that he must be a double—another Vacarius, 'who succeeded Roger as expounder of imperial law in this country[3].' When Selden conjectures[4] that the jurist, placed by the Monk of Eynsham in the third circle of Purgatory, was 'native-born or here only for teaching purposes,' one breathes a sigh of relief that this deceased lawyer is not identified with Roger and that so the career of the chameleon-like abbot is not pursued into the realms beyond.

[1] *Infra*, pp. 111 and 121.   [2] *Infra*, p. 125.
[3] *Infra*, p. 121.   [4] *Infra*, p. 139.

xxviii   INTRODUCTION

Selden was led into these errors by an important omission in the Paris MS. of the Chronicle of Robert of Torigny. Unfortunately this MS. was published in 1619 by Duchesne, in his *Gesta Normannorum in Francia* where Selden, under the year 1148, read as follows: 'Obiit Bechardus VI abbas Becci cui successit Rogerius magister Vacarius.' Here there is an accidental omission of a paragraph between Rogerius and magister, a paragraph which makes it clear not only that Roger and Vacarius were quite distinct persons, but also that the information concerning Vacarius was added, not as concerning the abbey of Bec, but because it was of a general character such as might commend it to the readers of the chronicle. The average monastic scribe was quite capable of omissions as deceptive and as difficult to detect as this one. Had Selden been dependent solely on this defective text, his mistake would be pardonable, but he read Robert of Torigny in MS.[1] also, for his friend Sir Symonds d'Ewes possessed one of the MSS. of the chronicle. This MS. omits the reference to Vacarius altogether and so does not confuse the abbot with the lecturer; hence Selden ought to have suspected that there was something seriously wrong with the text on which he was relying for the sole link connecting Roger with Vacarius. Even thus, however, there was ample evidence in his books that Roger the abbot, Vacarius the Lombard and Roger the jurist were three quite distinct persons—evidence rejected by Selden because it did not conform with his hypothesis that they were all three one and the same. In maintaining the indivisibility of this extraordinary trinity, Selden becomes both embarrassed and obstinate: nor does he take the reader into his confidence, for in referring to Robert of Torigny's obituary notice of abbot Roger, he is careful to omit the details provided in that notice, leaving his reader to infer that Roger as abbot was of that eminence and distinction which one would expect in a man who had already made his reputation as a jurist. In his eulogy of the late abbot, Robert of Torigny refers to his provision of better accommodation for the monks, his improvement of the water-supply, his building of guest chambers and his installation of improved heating

[1] *Infra*, p. 112, n. 1, and p. 113, n. 1.

INTRODUCTION

arrangements[1], activities which one would associate with an enterprising domestic bursar, but not with a pioneer exponent of abstract jurisprudence. Selden's treatment of this subject shows a perversity possible only in a man of absolutely assured reputation.

There are also several faults of method in the *Dissertatio*. Thus in the first section of chapter VIII Selden adduces a number of scattered and inconclusive references without any attempt at correlation or generalisation: what may have been literary embellishments or conventions he cites as direct evidence of Roman Law influence. He takes up much time with a discussion of Bracton's real name, and points out several mistakes in the printed editions of the *De Legibus*, but says nothing of the 'universitas regni et baronagium' or the 'reipublicae communis sponsio' as illustrating Bracton's conception of the Lex Regia. He does not even refer to Bracton's peculiar adaptation of Roman Law terminology to the discussion of the villein status. Important questions like the influence on English Law of the canon law he leaves untouched. Moreover his style is crabbed and difficult: he never spares the reader, incorporating into his text many discussions more fitted for foot-notes or appendices; he tends to diffuseness and redundancy; often an important principle is lost sight of in an elaborate discussion of some subsidiary theme. The only relief is provided by occasional touches of sarcasm—generally at the expense of the clergy. Incompetent editors, including the editor of the text to which his essay was an appendix, are castigated without regard for their feelings. These faults of pedantry were shared by many of the great scholars of the time: they help to account for the fact that, by his contemporaries, Selden was more respected than loved and that by posterity he is more frequently quoted than read.

But it would be worse than folly to reprint one of Selden's works merely in order to show its faults. His mistakes are often of some historical interest, for they reveal the prepossessions, the disabilities and the equipment of the seventeenth-century scholar. In addition, the *Dissertatio* abounds in proofs

[1] *Chronicle of Robert of Torigny* (Rolls Series, ed. Howlett), p. 286.

not only of profound learning but of cogent analogy and logical reasoning; examples are his discussion of the relationship between Bracton and *Britton*: his account of the forged Donation of Constantine: his balanced and judicious estimate of the precise influence of civil law principles on common law practice, and his determination, from internal evidence, of the precise period when *Fleta* was compiled. The austere standards and rigorous earnestness of Selden's scholarship found ample scope in the subject to which he devoted the *Dissertatio*, and if he sometimes errs through a plethora of material, he yet provides a sharp corrective to all that is superficial or pretentious. In an age of specialisation like the present, Selden may profitably be studied as an illustration of the fact that it is possible to combine minute research with wide intellectual interests. To-day, these are too often divorced.

The three topics of most general interest touched upon in the *Dissertatio* are: first, the real nature of the twelfth-century legal revival at Bologna; second, the use made by Bracton of his Roman Law sources; and, third, the general influence of Roman Law on English legal and constitutional principles. It is proposed here to supplement Selden's Essay by brief references to the results of some modern investigations on each of these three subjects.

I. With regard to the first topic, Selden clearly did not believe that Roman Law studies were in complete abeyance in the period between the fifth and twelfth centuries, for he cites such diverse writers as Isidore of Seville[1], Boniface of Mainz[2] and Hincmar of Rheims[3] to show that imperial jurisprudence was never entirely neglected in what have been termed the Dark Ages. But he took the view nevertheless that the work of Irnerius was in itself a revival and even a renaissance, for it was linked (in his opinion) with the discovery of the Pisan MS. of the Pandects after the destruction of Amalfi in 1137; and it had a semi-official aspect because it received the direct encouragement of the emperor Lothair[4]. It will be seen that Selden,

---

[1] *Infra*, p. 71.
[2] *Infra*, p. 75.
[3] *Infra*, p. 81.
[4] *Infra*, p. 91.

INTRODUCTION   xxxi

relying on Panzirol and Sigonius, believed Irnerius to have survived until about 1190, and so he had no difficulty in associating his teaching with the discovery of an important manuscript in 1137: like his contemporaries and predecessors also, he accepted the tradition that Lothair issued a decree enacting that the law of Justinian should supersede all other systems. Had Selden realised that Irnerius was born some time between 1050 and 1060 he might have been tempted to raise the question whether the study and teaching of this jurist constituted a real innovation, or whether it could be co-ordinated with the achievements of the immediately preceding centuries.

The most explicit statement concerning Irnerius is that by Odofred[1]:

Dominus Irnerius fuit apud nos Lucerna Juris, id est primus qui docuit in civitate ista (Bologna). Nam primo coepit studium esse in civitate ista in artibus: et cum studium esset destructum Romae, libri legales fuerunt deportati ad civitatem Ravennae et de Ravenna ad civitatem istam. Quidam dominus Pepo coepit autorite sua legere in legibus. Tamen quicquid fuerit de scientia sua, nullius nominis fuit. Sed dominus Yrnerius dum doceret in artibus in civitate ista cum fuerunt deportati libri legales, coepit per se studere in libris nostris et studendo coepit docere in legibus. Et ipse fuit maximi nominis, et fuit primus illuminator scientiae nostrae, et quia primus fuit qui fecit glossas in libris nostris vocamus eum Lucernam Juris.

This passage has been subjected to much critical examination. The first point of interest is its reference to the school of Rome, which disappeared with the sack of Rome by the Normans in 1084. This school is referred to by Cassiodorus and was recognised by Justinian as one of the three law schools: there is a tradition that from Rome, Charlemagne obtained 'artis grammaticae magistri' to act as teachers throughout the Empire[2]. Except by deduction from Odofred's statement there is however no evidence that the 'studium' at Rome included a law faculty. There is more evidence in regard to Ravenna. As the seat of the Byzantine Exarchate, Ravenna was a centre of secular studies in the early middle ages, and the anathemas

[1] Cited *infra*, p. 90.
[2] H. Fitting, *Die Anfänge der Rechtsschule zu Bologna* (Berlin, 1888), § xv (on the authority of Ademar of Chabanne's Chronicle).

xxxii INTRODUCTION

poured forth by Peter Damiani in 1045 show that Ravenna possessed a faculty of enterprising and secular-minded jurists. The canonical rules regarding marriage within the prohibited degrees were contested so successfully by the Roman Law professors of Ravenna that papal prohibition had to be invoked[1]. In addition, there was a school of Lombard Law at Pavia which had acquired celebrity from its association with Lanfranc. These facts, taken together with Odofred's reference to the transport of law books from Rome to Ravenna and then to Bologna, might be taken to justify the view that there was some kind of organised law-teaching in the schools of Italy before Irnerius began his studies. It has even been suggested[2] that the school of Ravenna developed advanced doctrines of equity, that in some respects it was the rival of the Bolognese school but declined because of the better climate and position of the latter, and because Irnerius raised the reputation of Bologna to a level attained by no other city.

Odofred, in the passage just quoted, refers to a predecessor of Irnerius—Pepo, who apparently acquired no reputation from his law-teaching. Most modern authorities have accepted this tradition; according to one writer he was a charlatan[3]. But Odofred's testimony on this point has been contested by Fitting[4], who argued, from the evidence provided by the record of a law-suit contested at Poggibonzi in 1076, that Pepo was a 'doctor legis' of some eminence, and that it was he, rather than Irnerius, who directed special attention in his studies and teaching to the Digests. The tradition at Bologna (where Odofred himself had been a student) was to regard Irnerius as the pioneer, but, if Fitting's conclusions are warranted, Pepo has at least an equal claim to that title.

Before directing his attention to legal studies, Irnerius, according to Odofred, was a teacher 'in artibus': that he was also a dialectician may be concluded from another reference by Odofred to the effect that Irnerius wrote a gloss even more obscure than the text which it was intended to elucidate[5]. The

---

[1] Fitting, § XVI.   [2] By Fitting.
[3] Cassani, *Dell' antico studio di Bologna*, 76, quoted in E. Besta, *L'Opera d'Irnerio*, I, 38.
[4] Fitting, *op. cit.* § XLII.   [5] *Ibid.* § XLV.

INTRODUCTION xxxiii

transition from metaphysics to abstract jurisprudence would not be a difficult one. But Odofred is wrong in his assertion that Irnerius was the first to write glosses on the law-texts, for there exist several specimens of such glosses prior to this period, of which noteworthy examples are the Turin Gloss on the Institutes, a Gloss on the *Epitome* of Julian and a tenth-century Gloss on the Code. So far from the gloss having been invented or even revived by the Bolognese school, it was a familiar method of comment at many periods of the early middle ages: it had been applied to new productions such as the *Brachylogus* and the *Exceptiones Petri*. These two names recall the fact that there exist original juridical writings of importance which may be placed in the barren period between the fifth and twelfth centuries. Ficker[1] conjectures that the *Exceptiones Petri* was originally compiled at Ravenna in the early part of the eleventh century: it afterwards, on this theory, was transmitted to southern France, where it received local additions: it crossed the Alps again and was given its definitive form at Pavia about the year 1063. The legal précis, known since the sixteenth century as the *Brachylogus*, is preserved in six manuscripts: its origin has been attributed by Fitting[2] to Orléans and its period has been described by the same authority as late eleventh or early twelfth century. Like the *Exceptiones Petri*, the *Brachylogus* is a concerted work showing a fairly high standard of juridical science, based not on the Breviary but on Justinian, and having characteristics which distinguish it from the products of the Bolognese school. This appears to provide one more indication that the work of Irnerius did not mark any definite breach with the past, but was preceded by a tradition of juristic activity and was paralleled by the almost equally important output of contemporary and immediately preceding schools, such as those of Ravenna and Orléans. It is an essential part of Fitting's thesis that this stream of legal learning between the fifth and the twelfth century was one of scientific jurisprudence, based primarily on direct access to the Corpus Juris, and not a mere adjunct to routine practice nor an educational convention.

[1] Quoted in Fitting, *op. cit.* § xxvi. See also Flach, *Études critiques sur l'histoire du droit romain* (1890), 187–203.
[2] *Op. cit.* § xxx.

Such is the theory of juristic continuity as it has been presented by its most able advocate—Hermann Fitting. It is in line with characteristic nineteenth-century evolutionary doctrines which trace the genesis of national jurisprudence not from the authority of the lawgiver, nor the genius of the innovator, but from the gradual growth of innumerable factors in the life and environment of the nation, doctrines expounded for the first time by the Italian Vico in the early years of the eighteenth century. Moreover it is a seductive theory, for one would fain believe that throughout the dark ages a flicker of ancient civilisation was kept alive by schools of scientific jurists. But it is based on a number of hypotheses, some slender, some fanciful. It has been assailed with considerable force and sarcasm by Flach[1]. He points out that Odofred refers only to the transport of law-books from Rome to Bologna *via* Ravenna, and, while he mentions the cessation of law-teaching at Rome, he gives no indication of any rivalry between Ravenna and Bologna nor of any noteworthy activity in the latter school prior to Irnerius. As regards Orléans there is no direct evidence of any school there before the twelfth century: the school of Orléans emerges from obscurity only when, in 1219, Honorius III forbade the teaching of Roman Law in Paris[2]. Equally, Flach discredits the theory that the *Brachylogus* is of French origin, because this attribution is based merely on a thirteenth-century gloss which, while presumably French, provides no proof that the text itself came from the same source[3]. Even if the French origin of the *Brachylogus* were proved, concludes Flach, it cannot be earlier than the end of the eleventh century, and so it supplies not a proof of the continuity of legal studies in France, but simply evidence of revival in France following on that of Bologna. So also it is unwarrantable to assume, from a few scattered and scanty references, that Roman Law was an essential or distinct part of the mediaeval curriculum. It was studied simply as a part of Rhetoric: the student of Grammar was made familiar with certain legal conceptions and phrases; he was too young to be introduced to abstract conceptions of jurisprudence. All that can be asserted with certainty is that

---

[1] In *Études sur l'histoire du droit romain* (1890).
[2] *Op. cit.* 110.   [3] *Ibid.* 112–17.

INTRODUCTION xxxv

in the period between the fifth and the eleventh century—generally designated the Early Middle Ages and more often the Dark Ages—the schools inculcated elementary and possibly stereotyped notions of law to serve as conventions for debate or embellishments for literary composition[1].

There is thus reason[2] for accepting, with certain reservations, the theory of Selden, which was substantially that of Savigny, whereby Irnerius is regarded not as a continuator but as an innovator. At Ravenna, the study of Roman Law does not appear ever to have emancipated itself from the requirements of the practitioner, and, at best, it had never been more than an adjunct to grammar and dialectic: at Bologna, on the other hand, it was an abstract study, based on the most scientific element in Justinian's legislation—the Digests. It is true that there are several surviving texts of the early middle ages showing a mixture of Roman and native law, but their standard is not high and they are inspired by a conception of law very different from that expounded by Ulpian and Papinian. It must be confessed that the attempts to create a passable bridge between the fifth and the eleventh century are handicapped by the lack of historical foundations: throughout that period, Roman Law was little more than a survival or reminiscence and the gloss helped to chain it to theology and dialectic. The importance of the Bolognese revival lay not only in the fact that Irnerius made possible a more accurate and detached study of Roman Law, but that he popularised a secular subject, independent alike of theology and the needs of the moment. That was more than a renaissance: it was a revolution.

[1] *Études sur l'histoire du droit romain*, 107.
[2] Flach's arguments had already, to some extent, been foreshadowed by Max Conrat (Cohn). In the preface to his edition of the *Epitome Exactis Regibus* (Berlin, 1884, pp. ccxlix–cclvii) Conrat adduced the following reasons for concluding that most of the juristic literature attributed to the early middle ages really belongs to a period after the eleventh century:

(a) In the early middle ages there is no evidence of any serious use of the Digests.

(b) The grammarians were not familiar with Justinian's legislation and in many cases were not aware of its existence.

(c) The manner in which the grammarians handle legal sources in this period is entirely 'unjuristisch.' An example is the Gloss on the Bamberg Codex of the Institutes (ninth–tenth centuries); it is 'childish' and attempts neither to explain nor illustrate the text. In many cases such glosses were content with supplying synonyms and have little more than a philological interest.

xxxvi INTRODUCTION

II. When we turn to the second subject—the use made by Bracton of Roman Law originals[1], it should not be forgotten that, in contrast with the academic Italian jurists of the twelfth century, Bracton, the thirteenth-century English judge, was writing his treatise with a practical object, and was not directly concerned with any law other than the native jurisprudence which he administered in his courts. His Roman Law scholarship must therefore be judged by standards very different from those which would be applied to professional and academic Romanists like Azo and Placentinus, for he was elucidating the principles of a system but recently emerged from custom, while the Italian revivalists were expounding from documents that had acquired the sanctity of classical texts. Since the publication of Güterbock's treatise, there has been considerable investigation into this subject: the critical editions of Bracton[2] and Vacarius[3], when completed, will help to throw further light on the origin and uses of Bracton's Roman Law learning.

Except in his study of Bracton's use of the Lex Regia, Selden's *Dissertatio* seldom probes beneath externals. On the subject of Donations, for example, he is content to say that Bracton[4] regards the law of Justinian as providing the sanction for the legality of Donations in the form of dower between man and wife. He does not realise the more general significance of Bracton's whole treatment of Donations, a treatment in which, for the first time, Bracton breaks away from Azo. Considering Donations as acquiring their force 'jure civili[4]' not, as in Azo, 'jure naturali,' Bracton defines Donatio as 'quaedam institutio quae ex mera liberalitate et voluntate, nullo jure cogente, procedit ut rem transferat ad alium[5],' a definition which, while recalling Azo, is used to provide for Donatio a much wider sphere than is found for it by the Bolognese master. For, as a judge, Bracton was called upon to decide in many cases where good faith rather than custom or enactment would be the dominant feature; the complex relations governing status and

[1] For a full discussion of this see Holdsworth, *History of English Law*, 3rd ed. II, 267–82.
[2] In course of publication by Dr Woodbine.
[3] In course of preparation by Prof. de Zulueta.
[4] *De Legibus*, f. 10B.
[5] *Ibid.* f. 11.

service in feudal society might rest on no more stringent basis than 'mera liberalitas et voluntas.' The twenty-one chapters which Bracton assigns to Donations are Roman in form but feudal in substance; the disentanglement of the two elements would provide one of the requisite preliminaries to a complete estimate of Roman Law influence on the substance of the *De Legibus*.

Selden notices[1] the very original interpretation given to the Lex Regia by Bracton. On this interpretation, the Lex Regia of the English constitution would consist of such concordats as Magna Carta and the Coronation Oath. By omitting all reference to a surrender of authority by the estates of the realm, Ulpian's absolutist maxim could be accommodated with the most advanced constitutional theories of thirteenth-century England, for, in Bracton's rendering, the king's will has the force of law only in so far as consistent with those fundamental principles to which the king himself has sworn allegiance But Selden's acquaintance with the texts of Bracton was apparently not such as to give him a hint of the profound modifications and even discrepancies which crept in mainly through the incorporation of glosses: he did not observe that the Montfortian 'Rex habet superiorem, deum scilicet: item curiam suam, videlicet comites et barones, quia comites dicuntur quasi socii regis, et qui habet socium habet magistrum[2]' is to be found in the same book as the maxim 'Parem non habet rex in regno suo[3].' Accordingly it was possible for posterity to deduce two quite different sets of maxims from the *De Legibus*: Thomas Cromwell and Robert Cecil are among those who quoted Bracton to prove that the royal prerogative is not controlled by human laws[4]: while fervid Milton[5] and the indefatigable Prynne[6] quoted Bracton on the other side, citing the 'socii' as the superiors and potential critics of the monarch.

[1] *Infra*, pp. 25–31 and especially 29.
[2] *De Legibus*, f. 34B. In his edition of Bracton (II, 110) Woodbine classes this passage as one of the 'addiciones.'
[3] *De Legibus*, f. 5B.
[4] *Parliamentary History* (1751), IV, 191 and 465.
[5] *Defensio pro Populo Anglicano*, ch. VIII.
[6] *A Plea for the Lords or...a Vindication of the Judiciary and Legislative power of the House of Peers* (1648), p. 22. Fabian Philipps (see *infra*, p. lxiv) in his *Established Government of England*... (1687), pp. 231 ff., tried to show that, in Bracton's use, the 'socii' were 'advisers,' not 'superiors.'

xxxviii INTRODUCTION

A few more instances will serve to show how elements from Roman jurisprudence were assimilated into Bracton's exposition and, in some cases, into the practice of English Law. Thus his discussion of homicide is based throughout on the treatise of the canonist Bernard of Pavia[1]: in Bracton's treatment of this subject the canon law influence helps to break up the old assimilation of delict with crime. This is seen in his statement that homicide and theft must be considered as volitional acts, the will to commit such acts being an essential accompaniment to the acts themselves: 'Crimen[2] homicidii non contrahitur nisi voluntas nocendi intercedat et voluntas et propositum distinguunt maleficium, et furtum omnino non committitur sine affectu furandi.' In accordance with the canonists' distinction between corporal and spiritual homicide a man, says Bracton, may commit homicide 'facto, praecepto, consilio et defensione[3].' It is thus a real advance that Bracton, using canon law sources, should distinguish and emphasise the element of moral guilt, because while that distinction was lacking, a criminal law, in the modern sense of the term, was impossible.

In matters of detail also the influence of the canon law on Bracton's exposition and on English practice was most pronounced. The terminology of English writs is often borrowed from that of papal rescripts: English lawyers adopt the canonist jargon when they speak of 'impetrating an original[4].' It is by the agency of the canon law that the ordeal is eventually displaced by other methods of trial. In procedure, the canon law influence can be detected in the wager of law and proof by charters. Even our land law was indebted to the same source, for the Assize of Novel Disseisin can be fathered on the canonists' 'actio spolii,' which in its turn can be traced to the interdict 'unde vi[5].' Moreover the canon lawyers gave currency

---

[1] This appears to have been noticed for the first time by Sir Travers Twiss (in his edition of Bracton, II, lix). For parallel passages see Maitland, *Bracton and Azo*, Appendix II.
[2] *De Legibus*, f. 136B.
[3] *Ibid.*
[4] For this, see Holdsworth, *History of English Law*, 3rd ed. II, 282. The 'original' was the papal rescript whereby a judge delegate was authorised to hear a case: William of Drogheda speaks of 'impetrating' such an 'original.' See also Maitland, *Canon Law in the Church of England*.
[5] Vinogradoff, *Roman Law in Mediaeval Europe*, 86.

INTRODUCTION xxxix

to many Regulae Juris which helped to confer an epigrammatic crispness on axioms and doctrines some of which were derived from Roman Law.

Two other lines of approach may be noted as necessary for the complete study both of Bracton's actual sources and of the more general contemporary influences which helped to mould whatever is not purely English in his doctrines. The first of these is Anglo-Norman customary law. In the thirteenth century English policy had not entirely lost the Norman-Angevin orientation of Henry II's day and, though Bracton would not have been so much at home in Normandy as would Glanvil, he nevertheless shared with his predecessor a personal acquaintance with Anglo-Norman custom: England and Normandy were, in his day, but recently disintegrated elements in a once homogeneous feudalism. A consideration of this will sometimes explain what otherwise might seem a mistake in Bracton, or a failure to interpret aright his Roman Law authorities: this might have saved the late Prof. Goudy[1] as well as Maitland[2] from the assumption, sometimes too-hastily adopted, that where Bracton differs from his Romanist authorities, the difference is generally due to a mistaken interpretation. The rehabilitation[3] of Bracton on these points is of more than academic importance, because only thus can the peculiar characteristics and the unique value of a pioneer English work be estimated.

One instance will serve to illustrate this. In the passage treating of Obligation as affected by the death of one or both of the contracting parties, Bracton distinguishes[4] between Obligatio 'simplex' and Obligatio 'duplex,' the latter being penal and for recovery. Such a double obligation is extinguished, so far as its penal element is concerned, when it passes to the heirs. Prof. Goudy[5] here accuses Bracton of confusing Obligatio with Actio and so misunderstanding his Roman original. But Bracton was not engaged on an abstract com-

[1] In *Essays in Legal History* (ed. Vinogradoff, 1913), 223.
[2] In his *Bracton and Azo*.
[3] See especially articles by Dr Woodbine in *Yale Law Journal*, xxxi, 827, and by Vinogradoff in *ibid*. xxxii, 751.
[4] *De Legibus*, f. 101.
[5] *Essays in Legal History* (*Two Ancient Brocards*).

position: his purpose was, as far as possible, to accommodate law and custom, as he knew them, with the Roman Law categories and definitions which he believed essential for the structure of his treatise. In this passage he was giving expression not to a solecism but to a principle of mediaeval custom thus expressed in the *Sachenspiegel*: 'He who takes the inheritance shall acquit debts to the extent of the goods transmitted to him by the inheritance. He is not bound to pay for theft, nor brigandage, nor gambling losses, nor any debt the equivalent of which he has not received in the inheritance, or for which he did not stand surety.' This came to be grouped under the general principle that the heir was bound by any obligation contracted by the ancestor if the heir had derived profit therefrom: obligations arising from delict and from contract were thus clearly distinguished. The source of Bracton's apparent misunderstanding is therefore to be found not in his imperfect knowledge of Roman Law, but in his practical acquaintance with English and Germanic custom[1].

Elsewhere the Roman moulds have to be distorted in order to hold their English contents. Thus he equates[2] the *ascriptitius* with the sokeman on the royal demesne who cannot be ejected from his holding: by *statuliber* he understands a runaway serf who, during residence for year and day in a privileged place can plead an 'exceptio privilegii' against the master's writ 'de nativo habendo': in Bracton's terminology he is in seisin of liberty. In adopting the distinction of mankind as falling into one of two classes, free or unfree, and in associating the villein with the *servus*, Bracton was straining both Roman terminology and feudal fact, for the disabilities of the thirteenth-century villein had been superimposed on a basis of freedom, and traces of the original independence still survived.

A second line of enquiry in reference to Bracton's use of Roman Law sources is the examination of his indebtedness to mediaeval Romanists other than Azo. Caillemer[3] has drawn attention to William of Longchamp's *Practica Legum et Decretorum* and the twelfth-century school of Norman-English

---

[1] I have borrowed this from Vinogradoff's article referred to above.
[2] *De Legibus*, Bk I, XI.
[3] In his *Droit civil dans les provinces Anglo-Normandes*, 1883.

INTRODUCTION   xli

lawyers. In the *Summa Pauperum* of Vacarius there are references to several Norman-English jurists such as Ascelin, Robert and Simon: it is of special interest to conjecture how far Bracton was influenced directly or indirectly by Vacarius. The question can be settled only by textual comparison, but even a critical edition of Vacarius might leave this question only partly solved, for Bracton may have used Vacarius indirectly or through other abbreviations. In his section on Obligations[1] there are at least four passages where Bracton's indebtedness to Roman Law cannot be traced directly to Azo and where, unless the substance was derived directly from the Corpus Juris, the debt must be due to some intermediate and undetermined source. That Bracton went directly to Code, Institutes or Digest for his references is, on the whole, unlikely: in many cases he must have used an abbreviation such as that of Vacarius. The accurate determination of these points is an essential preliminary to a complete estimate of Roman Law influence on the early development of English Law.

III. This leads naturally to the third and most important topic to be dealt with in this Introduction, namely, the general influence of Roman Law on English legal and constitutional principles. It is treated by Selden in his eighth and ninth chapters. He believed that Stephen's prohibitory edict proved no barrier to the progress of civil law studies in England and considered that these studies were specially fostered by the chancellor and his clerks, who, as learned ecclesiastics, were likely to respect civil law traditions in their legal administration. Bracton was not the only practising lawyer of his day familiar with Roman as well as English rule: there was the justiciar Hubert Walter[2] in Richard's reign, and chief justice John of Lexington[3], 'in utroque jure peritus,' who practised in the reign of Henry III. Edward I invited Francis Accursius[4], son of the great Glossator, to come to England in order to teach civil law at Oxford. It was Selden's opinion that, whatever influence the civil law has ever had on our common law, that influence was at its height in the reign of Edward II. He

[1] See *Bracton and Azo*, 161 ff.   [2] *Infra*, p. 141.
[3] *Infra*, p. 143.   [4] *Infra*, p. 145.

xlii   INTRODUCTION

illustrates, from his reading of the Inner Temple MS. of the Year Books of that reign, the use of Regulae Juris in court: when, however, he adds that nothing of this kind is to be found in the reign of Edward I, exception may well be taken, for there are several cases in the Year Books[1] of the first Edward where Roman Law maxims, such as 'melior est conditio possidentis' and 'volenti non fit injuria,' are freely bandied about as the common property of canonist, civilian and common lawyer. But, on the whole, Selden's contention is right: at no other period of our legal history are the commonplaces of Roman Law doctrine so frequently cited in court as in the reign of Edward II[2]. It was perhaps natural that, after the pioneer labours of Bracton and the formative work of Edward I, English lawyers should appropriate to themselves many of the conveniently condensed and axiomatic expressions of Roman jurisprudence. At this point, however, a caution is necessary. The quotation of maxims, whether from the civil law or any other source, is a popular habit with certain writers and speakers: such illustrations in court may have been little more than a matter of form, or a piece of ostentation. It is one thing to set off an argument with a general maxim which, when applied to the case, can be little more than a sententious embellishment or a 'showy proverb[3]': it is another thing to utilise a fundamental axiom of foreign jurisprudence for the elucidation of a native case. The frequency of civil law maxims in the Year Books of Edward II is, in itself, no evidence of any real Roman Law influence[4].

Nevertheless it must be admitted that the legal maxims have played some part in the development of our law: their conveniently terse and epigrammatic character could best be appreciated at a time when lawyers still felt the reproach that English Law was not a written law. The principal source of the Roman Law maxims is the title *De Diversis Regulis Juris* in the fiftieth book of the Digests. These date mostly from the re-

---

[1] Cf. 30–1 Edward I, p. 57 and 33–5 Ed. I, p. 9 (*Rolls Series Year Books*).
[2] 2–3 Ed. II, pp. 110 and 174–6: 1 Ed. II, pp. 31 and 71: 3 Ed. II (1309–1310), p. 25: 3 and 4 Ed. II (1309–1311), p. 200: 6–7 Ed. II (1313), pp. 9 and 70 (*Selden Society Year Book Series*).
[3] Pollock and Maitland, *History of English Law*, I, 196.
[4] But see Vinogradoff, 'Les Maximes dans l'ancien droit commun anglais' in *Revue historique de droit français et étranger*, 1923, p. 335.

INTRODUCTION xliii

publican, not the imperial period, and come into prominence when, mainly under the influence of Greek philosophy, lawyers begin to reflect on the principles of their subject and law comes to be regarded from its abstract and subjective[1] side. The scholastic methods of disputation welcomed general formulae which could be employed by the disputant as premises or arguments and, just as the didactic epigram was favoured by the mediaeval moralist, so the glossators loved to eke out their logical disquisitions with brocards[2]. In this way the juristic maxim came to have the same value for the legal commentator as the postulate for the mathematician and dialectician. Coke[3] defined a legal maxim as 'a sure foundation and ground of art, and a conclusion of reason, so called quia maxima est eius dignitas et certissima auctoritas, atque quod maxime omnibus probetur.' Noy, in his *Treatise of the Principal Grounds and Maxims of the Nation*[4], wrote: 'Every maxim is a sufficient authority to itself, and which is a maxim and which not shall always be determined by the judges, because they are known to none but the learned. A maxim shall be taken strict.' Most of the old law-books from Bracton to Coke use maxims and in the *Dialogue of Doctor and Student*[5] their authority is ranked with that of statutes. It would however be erroneous to hold that most of the civil law maxims are derived from Roman Law. Bacon[6] made a fair estimate when he said 'some of the rules have a concurrence with the Civil Roman Law and some others a diversity and many times an opposition.'

Latin legal maxims may be divided[7] into three classes according as they are (*a*) Roman, (*b*) Roman modified, (*c*) Indigenous. In the first class, that of maxims cited directly from the Corpus Juris, there are comparatively few, most having

---

[1] For a full and interesting account (with bibliography) of the general importance of the maxims, see Roscoe Pound, 'The Maxims of Equity' in *Harvard Law Review*, June, 1921. See also Ihering, *Geist des Römischen Rechts*, III, 49.
[2] For the suggested derivation of this word, see the above article.
[3] *Inst.* 1, sect. 3.
[4] 1641. [5] Bk I, ch. v.
[6] *Some Principal Rules and Maxims of the Common Law.*
[7] See an article by the late James Williams, 'Latin Maxims in English Law' in *Law Magazine and Review*, August, 1895. Williams' article does not seem to be very generally known: the present writer is indebted to it for a number of the above references.

xliv INTRODUCTION

been modified in one way or another. In this class are the following:

In testamentis plenius voluntates testantium interpretamur[1].
Quod initio vitiosum est non potest tractu temporis convalescere[2].
In pari causa possessor potior haberi[3] debet (or, in modern form, Melior est conditio possidentis).
Impossibilium nulla obligatio[4] est.
Semper in obscuris quod minimum est sequamur[5].
Nemo plus juris ad alium transferre potest quam ipse habet[6].

The most interesting example of the second class, *i.e.* modified Roman Law maxims, is the famous 'Actio personalis moritur cum persona.' This is compounded from the Digest dictum 'Beneficium personale est et cum persona extinguitur[7]' and the principle laid down in the Institutes, 'Est enim certissima juris regula ex maleficiis personales actiones in heredem non competere[8].' In this class of mixed maxims are some of Bracton's:

Non valet donatio nisi subsequatur traditio[9].
Pro possessione praesumitur de jure[10].
Juste possidet qui praetore auctore possidet[11].

But many of his maxims are his own or at least indigenous:

Nullum tempus currit contra regem[12].
Lex facit regem[13].
Solus deus heredem facit[14].

The glossators were responsible for a great many of these mixed maxims:

Habemus optimum testem confitentem reum.
Actori incumbit rei probatio.
Cessante ratione legis, cessat ipsa lex.
Ignorare leges est lata culpa.

Of the third class, that of maxims which nowhere find expression in Roman Law, some of the most typical examples are:

---

[1] D. 50. 17. 2.
[2] D. 50. 17. 29.
[3] D. 50. 17. 128.
[4] D. 50. 17. 185.
[5] D. 50. 17. 9.
[6] D. 50. 17. 54.
[7] D. 24. 3. 13.
[8] *Inst.* IV, 12. 1.
[9] *De Legibus*, f. 39 B.
[10] *Ibid.* f. 160 B.
[11] *Ibid.* f. 196 A.
[12] *Ibid.* f. 103 A.
[13] *Ibid.* f. 56.
[14] *Ibid.* f. 62 B.

INTRODUCTION xlv

Aequitas sequitur legem.
Ubi jus ibi remedium.
Interest reipublicae ut sit finis litium.
Mobilia sequantur personam.
Locus regit actum.

In this class is the maxim compounded from Glanvil[1]:

Hereditas numquam ascendit.

The canon law was the medium through which the greatest number of these Latin maxims were assimilated into modern jurisprudence. In the chapter *De Regulis Juris* appended to the *Liber Sextus* of Boniface VIII there is a collection of eighty-seven maxims, most of which are of extremely general purport, and of which many are familiar to us in other forms. Thus the current maxim 'impossibilium nulla obligatio est' appears in the Sext[2] as 'nemo potest ad impossibilia obligari': the rule 'in pari causa, potior est conditio defendentis' is paralleled[3] by 'cum sunt partium iura obscura, reo favendum est potius quam actori': the principle 'semper in dubiis benigniora preferenda' is matched by 'in poenis benignior est interpretatio facienda[4],' while our 'prior tempore, potior jure' has its parent in 'qui est prior tempore potior est jure[5].'

It was mainly because of their Latin dress and their epigrammatic conciseness that maxims such as these passed into the legal currency of nations which never 'received' the Roman Law in the ordinarily accepted sense of the term[6]. For this reason the study of their application in native law is a difficult investigation, since there are many etymological pitfalls, inevitable perhaps wherever Latin is used to convey general principles to men whose characteristic institutions and conceptions are described in a modern language. Behind many of

---

[1] 'Terra ista quae sic donata est...naturaliter quidem ad haeredes haereditabiliter descendit: numquam autem naturaliter ascendit' (Glanvil, *Tractatus de Legibus* (1780 ed.), VII, I.
[2] No. 6. [3] No. 11.
[4] No. 49. [5] No. 54.
[6] Of maxims in the Sext which might have a special meaning in mediaeval ethics, the following may be cited: Semel malus, semper praesumitur esse malus (in modern parlance, 'Give a dog a bad name and hang him'). In malis promissis fidem non debet observari (this might be developed into the principle that faith need not be kept with heretics). Qui tacet consentire videtur (a doctrine easily capable of casuist applications).

these maxims there lies a long and complicated history which only a perfected science of comparative jurisprudence could ever hope to unravel. But their wide currency, while it provides no proof of any 'reception' of Roman Law, is evidence that the mediaeval and the modern world have appreciated the two qualities characteristic of the Latin mentality—clarity and concision, qualities finding permanent expression in the common sense and logic of Roman Law, and profoundly influencing, at every stage of European civilisation, the basic conceptions of jurist and legislator.

How far has this country been affected by 'receptions' of Roman Law?

It is unquestionable that, by the beginning of the fourteenth century, English Law had experienced a modified reception which acted as a prophylactic against the epidemic of receptions in the sixteenth century. By Edward III's reign, the common lawyers had obtained all that they needed from the continental revival. They were not concerned with the work of Bartolus and the post-glossators, for the supremacy of native rule in their courts was practically assured. In this sense Selden was right in closing his account at the reign of Edward III. But the sixteenth century brought several threats to English insularity, and at times there was a chance that the supremacy of the common law would be contested by the restored jurisprudence of Rome. It is sometimes the duty of the historian to estimate the strength of influences which just failed of complete achievement, to speculate on the extent and nature of a fate averted.

An enquiry of this kind had no attraction for Selden. There was little of the imaginative in his composition: he took his stand on hard fact and definite proof: he might venture a suggestion on the origin of a word, but conjectures on what might have been, he would have considered outside his province. It was otherwise with the late F. W. Maitland, who devoted one of his most brilliant essays to the study of those foreign influences which, in the sixteenth century, nearly altered the course of our constitutional history. His *English Law and the*

INTRODUCTION xlvii

Renaissance[1] is a psychological study of the prepossessions of our sixteenth-century lawyers and the instincts of those contemporary publicists who were striving to emancipate English jurisprudence from what they considered its mediaeval solecisms. Nor were the publicists altogether without official support, for the Tudors gave a greatly enhanced importance to exceptional jurisdictions, like the Star Chamber, in which common law principles had only a limited application. Maitland's literary skill was so great that he was able to do justice to this intricate theme without upsetting the balance of historic truth. The common law was not uninfluenced by the assaults of its critics, but it managed to survive them: the fact of that triumph is of paramount interest for a study such as this.

The most emphatic plea for some kind of 'reception' in England was that made in the *Dialogue*[2] between Starkey and Pole. The latter criticised the common law on the following grounds:

There is no doubt but that our law and order thereof is over-confused. It is infinite and without order or end. There is no stable ground nor sure stay: but everyone that can colour reason maketh a stop to the best law that is beforetime devised. The subtlety of one sergeant shall evert and destroy all the judgments of many wise men beforetime received. There is no stable ground in our common law to lean unto....The statutes of kings also be overmany, even as the constitutions of the emperors were. Wherfor I would wish that all these laws should be brought into some small number and to be written also in our mother tongue, or else put into Latin.

Starkey considered that primogeniture was a good institution where provision could be made for the younger sons, but 'entails in mean families' are bad and would be removed by a land-law based on Roman jurisprudence. The civil law he regarded as an admirable subject of education for the nobility. Starkey and Pole are not the only instances of Englishmen who (partly by reason of education abroad) felt that the cumbersome dialectic of English common law pleading, its dependence on decided cases and its use of barbarous French and Latin jargons all needed drastic reform. The *Complaint of Roderick Mors*[3],

[1] Cambridge, 1901. It is a scarce pamphlet and might well be reprinted.
[2] Published by the Early English Text Society (1878).
[3] In Early English Text Society: quoted by Holdsworth, *History of English Law* (3rd ed.), IV, 259.

for instance, refers to 'the innumerable wiles, crafts, subtleties and delays that be in the common law.' These were the objections most patent to men who, like Starkey and Pole, had imbibed something of the literary culture of the Renaissance: there is an aesthetic element in this attitude, for their education had led them to despise the debased Aristotelian logic which supplied rigid forensic moulds to the mediaeval pleaders, and they equally abhorred the tradition which required Englishmen to use a jargon capable of such an effort as this: 'Il jecta des brickbats sur lui que narrowly mist[1].' This linguistic objection to the Latin and French of the common lawyers was revived in the seventeenth century, as may be seen from the play *Ignoramus* performed by a body of Cambridge undergraduates before James in 1618. In this satire, Ignoramus (the Common Lawyer) requires his clerk to write abbreviated Latin ('scribere cum dasho') in order to avoid mistakes in Latin and Law[2]. There is a tradition[3] that Selden took this skit as an attack on himself and his common law colleagues. As late as 1646 there was a protest[4] against the Latin and Norman-French of the Common Lawyers.

More serious than the linguistic objection was the half-expressed feeling that the common law and all its works were an inseparable element of the old 'popish' England which the reformers were so anxious to destroy. The feeling was clearly voiced[5] in 1558 by the Scottish Protestants when they advocated that the old clerical abuses should be judged by the New Testament, the Fathers and 'the godly approved laws of Justinian.' Horne, bishop of Winchester, justified Henry's assumption of the Supreme Headship of the English Church on the ground that 'it is the judgment of the most learned civilians and canonists that when the Clergy are faulty and negligent, it appertaineth to the emperor to call general councils for the reformation of the church[6].' The fact that most of the French sixteenth-

---

[1] Quoted by Maitland in *English Law and the Renaissance*.
[2] Act IV, sc. viii (1668 ed.).
[3] Mentioned in Paulus Colomesius' *Vie de Jean Selden* (MS. Bodley 1022, f. 20).
[4] John Cook, *Vindication of the professors and profession of the law* (1646).
[5] Quoted in Maitland, *English Law and the Renaissance*, 14.
[6] Strype, *Ecclesiastical Memorials*, I, 171.

INTRODUCTION	xlix

century jurists were Huguenots was not without its influence in England: Melanchthon was a Roman Law enthusiast, and in Edward VI's reign, when foreign influences were stronger than at any other period in the century, there were proposals for the foundation of a Civil Law college at Cambridge. Maitland conjectures that possibly Henry VIII had a legal reformation in his mind, perhaps a project for a reform of the Inns of Court or even for the introduction of a Civil Code[1]. Bucer speaks of such projects: the new Erastianism might find in Code and Digests the best armoury of weapons against the old Popery.

It was Maitland's purpose to show that though there was no violent conflict between native and foreign jurisprudence, there were in existence some of the elements of such a conflict. The New Learning emphasised many antitheses and contrasts: the political and economic difficulties of the century brought them into prominence, without always precipitating a contest. There existed a consciousness of the antithesis between clumsy case-law and the convenient code, between local, corruptible juries and impartial royal commissions, between the metaphysical abstraction of legal fictions and the mundane certainty of established fact, between the ideal of equality of all before the law and the convenience of 'laws of state,' between the democratic copyholders and the rightless tenants-at-will, between the academic necessity of forensic proof of guilt and the administrative convenience of acting on presumption or suspicion. The contrast between the old common law and the new foreign jurisprudence was a contrast between tradition and authority, dialectic and definition, 'constitutionalism' and political expediency. But the 'Marsilianism' or 'Byzantinism' of the Tudors was never pushed too far, and what would have produced a crisis under other dynasties was limited to a regime of executive efficiency. The Tudors were successful because they had no political theories.

But in spite of his literary skill and scholarly reserve, Maitland was inclined at times to push these contrasts too far, and to

[1] For an account of the canon law code drawn up in Henry VIII's reign but never promulgated, see Cardwell, *The Reformation of the Ecclesiastical Laws* (1850). There is a proposal for the introduction of some kind of civil law code in 'A discourse touching the reformation of the laws of England' (MS. Faustina, c. II, f. 5).

INTRODUCTION

assume that the common law was in even greater jeopardy than is warranted by the facts. Thus he attaches some importance to the fact that in 1535 the Year Books cease to appear. On the other hand Prof. Holdsworth has shown[1] that this need not be regarded too seriously, since the Year Books were not official publications: the printed collections were beginning to be available, and abridgments, such as Fitzherbert's, were being eagerly bought by practising lawyers. It should be remarked also that the great bulk of English legal literature of the first half of the sixteenth century was common law literature[2]. As regards the complaints of men like Starkey, it might be replied that the legal procedures of France and Germany were almost equally cumbersome and intricate[3]. Humanist dislike of mediaeval institutions must not be confused with national antipathy to these institutions. Nor is it even just to regard the English common lawyer as passing through a decline during the Renaissance, for the sphere of activity allotted to his rival the civilian was a limited one: the Press was pouring out common law books: the Inns of Court were the centres of a collegiate life so strong and characteristic as to justify, in later years, the remark of Noy[4] that 'every Inn of Court is a University.'

There was a slight decline in the business of the common law courts during the first half of the century and there were complaints of the civilians taking the bread out of the mouths of the common lawyers. In 1547 it was objected, in a petition, that 'the judges in Chancery are Civilians and not lerned in the Comen laws[5].' But the legal profession is apt to magnify any danger which threatens to diminish its business: the competition of rival jurisdictions was sometimes exaggerated, and, in particular, it was unjust to regard Chancery as administering a foreign system. The influence of canon law procedure[6] and of

[1] *History of English Law* (3rd ed.), IV, 262.
[2] The revival of the study of feudal law in Tudor times was connected with the increase in the efficiency with which Crown and Landlords asserted their feudal rights: cf. Court of Wards and Liveries.
[3] *Ibid.* 260.
[4] In a discourse at Lincoln's Inn, August, 1632. Noy referred to the civil law titles of 'Batchelor' and 'Doctor' as 'specious and grovelling titles' (Harley MS. 980, f. 153).
[5] For this see the articles by Prof. Holdsworth, 'Reception of Roman Law in the Sixteenth Century' in *Law Quarterly Review*, XXVII.
[6] Langdell, 'Development of Equity Pleading from Canon Law Pro-

INTRODUCTION   li

scholastic philosophy[1] on the development of equity have been estimated by recent authorities: it is established fact that English equity, as dispensed by the Chancery, was supplementary to common law, not in contradiction with it: the judges in Chancery owed more to common than to civil law, and in no sense of the word was Chancery ever a foreign or civilian institution. 'The common law,' wrote Bacon[2], 'hath a kind of rule and sway over the Chancery to determine what belongs to the Chancery.' Nevertheless it is an interesting historical fact that in early Stuart times Chancery was regarded as administering a system antagonistic to the common law. Coke resented what he considered its encroachments, and Ellesmere felt it incumbent on himself to prove that its jurisdiction was not affected by the Statute of Praemunire. 'The Chancery,' he wrote[3], 'as it judgeth in equity is part of the law of the land. Aequa justitia is part of recta justitia and should precede it[4].'

It may be possible to arrive at a more balanced conception of the extent of the sixteenth-century 'reception' in England if reference be made to some of the exceptional tribunals which played such an important part in Tudor administration.

Of these the chief is the Star Chamber which came to monopolise a large share of the Council's functions. In the fifteenth century the jurisdiction of the Council had included a number of cases which, for various reasons, such as the rigidity of common law procedure, could best be dealt with by a court endowed with summary and exceptional powers: these cases included matters arising from fraud, forgery, malicious indict-

cedure' in *Select Essays in Anglo-American Legal History*, II, 753 ff. Langdell shows that ecclesiastical procedure was never, as such, the procedure of Chancery but the latter followed the practice of church courts in its mode of taking the sworn testimony of witnesses and in requiring each party to submit to an examination under oath by the adversary. In the formal conduct of proceedings, the common law practice was followed (*op. cit.* 773). Moreover Chancery had a common law side as well as an equity side and the former is more ancient.

[1] Vinogradoff, 'Reason and Conscience in Sixteenth Century Jurisprudence' in *Law Quarterly Review*, XXIV, shows how the principles of equity were influenced by the philosophy of Gerson.

[2] Quoted in Holdsworth, *History of English Law*, IV, 282.

[3] See the tract *On the Jurisdiction of the Court of Chancery*, attributed to Ellesmere in *Collectanea Juridica*, 1791.

[4] It should be noted also that the Statute of Uses caused an infiltration of equitable doctrines into the Common Law and moreover the Exchequer had an equitable jurisdiction.

ments, cases affecting the rights of the crown, cases of trusts and uses, and cases where the suitors claimed that they were too poor to sue at common law[1]. There were frequent complaints that the Council ignored the forms of law and in 1346 the Commons had obtained the royal consent to the restriction that no man should be required to answer for his freehold before the Council—the only definite restriction which the Commons were ever able to impose on the jurisdiction of that body. Its methods of procedure were frequently attacked, in particular the system of inquisitorial examination, derived from the ecclesiastical courts, whereby the defendants, and sometimes both plaintiffs and defendants, were required to answer questions on oath. The writs of summons issued to the defendant contained no intimation of the charges to be preferred against him, and a person accused of felony was not allowed the use of counsel. But before we condemn the fifteenth-century council as arbitrary and unjust, it should be remembered that torture was frequently employed by the common law judges and that common law juries were notorious for bias and corruption.

The Star Chamber, as reconstituted by the Act of 3 Henry VII, was the most efficient engine of Tudor despotism. Its jurisdiction was so wide because it was never clearly defined: it could consider the intention as well as the act: it decided in many cases which otherwise would have led to murder or duel: it kept in their places the 'over-mighty subjects' who had played such havoc in Lancastrian and Yorkist times: it controlled the findings of juries, determined conflicts of jurisdiction and dealt with complaints concerning subordinate government officials[2]. The scriptural warning 'He that calleth his brother Raca shall be in danger of the Council[3]' had a literal significance in sixteenth-century England. The Star Chamber played a part similar to that of the Conseil Privé in seventeenth-century France[4], for it was able to withdraw the servants of the executive

[1] Baldwin, *The King's Council*, ch. XI.
[2] For the Star Chamber see I. S. Leadam, *Select Cases in the Star Chamber* (Selden Society): Tanner, *Tudor Constitutional Documents*, 249–57: and Holdsworth, *History of English Law*, IV, 84–107 and V, 155–214.
[3] These words are used by Hudson in his *Treatise on the Star Chamber*.
[4] For the French Conseil Privé see Marion, *Dictionnaire des Institutions de la France aux XVIIe et XVIIIe siècles*.

INTRODUCTION

from the procedure of the common law and so afford them a protection inconsistent with the English principle of the equality of all before the law. The strength of the Star Chamber jurisdiction lay in its flexibility: it dealt with exorbitant offences and 'exorbitant offences are not subject to an ordinary course of law': so far from being bound by precedent, it could 'make an order according to the necessity and nature of the thing itself.' Even a writ of Habeas Corpus was no bar to its proceedings. It summoned juries accused of giving a wrong verdict: it used torture when necessary: it could proceed on suspicion or information. The presumption was against the accused until his innocence was proved: there was no need for the conclusive proof required by common law rules. Perjury, forgery, conspiracy and attempted crime were its principal provinces, and in these spheres the activities of the Star Chamber have notably assisted the development of our criminal law Its special purpose was to deal with those offences which might in any way threaten the security of the state: the provision of a special tribunal for this purpose savours more of continental than of English principle and recalls a conception of sovereignty more akin to that of the civil lawyers than to that of Bracton and the common law.

Nevertheless it would be wrong to regard the Star Chamber as always necessarily antagonistic to native conceptions of law. Persons bringing their suits to the Star Chamber had to show cause why they did not resort to the ordinary tribunals. The procedure of the Star Chamber shows a mingling of English with foreign methods[1]: common law influence can be seen in the manner of pleading, the open hearing and the liberty of defence: while the foreign element is seen in the obligation of defendant to answer upon oath, in the secrecy of his examination and in the use of written evidence. The Star Chamber was harshest in extraordinary cases where torture was freely used. In these cases it was held to be justified by the necessity of maintaining ordered government, and it should be remembered that the political theorists of the sixteenth century were practically unanimous in their fear of anarchy and their apotheosis of uncontested and legitimate sovereignty.

[1] Holdsworth, *History of English Law*, v, 184.

liv INTRODUCTION

Similar principles are seen in the working of the Court of High Commission[1]. Trial was by witnesses: their evidence was weighed not by a jury but by the civil law rules of evidence: there was no separation, as in the common law, between the law and the facts. The initial presumption was against the accused, whose chief grievance was that he might be forced to incriminate himself by having to take the Ex-Officio oath. The Commissioners exercised their powers in virtue of the statutory legislation which had 'restored' to the Tudors that part of the prerogative formerly usurped by pope and bishops: this was its most objectionable feature in the eyes of the common lawyers, for they questioned the existence of any residuary judicial power in the crown. Coke[2] believed that the Commissioners had greatly exceeded their statutory powers as defined in the Act of Supremacy and, by subjecting that Act to 'a violent construction under mystical and cloudy words,' they had arrogated to themselves power to fine and imprison for offences not so punishable in the days of ecclesiastical jurisdiction. Unlike the Star Chamber, the Court of High Commission was regarded, by the common lawyers of the early seventeenth century, as an illegal tribunal.

On the other hand it may be noted that the Court of High Commission incurred less odium than did the Star Chamber It has been shown by a recent writer[3] that even in Laud's time only about five per cent. of the cases were initiated by the Commissioners themselves. Litigants frequently preferred to entrust their suits to the Commission because there was no jury to be corrupted, no judges to be bribed (the Commissioners were not dependent on fees): there was more scope for the evidence of witnesses, and the case need not break down with an error in pleading. There was less risk in attempting to establish a reasonable likelihood before incorruptible Commissioners than in attempting to prove a legal fiction to a judge and jury who might already have accepted their price.

There is an interesting apologia of this court from the pen of Richard Cosin[4], who maintained that, by the statutes, several cases other than matrimonial and testamentary cases pertained

[1] There is a good account in Usher, *Rise and Fall of the High Commission*.
[2] *Institutes*, IV, 74.   [3] Usher, *op. cit.* 323.
[4] *An Apologie for Sundrie Proceedings by Jurisdiction Ecclesiastical* (1593).

INTRODUCTION lv

to ecclesiastical courts. These included all 'cases of correction' and heresy: refusing to have a child baptised, or receive communion, or come to church. The office of the Commissioners he defines as 'enquiry'—equivalent to the civil law 'quaestio': the office of Informer is 'officium promotum.' 'When no prosecutor stirs, a court acts only on duty—officium merum, more worthy than the other course which is by a party[1].' The practice of Denunciation he condones[2], defining it as a 'special means of stirring up the Office, as in Ancient Rome...a relating of some man's crime unto a judge to the end to have the offender reformed or punished, yet without that solemn description by the Denouncer which the law requires in an accusation.' So too Fame may sometimes take the place of accusation: when based on strong presumption, it takes the place of proof: adultery, for instance, can often be proved only presumptively. In these ways, says Cosin, the Commission may justifiably dispense with the common law principle that no man is to be condemned without an accuser. The third part of his *Apologie* contains a defence of the system whereby the Commissioners required the accused to answer on oath: this practice Cosin justifies by civil and canon law procedure and by the fact that it inflicts no injustice on the innocent.

The Council of the Marches[3] provides another illustration of a Tudor tribunal unfettered by common law rules. The jurisdiction of the Council of the Marches was not clearly defined until 1574, when full instructions were issued to its president, Sir Henry Sydney: these instructions were a model for later regulations[4]. The Council consisted of twenty councillors, who, as a body, or any two of them, were empowered to decide 'all manner of complaints and petitions...concerning as well the titles of lands and other hereditaments, as also personal, real and mixed actions, causes or matters, civil or criminal, exhibited or put unto them by any poor persons that shall manifestly appear not to be able to sue or defend at the common law, or by any person like to be oppressed by maintenance, riches, strength, power, degree or affinity of the parties' adversaries.'

---
[1] *An Apologie* etc. II, 35. [2] *Ibid.* II, 38.
[3] For this see C. A. J. Skeel, *The Council of the Marches of Wales* (1904).
[4] *Ibid.* 89.

In addition, the Council had to examine into all charges of perjury against juries in Herefordshire, Worcestershire, Gloucestershire and Haverfordwest. The Council of the Marches could employ torture and was empowered to deal with persons spreading rumours or seditious tales. Local courts and mayors of towns were subject to its jurisdiction, and it dealt with misdemeanours committed by Sheriffs, Justices of the Peace, Bailiffs, Lieutenants, Escheators, Gaolers, Clerks and all officers and ministers of justice within the area of its jurisdiction. Like the Star Chamber it was therefore an administrative court. It did not however encourage litigation, for no actions of replevin, debt, detinue or trespass on the case could be brought before it, unless the bill was signed by at least two of the Council.

The complaints against this tribunal were due mainly to its interference with common law courts, its extension of jurisdiction to cases of title and legacies, and its punishment of offenders already punished by other courts[1]. As a prerogative court it incurred the jealousy of Westminster Hall. Many convicted by the Council lamented that their case had not gone before a jury: in addition there was considerable uncertainty regarding this Council's procedure, for its instructions were issued by the Crown and always liable to change. Its criminal jurisdiction was abolished in 1641 and it disappeared altogether in 1689.

Like the Court of High Commission, the Council of the Marches had its apologist. The *Dialogue on the Government of Wales* between Barthol, a doctor of the civil law, and Demetus, a Pembrokeshire man, was written in 1594 by George Owen of Henllys[2]. Demetus considered that the Council was carrying out functions similar to those of Chancery and Star Chamber and conferring benefits not easily obtainable in common law courts. 'Generally it is the very place of refuge for the poor oppressed of this country of Wales to fly unto...the more for that it is the best cheap court in England and there is great speed made in the trial of causes.' Cheapness and expedition were thus among the benefits which litigants might find in the procedure of this Council, advantages not always characteristic of the common law courts.

[1] *The Council of the Marches of Wales*, 121 ff.   [2] *Ibid.* 127.

INTRODUCTION lvii

The Court of Requests, as constituted by Henry VII, was intended for civil causes; Wolsey gave it a permanent home in Westminster Palace, 'for the expedition of poor men's causes depending in the Star Chamber[1].' It was never a statutory court, but simply an offshoot from the Council: its judges, recruited from the Star Chamber, were called Masters of Requests—probably on the French model. Among its activities was the protection of copyhold tenants from harsh manorial courts and the oppression of the landed nobility: Wolsey's association with this court won for him the unanimous hatred of the aristocracy. In Elizabeth's reign it was 'a court of conscience appointed to mitigate the rigour of proceeding in law,' *i.e.* a court of equity: its procedure, as Sir Julius Caesar tells us, 'was altogether according to the process of summary causes in the civil law[2].' It issued numerous injunctions staying suits at common law and, while the judges of this court often consulted the common law judges, there was often collision and enmity between the two. The common lawyers began to attack it in 1590; in 1614 it was decided that all matters of equity must be decided in Chancery: thereafter, the Court of Requests was regarded as illegal and openly defied. It disappeared with the Star Chamber, Council of the North, and the Council of the Marches in 1641.

It may be seen from the above that the activities of Star Chamber, Court of High Commission, Council of the Marches and Court of Requests give some indication of civil law influence, but it would be wrong to assume therefrom that there was a 'reception' of Roman Law in sixteenth-century England. The characteristic of these courts was not that they could use civil law doctrines, but rather that they were not bound by any stereotyped procedure at all: in their methods they were eclectic, and they subordinated judicial conventions to what they conceived to be the interest of the state. Where they had to deal with a case involving principles outside the common law, they did not hesitate to employ civilians or canonists, but this practice did not diminish, to any appreciable extent, the scope of common law jurisdiction. If there was a 'reception' in Tudor

[1] *Select Cases in the Court of Requests* (Selden Society), XIII.
[2] *Ibid.* XX–XXI.

England, its most noteworthy features are that the civilians and canonists were kept within certain allotted spheres of activity: that they did not have a complete monopoly even in the prerogative courts, and that they had exclusive audience only in the ecclesiastical courts, the court of Admiralty[1], and the court of the Constable and Marshal[2]. So far from there being an assimilation of civil jurisprudence with common law practice, there was segregation of civilian and canonist from the common lawyer, a process accompanied by the growth of a strong class and national consciousness among the exponents of native jurisprudence. In 1511 Dr Bodewell, Dean of Arches, founded the College of Advocates for practitioners in the Ecclesiastical and Admiralty courts[3]: with Doctors' Commons were thus closely associated those miscellaneous surviving jurisdictions which still owed allegiance to civil or canon law. This intimate connection between Admiralty and Ecclesiastical cases, as controlled by other than common law principles, is still symbolised by the present Probate, Divorce and Admiralty Division of the High Court, a title which helps to convey something of the historic fact that the jurisprudence of ancient and mediaeval Rome, while admitted in the past into certain spheres of our national life, is something quite apart from the domain of our native law.

The Tudor theory of sovereignty, while it does not reveal any direct debt to Roman jurisprudence, is nevertheless such as would be better appreciated by the civilian than the common lawyer. In this respect Tudor principles of government were influenced, to some extent, by the absolutist conceptions of empire popularised on the continent by the reception of Roman

---

[1] For the court of Admiralty, see Marsden, *Select Pleas in the Court of Admiralty* (Selden Society) and T. L. Mears, 'The History of Admiralty Jurisdiction' in *Select Essays in Anglo-American Legal History*, II, 312–64.

[2] The criminal jurisdiction of the Constable ceased in 1514 when Buckingham was removed from the office. For an early seventeenth-century account of the jurisdiction of the Marshal's Court see Harleian MS. 305, f. 59, where the special jurisdiction of this court is defined as (I) cognizance of contracts touching deeds of storm and war out of the realm, and (II) all matters of war within the realm. For an account of a court of chivalry held in 1623 by the Earl Marshal, Thomas of Arundel, see Harleian MS. 4128.

[3] For the organisation of the civilians and canonists practising in these courts see W. Senior, *Doctors' Commons and the Old Court of Admiralty* (1922).

INTRODUCTION   lix

Law doctrines; while refraining from the challenge implied by the assertion of constitutional dogmas, the Tudors ruled by a tacit Lex Regia which gave them all the powers of the civil law *princeps*. This may be inferred, not from the language of Henry VIII or Elizabeth, but from the arguments of their apologists and the tenor of some Tudor statutes. Selden's discussion of the Lex Regia and its English prototypes might have been enriched by a reference to such a statute[1] as 31 Henry VIII, c. 8:

...considering that sudden causes and occasions...do require speedy remedies and that by abiding for a Parliament in the meantime might happen great prejudice to ensue to the realm...it is therefore thought in manner more than necessary that the King's Highness of this realm for the time being with the advice of his Honourable Privy Council should make and set forth proclamations for the good and public order and governance of this his realm...for the defence of his royal dignity and the advancement of his commonwealth.

This is entitled 'An Act that proclamations made by the King shall be obeyed.' Names like Erastianism or Marsilianism conceal the Roman Law origin of such principles. Even more striking is the right to a *non-obstante* claimed in Henry VIII's 'Act giving authority to such as shall succeed to the crown of this realm when they shall come to the age of twenty-four years to make frustrate such acts as shall be made before in their time[2].' In this way the English monarch was given the right to repeal all acts passed during his minority. It was observed by Blackstone[3] that when a royal grant was allowed to contain and give effect to these words, 'non obstante aliquo statuto in contrarium,' it must have set the prerogative above the laws. Now, the *non-obstante* clause is of canonical origin: it was used by the papacy for the purpose of raising money in England, and was first imitated by our Henry III[4]. From thence it is not a distant step to the theory that the laws are the king's laws, not the laws of the realm, a view definitely propounded by James II's judges when they approved the dispensing power on the ground 'that the laws are the king's laws: that the king might dispense with

[1] *Statutes of the Realm* (1817 ed.), III, 726–7.
[2] 28 Henry VIII, cap. XVII (*Statutes of the Realm*, 1817 ed., III, 673).
[3] *Commentaries*, I, cap. IX.
[4] For instances, see Prynne's *Animadversions on the Fourth Institute* (1669 ed.), pp. 129–51. For the documents, see Prynne's *Exact History of the Pope's Intolerable Usurpations*, IV, ch. I (1665).

the laws in case of necessity, and that the king is judge of that necessity.' This was the most definite assertion of the principle and the last, for the Bill of Rights removed the dispensing power.

Occasionally the English apologists of absolutism have drawn upon Roman Law precedent, though this is so rare that the most noteworthy instances can be speedily indicated. Thus in a treatise, *Regal and Ecclesiastical Power*, dedicated to the Protector Somerset, Henry Lord Strafford maintained that as Justinian had made 'laws and ordinances of faith, of heretics, of religious men...and all such cases, so it appertaineth to the English monarch to regulate the temporal affairs of church and churchmen[1].' Despotism, he holds, is not without divine sanction, for 'God sometimes suffereth tyrannical power to punish the people[2].' This has its parallel in some of the political thinking of seventeenth-century France, where it was maintained that, as work is necessary for a donkey and leeches for a swollen body, so the absolute rule of the monarch preserves the body politic from disease and decline[3]. In this respect it may be noted that the best exposition of Absolutism, based not on Divine Right but on Roman Law, is to be found in the three *Regales Disputationes*[4] of Alberic Gentili, who held the post of Professor of Civil Law at Oxford, and is best known as a pioneer in the history of international law. Applying the Lex Regia to James I, he argues that the royal prerogative is unlimited: 'princeps est deus in terris'—but he is the God of Code and Digest, not of the Old Testament. The contention of Vasquius that the state is in the interests of the governed, he confutes[5]. 'Qui habet potestatem omnem, is est legibus solutus omnibus: sed princeps habet potestatem omnem, ergo[6]....' But Gentili was not an Englishman and such theories never obtained a firm hold in this country.

When Cowell expressed similar views in English, he took a greater risk. A civil lawyer, like Gentili, he believed that common and civil law were 'on the same foundation' and in

---

[1] *Regal and Ecclesiastical Power*, 79.   [2] *Ibid.* 20.
[3] See especially the political maxims of Richelieu in *Mélanges Historiques* (ed. Hanotaux), vol. III (*Coll. des documents inédits sur l'histoire de France*). See also the *Prince* of Balzac (1631).
[4] 1605. Dedicated to James I.
[5] *Regales Disputationes*, 6.   [6] *Ibid.* 36.

INTRODUCTION lxi

his law dictionary, the *Interpreter*, he propounded views on the prerogative which raised the ire of the parliamentary lawyers. In 1603, at the request of Bancroft, he drew up arguments[1] to prove 'that the king hath power to hear and determine all kinds of causes when it shall so please his majesty': it was the attempt of James I to act on this principle that led Coke to draw his fundamental distinction between the king as person and as institution, perhaps the most important constitutional distinction evolved in the whole course of the seventeenth century. But Cowell was too late in James's reign as Filmer, the apologist of Divine Right, was too late in the reign of Charles II. In 1609 the following of Cowell's opinions were condemned by the House of Commons[2]:

1. That the king is 'solutus a legibus[3].'

2. That it is not necessary for the king to summon a parliament in order to make laws, since he can legislate by his absolute power.

3. That it is a favour, on the part of the monarch, to admit the consent of his subjects in the matter of subsidies.

The same parliament condemned the assertion of Blackwood that 'we are all slaves by the conquest.' Against these doctrines, the parliamentary lawyers developed the theory that there existed fundamental laws of remote antiquity, whereby the monarch was merely an estate of the realm, pledged to the co-operation of the other estates in all his legislative acts. It was part of this view that the common law was in existence before the Conquest, a view which found ample confirmation in Horn's *Mirror of Magistrates* and afterwards led to the strange notion that the real fount of English jurisprudence was to be found not in Bracton nor in Magna Carta, but in the Laws of Edward the Confessor[4].

[1] Lansdowne MS 211, f. 141.
[2] W. Petyt, *Miscellanea Parliamentaria* (1680), 65.
[3] Throughout the sixteenth and seventeenth centuries, the maxim 'princeps legibus solutus' was taken to mean that the monarch might dispense with all his laws, whereas all that this maxim of Ulpian may have really meant was that the prince could dispense with private and police law. See Esmein, 'La Maxime Princeps Legibus Solutus' in *Essays in Legal History* (ed. Vinogradoff, 1913).
[4] Cf. John Lilburne, *The Just Man's Justification* (1646), where there is a plea for the restoration of local autonomy in England. The common law, he declares, is a badge of slavery derived from the Norman Conquest: common law courts had been set up in opposition to the laws of Edward the Confessor.

Probably the most eloquent plea for the use of civil law in English practice was that made by Sir Robert Wiseman in his *The Law of Laws, or Excellency of the Civil Law* (1657). Wiseman grounds his contention not only on the advantages of using the civil law for international relations and for questions of royal succession and donation, but also because, in his view, the civil law is more equitable than the common law. Thus primogeniture, he holds, is in contradiction with the original law of nature: the civil law, on the other hand, making no difference 'between land and goods, nor between eldest and youngest, divides the whole estate, real and personal equally amongst the children.' So, too, the civil law is less likely to permit injustice through fraudulent interpretation, or constructions that keep the words of a law while perverting its spirit: it does not cause a man to lose his case through lack of witnesses: it enjoins a man to answer, though against himself, rather than permit that the truth should suffer[1]. 'He that is cast by his own confession is more powerfully condemned than he can be by any kind of evidence whatever.' Moreover the civil law, instead of requiring direct and positive proofs, will admit 'strong and forcible presumptions[2].' Hence its utility from the point of view of state interests. 'The extremities of a nation must be provided for by fitting and convenient means, though the exactness of right and justice seem to be infringed[3].' Wiseman suggests that the civil law should be received in England provided it was (*a*) by consent, (*b*) to supply defects in our laws and (*c*) applied to those cases 'where there is greatest need of equity and a good conscience[4].'

Neither in the Civil War struggle however nor in the Revolution settlement was there any question of principle involving the reception or rejection of civil law doctrines. The Bill of Rights limited the prerogative and asserted the legislative supremacy of parliament, leaving the theory of Divine Hereditary Right as an agreeable sentiment to be entertained by those who found precedents for absolutism not in the Digests but in the Bible. Long before the fall of the Stuarts, the civil law had become of little importance in England: there was still, especially

---

[1] *The Law of Laws...*, 14–16. [2] *Ibid.* 17.
[3] *Ibid.* 34. [4] *Ibid.* 108.

INTRODUCTION										lxiii

after 1660, some scope for the civilian as diplomatist[1], though even in this sphere he was frequently invoked merely as a consultant: there was a school of distinguished civilians[2], including Gentili and Zouche, which did much for the development of international law, but this was of more academic than practical importance: the procedure of the Admiralty courts still rested mainly on civil law principles, but chiefly in the form of the Law Merchant, and in the seventeenth century the Law Merchant was coming to be regarded as part of the common law[3]. With the abolition of the Star Chamber and other prerogative courts in 1641, there passed away any immediate[4] danger of this country being subjected to a system of administrative law. The Renaissance was succeeded by a period of decline in the influence of Roman Law, though that influence penetrated to Sweden and Denmark where, in order to control an over-mighty nobility, a Lex Regia was passed by the Estates of each country, conferring practically limitless powers on the monarch[5]. In Italy and Germany, Roman Law studies played an important part in the speculations of the philosophers Vico and Leibnitz, inspiring the first[6] to seek, in the general history of civilisation, a process of evolution similar to that exemplified in the development and decay of Roman institutions, and tempting the second to think of reducing the principles of jurisprudence to the certainty and consistency of mathematical[7] axioms. In England and France, on the other hand, the theory of Divine Hereditary Right held sway, and the religious sanction needed no support from pagan precedent. In this way England recovered something of her insularity; having absorbed just enough of Romanist influence to give some doctrinal consistency to heterogeneous native rules and precedents, the common law of England became entrenched as a national and

---

[1] For this see E. Nys, *Pages de l'histoire du droit en Angleterre: le droit romain, le droit des gens, et le collège des docteurs en droit civil.*
[2] For these see Pillet (ed.), *Les Fondateurs de Droit International.*
[3] See Holdsworth, *History of English Law*, IV, 238 ff.
[4] For some recent tendencies to 'officialise' law in England, see Dicey, *Law of the Constitution* (1915 ed.), XLII ff.
[5] In Denmark, this took place in 1661; in Sweden in 1682.
[6] In his *Scienza Nuova*.
[7] See Leibnitz' *Opera*, ed. Dutens, vol. IV, 92–158, and G. Hartmann, 'Leibnitz als Jurist' (in *Festgabe Rudolph v. Ihering*, 1892).

lxiv INTRODUCTION

assertive institution which no monarch could ever hope to over-ride.

Of English apologists for absolutism, the last to make any use of civil law doctrines, as distinct from Divine Right theories, was an obscure though learned writer named Fabian Philipps[1], who devoted all his money and energies to the declining Stuart cause. His literary activities stopped short at the significant date 1687. In his *Regale Necessarium, or the Legality, Reason and Necessity of the Rights and Privileges claimed by the King's Servants* (1671), he noted, among his sources, 'the civil law, that great repository of reason and prudence[2],' and, with the help of vast legal and historical erudition, he tried to show that the servants of the executive should not be obliged to appear in a court of justice until a licence therefor had first been obtained from 'the Lord Chamberlain, or other royal officer.' He indulges in some curious perversions of English history in order to justify this principle. Thus, according to this writer[3], the Common Pleas were established in a definite place, in order to do justice to the people, while the Marshal's Court continued to follow the king, dealing with all cases where the royal servants were concerned, and so securing to them a special protection from the law of the land. The judges, he holds[4], were accustomed in the past to give unquestioned obedience to any expression of royal pleasure where a servant of the executive was concerned. Philipps was nothing if not thoroughgoing. The king could, by licence, accord the protection of servant to any of his subjects[5]: the whole of the nobility and bishops should, he claims, enjoy immunity from arrest for any civil suit[6]: parliament should content itself with its one indisputable privilege—the right to petition[7]: the feudal aids ought to be restored to the monarch[8]: the king, as fountain of justice, should be a real fountain, emitting two separate streams, one for his

---

[1] 1601–1690. He was a barrister of the Middle Temple and was active in the protests against the execution of Charles I. After 1660 he held some minor government appointments.
[2] *Regale Necessarium*, dedication.
[3] *Ibid.* p. 93.
[4] *Ibid.* p. 392.
[5] *Ibid.* p. 365.
[6] *Ibid.* p. 413.
[7] *Ibid.* p. 375, and *Investigatio Jurium Antiquorum* (1686), *passim*.
[8] See his *Tenenda non Tollenda, or the Necessity of preserving Tenures in Capite and by Knight Service* (1660).

INTRODUCTION   lxv

subjects, the other for his servants[1]. These views would be too ludicrous for mention here were it not that they are supported by copious citations from that jurisprudence which, more than any other, has provided arguments for the apologist of uncontrolled prerogative. Had he written in Tudor times Philipps might have been interesting: under the later Stuarts, his views are merely pathetic.

Thus in a strict sense Selden is justified in terminating the period of Roman Law influence in England at the beginning of the reign of Edward III. Thereafter the supremacy of the common law was sometimes threatened but never really endangered and, in the Civil War struggle, the common lawyers could argue, on behalf of their system, not only its continuity but its (supposed) immemorial antiquity. This was the greatest element of strength in the opposition to the Stuarts, for it associated the parliamentarians with tradition and precedent, while discrediting the executive with the imputation of innovation and encroachment. Historical examination of the position taken up by the opposition prior to 1641 does not always justify the claims of the parliamentary lawyers, but it was sufficient that many of these claims were uncontested by the Royalists, and with a constitutional lawyer like Selden as advocate, judgment was likely to go against the other side by default. It should not be forgotten that the author of the *Dissertatio* had been the mover in the Commons of the Petition of Right. As early as 1628 he had indignantly repudiated the suggestion that civil law principles had ever been of force in English government. Speaking in the debate on the Liberty of the Subject in March of that year, he brushed aside the argument that there were considerations of state[2]: 'I understand not matters of state: I expected not this objection in a course of justice.' On the subject of the proposed commissions for martial law, he was even more explicit: admitting that such commissions had been issued in Henry VIII's reign, he showed that they had never been executed: as for the prerogative of the Marshal's Court, its

[1] *Regale Necessarium, passim.*
[2] See the reports of Selden's speeches in Wilkins' edition of his works (1719), III, pt. II, 1932 ff.

jurisdiction was limited to cases arising in the continental possessions of the crown and, at home, had cognizance only of warfare but not of rebellion. 'The sitting of the Courts at Westminster is a badge of peace, though in other parts of England there be war. What part of England is free from an army, there is *tempus pacis*, if the sheriff can serve his writs. The nature of the Marshal's Court is according to civil law. Can there be a commission to determine life and death according to the civil law?' These words of Selden are the best answer to the question whether civil law principles were admitted into the constitutional doctrines of seventeenth-century England and the best justification for his confining the scope of his *Dissertatio* to mediaeval times.

Selden's inscription on his books περὶ παντὸς τὴν ἐλευθερίαν was no academic convention: he was inspired by a genuine love of liberty when it might have suited his personal advantage to range himself on the side of the prerogative, and at a time when public assertions of general principle were often attended with peril, he proclaimed 'that the liberty of the subject is the highest inheritance that he hath.' The most disinterested figure in an age of fierce personalities, aloof from personal motives and party prepossessions, seeking not fame but truth in an erudition more vast than was ever garnered by any other human mind, Selden stands out alone in a century of great men and unique in the history of his race. His *Dissertatio ad Fletam* should be read not as the pedantic exercise of a recluse, but as the mature work of a great scholar who, in his person, had already vindicated[1] those ideals of personal liberty which are part of our greatest heritage from the past.

[1] He was imprisoned in 1621 for his part in the Commons' protestation and in 1629 for his opposition to Tunnage and Poundage proposals.

IOANNIS SELDENI
AD FLETAM DISSERTATIO
1647

IOANNIS SELDENI
AD FLETAM DISSERTATIO

Caput Primum

   I. De Editione.
   II. Scriptorum Classis cui accensendus est Fletae autor.
   III. De ejusmodi scriptorum usu et autoritate.

   I. Luce jam demum fruitur typographica commentarius hic Juris Anglicani vetustus, Fleta dictus, tamdiu totiesque a studiosioribus desideratus. E codice veteri manuscripto qui pars est Thesauri Cottoniani singularis ac penes me diu mansit manetque et quantum scio, est unicus, ipsoque autore aliquantulo tantum recentior (unde nonnulla pridem desumpta sunt exemplaria) editionem qualemcunque bibliopolae nonnulli per conductam sibi librarii certe nec satis periti nec diligentis satis operam procurarunt. Neque enim editio omnino mea est. Nec sane si fuisset, vocabula exemplaris veteris, ad forensis scriptionis formulam, tot decurtata et veluti 'notis levibus pendentia verba' (ut de veterum formulariorum scriptione dixit Manilius) adeo retineri permisissem, nec sine commodiori lectoribus ornatu ac dispositione, nec cum frivolis aliquot in margine notulis indiciisque intempestivis, ut uberrimam mendorum aliorum segetem praeteream, cudi sivissem; nedum tractatulum Gallicanum 'Fet Assavoir' a primis, ut fieri assolet jurisconsultis, vocibus denominatum et in vetustis juris nostratis collectaneis mss. satis obvium, ad calcem codicis quasi pars ejus esset assui perperam admisissem. Tametsi interim verum sit, exemplari veteri, unde editio fit, illum esse subjunctum, nec sane charactere omnino dispari. Sed alia inter hunc et Fletam intercedit cognatio nulla. Simulac autem cusus est, instantius efflagitarunt editores ut et titulum ego et de libro, autore, nomine aliquid adjicerem. Quod nec aegre impetratum est; dum scilicet per valetudinem dierum aliquot non satis integram, otio abundabam continuo eoque domestico, sed interea studiis diffusioris indaginis rebusque gravioribus nimis inidoneo ac impari.

   II. Autor hujus scripti hactenus est plane incognitus. Connumerandus vero est quisquis ille fuerit, vetustioribus illis,

JOHN SELDEN'S
DISSERTATION ANNEXED TO *FLETA*

Chapter I

I. The edition.
II. The class of writers to which the author of *Fleta* belongs.
III. Concerning the use and authority of such writers.

Faults of the edition

I. This ancient commentary on English Law, called *Fleta*, at last appears in print as scholars have so long and so often desired. An old and, so far as I know, unique MS.[1], forming a remarkable item in the Cottonian collection, of a period only slightly later than that of its author, and of which some copies were made in the past, has long been and still is in my keeping: from this MS. some booksellers have produced an edition of a sort by the help of a paid editor of insufficient experience and diligence. In this I had no hand whatever, otherwise I would not have retained so many of the MS. legal contractions, like 'words hanging on small signs' as Manilius[2] said of the style of the old legists, nor would I have allowed it to go to press without a more tasteful and orderly arrangement for the reader. I would have omitted several irrelevant marginal notes and references (not to mention a plentiful crop of other errors), and I would not have tacked on, as an integral part, the mediaeval French tract known from its opening words as *Fet Assavoir*[3] which is so frequently met with in old MS. collections of our law. Beyond the fact that this tract is annexed to the MS. from which the edition [of *Fleta*] is compiled and is in a similar hand, there is no connection between it and *Fleta*.

The publishers request a preface

The text was no sooner printed than the publishers earnestly begged me to add a chapter dealing with the book, the author and the name, a request readily complied with, as, owing to a slight indisposition of some days' duration, I had an uninterrupted period of domestic leisure incompatible with more extensive studies or more weighty affairs.

Place of Fleta *in legal literature*

II. The author of this treatise is so far completely unknown. Whoever he was, he may be classified with such old writers as

[1] Now MS. Julius B. VIII in the British Museum. It bears Selden's autograph.
[2] M. Manilius, *Astronomica*, IV, 210.
[3] Many MS. copies are imperfect. See Royal MS. 9A, VIII, 35 for the complete text: only about half was printed in the 1647 edition. It has been reprinted by Woodbine in *Four Thirteenth Century Law Tracts* (Oxford, 1910). Woodbine assigns its authorship to Hengham. It was a compilation for convenience in pleading and many MS. copies have survived.

Ranulpho de Glanvilla (saltem si ille autor sit libelli ejus nomine editi, qui ad tempora Henrici regis secundi spectat) viro spectatissimo summaque apud Henricum illum pollenti gratia et primarium in regimine publico locum occupanti; Henrico de Bracton qui, sub annis Henrici tertii posterioribus, judiciis cum primis praefuit; autori anonymo regii Bractonii illius compendii, non sine insequentibus aliquot Edwardi primi legibus intersertis, 'Breton' et 'Britton' nuncupati (de quo plura mox); Radulpho de Hengham, Gilberto de Thornton qui sicut et alter ille uti et anonymus hic noster (qua de re plura inferius) sub Edwardo primo scripserunt, atque Andreae Hornio qui sub Edwardo secundo, aliisque id genus sive in archivis fiscalibus servatis sive in curiosorum bibliothecis delitescentibus. Jam dictorum inquam classi cum primis est Fletae autor accensendus. Priscam scilicet (quemadmodum et illi aliter atque aliter pro aetatum et judiciorum discrimine) Juris Anglicani faciem exhibet, qualis erat ea sub Edwardo primo. Cum reliquis illis idem haud parum praestat juris nostratis studiosioribus et qui penitus originem ejusdem et processum introspicere gestiunt, quod in Jure Caesareo jam praestarent Papirii, Tuberonis, Juliani, Proculi, Flavii, Aelii, Catonis, Sabini, Bruti, Alpheni, Labeonis, Papiniani, Neratii, Jaboleni, Celsi, Pomponii, Neratii Scaevolae, Gaii, Pauli, Ulpiani, Callistrati, Modestini id genus[1] aliorum complurium libri desideratissimi, si jam extarent integri. Habet quidem hic non pauca Bractonio et Thorntonio usque adeo consona ut etiam verbis saepius haud discrepet. Sed interim quamplurimum docet alia nec apud eos nec alibi in libris quos terimus reperta; maxime libro secundo.

III. Scriptores hujusmodi apud nos inter eos quorum doctrina pro ornamentis tantum orationis, in disputationibus juris nostri forensibus scholasticisque esse possit nec autoritatem in se ferat, vulgo censeri solent; idque non sine autoribus[2] magnis. Quod mea sententia (tantorum virorum pace dictum sit) non citra errorem ex incogitantia ingentem ortum propagatumque. Tametsi enim ob vetustatem et intervenientes quae insequutae sunt juris mutationes admodum multiplices, autoritatem in quamplurimis jam non praestent ejusmodi quae decisionibus, judiciis, consultationibusve per se solum sufficiat, innumera nihilominus continent quae aut etiamnum manent integra nec omnino abrogata (ut in materie maxime feudali, criminali, haereditaria, contractibus, translatione dominii, aliis aliquot

---

[1] Videsis l. 2, D. tit. de Origine Juris.
[2] 35 Hen. VI. Fitzherb. tit. Gard. 71, Plowden., Comm. Part. 1, f. 157, atque inde alii.

PLACE OF *FLETA* IN LEGAL LITERATURE

(*a*) Ranulph de Glanvil[1], high in the public service and favour of Henry II (assuming him to be the author of the work attributed to him), (*b*) Henry de Bracton[2], a particularly notable judge in the later years of Henry III, (*c*) the anonymous author of an official summary of Bracton, embodying some of Edward I's subsequent legislation and called *Breton* or *Britton*[3]—of which more anon, (*d*) Radulph de Hengham[4], who, like (*e*) Gilbert de Thornton and the anonymous author here considered, wrote in Edward I's reign, (*f*) Andrew Horn[5] of Edward II's time, and other such commentators whose works are preserved in public or private archives. With these the author of *Fleta* should be specially classed because he expounds the law of Edward I's time, as do the above writers for their periods and according to their respective abilities. Like these also he is of great service to industrious researchers into the origin and development of our legal system, a service similar to that which would be afforded for the study of civil law by Papirius, Tubero, Julian, Proculus, Flavius, Aelius, Cato, Sabinus, Brutus, Alphenus, Labeo, Papinian, Neratius, Jabolenus, Celsus, Pomponius, Scaevola, Gaius, Paul, Ulpian, Callistratus, Modestinus and others of that class[6], if only, as one would wish, they were extant complete.

Identity with Bracton and Thornton

The author of *Fleta* shares so many things with Bracton and Thornton that often the very words are identical but, especially in his second book[7], he expounds several things not to be found in Bracton or Thornton nor in any other source examined by us.

The value of ancient legal writings

III. Though popular opinion, not without great authority on its side, regards such writers as unauthoritative and providing merely an elegance of style for the discussion of legal questions in our courts and universities, yet in my view, with all due deference, this is quite wrong. For though, on account of antiquity and many subsequent legal changes, these writings have not an inherent authority such as would suffice by itself in judicial decisions or opinions of counsel, they yet contain many things either still valid or not completely

---

[1] His *Tractatus* was first printed about 1554.
[2] The *De Legibus* was first printed in 1569.
[3] There were editions in 1540 and 1640.
[4] Hengham's *Magna Summa* and *Parva Summa* were edited by Selden in 1616. The *Magna Summa* has been reprinted by Woodbine (*Four Thirteenth Century Law Tracts*). The *Judicium Essoniorum* (Camb. Univ. MS. Dd. VII, 14) and the *Modus Componendi Brevia* (Royal MS. 9A, VII, 50) have also been attributed to Hengham.
[5] The *Mirror of Magistrates* was first printed in 1640.
[6] For these see *Jurisprudentiae Anteiustinianae Quae Supersunt*, ed. Seckel (and others) in Teubner Series 1868–1908.
[7] In the final chapters of Book II there are many extracts from Walter of Henley's *Husbandry*. See Lamond's edition of Walter of Henley, xxxii ff.

etiam quotidianis) aut quae mores majorum legesque avitas mutationibus ejusmodi priores copiosius ostendunt. Atque ita certe tam autoritatem e qua juris interpretatio pendeat eos habere manifesto in disputationibus forensibus scholasticisque est agnoscendum quam ornamento esse. Dubitarine potest quin, si Romanorum quos diximus veterum scripta juridica nobis non adeo invidisset temporis injuria, ingens inde et lux et autoritas accessisset Pandectis (quae illorum fragmentis tantum aliquot ad Triboniani in jure novando dirigendoque sensum aptatis refertae sunt) et utrique Codici Novellisque Justinianeis rite intelligendis explicandisque? Certe lucis ejusmodi saepe nimis ex jactura illa immani infeliciter caremus. Ac specimina ea de re habentur non contemnenda ex pauculis Gaii, Ulpiani, Pauli ipsorum reliquis quae non interiere atque id genus aliquot aliis. Quinimo autores ejusmodi veteres ad eos qui sunt recentiores atque in studiis foroque maxime obtinent, ita se ferme habent ut sanctiones legesque antiquitus latae ad eas quibus ipsae sive abrogatae, sive mutatae, sive novatae fuerint. Lex etiam ipsa abrogata, nedum mutata aut novata, abrogandique, mutandi, novandi ratione diligentius perpensa (neque enim sine hujusmodi concursu praevio bene decernit jurisconsultus) autoritatem plane praestat amplissimam[1] juri novissimo atque in re praesenti rite capiendo. Ita in jure caesareo, Codex Theodosianus et quae cum eo eduntur, Codici, in non paucis, Justinianeo. Ita compilationes decretalium antiquae illae quatuor ab Antonio Augustino uti et quinta seu Honoriana ab Innocentio Cironio jam nuper edita Gregorianae juris pontificii corporis parti, uti et Burchardus et Ivo, id genus alii, Gratiani maxime syntagmati. Ita et Orientalibus, quamdiu Basilicorum Leoninorum usus eis olim mansit, adjumento proculdubio fuere maximo ipsae Justinianeae Pandectae codicesque reliqui unde conflata Basilica illa, quibus dum haec scribimus, primo fruimur ex editione V.C. Caroli Annibalis Fabroti. Quale itidem plane dicendum de priscis apud nos alibique legibus innumeris, quae aut esse desiere aut mutatae sunt novataeve. Neque sane excogitari

---

[1] D. tit. de Legibus, 26, 27, 28 et ibi gloss. et DD. Constant. Rogerius de Juris Interp. cap. 11. Alderanus Mascardus, Conclus. de Statutorum Interp. 2 etc.

VALUE OF OBSOLETE LAW BOOKS

abrogated, especially in questions of tenure, felony, inheritance, contract, conveyancing and other everyday matters. They may contain many things which reveal ancient laws and customs prior to these changes. Clearly therefore, in both abstract and concrete cases, they provide not only a literary embellishment, but a confirmation on which the interpretation of the law may depend. Had the above-mentioned legal treatises of the Romans been preserved in their entirety, can it be doubted but that they would have afforded great light and authority for the proper understanding of both Code and Novels of Justinian as well as of the Pandects? These last are filled with only some fragments of such writings, adapted by Tribonian to his special task of reviving and regulating the law, and the extent of our loss may be inferred from the few but not to be despised fragments that remain of writers like Gaius, Ulpian and Paul.

Their relationship to modern writings

Ancient writers of this type bear the same relationship to modern and authoritative writers as do obsolete laws to those laws by which they are annulled, changed or renewed. Even an abrogated law, not to mention an altered or revived one, provides the new law with its fullest authority[1] and best interpretation if the reason for the abrogation, change or renewal be carefully considered. Without such preliminary survey the jurist cannot form an accurate judgment. In civil law, this function was to a large extent fulfilled by the Code of Theodosius and its appendices, in relation to that of Justinian. The same holds of the four old compilations of Decretals drawn up by Antonius Augustinus[2], together with the fifth or Honorian Decretal recently published by Innocent Cironius[3], in relation to the Gregorian section of the Canon Law code[4]; and this is also true of writers like Burchard[5] and Ivo[6] in relation to Gratian's compilation[7]. In the East, so long as the Basilica of Leo were in force, great service was doubtless afforded by the Pandects of Justinian and by other Codes from which the Basilica (available now in the edition of Fabrot[8]) were themselves compiled. This may be said of innumerable old

---

[1] D. 1. 3. 26, 27 and 28.
[2] *Juris pontificii veteris epitome*, Rome, 1611–13.
[3] Drawn up by Honorius III in 1216: published by Cironius in 1645.
[4] Compiled, 1230–4, by Raymond of Peñaforte at request of Gregory IX. See *infra*, p. 111, n. 6 and 191, n. 1.
[5] Bishop of Worms, died 1023. His *Collectarium* or *Decretum* was compiled between 1012 and 1023 and was first printed at Cologne in 1548. His *Decretum* is semi-religious and philosophical. See Diederich, *Das Dekret des Burchards von Worms* (Breslau, 1908).
[6] Bishop of Chartres, died 1117. Between 1095 and 1117 his *Decretum*, *Panormia* and *Tripertita* were compiled. See Menu, *Recherches sur les recueils...attribués à Yves de Chartres* (1880), and Fournier, in *Revue des Questions historiques*, LXXII, 51 ff.
[7] *Circa* 1150. See *infra*, p. 101 and n. 5.
[8] Βασιλικῶν *libri sexaginta*, Paris, 1647.

potest, scriptorem haberi juris omnino aliquem cujus autoritas singularis, quantum ad tempora insequentia, non decrescat pro varia morum legumque superinductarum ratione ac usu. Sed interim in his tantum decrescit quae ab ita superinductis mutantur; in quibus nihilominus ipsis usque adeo firma permanet, ut jus pristinum, cujus in novissimo interpretando usus est sicut tralatitius ita etiam pernecessarius eximiusque, inde sit imprimis ediscendum. Summa est, veterum hujusmodi usum simul ac autoritatem esse ferme qualis est epocharum sive a quibus sive per quas temporum motuumve deductiones fieri solent et calculus.

Caput Secundum

    I. De Gilberti de Thornton capitalis sub Edwardo primo justitiarii Summa MS. in quam Bractonium redegit.
    II. De variis Bractonii nominibus.
    III. De compendio juris gallicano, Britton dicto.
    IV. Summae Thorntonianae titulus, partiumque, quarum pleraeque mutilae, lemmata.

I. Quemadmodum autem 'Fletae' autor, in non paucis tam sententiis ac periodis integris quam rebus ipsis, sequax est et Bractonii et Thorntonii, ita Thorntonius ipse Bractonii, ut scilicet ejusdem epitomator; de quo utpote adeo Fletae congenere atque scriptore quasi incognito, etiam ferme inaudito, pauca liceat adtexere. Gilbertus ille de Thornton sub Edwardo rege primo, cum potestate summa seu quae capitalis justitiarii vocatur, judiciis praefuit; quod nec ignorat quisquam sive archivis nostris sive juris annalibus non alienus. Anno autem ejusdem regis vigesimo Bractonium in compendium summa cum diligentia redegit, unde etiam de singulari Bractonii, qui Fleta paulo vetustior est, in jure sub Edwardo illo (cujus etiam annales juridici in foro hactenus obtinuere atque in rebus gravissimis etiamnum[1] obtinent) discutiendo autoritate est dijudicandum. Penes me habeo compendii illius codicem manuscriptum autori, quod ex charactere scimus, satis coaevum. In bibliotheca quae olim erat Burleiana reperi. Neque exemplar aliud mihi aut visum aut auditum. In partes tribuitur octo. Sed nimis est mutilum. Vocatur in fronte 'Summa de legibus et consuetudinibus Angliae a Magistro Henrico de Bryctona composita tempore regis Henrici filii regis Johannis'; adjecto dein, abbreviatam esse a Thorntonio.

---

[1] Ut ex temp. Ed. I cas. Cobledike in cas. Calvin. Cok. relat. part. 7 et saepissime in Fitzherberti Breviario liquet.

laws, both in England and abroad, which have either been rescinded, changed or renewed.

Changes in law illustrate existing law

But while it is true that the authority of every legist in relation to later times must decrease in proportion to the different nature of subsequent legislation and custom, yet this authority is lessened only in respect of matters actually changed. Such changes may, however, serve to reveal the original law which is used in interpreting most recent law in a traditional as well as exemplary manner. To sum up, the use and authority of these ancient writers is like that of Epochs[1], in reference to which calculations of time and motion are made.

Chapter II

   I. The MS. summary of Bracton by Gilbert of Thornton, chief justice in Edward I's reign.
   II. The various names of Bracton.
   III. The Norman-French law manual called *Britton*.
   IV. The title of Thornton's *Summa* and the subjects of its sections, many imperfect.

Thornton

I. As the author of *Fleta* frequently follows Bracton and Thornton not only in sentences and whole paragraphs but in subject-matter also, so Thornton the epitomizer follows Bracton. It may be permissible to say something of Thornton as an almost unknown writer and of the same class as the author of *Fleta*. As every student of our archives and Year Books knows, he was chief justice in Edward I's day. In the twentieth year of that reign he carefully digested Bracton's book into a compendium, whence we may infer the great authority of Bracton (who is a little earlier than *Fleta*) in the legal questions of that reign, the Year Books of which had and still have great weight in important matters. In my possession there is a manuscript copy[2] of this *Summa* which, judged by the handwriting, is presumably coeval with the author: this I found in the old Burghleian library. I have neither seen nor heard of any other copy. Divided into eight parts and very imperfect, it is entitled 'A Summa of the *De Legibus et Consuetudinibus Angliae* compiled by Henry de Brycton in the time of King Henry, son of King John,' and it is added that the abbreviation is the work of Thornton.

[1] As late as the seventeenth century it was a current belief that human history consisted of a definite number of epochs—seven was the number generally chosen. In mediaeval times it was often supposed that the Holy Roman Empire would be succeeded by the reign of Christ, or the Church, then Anti-Christ, then the Judgment.
[2] Now lost. See *supra*, p. xxii.

II. Neque mirum videatur 'Henricum de Bryctona' heic nuncupari eum quem vulgo, uti in libris ejus editis, Bracton vocitamus. Nomen ejus perquam variatim scribi solebat. Et ubi in editorum initio legitur 'ad instructionem saltem minorum ego Henricus de Bracton animum erexi' etc. codicum MSS. alii habent tantum 'ad etc. ego talis' etc. alii 'ego talis H. animum erexi' etc. Ac perpulchrum inter alia penes me est ejusdem nec Edwardi primi initiis sed autore ipso paulo recentius exemplar, quo post lemmata capitum recensita subjicitur 'expliciunt capita Britonis.' Et Bracton igitur et Brycton et Britton et Briton etiam et Breton (ut statim ostenditur) aliterque appellatus est. Unde et compendium illud sequentibus aliquot legibus auctum, 'Britton' dictum, nec, sine errore manifesto Johanni Bretoun episcopo Herefordensi annis compluribus ante ejusdem conscriptionem mortuo tribui solitum, nomen velut ab autore, unde nomine jussuque regio descriptum est, primario sumpsisse autumo. Id quidem agnoscendum est ex eo quod in ejusdem editis legitur[1] de errore nominis in rescriptis regiis, verum illi videri nomen fuisse de Bracton. Sed interim aliis quae memoravimus nominibus vocatum etiam antiquitus aliterque eum esse certo est certius. Atque in loco illo de nominis errore, ita allato ut suum pro exemplo habeatur, variant codices manuscripti. E meis habet unus isque proximo post autorem seculo exaratus, pro eo quod in editis ibi legitur, 'item si erratum sit in syllaba, ut si quis alium nominet Henricum de Brathon si nominare deberet eum de Brachiton. Item idem erit in litera, ut si quis erraverit sic nominando Henricum de Brochton et nominare deberet eum Henricum de Braketon.' Et codices ibi alii aliter aliterque. Quinimo sub Edwardi primi initiis tum eum expressim nominari solitum Henricum de Breton tum librum ejus Brettone et Breton dictum esse satis liquet ex syngrapha R. de Scardeburgh, Thomae Bec archidiacono Dorsetiensi confecta, de libro illius quem per Thomae istius manus a Roberto Bathoniensi episcopo commodatum acceperat. In archivis[2] titulus est 'Litera R. de Scardeburgh per quam recepit ex mutuo de Magistro Thoma Bec quendam librum, qui vocatur Brettone.' Ipsa autem syngrapha sic. 'Universis praesentes literas inspecturis R. de Scardeburgh archidiaconus salutem in Domino sempiternam. Noveritis me recepisse et habuisse ex causa commodati librum quem dominus Henricus de Breton composuit, a venerabili patre domino R. dei gratia Bathoniensi episcopo per manum magistri Thomae Beke archidiaconi

---

[1] Lib. 4., de Assisa Nov. Disseis. cap. 20, § 4, fol. 188 b.
[2] In codice MS. Bullarum etc. apud camerarios Scaccarii fol. 175.

VARIATIONS OF BRACTON'S NAME

Relationship of Bracton to Britton

II. It need not occasion surprise that the writer whom we know in the printed texts as Bracton should here be called Brycton, for his name was variously written. Where, at the beginning of the printed editions we read 'ad instructionem saltem minorum ego Henricus de Bracton animum erexi' etc., some of the MSS. have simply 'ad...etc., ego talis' etc., others 'ego talis H. animum erexi' etc. Among my MSS. there is a very perfect one of Bracton not later than the early years of Edward I and slightly later than the period of the author himself, in which there are appended to the enumeration of the chapter-headings, the words 'Here end the chapters of Briton[1].' Thus Bracton was styled Brycton, Britton, Briton and even, as will be shown, Breton. This is my reason for holding that the compendium, embodying some later legislation, called *Britton* and attributed erroneously to John Bretoun Bishop of Hereford (who died some years before its compilation) really derived its name from that of the author summarised—Bracton, and was so copied therefrom in the royal name and by royal command.

The name Bracton

That Bracton appears to have been his real name may be inferred from the place in the printed texts referring to mistaken names in the royal writs: it is certain however that, even anciently, his name had the above and other variations. At the point where his own name is quoted to illustrate mistakes in names the MSS. show considerable differences. One of mine, of the fourteenth century, has the following variation on the reading found in the printed texts—'If there be a mistake in a syllable, as Brathon instead of Brachiton, or in a letter as Brochton for Braketon.' Other MSS. have other variations. But that in the early years of Edward I's reign he was expressly named Henry de Breton and his book called *Brettone* or *Breton* may be deduced from the bond of R. de Scardeburgh given to Thomas Bec, archdeacon of Dorset, promising to return a book named *Brettone* borrowed, by means of the said Thomas from Robert, bishop of Bath. The words[2] of the bond are: 'To all whom it concerns...R. de Scardeburgh, archdeacon...I have received on loan the book which Henry de Breton composed, from the bishop of Bath, by the hand of Master Thomas Bec, archdeacon of Dorset, which book I promise to restore on the feast of St John Baptist 1278. Given at Dover...1277.'

[1] The editor cannot identify this MS. Harleian MS. 817 ends 'explicit Breton': Add. MS. 24067 has 'Bretton.'
[2] Translation slightly abridged.

Dorsetiae, quem eidem restituere teneor in festo sancti Johannis Baptistae, A.D. MCCLXXVIII. In cujus rei testimonium praesentibus sigillum meum appensum, datum Doveriae die veneris post purificationem Virginis Gloriosae, anno MCCLXXVII.'

Annus fuit hic Edwardi primi sextus. Nec quis horum erat qui Bractonium ipsum in vivis cognoscere non potuisset. Sed de nomine insuper testimonia sunt palmaria in archivis ipsis ubi codicilli[1] praefecturae Bractonii. Ibi crebro Henricus de Bretton nominatur uti et subinde etiam de Bratton.

III. Verum quidem est pro recepto haberi, compendii quod vocitamus 'Britton' autorem fuisse Johannem Bretoun seu Bretun (quem et Bectonum falso nuncupant aliqui[2]) episcopum Herefordensem Henrico nostro coaevum jurisque Anglicani peritum. Etiam in editione Matthaei monachi Westmonasteriensis seu Florilegi Londinensi, anni MDLXX ejusque in Germania sequaci expressim fit ille auctor ejusdem compendii. Verba sunt in editione illa; 'obiit hoc anno (MCCLXXV seu III Ed. I) Johannes Bretoun episcopus Herefordensis qui admodum peritus in juribus Anglicanis librum de eis conscripsit, qui vocatur le Bretoun.' Atque hoc nomine designatur proculdubio aut opus illud Bractonii latinum aut gallicanum illud minus. Utrumque enim idem ut vides antiquitus sortiebatur nomen. Sed sive hoc sive illud innuatur hallucinationem esse scriptoris quicunque temere inserserit palam est. Neque enim ipsius monachi est, ut statim ostendetur. De latino Bractonii opere nemo puto dictum admittet. Et qui de gallicano admiserit, nae illi etiam est admittendum ut qui anno Edwardi primi tertio in vivis esse desierit (tunc enim mortuus[3] est episcopus ille Herefordensis) sanctiones[4] in scriptis suis Parlamentarias decennio ampliusque post latas intersereret. Certe et Gallicani illius tractatus seu compendii habeo exemplar pervetustum cui subjicitur, 'Ici finist le Brecton que contient IV lieures' (ita enim distinguitur) 'en les queux chascun maniere de plee est contenue.' Et memini me olim alicubi ad calcem ejusmodi exemplaris legisse distichon rhythmicon, cujus verba non satis teneo cuncta. Sed primum versum terminavit 'Brato' pro autoris nomine et secundum 'et dixit talia nato.' Quae quidem etiam adstruunt, Henrici de Bracton seu Breton nomen in codice quod Britton et Breton vulgo vocitamus, intelligi, ut primarii autoris

---
[1] Vide Rot. Claus. 43 Hen. III dorso 7 et dors. pat. 43 Hen. III et quae in id genus tabulis antecedunt.
[2] Balaeus, Pitsaeus etc.
[3] Vide Notas ad Rad. de Hengham, pag. 129.
[4] Vide Britton, c. 14, c. 36, etc., ubi statuta 13 Ed. I seu West. II habentur.

THE AUTHORSHIP OF *BRITTON*

The forms Bretton and Bratton

This was in the sixth year of Edward I. It was not impossible for any of these men to have known Bracton personally. There is additional evidence about the name in the documents relating to Bracton's judicial activities preserved in our public archives[1]. There he is frequently styled Bretton and often Bratton.

Authorship of Britton

III. Popular opinion regards the author of the compendium called *Britton* as John Bretoun, or Bretun or (wrongly) Becton, Bishop of Hereford, a man skilled in English Law and contemporary with our Henry[2]. This is expressly stated in the 1570 London edition of the Chronicle of Matthew of Westminster[3], or Florilegus, and is repeated in the later German edition[4]. The reference is: 'There died in this year (1275 or 3 Edward I) John Bretoun, bishop of Hereford, highly skilled in the laws of England and author of a book thereon called le Bretoun.' Obviously this name may refer either to the Latin work of Bracton or to the compendium in Norman-French, the same name being anciently assigned to each, but whichever is intended there is obviously a mistake for, as will be shown presently, the above statement was not made by Matthew himself. The statement cannot refer to the Latin work of Bracton: nor can it be affirmed of the Norman-French compendium, for a man who died in 1275, as did this Bishop of Hereford, could not have referred to parliamentary enactments made more than ten years later[5]. I possess a very old copy of this French treatise or compendium concluding with the words 'Here end the four books of le Brecton[6] containing every type of plea,' and I remember reading somewhere, at the end of some such copy, rhyming verses of which the first line ended with 'Brato' (for the author's name) and the second with 'et dixit talia nato[7].'

---

[1] In the Calendar of Close Rolls (1242–7) the name appears in three places as Bratton: in *ibid.* 1247–51 it appears five times as Bretton. Bratton is probably correct: cf. Madox, *Baronia Anglica*, 102, 104.
[2] Presumably Henry III or Henry of Bracton.
[3] The existence of Matthew of Westminster has been doubted: see preface to the *Flores Historiarum* in the Rolls Series (1886).
[4] Frankfort, 1601.
[5] Wingate, who edited the 1640 edition, conjectured that the book was examined after the bishop's death and more recent statutes incorporated. This is rejected by Britton's most recent editor (F. M. Nicholls, 1865). On the other hand the book may have been written by John le Breton, who in 1305 became a Justice of Trailbaston.
[6] Cambridge MS. Gg. v, 12 ends 'Ici finist le livr de Brectoun.' Among the British Museum MSS. of *Britton* occur the forms Bratton (Harleian MS. 489) and Bruton (Harleian MS. 4656).
[7] This MS. cannot be traced.

unde desumptus est, utcunque ipso recentioribus aliquot rebus auctus. Etiam in annalibus nostris juridicis[1] plane codex ille 'Britton' dictus, 'Bracton' nuncupatur. Sic codicem Justiniani recte vocamus, licet interspersus fuerit, multis post Justinianum seculis, tum Novellis ejusdem tum Fredericianis constitutionibus aliquot. Sic Xiphilinum saepe Dionem, Justinum Trogum Pompeium, Florum etiam Livium, id est epitomatores ipsos autorum suorum nomine indigitamus. Et quod ad locum illum in editione quam diximus 'Florilegi' attinet; nec omnino habetur is sive in editione prima anni 1567 sive in codicibus ejusdem MSS. veteribus qui in bibliothecis et Lambethana et Westmonasteriensi asservantur. Adeoque a sciolo aliquo temere ingestum dubitare nequeo.

IV. Opus quod diximus 'Thorntonii,' esse Henrici de Bracton (illud enim retinemus nomen quod Brycton apud eum sit) summam abbreviatam palam est. Verba tituli integra damus. 'Incipit summa de legibus et consuetudinibus Angliae a Magistro Henrico de Bryctona composita tempore Henrici filii regis Johannis, quam quidem summam Dominus Gilbertus de Thornton tunc Capitalis Justitiarius domini regis in Anglia secundum statuta et leges tunc usitatas, ad utilitatem posterorum diligenti studio postmodum abbreviavit sub compendio, anno regni regis Edwardi filii regis Henrici vicesimo. Et ipse idem dominus Gilbertus tempore illo scientia, bonitate et mansuetudine floruit eleganter.' Sensus est, Thorntonium dum Capitalis erat Justitiarius, sub Edwardo scilicet primo, compendium hoc seu breviarium fecisse, idque juxta statuta et leges tunc usitatas. Id est Bractoniana exhibuit quatenus in legibus et statutis tunc usitatis rite intelligendis posteritati esse possent adjumento. Neque enim statuta ipsa quae post Bractonium et ante scriptionis tempus intervenere veluti de Dotis, verbi gratia petitione[2], de Homicidio ex infortunio[3], de Donis Conditionalibus[4], ejusmodi aliis aliquot, omnino memorat. Praetermittit perplurima ut epitomatores solent. Nec vero Bractonii methodum semper sequitur, alia interdum usus, uti et distributione alia, quod ex partium ejus octo hac serie luculentius est videre. In fronte sequitur, 'Et notandum est quod praesens opus in octo partes dividitur.'

'Prima pars tractat de Personis et earundem variis conditionibus, de Rebus et Rerum divisionibus, de Donationibus et Confirmationibus.

Secunda, de Actionibus et Obligationibus, de Poenis et Judicum Potestatibus, de Itinere Justitiariorum et eorum Capitulis.

[1] Conferat 35 Hen. VI, fol. 42 cum 35 Hen. VI, tit. Gard. 71.
[2] 3 Ed. I. West. I, c. 49.   [3] 6 Ed. I. Gloc. c. 9.
[4] 13 Ed. I. West. II, c. 1.

The title Britton derived from Bracton

These things mean that, though the writing commonly called *Britton* or *Breton* contains matter of a later date, yet the name Bracton or Breton occurring therein is to be understood as derived from the name of the primary author. Similarly in our Year Books the compilation called *Britton* is referred to as *Bracton*. Thus we speak of Justinian's 'Code' though it was, much later, enlarged by the Novels of this emperor and by some constitutions of Frederick: in the same way we often refer to Xiphilinus[1] as Dio, to Justinus[2] as Trogus Pompeius, to Florus[3] as Livy, that is, we indicate the epitomizers by the names of their original sources. As regards the passage adduced from Florilegus, it is to be found neither in the first printed edition of 1567 nor in the old MSS. of the work preserved in the libraries of Lambeth[4] and Westminster. There can be little doubt but that it was rashly inserted by some smatterer.

Title of Thornton's treatise

IV. The treatise called *Thornton*[5] is obviously a summary of Bracton. Here is the full title: 'The Treatise of the Laws and Customs of England compiled by Henry de Brycton...reduced to an abbreviation by Master Gilbert Thornton, then Chief Justice of England, in the twentieth year of king Edward, for the benefit of posterity and according to the laws and customs then in force. This master Gilbert excelled in learning, integrity and clemency[6].'

Its contents

Thornton's purpose being thus to elucidate the law as it was in the time of Bracton, he makes no reference to those statutes passed in the period between Bracton's death and the date of his compiling the *Summa*—such as, for instance, the statutes dealing with pleas in dower, the issue of writs by Chancery in cases of homicide, and grants of lands on conditions (De Donis Conditionalibus). Like most epitomizers, he omits a good deal, nor does he always follow Bracton's arrangement, using, as he does, a different system and distribution of contents, as may be seen from a list of the eight parts of the book:

1. Persons and their various conditions, Things and Divisions of things, Donations and Confirmations.

2. Actions, Obligations, Penalties, Powers of Judges, the Eyre of Justices and their Commissions.

---
[1] Xiphilinus, Ἐκ τῶν Δίωνος...ἱστοριῶν ἐπιτομή, Paris, 1551.
[2] Justinus, *Epitome in Trogi Pompeii Historias*, Rome, 1472.
[3] Florus, *Ex T. Livii Decadibus...Epitome*, Venice, 1520.
[4] MS. 188 in M. R. James' *Catalogue of the Lambeth MSS.* (Camb. 1900).
[5] See *supra*, p. xxii.
[6] Selden's sentence repeating this information is omitted.

Tertia, de Criminibus et Homicidio et de Appellis et Feloniis.
Quarta, de Vetitis Namiis et Disseisinis.
Quinta, de Communia Pasturae et ejusdem ammensuratione, de Assisa Mortis Antecessoris, de Damnis et Convictionibus.
Sexta, de Brevi de Recto, de Summonitionibus et Essoniis.
Septima, de Exceptionibus et regiis Prohibitionibus, de Bastardia et Gradibus Successionis.
Octava, de Homagiis et Releviis, Haereditatibus et Donationibus propter Nuptias, et Dotibus mulieribus assignandis.'

Et quantum ad methodum sane et distributionem attinet, etiam aliter aliterque se habent ipsae in codicibus MSS. Bractonii. Perpulchrum habetur et vetustum in bibliotheca Oxoniensi publica exemplar quo, Henrico de Bracton nomine apposito, nulla omnino distributio est in libros, ut in editis; sed ita in centenas tantum, ut post decem centenas numeris suis designatas sequantur capitula insuper 67 adeoque opus integrum ex capitulis 1067 constet. Alii codices perpetuam capitum seriem usque in finem habent. Ceterum adeo mutilus est codex MS. Thorntonii ut quum partis primae capita, cum lemmatibus singulis adjectis numerentur 58 uti et partis secundae capita 19 reliqua post caput primae 42 et post secundae caput 10 praeter aliquantulum noni, omnino desiderentur. Quale pariter dicendum de parte tertia cui numerus capitum 31. Sed quae octavum intercedunt et vigesimum desunt. Quartae tribuuntur capita 26. Quinta capita habuit 18 quorum praeter partem decimi sexti restant tantum postrema bina. Sexta integra est, cui capita 21. Septimae erant capita 25. Sed desunt quae decimum quintum sequuntur. Octavae sunt 14 eaque integra. Incipit non aliter atque Bractonius ipse, nec aliis in proemio verbis quam ille in editis utitur, demto quod Bractonii nomen non interserit, prima persona interim ut apud Bractonium usurpata, atque eodem modo quem habent codices hujus MSS. 'Ego talis animum induxi.' Postrema item ejusdem verba et caput partis octavae postremum integrum, eadem ferme sunt ipsissima quibus finitur Bractonius. Jussu autem regio aut non sine regis auspiciis conscriptum esse hoc Thorntonii opus par est ut credamus ex eo quod in Annalibus[1] juris nostri habetur Edwardum illum (male in impressis vocatur secundus) tum leges moresque regni in scripta redigere universos voluisse, tum libros aliquot alios, praeter notissimum illum 'Britton' dictum, opera jurisprudentiorum qui sub eo floruere eam in rem confecisse, idque veluti suos. De Brittonio plane intelligendum illud Prisoti summi causis civilibus quae Communia Placita vocamus sub Henrico Sexto rege praefecti,

---

[1] 35 Hen. VI, fol. 42 a.

3. Crimes, Homicides, Accusations and Felonies.
4. Withernams and Disseisins.
5. Common of Pasture and its apportionment, Assize of Mort d'Ancestor, Damages and Convictions.
6. The Writ of Right, Summonses and Essoigns.
7. Exceptions, Royal Prohibitions, Bastardy and the Order of Succession.
8. Homage and Relief, Inheritance, Marriage Settlements and Dower.

Division of chapters in Bracton MSS.

As regards system and arrangement the MSS. of Bracton show some variations. In the Bodleian Library, Oxford, there is an old and very fine specimen[1] bearing the name of Henry de Bracton, which, unlike the printed editions, is not divided into books but into hundreds, and after ten sets of each a hundred chapters there remain over 67, so that the whole work consists of 1067 chapters. The other MSS. have a continuous series of chapters throughout.

Lacunae in the MS. of Thornton

The MS. of Thornton is however so imperfect that while the chapters of Part 1, together with the added titles, number 58, all after the 42nd chapter is wanting: of the 19 chapters in Part 2, all after the 10th and a part of the 9th are missing. There is a gap between the 8th and 20th of the 31 chapters of Part 3: Part 4 is assigned 26 chapters: Part 5 had 18, of which, except a portion of the 16th, only the last two survive. Part 6 is entire (21 chapters): Part 7 had 25 chapters, but all after the 15th are lacking. Part 8 is complete—14 chapters. The opening words are identical with those in Bracton, except that Bracton's name is not used: he occasionally, like Bracton, employs the first person and prefaces with Bracton's words 'Ego talis animum induxi[2].' The whole of the last chapter in Part 8 and the concluding words are practically the same as the final part of Bracton.

Date of Britton

There is reason to believe that Thornton's *Summa* was written by royal command or under royal auspices, for it is recorded in the Year Books that this Edward (by a printer's error called Edward II), wishing to reduce all the customs and laws of the realm to writing, caused some lawyers of his time to compile, as royal productions, other legal manuals in addition to the well-known *Britton*. The remark of Prisot, Chief Justice of Common Pleas, in a case arising in Henry VI's reign from a statute of 3 Edward I concerning the

---
[1] Now MS. Bodley 344.
[2] The texts of Bracton have 'erexi' not 'induxi.' See *supra*, p. 10.

ubi dum fiunt in foro verba de statuto anno tertio[1] Edwardi
primi de pupillari aetate edito, "cest estatut (inquit[2]) fuit fait
en temps le roy E. le 2 (plane legendum E. le 1 pro Edwardo
primo) le quel roy fuit in purpose daver mise tout en certein,
per que il fist un liver deux ans apres cest estatut fet et en que
cest estatut est reherse.' Ipsissimum hoc statutum habetur in
'Brittonio[3],' nec dubitari solet quin codex ille heic intelligendus.
Sed interea nec puto dubitandum quin pro 'deux ans' legendum
sit 'douze ans.' Nam in codice illo expressim memorantur
etiam statuta[4] anni ejusdem regis decimitertii, seu quae Westmonasterii secundi dicimus, unde manifestum sit haud biennio
post tertium annum, illum fuisse conscriptum, sed post decennium saltem inde elapsum, ut ante etiam monuimus. Sed si
Prisoto sic credendum, conscriptus ita erat sub annum Edwardi
primi decimum quintum, non omnino quintum ut volunt qui
ex depravata heic lectione secure nimis hallucinantur. In alio
autem exemplari annalium juridicorum, unde illud Prisoti sum-
tum, aliorum item librorum ejusdem regis jussu conscriptorum
mentio expressa. Verba sunt[5], 'le quel roy' (scilicet Edwardus
primus ut in editionibus correctioribus[6]; nam in aliis[7] mendose
itidem legitur Edward le second) 'fuit appurpose daver mise
tout en certein et en escripture et commence de ceo faire liver
de et par plus sages homes del ley deins le realme s. juges et
autres. Il fist un liver deux ans' (lege 'douze ans') prochein
apres le fesance de cel estatute.' Atque ex hisce Thorntonii
codicem fuisse non videtur ambigendum. Certe in ipsius initio,
quod, ut apud Bractonium, est 'In rege qui recte regit...' prima
vox ampliori et eleganti pingitur ducto auro ac coloribus varie-
gato, intra quem in solio habituque regio ad hunc modum
residens rex ille judices sex habitu ornatos forensi solennique
ac coram adstantes adloquitur. Quasi inde regium jussum ad
librum illum sic attinuisse ipsumque regem veluti ejusdem
autorem (qualis saltem Justinianus 'Tribonianeorum' erat)
fuisse, legesque ac mores Anglicanos in eo judicibus ac turbae
forensi indicasse ibi innueretur. Neque epitomator solum sed
etiam subinde est interpres egregius Thorntonius et expositor.
Exempla autem ac decisiones forenses quas non paucas memorat
Bractonius praetermittit hic, uti etiam ferme quas habet ille[8] e
Juris Caesarei libris locorum citationes pessime ab editoribus
tractatas. Atqui illas non praetermisit omnes. Qua de re, uti

---

[1] West. I, c. 22.   [2] 35 Hen. VI. Fitzherb. tit. Gard. 59.
[3] Cap. 67.   [4] West. II, c. 1 et 38. Britton, cap. 36 et 14.
[5] 35 Hen. VI, fol. 42.   [6] Anni 1601.   [7] Anni 1557.
[8] Lib. 2 de Acq. Rerum Dom. cap. 12. Lib. 3 de Actionibus, cap. 8, § 3, cap. 3 et cap. 12, § 5.

OFFICIAL LAW BOOKS

age of wards, clearly refers to *Britton*: 'This statute was made in the reign of Edward II (read Edward I), who wished to have everything clearly defined and who, for this purpose, compiled a book two years after passing this statute in which the statute is cited.' The statute referred to is to be found in *Britton*. But I think that for 'two years' (deux ans) should be read 'twelve years' (douze ans), for in *Britton* the statutes of 13 Edward I (called Westminster 11) are expressly mentioned: hence obviously the book must have been written not two years after 3 Edward I but at least ten years thereafter, *i.e.* if Prisot is to be believed, 15 Edward I, not 5 Edward I.

Thornton's Summa *compiled by royal command*

In another copy of the Year Books[1] from which this statement of Prisot is taken, mention is made of other manuals written by command of the same king. The words are: 'which king (Edward I in corrected texts, Edward II in uncorrected texts), desiring to have everything defined and expressed in writing, commenced a book by the help of his wisest lawyers, *i.e.* judges and others. He completed a book two years (read twelve years) after making this statute.' There is no doubt that Thornton's compilation was of this class. Like Bracton, he begins with the words 'In rege qui recte regit' and the first word is drawn on a larger scale, tinted with gold and colours, while within is depicted the king seated on his throne addressing six judges, dressed in their robes and standing solemnly in his presence[2]. In this way is conveyed the impression that the book appeared by royal mandate and as if with the king for author (in the sense, at least, that Justinian was the author of the Tribonian collections) and that he was thus declaring the laws and customs of England to the legal fraternity.

Thornton not a mere epitomizer

Thornton however is not merely an epitomizer but an interpreter and commentator of some eminence. He omits many illustrations and precedents recorded by Bracton and nearly all the latter's quotations from civil law books—these last have been badly handled by Bracton's editors. Of this matter and of the use of imperial law

---

[1] Selden here refers to the printed text of the Year Books printed by R. Tottell in 1567. For the literature of the Year Books see Holdsworth, *History of English Law*, 3rd edition, II, 528 ff., and Maitland's preface to the third volume of the Selden Society Year Book series.

[2] This illumination is lacking in the Lincoln's Inn MS. considered by Woodbine to be a copy of Thornton.

insuper de Juris Caesarei apud scriptores hosce Fletaeque autorem usu atque etiam de eodem in hac insulae parte olim recepto, intermisso, restituto, temperato et cancellis cohibito paucula subjiciemus quae studiosioribus satis grata fore non dubitamus.

Caput Tertium

    I. Librorum Juris Caesarei usus prisci apud Juris Anglicani consultos, qua tales, vestigia manifesta tam in Thorntonio et Fletae autore quam Bractonio.

   II. Eorum Legis Regiae in Pandectis l. 1. tit. de Constitutionibus Principum lectio sensusque, etiam qua in Caesareis est, perquam singularis et mirus.

  III. Diversae interpretum coaevorum de Lege Regia illa sententiae.

  IV. Quaenam vera; et quid illa Lex.

   V. Quanam ab jurisconsultis nostratibus illo in seculo sub ratione ita adhibitum Jus Caesareum, maximeque Lex illa Regia.

I. 'Lex,' inquit Thorntonius[1], 'gravem poenam infligit judici corrupto per munera sordida ut C. ad legem milit.' (sic MS. sed legendum 'C. ad legem Juliam' quae est repetundarum) 'l. omnes, ubi dicitur quod omnes cognitores et judices a pecuniis manus abstineant ne alienum jurgium putent suam praedam.' Atque ita e Codice Justinianeo eandem citaverat legem Bractonius[2], quod ex MSS. constat, utcunque in ejusdem editione tam seculi superioris, quae prima fuit, quam jam nupera (quarum utraque se fingit factam ingenti cura atque e codicibus MSS.) perperam legatur, 'ut C. ad legem vel repetet l. omnes' pro 'ut C. ad legem Jul. repetund. l. omnes' et pro 'a pecuniis' ridicule substituatur 'a re cuivis'; uti et paulo post ibi 'ut C. s. l. ultima' pro 'ut C. e' (pro 'eodem titulo') 'l. ultima,' qua poena quadrupli illic memorata a Theodosio et Valentiniano irrogatur. Atque in editionibus illis utriusque menda sunt perplurima eaque crassissima, partim e librariorum inscitia, partim ex operarum incuria. Alias adhibentur item leges ipsissimae tum a Bractonio tum a Thorntonio e corpore Justinianeo citatae, adjectis ab utroque, designatisque more jurisconsultorum caesareorum, locis quos praeterit omnino Fletae autor, ipsas interea leges expressius, easque velut vim heic tunc obtinentes pariter recitans. Verbi causa; Fletae autor de Donationibus inter virum et uxorem loquens, 'Verba,' inquit[3], 'legis sunt ejusmodi, si in nomine et substantia nihil distet a dote....' Quae inde sequuntur in lege ipsa quam innuit, ab ipso Justiniano[4] lata, ibi subjicit, quemadmodum itidem et Thorntonius[5] et Bractonius[6]. Horum autem uterque in MSS. suis locum etiam ipsum legis qui

[1] Part. 1, cap. 11.   [2] Lib. 3 de Actionibus, cap. 8, §3.
[3] Lib. 3, cap. 3, §§ 15 et 16.   [4] L. 20, C. tit. de Donat. ante Nuptias.
[5] Part. 1, cap. 33.   [6] Lib. 2 de Acquir. Rer. Dom. cap. 12.

by these writers, including the author of *Fleta*, together with its former reception, discontinuance, restoration and reduction to strict limits in this part of Britain we shall add some remarks. These we hope will be acceptable to scholars.

Chapter III

I. The undoubted evidences, in *Thornton*, *Fleta* and *Bracton*, of the former use of civil law books by English jurists.
II. Their interpretation, remarkable and unique even among civil lawyers of the Lex Regia enunciated in the Digests.
III. Different contemporary interpretations of the Lex Regia.
IV. The true interpretation and the law itself.
V. For what motive the civil law and particularly the Lex Regia was utilised in those days by our lawyers.

Civil Law quotations in Thornton and Bracton

I. 'The law,' says Thornton, 'inflicts a heavy penalty on the judge corrupted by bribes as enacted in the Code[1]...the words being "all kinds of judges must abstain from bribes lest they come to consider the disputes of others as their prey."' Bracton, as the MSS. show, cited the same law from Justinian's Code, though in both the printed editions (one of last century[2], one of recent date[3]), each claiming to be based on a careful collation of the MSS., it is quoted wrongly; and there are, in addition, many gross mistakes[4] due to the ignorance of the editors and the carelessness of the printers.

Bracton, Thornton and Fleta *on Donations*

Elsewhere the actual laws from the Corpus of Justinian are cited by both Bracton and Thornton, who, in the manner of Civil Lawyers, give their references, which the author of *Fleta* omits. Equally with the other two, however, *Fleta* quotes these same laws as if they were valid in this country at that time. For instance, on the subject of donations between husband and wife, *Fleta* writes 'the words of the law are these' and goes on to quote the rest of the passage from the law of Justinian here referred[5] to, in the same way as do Bracton and Thornton, who, however, add references. The printed editions of Bracton make a mistake in this reference and misquote Justinian's

[1] C. 9. 27. 3.
[2] 1569.
[3] 1640.
[4] For instances see Selden's text.
[5] C. 5. 3. 20.

praetermittitur in Fleta, sic addidit, 'C. tit. de Donationibus ante nuptias l. cum multae,' pro quo in editis Bractonii male legitur 'cum milite'; et pro eo quod est in ipsa lege (uti et a Thorntonio et Fletae autore recte exhibetur) 'Sancimus omnes licentiam habere...,' e quibus verbis utpote in persona Justiniani prolatis totam vim legis pendere nemo non videt, pessime exaratur 'Scimus omnes licentiam habere....' Sed hujusmodi in Bractonii editis sunt creberrima menda, etiam et non raro in exemplaribus ejus MSS. licet vetustis, aliquot. Atque ita plane apud triumviros hosce usurpatur Justinianeum illud sub legis nomine et Constitutionis et Inhibitionis, perinde ac si etiam apud Anglos jus Donationis inter conjuges inde vigorem contraxisset. Et 'fraudem fieri Constitutioni' aiunt Bractonius[1] et Thorntonius, et 'fraudem inhibitioni' Fletae autor, si quid aliter in conjugum donationes fiat quam sanctio illa Justinianea praescripserit. Alibi item in Fleta[2] legitur, 'Donationes etiam post feloniam perpetratam factae perfectae erunt et perpetuae, nisi donatores hujusmodi de feloniis suis in vita convincantur.' Quod juri quo utimur et avito plane consonum est. Sed statim in Fleta subjungitur; 'Et ad hoc facit lex Imperatoria, post capitale crimen contractum donationes valent, nisi condemnatio fuerit subsecuta.' Id est, l. 15. D. tit. de Donationibus e Marciani Institutionibus sumpta, quae etiam citatur Bractonio[3] sic, 'et ad hoc facit lex F. (pro ff.) de Donationibus, post contractum...,' alibique, 'convenit lex cum consuetudine Anglicana ff. de Donation. l. post contractum, ubi dicitur quod post contractum capitale crimen donationes factae valent nisi condemnatio subsequuta sit.' Atque loco priori, 'innuit ergo,' inquit ille[4] recte, 'quod, nisi fuerit subsequuta, valent Donationes, et, si fuerit, quod non valent.' Et utrique sic legitur illa lex ut in vulgaribus rudioribusque Pandectarum editionibus habetur, praetermissa quae in politioribus occurrit voce expressim negativa. Nam in Florentinis ita se habet, 'post contractum capitale crimen donationes factae non valent ex constitutione divorum Severi et Antonini, nisi condemnatio secuta sit.' Quae locutionis formula mira non penitus perpendenti videatur, quasi scilicet donationes damnatorum valerent, quales, nisi damnarentur, forent irritae. Sic enim verbo tenus sonare videtur. Substituendum igitur volunt aliqui 'si' pro 'nisi.' Tunc enim ex condemnatione sola irrita fit rei donatio. Et de lege illa perquam variae occurrunt doctorum opiniones. Et Bartolus de ea; 'ista

---

[1] Ibid. lib. 2, cap. 5, § 5.   [2] Lib. 3, cap. 10, §§ 2 et 3.
[3] Lib. 2 de Acquir. Rer. Dom. cap. 5, § 5 et cap. 13 ad finem.
[4] C. tit. de Donat. inter Vir. et Ux. L. 24 et L. 31. D. dict. tit. in fine.

sanction of the law, reading 'we know that everyone is permitted' instead of 'we decree....' Mistakes indeed are common in the printed editions and even in some old MS. copies[1]. But the point is that our legal triumvirate annex this enactment of Justinian as a law, an ordinance and a prohibition, just as if the English law of donations between husband and wife derived its force therefrom. 'It is a fraud on the ordinance,' say Bracton and Thornton, 'a fraud on the inhibition,' says *Fleta*, if anything is done in conjugal donations otherwise than as prescribed by this enactment of Justinian.

In another part of *Fleta* we read 'Donations made after the commission of a felony will be valid and perpetual unless the donors are convicted of such felony in their lifetime'—an opinion consistent with the law of those days and of ours. But *Fleta* immediately adds: 'This is the effect of the imperial law that donations are valid even after the commission of a capital offence, unless conviction has ensued.' This title in the Digests[2] (from the Institutes of Marcian) is quoted in two places by Bracton: in the one[3] (where he cites the Digests wrongly[4] as *F.* instead of *ff.*) he says 'this is the effect of the law in the Digests...concerning donations,' and in the other[5], he states that 'consistently with English custom, the law in the Digests concerning donations...enacts that, after the commission of a capital offence, donations are valid unless conviction has ensued.' In the first of these two places he says rightly 'hence the implication is that donations are valid, unless conviction has ensued; and invalid, if conviction has ensued.'

Both writers however read this law as it is found in the inferior editions of the Pandects, omitting the express negative to be found in the more accurate editions. In the Florentine recension it reads thus: 'after the commission of a capital crime, donations are invalid, from a constitution of the emperors Severus and Antoninus, unless (nisi) conviction has ensued.' This singular method of expression may seem to imply that donations of convicted persons were valid only if conviction had ensued. Some would insert 'if' for 'unless' thus making conviction invalidate donations.

[1] For instances see Selden's text.
[2] D. 39. 5. 15.
[3] *De Legibus*, f. 12b.
[4] The traditional mediaeval method of referring to the Digests was 'ut ff.' The reason for this contraction does not appear to be known.
[5] *De Legibus*, f. 30b.

est valde notabilis lex et habet materiam quotidianam et legitur duobus modis....' Certe sensum fuisse post condemnationem non valere non dubito, quod satis fit e Graecorum ejusdem quasi versione, Τοῦ δωρησαμένου κεφαλικῶς καταδικασθέντος αἱ παρ' αὐτοῦ μετὰ τὸ ἁμάρτημα γενόμεναι δωρεαὶ οὐκ ἰσχύουσιν. Sic in Basilicis[1]; id est, 'si is qui donavit capitali supplicio damnatus sit, post crimen admissum donationes ab eo factae non valent.' Unde puto legisse etiam Graecos 'non valent' in ipsis Digestis. Et quod ad vocabulum 'nisi' attinet, etiam in ipsa Florentinorum editione Taurelliana, ejusque sequacibus quasi dubitanter est insertum. Certe retinendum censuerit quisquis archaismum heic locum[2], ut in aliis crebro, habere admiserit. Scilicet si vocabulum 'nisi' dividatur heic in 'ni si,' id est apud veteres 'non si' (nam 'ni' pro 'non' usurpari agnoscunt Grammatici[3]) sensus erit apertus; 'non valent donationes,' quae verba fuerint constitutionis imperatoriae, quibus explicandi gratia sic adjecerit Marcianus, 'ni si condemnatio secuta sit,' id ita est, 'non, si condemnatio sit secuta'; quod etiam est consonum ipsi juri receptissimo. Sed ex archaismo hujusmodi opem heic nec accersendam nec satis praestitam sentio. Aut 'ni' expugnas, aut substituas 'non.' In impressis item Bractonii citatur[4] 'l. 13 in bonae fidei C. tit. de Pactis' (sed satis perperam) atque inde dicitur probari pacta ex intervallo donationibus adjecta, nec incontinenti, eis non inesse. Verum in codicibus MSS. quibus utor locus ille non omnino sed sensus tantum adfertur.

II. Specimen autem prae reliquis, juris Caesarei sic ab jurisconsultis nostratibus tunc adhibiti peregregium est illud quod de potestate principis seu regia, e Pandectis, sed non expressim memoratis, Bractonius exhibet. 'Nihil aliud,' inquit[5], 'potest rex in terris, cum sit Dei minister et vicarius, nisi id solum quod de jure potest. Nec obstat quod dicitur, "quod principi placet[6] legis habet vigorem" quia sequitur in fine legis, "cum lege Regia quae de imperio ejus lata est," id est, non quicquid de voluntate regis temere praesumtum est [sed animo condendi jura]' (redundant haec verba hoc in loco, tametsi ad rem ipsam primario spectent, nec in MSS. Bractonii quibus utor habentur, nec in Thorntonio aut Fleta) 'sed quod consilio magistratuum suorum, rege autoritatem praestante, et habita super hoc de-

[1] Lib. 47, tit. 1.
[2] Cujac. Observat. 3, cap. 38. Alberic. Gentil. de Libris Jur. Civ. cap. 3.
[3] Priscianus, lib. 15 et Donatus ibi.
[4] Lib. 2, c. 6, § 12.
[5] Lib. 3 de Actionibus, ibid. c. 9, § 3.
[6] L. 1, D. tit. de Constit. Principum.

Solution of the difficulty

There are various opinions about this law. Bartolus refers to it as 'a very notable law of every-day application and read in two ways.' That its intention was to invalidate donations after conviction there can be no doubt, as is clear from the Greek version in the Basilica: 'if a man making a donation be condemned to capital punishment, his donations are invalid if made after committing the crime.' Hence I infer that even in the Digests the Greeks read 'are invalid.' As regards the word 'unless' (nisi) it is inserted in the Torellian[1] and succeeding[2] editions of the Florentines as if with some doubt. Whoever is for invoking an archaism of this kind will admit that, as in other cases, the principle applies whereby the word 'nisi' may be divided into 'ni' and 'si,' or the old 'non si' (grammarians allow the usage of 'ni' for 'non'); the meaning will thus be clear: 'Donations are invalid' (these we may assume to have been the words of the imperial constitution, to which for purposes of explanation, Marcian may have added) 'not if conviction ensues,' and this is consistent with the generally accepted opinion of that law. But in my view nothing is gained by retaining such an archaism; delete 'ni' or substitute 'non.'

A wrong reference in an edition of Bracton

In the printed copies of Bracton there is a reference[3] stated to provide proof that agreements annexed to donations and made not immediately after but at an interval are no part of such donations. In my MSS. copies is to be found only the principle, not the reference.

Bracton and the Lex Regia

II. A specially noteworthy instance of the use of civil law at this time by our lawyers is the passage in Bracton, derived though not actually cited from the Pandects, concerning princely power. 'A king,' he says, 'can act no otherwise in his dominions than as authorised by law, since he is God's servant and delegate. Let it not be objected "what pleases the prince has the force of law," because this law goes on to say "in accordance with the Lex Regia formulated in regard to his authority..." *i.e.* the maxim refers not to any rash presumption of the royal pleasure (but to what the king does with the intention of legislating): rather it is to be understood as meaning what shall be agreed upon after mature deliberation and with the counsel of his ministers, the king furnishing the requisite authority.' *Fleta* and Thornton speak to the same purpose[4] and in

---

[1] The Torelli brothers published their edition of the Florentines in 1553. For the Torellis see Stintzing, *Geschichte der deutschen Rechtswissenschaft*, I, 204 ff. 'Si' appears as 'nisi' in Haloander's edition (Nuremberg, 1529).
[2] 1571 and 1576.
[3] C. 2. 3. 13.
[4] See Selden's text for the quotations: they are practically identical with those from Bracton.

liberatione et tractatu recte fuerit definitum.' Tantundem et totidem ferme syllabis Fleta[1]; 'quia sequitur,' inquit, 'cum lege regia quae de imperio ejus lata est.' Thorntonius item; parili sic adjuncta ratione; 'quia sequitur in fine legis cum lex regia' (sic codex MS. pro 'lege'[2]) 'quae de imperio ejus lata est, et non quicquid de voluntate regis temere praesumtum est....' Ex hisce duo sane sunt inprimis advertenda. Posterius autem non sine stupore. Prius est, Jus Caesareum in illustri illa gravissimique momenti de potestate apud Anglos regia, quaestione discutienda, tunc locum, ex horum omnium sententiis adeo esse sortitum, ut quod ex eo velut in autoritatem usumve obvium recepto posset objici, id responsione seu interpretatione necessario indigere existimaretur, adeoque in rebus quarum in ratione, regiminis reipublicae populive Anglicani versaretur cardo, vigorem prae se ferre. Posterius autem est, autorum horum quemlibet legem illam e Pandectis sibi allatam tum legisse tum intellexisse (si eos omnino capio) aliter prorsus quam legi solet intelligive sive a Graecorum sive a Latinorum scriptorum opinor aliquo. Conjicitur Lex illa Regia tum in Pandectas[3] tum in Institutiones[4] ex Ulpiano. 'Quod principi placuit' (sic utrobique) 'legis habet vigorem; utpote' (sed Institutionibus deest 'utpote') 'cum Lege Regia, quae de imperio ejus lata est, populus ei et in eum omne suum imperium et potestatem conferat,' ut in Florentinis; aliis habentibus 'contulerit' pro 'conferat'; uti et Institutionum exemplaribus aliis 'concedat,' aliis 'concesserit' et 'concessit' pro eodem. Ubi 'cum' (quod et 'quum' legitur in accuratiori editione Cujaciana aliisque ejusdem libentius sequacibus) pro conjunctione causativa sive verbo 'conferat' aut 'contulerit' sive voci 'concedat,' 'concesserit' aut 'concessit' inserviente plane sumendum. Justinianus etiam ipse alibi[5],—'Lege antiqua quae Regia nuncupabatur omne jus omnisque potestas populi Romani in Imperatoriam translata sunt potestatem.' Et Arcadius Charisius[6], 'Regimenta reipublicae ad Imperatores perpetuo translata esse' ait, legem hanc Regiam innuens quae etiam 'Lex Imperii[7]' et 'Augustum[8] Privilegium' in Codice dicta. Pomponius[9] item, 'Constituto principe, datum est ei jus, ut quod constituisset ratum esset.'

[1] Lib. I, c. 17, § 7.
[2] Part. II, c. 12.
[3] L. 1, tit. de Const. Princip.
[4] Tit. de Jur. Nat. § Sed et Quod.
[5] L. 1, § Cum itaque. C. tit. de Vet. Jur. Enucleando.
[6] L. 1, D. tit. de Offic. Praefecti Praetorio.
[7] L. 3 ex imperfecto C. tit. de Testamentis.
[8] L. unica, § 14, haec autem C. tit. de Caducis Tollendis.
[9] L. 2, D. tit. de Origine Juris, § 11.

almost the same words. The words in brackets, though very much to the point, are not to be found in my MSS. of Bracton, nor in Thornton nor *Fleta*.

Peculiar interpretation of the Lex Regia

Two things may be noted in regard to the above. The first is that in a matter of great import, namely the English royal prerogative, the civil law was held by these writers to have acquired such a place, that whatever could be adduced from it by way of authority or tradition must require a formal opinion or interpretation. The imperial law had thus acquired a sanction in matters on the interpretation of which turned the hinges of the English commonwealth. The second (and astonishing) thing is that these writers, if I understand them aright, interpret that law quite otherwise than any Greek or Latin writer.

Orthodox views on the Lex Regia

The Lex Regia is inserted in the Pandects[1] and the Institutes[2] from Ulpian: 'What pleases the prince has the force of law since ('cum') by the Lex Regia enacted in reference to his government, the people transfers ('conferat') to him and on him all its power and authority.' This is the Florentine version: others have 'transferred' for 'transfers' and some copies of the Institutes have 'concedes,' others 'had conceded' and 'conceded,' 'cum' (read 'quum' in the more accurate versions of Cujas and his followers) being taken for a causative conjunction linked with the verb 'confers' or its variations. So too Justinian says elsewhere: 'by the old Lex Regia all the power and authority of the Roman people were transferred to the imperial prerogative.' With reference to this Lex Regia, called also in the Code 'the law of empire' and 'the imperial prerogative,' Arcadius Charisius[3] writes: 'the control of the state is transferred for all time to the emperors'; while according to Pomponius[4], 'when a prince is constituted he is given the right that whatever he decrees shall hold good.' The Greeks, omitting for the most part the qualification

---

[1] D. 1. 4. 1.
[2] Inst. 1. 2. 6.
[3] Roman jurist, early fourth century.
[4] D. 1. 2. 2. 21.

Graeci vero, praetermissa plerunque ratione illa Ulpiani pronuntiant heic rotundius, "Ὅπερ ἀρέσει τῷ βασιλεῖ νόμος ἐστίν 'quod principi placuerit lex est'; quod scilicet ita placuerit ut animus jus condendi simul adfuerit. Sic in Basilicis[1], sic apud Harmenopulum[2], alibi, unde τὰ βασιλέων δόγματα[3] 'principum dogmata' seu decreta pars est juris apud illos etiam civilis. Sed Theophilus Antecessor ubi quartum juris condendi autorem, post tres illos Populum, Plebem, Senatum facit Principem Romanum, καὶ τί, inquit[4], ἔστι βασιλεύς; ἐστὶ ὁ κράτος τοῦ ἄρχειν παρὰ τοῦ δήμου λαβών. 'Et quid est Princeps? Princeps est qui potestatem imperandi a populo accepit.' Ita Legem Regiam, ut Ulpianus, intellexit. Et scholiastes ibi, βασιλεὺς νομικός 'princeps legitimus'; cui scilicet potestas sic concessa. Unde in Leonis et Constantini Epitome[5] vocatur Imperator ἔννομος ἐπιστασία 'legitima praefectura.' At vero triumviri jam dicti nostrates ita legisse mihi plane videntur omnes ut pericopen ad hunc modum aut sensum fuisse integram non dubitarent. 'Quod principi placet legis habet vigorem, cum lege regia quae de imperio ejus lata est'; quibus verbis etiam innuunt finiri hanc legem, idque satis expressim tum Bractonius tum Thorntonius. Adeoque 'cum' non ut conjunctionem sed ut praepositionem intelligunt, quemadmodum et Fletae autor, sensumque suum esse, legis quidem habere vigorem quod principi placuerit, ita tamen ut ejusmodi placitum cum Lege Regia quae de imperio ejus seu regimine lata est rite componatur perpendaturque, neque aliter atque juxta eandem legem vigorem sortiatur, nec de vigore illo aliter decernatur atque legis illius regiae conditionum ac temperamentorum qualiumcunque sine quibus collatum non est imperium, ratio permiserit singularis, juxta ea quae ibi statim subduntur de singulari apud nos tam de legibus in Ordinum Comitiis ferendis quam de Judiciis legitime exercendis. Neque illud de 'imperio et potestate omni a populo concessa' in lege illa omnino videntur hi ibi agnovisse, quasi exemplaribus suis plane defuisset. Certe Bractonii seculo adeoque deinceps Digestorum exemplaria heic studiosis habita non minus atque alias apud gentes integra ac ut libros alios describi solita satis constat, tametsi alia non reperirentur argumenta (quibus sane non caremus ut mox ostenditur) ex ipsius exemplis de Contractuum formulis allatis, ubi[6] de Codice et Digesto heic describendo ut re usitatissima loquitur. Unde

---

[1] Lib. 2, tit. 6.   [2] Lib. 1, tit. 1.
[3] Michael Psellus in Synopsi Juris.
[4] Inst. tit. de Jure Nat. Gent. et Civili.
[5] Tit. 2.
[6] Lib. 2, de Acquir. Rer. Dom. c. 6, fol. 19.

in Ulpian's definition, say roundly 'the king's will is law'—will in the sense of the will to make laws. So in the Basilica and in Harmenopulus[1] elsewhere: whence the resolutions or decrees of kings form a part of Greek civil law. Theophilus Antecessor[2], placing the Roman prince after people, plebs and senate, as the fourth source of law, asks: 'what is a king? A king is one who has received the power of ruling from the people,' *i.e.* he interprets the Lex Regia in Ulpian's sense. The scholiast here adds 'a lawful prince,' as one to whom power has been granted, and in the Epitome of Leo and Constantine the emperor is called 'a legitimate government.'

English interpretation of the Lex Regia

But our triumvirate appear to have interpreted the passage as though they did not doubt that an abbreviation in the following form and sense was its complete text: 'what pleases the prince has the force of law in accordance with the Lex Regia enacted concerning his power.' So expressly Bracton and Thornton. These two writers, like *Fleta*, translate 'cum' as a preposition not a conjunction, interpreting the maxim to mean that the royal will has the force of law only so far as consistent with the Lex Regia and acquiring its authority thereby. In this view, nothing is to be determined of the prerogative except as allowed by the characteristic sense of the various stipulations of the Lex Regia—an interpretation occurring before a passage concerning our remarkable characteristic of administering justice according to law and legislating in assemblies of Estates. Our trio seems to omit entirely the clause 'all their power and authority conceded by the people' just as if it was wanting in their copies. In Bracton's time, English as much as foreign scholars had complete copies of the Digests, which were transcribed like other books, and this is sufficiently shown in Bracton's discussion of Contract formulae where he speaks of transcribing Code and Digest as a very common affair in this country.

---

[1] Greek jurist, *c.* 1320–80. Author of the Πρόχειρον Νόμων.
[2] The quotation is from *Theophili Antecessoris Institutionum Libri IV*, p. 19 (Paris, 1638). See Ferrini, *Institutionum graeca paraphrasis Theophilo Antecessori vulgo tributa* (Milan, 1884–7).

magis mirandum quanam evenerit ratione ut non solum ipse adeo judiciis forensibus clarus et, si biographis[1] scriptorum nostratium fides, Professor Juris Utriusque Oxoniensis, verum etiam Thorntonius juris alias peritissimus et Fletae autor adeo diversam lectionem sensumque diversum atque interpretibus aliis universis adeo alienum in illustrissimo Juris Caesarei loco illo explicando tam fidenter admiserint. Tametsi interea, quantum ad rem ipsam, qua de apud eos agitur, et constitutionem Imperii Anglicani attinet, nulla scilicet verborum Ulpiani seu Justiniani ratione habita, subtexant eorum singuli id quod vero est perquam consonum et receptissimum; de Ordinum nempe Comitiis intellectum, ut opportet; qua de re item videndus Bractonius in prooemio. Quinetiam vetus est apud me in codicem illum quem 'Britton' vocitamus (sed in praevia tractatuum voluminis in quo continetur recensione antiqua, 'Bracton de Legibus Angliae,' juxta capite in superiore dicta, appellatum) commentarius MS. cujus in fronte verborum illorum 'Quod principi placuit...' sensus, qualis apud Bractonium exhibetur ipsissimus.

III. Quod vero ad decantatissimae illius Legis Regiae, qua in Caesareo corpore habetur, tum lectionem tum sensum apud alios attinet, id quidem advertendum est, in exemplaribus aliquot Digestorum Bractonio tum coaevis tum vetustioribus lectionem a superius e Justiniano allata diversam habitam atque etiam ab interpretibus aliquot adprobatam. Odofredus[2], Bractonio coaevus, in codice suo legebat 'utpote cum lex regia lata est, populus ei et in eum imperium et potestatem conferret.' Ita deerat 'omne suum.' Atque 'alias,' inquit Odofredus, 'in litera est, concessit[3]. Et haec est bona litera.' Sensus autem legis illius apud interpretes Bractonio coaetaneos et qui post instauratum in Occidente jus Caesareum praecesserunt, varius erat. Fuere enim etiam tunc qui ita omnimodum imperium et potestatem a populo Romano in Principem translatam esse, Lege illa voluerint, ut populum inde plane potestate ac imperio nudatum omnimodo ac destitutum assererent. Hostiensis; 'alii dicunt,' inquit[4], 'quod nec Populus nec Senatus potest hodie condere legem generalem, sed tantum Princeps, quod verius credo.' Tantumdem videre est apud Accursium[5]. Atque in

---

[1] Balaeus, Cent. 3, Script. 98. Pitsaeus, art. 13, Script. 335.
[2] Ad L. 1, tit. de Const. Prin.
[3] Sic apud Angelum Perus. ad dict. legem et vide Francisc. Conn. Juris Civ. lib. 1, cap. 16 et edit. Instit. Cujacianam et Baudozianam tit. de Jur. Nat. § Sed et Quod.
[4] Summ. tit. de Const. Prin. § 9 etc.
[5] Gl. ad D. tit. de Legibus 19 'non ambigitur.'

Why this interpretation is remarkable

For this reason it is all the more difficult to understand why not only so eminent a judge as Bracton who, according to his English biographers professed Civil and Canon Law at Oxford[1], but also such a skilled lawyer as Thornton, as well as the author of *Fleta*, should, on such a celebrated passage, give an interpretation so completely at variance with the universal one. Nevertheless, when they treat of their own subject and of the English constitution, apart altogether from Ulpian and Justinian, they each adduce much that is consistent and valuable, especially in regard to the meetings of the Estates. For this, see Bracton's prolegomena.

Reference to a MS. Britton

I possess an old MS. commentary[2] on the so-called *Britton* (referred to as Bracton in the ancient list of contents prefixed to the volume of tracts containing the MS.—see previous chapter of this Essay), and there the words 'Quod principi placuit...' are given the same interpretation as in Bracton.

Odofred's textual variations

III. In regard to the interpretation put upon this famous Lex Regia (as found in the Corpus Juris) we may note that some copies of the Digests, both coeval with and earlier than Bracton, give a reading different from the one already cited, and preferred by some scholars. Odofred[3], a contemporary of Bracton's, omitted in his text the words 'all their' before 'power and authority.' "Elsewhere," says the same writer, "the reading is 'concessit' and that is a good reading."

Confusion of Lex Regia with Lex Hortensia

Among Bracton's contemporaries and immediate predecessors there was a difference of opinion about this law. Some maintained its purport to be that all power was transferred to the prince by the people, who were thereby stripped of every vestige of sovereignty. This view is to be found in Hostiensis and Accursius, possibly also in Martinus: it will be considered later. Another interpretation

---

[1] There is no proof that Bracton ever studied at Oxford, Bale being the earliest authority for the statement that he did. See Maitland, *Bracton and Azo*, xx ff. Maitland suggests that, while at Exeter, Bracton may have received some instruction in Roman law from Thomas of Marlborough (afterwards abbot of Evesham and formerly a teacher of Civil Law at Oxford).

[2] This MS. cannot be identified.

[3] *Commentaria*, 1550, I, 17–17 b.

his, puto, erat Martinus. Et hac de sententia plura mox. Eorum alii potestatem quidem ac imperium Principi inde voluere concessum leges pro libitu condendi, sed ita tamen ut concessione ejusmodi populi potestas neutiquam minueretur, atque ut tam Plebiscitorum quam Senatusconsultorum non solum veterum sed quae insequerentur vis ut antea maneret integra. Scilicet ut Princeps, Populus, Senatus, Plebs parem invicem (quod merito mirere) hac in re potestatem tenerent. Hoc satis liquet ex Azone[1], Accursio, Hostiensi[2] et Odofredo[3] Bractonio aut paulo vetustioribus aut coaevis. Atque posterior haec opinio nata est partim ex eo quod legem heic Regiam intellexerint pro lege Hortensia, forte sane maxime, ex eo quod professores aliquot ac studiosi eo in aevo juris hujus quod ita paulo ante occidentalibus instauratum est, cautius timerent, ne si Principibus ex eo potestatem tantam, quanta in priore sententia habetur, tribuerent, populis civibusque per Europam passim libertate moribusque avitis potestati ejusmodi haud parum dissonis gaudentibus, nimium displicerent nec recens enascenti professioni suae satis prudenter consulerent. Et notissima est inter Martinianos et Bulgarianos[4] de Principis etiam ex hac lege potestate, seculis in illis vetustioribus controversia. Anno autem ab urbe condita 422 seu ante Christum 330[5] a Q. Hortensio dictatore lata est lex[6] 'ut eo jure quod plebs statuisset, omnes Quirites tenerentur,' unde factum est ut inter leges qualescunque ante receptas sive veterum regum, sive Senatus, sive alias, et Plebiscita, 'species[7] constituendi' (ut ait Pomponius) 'interessent, potestas autem eadem esset.' Atque hinc, ait Justinianus[8], 'Plebiscita non minus valere quam leges coepisse'; tametsi apud Livium[9] habeatur L. Valerium et M. Horatium Consules sub annum centesimum ac vigesimum ante legem Hortensiam, 'omnium primum, quum veluti in controverso jure esset, tenerenturne patres plebiscitis, legem, centuriatis comitiis, tulisse, ut quod tributim plebes jussisset, populum teneret.' Sed mira sane ex lege Hortensia huc allata ratio ab Accursio, Odofredo, aliis. Accursii verba; 'Regia, scilicet lata ab Hortensio mirabili oratore, ut supra de origine juris, l. 2 § deinde cum esset. Sed de populo et plebe ibi dicit. Dic ergo heic Regia, id

---

[1] Summ. ad C. tit. de Legibus et Constit. Princ. § 8.
[2] Locis citatis.
[3] Ad dict. legem.
[4] Jo. Quintin. in Aristocrat. Christ. Civit. tit. de Regis Imperio.
[5] Epit. Livii, lib. 2.
[6] Laelius Felix apud A. Gell. lib. 15, cap. 27.
[7] L. 2, D. tit. de Orig. Jur. § 8.
[8] Instit. de Jur. Nat. et Gent. § Plebiscitum.
[9] Dec. 1, lib. 3, cap. 55.

III III   LEX REGIA AND LEX HORTENSIA

inferred that power was conferred on the prince in order that he might freely legislate, but in such a way that neither the power of the people nor the force of plebiscita and senatus consulta, old or new, should be diminished. This remarkable view, giving an equal share of power reciprocally to prince, people, senate and plebs is also to be found in Accursius[1], Hostiensis[2] and Odofred[3], as well as in Azo[4]. It arose partly from a confusion between Lex Regia and Lex Hortensia, but mainly because these exponents of the recently-revived civil law hesitated to attribute to the prince such an authority as that allowed by the former of these two interpretations lest, at a time when European countries were enjoying free institutions and traditions quite inconsistent with such a degree of princely power, they might give offence and so damage the interests of their infant profession. Noteworthy also in this respect is the old controversy between the followers of Martinus and Bulgarus on the subject of princely power[5].

Explanation of this confusion

In B.C. 330 a law was carried by the dictator Hortensius that all Romans should be bound by enactments of the plebs[6], with the result that though plebiscites differed in form from other kinds of legislation, they[7] had equal force with them. From the Lex Hortensia Justinian[8] says that plebiscites acquired equal force with statutes, though Livy attributes the same effect to a statute carried by the consuls Valerius and Horatius one hundred and twenty years earlier. But the argument adduced by Accursius, Odofred and others from the Lex Hortensia is certainly surprising. The Accursian Gloss[9] says 'Regia, viz. carried by the wondrous orator Hortensius as stated above. There the reference is to the populus and plebs. So explain Regia here as Regal.' Accursius admits perforce that the Lex Hor-

---

[1] For the Glossa Ordinaria of Accursius see vol. VI of Genevan (1625) edition of the Corpus and Savigny, *Geschichte des Römischen Rechts im Mittelalter*, V, 279–305.

[2] Henry of Susa, afterwards Cardinal-Bishop of Ostia, retained in the pay of Henry III of England.

[3] For Odofred see Savigny, *Geschichte des Römischen Rechts im Mittelalter*, V, 324–344, and Tamassia, *Odofredo*. Odofred began his teaching in 1229; he is said to have taught at Padua and in France. He was supposed to be a rival of Accursius and is condemned by Savigny as unoriginal.

[4] For Azo's discussion of the subject see his *Summa Codicis* (Basle, 1563), 23–27. He says 'a populo autem Romano forte et hodie potest condi lex' (p. 24).

[5] Selden's authority at this point (Quintin, *Christiana Civitatis Aristocratia*) refers to a debate between Bulgarus and Martinus on the limits of princely power. Martinus held that the Emperor had the ownership of all within his power: Bulgarus left rights of private property intact. Cf. also the declaration of the Four Doctors at the Diet of Roncaglia (1158).

[6] Aulus Gellius, XV, 27, 4; cf. also *Jurisprudentiae Anteiustinianae Quae Supersunt* (Teubner), 5th ed. Index vol. p. 145.

[7] D. 1. 2. 2. 8.   [8] Inst. 1. 2. 4.

[9] D. 1. 4. par. 1.

est, Regali.' Agnoscit, quod facere necesse erat, in lege Hortensia, Populi et Plebis, seu Patrum et Plebis potestatis tantum mentionem fieri expressam. Quomodo igitur ibi quid de Regia lege praescribitur? 'Dic ergo' inquit 'Regali'; quod, si bene capio, juxta eum innuit, legem Hortensiam de jure regali id est regiminis seu gubernandi jure, latam et Plebi et Senatui (e quibus partibus seu ordinibus binis tunc integrum populi Romani corpus constabat) parilem concedentem potestatem, ita etiam intelligendum, ut, postquam Princeps super Populo adjectus est, haud dispari ratione itidem et illi, ut in regimine, parti tertiae, parilis ex ejusdem legis sensu potestas concessa admitteretur. Neque aliter video undenam velint illi veteres legem heic Hortensiam locum omnino habere ullum. Atque hinc ea quae Justinianus habet de singulari Plebiscitorum ac Senatusconsultorum vi, interpretabantur illi qui in hac fuere sententia; quasi ex ipsis ejusdem verbis ad Senatum Populumque Romanum in eis ferendis, eadem ipsa, quae olim in republica libera, potestas ac imperium etiamnum attineret. Disputarunt etiam an potestas sic concessa a populo jure revocari potuisset, ut a delegante potestas[1] delegato concessa.

IV. Sed certo certius est priorem sententiam veram esse, de populo scilicet, omnimodo imperio ac potestate, in legibus ferendis, plane ex lege illa Regia nudato. Quod tum ex Justiniano ipso tum ex veterum recentiorum interpretibus illustrissimis constat. Verba ipsa de lege illa ex Justiniano ante allata satis heic probant: quibus accedat et illud Constantini[2]: 'inter aequitatem jusque interpositam interpretationem nobis solis et oportet et licet inspicere' (ubi Graeci[3] μόνος νόμον τέμνετο ὁ βασιλεύς, 'solus princeps legem dirimat') item et illud Justiniani[4] ad Demosthenem praefectum praetorio: 'si imperialis majestas causam conditionaliter examinaverit et partibus cominus constitutis sententiam dixerit, omnes omnino judices qui sub nostro imperio sunt, sciant hanc esse legem, non solum illi causae pro qua producta est sed et omnibus similibus. Quid enim majus, quid sanctius....' Vetustiorum heic interpretum aliquot sententia supra indicatur, quibus adjicias Gallicanam Ulpiani de lege Regia verborum versionem pervetustam MS.: 'Ce que plest au Prince a force de ley, pur ce que li peuples li ottroia en la ley Royall que fu fait de l'empire tout le commandement et toute la poeste que il avoient et le mistrent sus lui et en lui.' Quod vulgares ibi interpretes, eis quos diximus recentiores

[1] Odofred. ad dict. legem et videsis ibi Raphael. Fulgosium etc.
[2] C. tit. de legibus.   [3] Basilic. lib. 2, tit. 6. 6.
[4] L. 12, C. tit. de Leg. et vide Basilic. lib. 2, tit. 6. 17, et vide tit. de Crim. Sacrilegii.

tensia dealt expressly only with the powers of the populus and plebs, or senate and plebs. So how is there any enactment in it about the Lex Regia? Call it 'Regal[1]' he says, meaning, if I understand aright, that the Lex Hortensia dealt with the regal [governing] power, and gave it equally to populus and plebs, into which the Roman state was then divided, so that when the princeps was set over the populus he was given a similar power in the sense of the Lex Hortensia, as being a third element in the government [regimen]. Otherwise I cannot see how these old writers applied the Lex Hortensia to this question. Hence, those holding this opinion understand Justinian's remarks on the great power of plebiscita and senatus consulta as if the same power and authority to make laws, formerly found in the Republic, still pertained to the senate and people of Rome.

Debated whether power could be revoked

It was likewise debated whether power thus conceded by the people could, like power entrusted to a delegate, be revoked[2].

Correct interpretation of Lex Regia

IV. But it is quite clear that of these opinions the first is the correct one, namely that by the Lex Regia the people were deprived of all law-making authority. This is shown by Justinian himself and by the most eminent of ancient and modern commentators. To these may be added the words of Constantine[3]: 'The function of interpretation, which mediates between law and equity, belongs to us alone.' The Greeks have: 'it is for the king alone to adjust the law' and there is the order of Justinian[4] to Demosthenes, Praefectus Praetorio, that where an imperial decision has been given, the judges are to regard it as law not only for that but for all similar cases. As a confirmation of this opinion may be added the reading (in the first or correct sense) of the Lex Regia to be found in an old Norman-French translation of Ulpian[5]. The opinion of more recent critics is sufficiently obvious.

---

[1] In the sense of 'governmental' rather than 'royal.'
[2] Selden's authority for this is (in addition to Odofred) Fulgosius' *Repetitio in Authenticum* (in vol. III, *Repetitiones Juris Civilis*, Leyden, 1553).
[3] C. 1. 14. 1.
[4] C. 1. 14. 12.
[5] Cannot be identified. The reading is simply a Norman-French translation of Ulpian's maxim as given *ante*, p. 26.

habent cuique obvium est. Legem vero Hortensiam quam ita huc vetustiores perperam torserunt, non omnino ad legem Regiam heic attinere, nedum ea innui, admittunt doctiores politioresque recentiorum, quorum quidem nonnullis[1] etiam legitur lege Remnia pro Regia. Regiam autem legem dici posse nemo non videt dupliciter, aut velut a rege latam, aut de rege seu regia potestate. Notione priore leges habentur regiae Romanorum perplurimae apud Dionysium Halicarnasseum[2] quas etiam diligenter exhibet Fulvius Ursinus[3]. Etiam in Codice[4] memoratur Lex Regia de praegnante muliere humanda, a regum veterum aliquo lata. Posteriore autem notione plane dicitur heic Lex Regia, atque pro ea recte sumitur (nam aliae prorsus rejiciendae sententiae) qua populus Romanus omne imperium et potestatem suam in Octavium Augustum Caesarem ejusque successores transtulit, nec pristinum sibi omnino retinuit, qua de re quidem satis expressim Dio Cassius in Augusti historia[5] Et Suetonius[6] de Caesare illo, 'tribunitiam potestatem perpetuam recepit...recepit et morum legumque regimen aeque perpetuum.' Sed et vetus extat Romae in basilica Lateranensi seu inde in Capitolium translata tabula aerea in qua legis Regiae ipsius Vespasiano Caesari instauratae habetur fragmentum, unde sensum Legis heic apud Ulpianum Regiae elicere non est difficile. Inter alia ibi summi ac solius imperii capita quae Vespasiano velut haereditaria confirmantur a populo, eodem scilicet modo quo antea eis fruebantur Augustus, Tiberius ac Claudius, habetur et hoc, 'Utique quae ante hanc legem rogatam acta, gesta, decreta, imperata ab imperatore Caesare Vespasiano Augusto, jussu mandatove ejus a quoquo sunt, ea perinde justa rataque sint acsi populi plebisve jussu acta essent.' Describitur fragmentum integrum apud Janum Gruterum[7], Fulvium Ursinum[8], Antonium Augustinum[9], Franciscum Hotomannum[10], Barnabam Brissonium[11], alios. Atque, sensu jam dicto, legem hanc Regiam apud Ulpianum seu Justinianum sumendam haud pauci consentiunt interpretum recentiorum. Praeter eos qui aut ad Digesta et Institutiones in sede hujus legis aut de imperio et jurisdictione integra volumina scribunt, consulas Augustinum et Hotomannum locis indicatis, uti etiam Joannem Corasium[12], Ludovicum Charondam[13], Petrum Tholosa-

---

[1] Alciat. ad tit. de Verb. Signif. 15, Jo. Coras., Miscell. lib. 6. 8.
[2] Antiq. Rom. lib. 2. [3] In Notis ad leges et Senatus consulta, pag. 42.
[4] Tit. de Mortuo Infer. 2. [5] Lib. 53.
[6] In Octav. cap. 27. [7] Inscript. pag. 242.
[8] In Leg. et Senatusconsultis marmoreis. [9] De Legibus pag. 125.
[10] Antiq. Rom. lib. 1. [11] Formular. lib. 2.
[12] Miscell. Juris, lib. 6, cap. 8. [13] Pithanon lib. 1, cap. 2.

Vespasian's Tablet

Among modern commentators the more reliable deny that the Lex Hortensia, twisted by these old writers into its wrong context, has anything whatever to do with the Lex Regia, and some even read Lex Remnia for Regia. It is obvious that a law may be called 'royal' in two senses—either as enacted by a king or as concerning his power or person. In Dionysius of Halicarnassus are to be found a great many royal laws (leges regiae[1]), and in the Code[2] there is mention of a lex regia concerning burial, formulated by some old king. But the Lex Regia we are considering is clearly of the second type and should be understood as that law by which the Roman people transferred all power and authority to Octavius Augustus Caesar and his successors, retaining for itself nothing whatever of its former prerogative. On this subject consult Dio Cassius, in his History of Augustus. Suetonius says of the same emperor: 'he took upon himself the perpetual tribunitial power as well as the permanent control of laws and customs.' There is a brass tablet[3] to be found in the Roman Church of St John Lateran (or transferred therefrom to the Capitol) on which is inscribed a fragment of the Lex Regia itself as renewed for Vespasian, and from this we may deduce an interpretation of the Lex Regia in Ulpian's sense. Among various headings inscribed there concerning the sole and supreme power confirmed by the people on Vespasian as his inheritance, that is, in the same way as hitherto enjoyed by Augustus, Tiberius and Claudius, there occurs this, that whatever had been decreed by Vespasian before the enactment of this law should be held valid as if passed by order of people or plebs. The fragment is completely transcribed by Gruter, Ursinus, Brisson[4], Augustinus, Hotman[5] and others. That the Lex Regia of Ulpian and Justinian should be understood in this sense is the opinion of not a few modern commentators. In addition to those who have discussed this law by way of commentary on the appropriate passages in the Digests and Institutes, or have written specifically on the subject of royal prerogative, consult Augustinus, Hotman, Coras, Charondas, Peter Gregory of Toulouse, Francis Conant[5] and especially the observations of Francis Amaya[6]. This by the way.

---

[1] Dionysius refers to the legislation of Romulus. For such 'leges regiae' see Girard, *Textes de droit romain*, 3-9.   [2] It is really D. 11. 8. 2.

[3] *Corpus Inscriptionum Latinarum* (1876), VI, No. 930. Now in the Capitoline Museum.

[4] J. Gruter, Flemish philologian (1560-1627): F. Ursinus, Italian philologian (1530-1600): B. Brisson, French jurist (1531-1591).

[5] Hotman, Coras, Charondas, Peter Gregory of Toulouse and Francis Conant were sixteenth century jurists and either officials of the Parlement or professors. Hotman was the author of the *Franco Gallia* and the *Anti-Tribonianus*. Antonius Augustinus was born at Saragossa in 1517 and became archbishop of Tarragona in 1574. Selden made liberal use of Augustinus' numerous writings on law and antiquities.

[6] Spanish antiquarian, sixteenth–seventeenth centuries. Bishop of Cuença.

num¹, Franciscum Connanum², et sane prae aliis Franciscum de Amaya in Observationibus³, qui rem copiosius explicat. Sed haec obiter.

V. Atqui interea, e locis superius ex Jure Caesareo ab jurisconsultis nostratibus Fletae utputa autore Bractonio et Thorntonio celeberrimis ac judiciis cum primariis (quantum ad posteriores binos attinet) praefectis, ita allatis expressimque indicatis, atque in rerum quas tractant probationem et argumenta sic adhibitis, idque velut aut autoritatem aut saltem rationem cogentem prae se ferentibus, manifestum sit usum qualemcunque neque eum adeo obscurum apud majores nostros eo in saeculo juris ejusdem atque illius librorum in discussionibus nostris etiam ex jure Anglicano definiendis invaluisse. Non quidem omnino quasi regnum hoc seu rempublicam Anglicanam Caesaribus jurive Caesareo subjici aut regimen heic inde pendere omnino, aut jus Anglicanum ante sive scripto sive moribus constitutum inde mutationem recipere voluissent (nam passim etiam jus hoc, qua multifariam a Caesareo discrepat eique plane adversatur, ut sequendum docent ipsi), sed ut tum ubi deesset nostri juris praescriptum expressius, ad rationem juris etiam Caesarei ratione suffultam recurreretur, tum ubi jus utrumque consonum, etiam Caesarei quasi firmaretur explicareturve res verbis. Quod certe alias apud gentes Occidentis olim hodieque factum scimus. Et certe in illustri illa de regia potestate apud nos quaestione definienda, locum ex autoritate sui habere nequibat ullum illud Ulpiani de Lege Regia, cum nec vim in regimine publico nostrati ullam omnino ex autoritate sui sortiretur jus Caesareum. Nec quidem ab autoribus quos heic diximus nostris revera adhibetur dictum illud Ulpiani aliter atque moribus Anglicanis etiam ipsis quibus semper usi sumus, aut consonum esse aut saltem non dissonum sed satis adaptandum ipsi, prout ostendimus, utcunque hallucinati, existimarent. Verus autem ejusdem, qua pars juris Caesarei est, sensus qualis supra exhibetur, regiminis Anglicani uti et rerumpublicarum per Europam Christianam plerarunque constitutioni omnino adversatur, utpote quae in Principem Romanum aperte omnimodam transtulerit potestatem et imperium, quantum scilicet ad homines conditionis liberae regendos in principem citra tyrannidem transferri potuerit. Breviter rem ipsam explicat Cujacius⁴; 'Augusto illo privilegio eadem est potestas

---

[1] Syntagm. Jur. lib. 47, cap. 20.
[2] Comm. Jur. Civil. lib. 1, cap. 16, vide item Edmund. Merill. Observat. lib. 2, cap. 19.
[3] Lib. 1, cap. 1, § 19, etc.   [4] In Paratit. D. lib. 1, tit. 1, cap. 4.

English use of Civil Law

V. Considering the above-mentioned citation of passages from imperial law by such distinguished lawyers as Bracton and Thornton as well as by the author of *Fleta*, and considering also that such passages are quoted as providing proof or evidence in questions under discussion, whether by weight of authority or cogency of argument, it is clear that among lawyers of that time there prevailed, even in the debatable points of English common law, some kind of use of imperial law not very difficult to determine. They did not assume that England was in any way subject to the empire or to imperial law, nor did they infer that English law, already established by custom and writing, should be changed: on the contrary they teach, in the many cases where civil and English law differ, that the latter is to be followed. Their meaning was that where our law lacked an express rule, recourse might be had to the civil law as grounded on reason and, where the two systems agreed, then the matter in question might, as it were, be confirmed and elucidated by the civil law analogy[1]. This practice was and is followed elsewhere among nations of Western Europe.

Ulpian's statement of the Lex Regia inconsistent with English constitutional principles

Thus in the famous question of the prerogative, as debated in this country, Ulpian's opinion on the Lex Regia could not in itself have any weight, since the imperial law has never by its own authority had any part in our government. Ulpian's maxim is interpreted (or rather misinterpreted) by our three authors only in so far as consistent or at least not inconsistent with our immemorial customs. Indeed the correct interpretation of that maxim, in so far as it is a part of civil law, is completely opposed to the English constitution and to that of most Christian states, since by it all power is transferred to the Roman prince, as much, that is, as could be conferred on a ruler of free men as distinct from a tyrant. Cujas says: 'By that sacred ordinance the Roman prince has the same power as the

---

[1] Cf. the words of Tindal, C.J., in Acton *v.* Blundell (1843): 'The Roman Law forms no rule binding in itself on the subjects of these realms, but in deciding a case on principle, where no direct authority can be cited from our books, it affords no small evidence of the soundness of the conclusion to which we have come if it proves to be supported by that law' (quoted by Scrutton, 'Roman Law influence on English Law' in *Select Essays in Anglo-American Legal History*).

Principis (Romani) quae Populi fuit,' alii doctissimorum tantundem. Nec quidem sive Plebiscitis sive Senatusconsultis post latam illam seu in usum revocatam Legem Regiam vis inerat alia praeter eam quam Augusti permittebant ipsi. Sed vero haud pauci sunt scriptores[1] qui jus illud vetus Caesareum popularium suorum juri pariter adaptare satagentes, ita translationem illam seu, ut illi potius volunt, communicationem imperii moderari et temperare ex pactis ac conditionibus tacitis variatim conantur, ut etiam ab Ulpiani Justinianique dum eos interpretantur mente, quantum video, non vereantur longe nimis discedere, aliam scilicet et Caesaribus priscis (quorum in regimine aliorum principum ratio non ita habenda) prorsus imparem potestatem ac multo quam admittit vetustas Romana minorem adserentes. Neque hisce melius ii qui singulis Principibus Romanis singulas Leges Regias easque diversas latas volunt[2], nec unicam, ut ante omnibus hac de re aut latam aut pro lata habitam. Et perperam nimis sententiam illam de omnimodo in Caesares quantum scilicet transferri ut dictum est potuerit, imperio translato, velut semper assentatoriam damnant. Certe non magis principi cuiquam assentari dicendus est quisquis de immenso veterum Principum Romanorum imperio illo quid ei adfirmaverit, quam is qui summo Turcarum aliive ejusmodi Principi angustos regum Spartanorum veterum potestatis cancellos aliasve regiminum habenis variatim temperatorum formas ostenderet, dicendus foret ei aut convitium inferre aut majestatem dignitatemve minuere. Nec in imperio quidem nunc dicto Romano, quod Germanicum est, successio habetur in jura Justinianea, qua Justinianea aut Romanis vetera. Neque ibi, nedum alibi capita de principum potestate ejusdem juris vim habent ullam aliter atque a legibus moribusque recentioribus, iisque perquam variantibus, id est, Capitulatione Caesarea seu Lege Regia Germanorum diversimode est permissum. De Capitulatione ac Lege illa consulas Benedictum Carpzovium in tractatu[3] de ea uti et de simili apud alias gentes ante annos aliquot edito. Superius vero dictis de Juris Caesarei heic qualicunque inter Juris Anglicani peritos, idque qua tales, usu antiquitus admisso adjicere etiam heic visum est non intempestivum, quando, quomodo atque unde usus ejusmodi initia heic sumserit, creverit, inoleverit, idque aliquatenus tam in foro quam in studiis

---

[1] Fran. Suarez, Defens. Fid. Cath. advers. Anglos lib. 3, cap. 2, § 12, Fran. de Amaya, Observat. Juris lib. 1, c. 1, § 45, etc. Tobiam Paurmeister, lib. 1, de Jurisdic. Imper. Rom. cap. 19, § 7, etc.

[2] Marius Salomonius, lib. de Principatu Paganin. Gaudent. Juridic. lib. 2, cap. 26, etc. Vide Henric. Bouricium lect. Jur. cap. 7 et Francis. Conan. Comm. Juris lib. 1, cap. 16. Rivall. Hist. Juris Civilis, lib. 2.   [3] 1622.

people formerly had' and other eminent scholars write to the same effect. This Lex Regia once enacted or renewed, the decisions of plebs or senate had just as much force as the emperors pleased.

Ulpian and Justinian must be interpreted strictly

Nevertheless some writers with the object of adapting this old imperial rule to the law of their country, try to show that the transference or, as they prefer, the sharing of sovereignty was controlled by stipulations, expressed or implied. These commentators, while claiming to interpret Ulpian and Justinian, depart, in my opinion, very widely from their authorities in attributing to the original Caesars (whose principles of government are not to be taken thus as a model for other rulers) an authority much less than what antiquity acknowledges them to have possessed. Nor is it a sounder theory to hold that there never was enacted any single or original Lex Regia, but that separate and distinct ones were passed for the various Roman emperors. It is a mistake to condemn as mere flattery the interpretation which regards all sovereignty as having been transferred to the Caesars in the manner already specified. For in truth it can no more be called flattery of the monarch to emphasise the unbounded sovereignty conferred on the old Roman emperors than it could be called an abuse or diminution of majesty to bring to the notice of a ruler like the Sultan of Turkey such a limited and regulated monarchy as that of the ancient kings of Sparta. Nor in what is now styled the Roman empire, that is the Germanic empire, is there any inheritance of the laws of Justinian as such. The civil law doctrine of sovereignty has no more force there, much less anywhere else, than what is allowed by diverse modern laws and customs, like the imperial Capitulation or Lex Regia of the Germans. For the study of this and similar institutions, consult the treatise of Carpzovius[1].

Scope of the Dissertatio

We may here add some remarks on when, how and why this use of the civil law in England commenced, developed and became established, not only in the courts but in the writings and studies of scholars, and also when it fell into decay. It will also be considered to what extent, if any, the imperial law was in vogue here in much earlier times. A summary of these points may be thought both relevant and useful by more enquiring readers.

---

[1] Saxon jurist, 1595–1664. His writings were of great practical importance: see Stintzing, *Geschichte der deutschen Rechtswissenschaft*, II, 55–100. Selden's reference is to the *De Capitulatione Caesarea sive de Lege Regia Germanorum* (1622).

scriptisque (ut infra ostenditur) et demum quando in desuetudinem abierit. Qualis item, in seculis diu ante initia illa retro actis, usus juris ejusdem sive illius intermissio heic haberetur. Nam et operae forte pretium nec loco huic alienum existimabitur puto curiosioribus compendio haec indicare.

Caput Quartum

    I. Usus Juris Caesarei in hac quam incolimus Angli Britanniae parte, Romanis heic summa rerum potientibus.

   II. Cerni ejusmodi usum tum in coloniis huc deductis tum in civili rerum heic tunc administratione.

  III. Papinianus, jurisconsultorum veterum ille facile princeps, in Britannia judiciis ex Jure Caesareo exercendis praefuit; Eboraci, alibi. Forte etiam Ulpianus et Paulus praeter id genus alios his coaetaneos.

  IV. Duravit hic ejusmodi Juris Caesarei usus, per annos 360 aut circiter.

I. Usus Juris Caesarei in hac Britanniae quam incolimus Angli parte, in triplici reperitur genere. Primum est ejusdem ut in regimine, plane supremi et heic quasi universalis. Secundum est, ut adscitii tantum seu immixti, atque juri Anglicano tam Civili quam Pontificio non solum interpretationem saepius ex ratione sua in studiis foroque praestantis, verum etiam, ubi aut deerat expressius in Anglicano praescriptum, aut huic, ut in non paucis, illud omnino erat consonum, velut autoritatem, non ex condentium potestate sed ex utentium heic consensu seu admissione, subministrantis. Tertium, ut consistoriis aliquot tantum causisque aliquot singularibus veluti militaribus, nauticis, testamentariis, adstricti, adeoque cancellis ita coerciti ut extra eos ex more non fuerit ejusdem usus admissus. Sic Rhodiorum leges nauticae Romae, sic Oleronianae nobis aliisque gentibus Christianis maritimis receptae. De primo et secundo genere heic maxime agemus; cum genus tertium nemini non sit notissimum. Quod ad primum attinet; habebatur illud tantum Romanis heic rerum summa potientibus. Usus ejusmodi coepit Claudii Caesaris tempore. Nam 'Britanniam a Julio Caesare in latas leges jurare compulsam,' quod temere scripsit Monachus Malmesburiensis[1] aliique ejusdem aliorumve similium heic sequaces, non omnino est admittendum. Claudius autem, ut Ethelwerdus ait, 'Britonum reges subjecit servire sibi' et australiorem insulae partem in Romanorum potestatem redegit. Atque ab ejus tempore quo primum huc deductae coloniae, duravit heic usus ille usque in tempora illa quibus adeo inclinavit

---

[1] De Gest. Regum Angliae lib. 1, cap. 1.

Chapter IV

I. The use of imperial law in this country during the Roman occupation.
II. Its use in the settlements established here and its influence on public administration.
III. Papinian, by far the greatest of the old jurists, administered imperial law in this country at York and elsewhere. Possibly also Ulpian and Paul, besides other such contemporaries, did so likewise.
IV. This use of imperial law lasted about 360 years.

Roman law influence on Britain

I. The application of imperial law in this country is found in three forms; the first, in which its use was in the government, clearly a supreme government, was here an almost universal use. The second is the mixed or derived kind by which the imperial law provides, for English civil and ecclesiastical law (generally by inference), not only an interpretation, in both theory and practice, but also a kind of confirmation, due, not to any legislative force, but to the agreement and consent of its exponents in matters where English jurisprudence either supplied no rule or was consistent with imperial law. The third form is that practised in certain courts or confined to a particular class of case, such as matters military, maritime and testamentary, where its use was so strictly controlled that outside these limits it was generally disallowed. Such were the Rhodian maritime laws[1] adopted by Rome, and the laws of Oleron[2], the latter accepted by us and other Christian nations. We are concerned here mainly with the first and second use: the third is known to everyone.

Roman law influence dates from Claudius

As regards the first type, this began with the Emperor Claudius and lasted as long as the Romans were supreme in this country. That Britain, in the words of the monk of Malmesbury[3] and others, was compelled by Julius Caesar to swear allegiance to enacted laws cannot be upheld. Roman rule in the southern part of Britain dates from Claudius, as Ethelwerd[4] affirmed, and from that time this use remained until, with the decline of the Roman empire, the yoke

---

[1] For these see W. Ashburner, *The Rhodian Sea Law* (Oxford, 1909).
[2] Selden's MS. *Commentarii de rebus Admiralitatis* contained a French version of the laws of Oleron (now MS. Bodley Arch. Seld. B. 27). This was printed in the *Black Book of the Admiralty* (Rolls Series, vol. I, 1871). *Les jugements d'Oleron* was printed at La Rochelle in 1571. See H. L. Zeller, 'Das Seerecht von Oleron nach der inkunabel Treguier,' in *Sitzungsberichte der Heidelberger Akademie der Wissenschaften*, 1915).
[3] *De gestis regum anglorum* (Rolls Series, 1887), VII.
[4] *Ethelwerdi Chronicorum Libri IV* (1596), I.

heic Romanum imperium, ut excusso ejusdem jugo, incolae in sui potestatem reversi suique facti juris Caesareum omnino rejecerint, saltem ita neglexerint ut cito evanesceret, qua tale; utcunque ejusdem reliquiae aliquot quae sic inoleverant ut juris Britannici naturam induerent, necessario forsan (quod nec aliter fieri potuisse videtur) essent retentae.

II. Cernitur autem hic usus potissimum in coloniis sic huc deductis, tum in civili rerum per intervallum quod diximus heic administratione. Colonias ipsas jure in provinciis uti solitas Romano, adeoque sub Caesaribus Caesareo urbisque ipsius meras fuisse expressimasque imagines satis est tralatitium[1]. Et diserte Tacitus[2] coloniam heic primam, seu quae Camaloduni erat, non solum ut adversus rebelles esset subsidium sed 'imbuendis sociis ad officia legum' ait huc deductam. Quo plane innuitur etiam Britannos, quotquot aut socii essent seu ut Romanis amici aut subditi seu in potestatem bello redacti, tunc imbuendos ad officia legum seu Juris Caesarei observationem, et proculdubio etiam sic fuisse a colonia hac aliisque similibus imbutos. Id sane quod haud difficile erat alia ex causa non ita obscura. Jure enim pristino quod totum erat Druidum disciplina (ut ex Julio Caesare ac perquam probabili doctorum virorum conjectura qui disciplinam illam pariter apud Gallos Britannosque in rebus omnimodis, tam profanis quam sacris, administrandis viguisse sentiunt, est eliciendum) jure inquam illo, tam apud Britannos, ut par est credere, quam Gallos, prorsus a Claudio sublato[3], facilius multo erat novum adeoque Caesareum seu victoris jura passim introducere. Alia ad colonias hujus provinciae (quorum nomina habemus quatuor aut quinque, et dubitandum non est complures fuisse alias) hoc nomine spectantia alibi[4] congessimus, neque heic iteranda duximus. Civilis autem rerum heic sub Romanis administratio in qua juris Caesarei usus primi habetur generis, satis visitur in officiis seu dignitatibus Vicarii Britanniae, qui Praefecto Praetorio Galliarum suberat, consularibus, praesidibus, pro-praetoribus, id genus reliquis quorum, ut in hac insulae parte suo regentium jure, mentio expressior tum in Notitia Dignitatum Imperii Occidentis tum in Romanis in Britannia apud doctissimum Gulielmum Camdenum e veteribus eos accuratius exhibentem. Et quod de Gallia dixit Julius Caesar, de Britannia hac itidem tunc plane dicendum. 'Respicite,' inquit ille, 'finitimam Gal-

---

[1] Vide Agellinum, lib. 16, cap. 13. Sigonium, Rossinium, etc.
[2] Annal. XII, 32.
[3] Sueton. in Claudio, cap. 25, vide Plin. lib. 30, cap. 1.
[4] Not. in Fortiscut. p. 9.

was thrown off and the inhabitants, restored to their own jurisdiction, either rejected the imperial law or so neglected it that it soon disappeared. Nevertheless there naturally survived such remains as had taken root and had assumed the form of British law.

Roman settlements in Britain

II. The first use is seen chiefly in the introduction of settlements and in the direction of public affairs during this period. These settlements, as express reproductions of the City itself, are known to have used Roman law in provincial administration and, afterwards, under the Caesars, imperial law. Tacitus asserts that the first settlement—at Colchester—was founded not only as a military outpost but for imbuing into the allies a respect for the laws. By allies he obviously means Britons, either such as were friendly to the Romans, or reduced by them to subjection, and doubtless they were brought to respect the imperial laws by this and similar settlements. Moreover it was easier to introduce everywhere the new or imperial legislation because Claudius had completely abrogated, in Britain as in Gaul, the original law consisting wholly of the Druid cult, which, as we learn from Julius Caesar[1] and the very credible opinion of investigators, held sway in all things, sacred and profane, in Britain and in Gaul. There remain four or five names of such Roman settlements in Britain and undoubtedly there were more, but as we have treated of this matter elsewhere[2] we need not repeat it here.

Civil administration of Roman Britain

It is in such offices as Vicar of Britain (subordinate to the Praetorian Prefect of Gaul), Legate, Governor and Pro-Praetor, who administered this country by their native jurisprudence and to whom there are direct references in the learned works of Camden, that one may trace the civil administration of our country under Roman rule and therein the first of the three specified types of use of imperial law. What Caesar said of Gaul may also be applied to Britain at that time—'Look at neighbouring Gaul—reduced to a province, its

---

[1] *De Bello Gallico*, VI.
[2] In *England's Epinomis*, II, and *Analecta Anglo-Britannica*, V–VIII.

liam, quae in provinciam redacta jure et legibus commutatis perpetua premitur servitute[1].' Prae aliis autem illustre est exemplum Septimii Severi Augusti, qui sub annum Christi 200 ἐς δύο ἡγεμονίας (sic Herodianus[2]) τὴν τοῦ ἔθνους ἐξουσίαν 'in duos principatus' seu 'praefecturas gentis imperium seu potestatem' distribuit, quod a doctis aliquot accipitur pro binis regimentis[3] seu praefecturis praetorianis id est binis praefectis praetorio qui in praefecturis suis singuli jus dicerent heic Romanum. Dein etiam idem Augustus filios suos Bassianum et Getam Caesares seu designatos successores, ut ab urbis deliciis eos abstraheret, secum in Britanniam ducens Getam juniorem, juri tantum heic dicundo praefecit, assignatis ei, ex amicorum senioribus seu praecipuis, adsessoribus. Sic Herodianus[4], Γέταν καταλιπὼν ἐν τῷ ὑπὸ Ῥωμαίους ἔθνει δικάσοντά τε καὶ τὰ λοιπὰ διοικήσοντα πολιτικὰ τῆς ἀρχῆς (δοὺς αὐτῷ συνέδρους τῶν φίλων τοὺς πρεσβυτέρους) τὸν δὲ Ἀντωνῖνον παραλαβὼν ἐπὶ τοὺς βαρβάρους ὑπήγετο id est, 'Getam in gentis parte quae Romanis suberat relinquens ut scilicet jus diceret et reliquas imperii res civiles administraret' (datis ei ex amicorum senioribus synedris seu adsessoribus seu consiliariis) 'Antoninum' (id est Bassianum; licet revera uterque hoc nomine etiam patre superstite frueretur) 'secum adversus barbaros eduxit.' Atque erat quidem hic Geta 'Moribus asperis, sed non impiis, et tractator' (quasi 'scholasticus' diceres) 'ac in literis assequendis et tenax veterum scriptorum et paternarum etiam sententiarum memor,' quod ait Spartianus[5]. Quicquid igitur Britanniarum tunc erat Romanorum in potestate, seu pars ab muro illo seu vallo Pictico qui Cumbriam intersecat meridionalis, Antonino Getae jam velut heic Praefecto Praetorio seu ab Imperatore secundo ac imperii participi in administratione civili jureque dicundo suberat.

III. Nec sane dubitandum videtur quin inter assessores seu consiliarios illos etiam et inter eos qui ipsi Augusto judicia quotidie[6] a tempore matutino usque in meridiem exercere solito, utpote et juris peritissimo, adsiderent, locum haberet heic primarium Aemylius Papinianus Asylum Juris veteribus dictum, seu ille omnium qui sunt, qui erunt, quique fuerunt juris peritissimus (ut Cujacii[7] de eo fertur judicium) atque

---

[1] Comm. lib. 7.   [2] Hist. 3.
[3] Richardus Vitus, Hist. Brit. lib. 5, not. 11. De 'regimenti' voce consulas Charisium D. tit. de Praef. Praet. et Festum in verb. 'regimen.'
[4] Hist. 3 (14).   [5] In Antonino Geta.
[6] Xiphilinus e Dionis lib. 76.
[7] In Epist. ad Bedinger praefix. Codici Theodos. quem et videsis in praefatione ad Papiniani Opera.

laws and customs changed, it is oppressed by perpetual subjection.' The emperor Septimius Severus set a remarkable precedent when, about A.D. 200, he divided 'the government of the people into two hegemonies' (Herodian). Some scholars interpret this to mean a pair of governments or praetorian prefectures under two prefects who would each in his province administer Roman law.

The Emperor Severus

The same emperor, in order to withdraw from the temptations of the city his two sons and intended successors, Bassianus and Geta, brought Geta with him to Britain and 'left him there in charge of supreme judicial and administrative duties, assigning him assessors [σύνεδροι] from his oldest or most distinguished friends[1]. This done, he took his elder son Antoninus (Bassianus) with him against the barbarians.' Of Geta, Spartian says that 'though harsh, he was not irreligious: respectful of his father's opinions, he was faithful in his studies to the old writers and was an amateur' (as if to say, something of a student). All therefore of Britain that was in Roman occupation, *i.e.* the part south of the Pictish rampart cutting across Cumberland, was subject, in matters of administration and judicature, to Geta as praetorian prefect, or partner and next in place to the emperor.

Papinian

III. There seems little doubt but that among those assessors or councillors referred to, and even among those who assisted the emperor himself in the daily routine of his judicial functions, the chief place was held by Aemilius Papinian[2], called by the old writers 'the sanctuary of the law' and by Cujas, 'the greatest jurist of all time.' In the age before Justinian his authority was so great that

---

[1] Selden quotes, translates and paraphrases this passage from Herodian, interpreting ἐν τῷ ὑπὸ 'Ρωμαίους ἔθνει to include Britain.
[2] For Papinian see E. Costa, *Papiniano* (Bologna, 1894).

autoritatis ante Justinianum prae reliquis tantae ut ubi pares erant sententiae invicem inversae ea praevaleret[1] in qua fuisset Papinianus, qui et amicissimus Severo Augusto cum eo simul professus est sub Cerbidio Scaevola et sibi praecipue utrunque Augusti filium habebat commendatum. Nimirum certissimum est non solum in Britannia hac parte Septimio Severo[2] ut comitem eum adfuisse, verum etiam in urbe Eboraco egisse ubi Augusti praetorium erat ac tribunal in quo judicia non solum ipsum Augustum sed etiam Getam subinde cum consiliariis illis exercuisse non est quod ambigamus. Ita expressim ex Dione Xiphilinus[3] de Papiniano; ubi Bassiani meminit in via occidere tentantis patrem; 'qui tamen nullum' inquit, 'verbum fecit sed in tribunal (Eboraci) ascendens peragensque quae necessaria erat, revertit in praetorium καὶ καλέσας τόν τε υἱὸν καὶ τὸν Παπινιανὸν καὶ τὸν Κάστορα et accersitis filio et Papiniano et Castore verba de facinore ad filium habet, in quibus 'si me cupis' ait 'interficere, heic me interfice...quod si id recusas et times tua manu facere, adest tibi (Παπινιανὸς ὁ ἔπαρχος) Papinianus praefectus cui jubere potes ut me interficiat. Omnino enim faciet quicquid abs te quum imperator sis, mandatum fuerit.' Sic ille. Scilicet erat Papinianus Praefectus Praetorio[4] tam Severo quam Antonino Caracallae seu Bassiano successori. Solem igitur illum ac asylum juris et doctrinae legalis thesaurum (sic enim Spartiano[5] nuncupatur et elogiis sane miris passim in corpore Justinianeo ornatur) jus in Britannis nostris Caesareum dixisse ac docuisse ut satis palam est, ita etiam in senioribus amicorum Getae[6] heic judiciis praefecti pro consiliariis ei assignatis, primarium fuisse credendum. Is erat cujus opera ante annum tertium studiosis ob mirum acumen et subtilitatem attingere fas non erat, unde postmodum Papinianistae[7] solenniter dicti. Ceterum in Britannia fuisse eum non video quenquam jurisconsultorum biographorum omnino memorare. Nec praeter Dionem Cassium (quem sane etiam in judiciis heic cum Severo adfuisse aequum est ex ejusdem scripto[8] suspicari) historicorum veterum quisquam id tradidit. Quin et Paulum ac Ulpianum aliosque aliquot ejusdem temporis

---

[1] C. Theodos. lib. 1, tit. de Responsis Prudentum.
[2] Spartian. in Ant. Caracalla.
[3] Hist. 76. In Severo et vide Guil. Camd. Brit. p. 572.
[4] L. lecta est 40. D. tit. de rebus creditis et Spartian. in Antonino Caracalla, Fr. Conanus Comm. Juris lib. 4, cap. 13, Guid. Panzirol. de Claris Leg. Interp. lib. 1, cap. 55, etc.
[5] In Severo.
[6] Videsis Jo. Bertrand. de Jurisperitis lib. 1 in Papiniano.
[7] Hist. Juris a Justiniano comp.
[8] Hist. 76.

where opinions were evenly divided and mutually contrary, that one would prevail with which Papinian concurred. Friend of Severus and fellow-student with him under Scaevola, it was to him that the special charge of the emperor's two sons was entrusted. It is certain that he not only acted as minister of Septimius Severus in Roman Britain, but that he also practised at York where the imperial residence and tribunal were situated, and where justice was doubtless administered by this emperor and afterwards by Geta, with the help of such assistants.

Severus and Bassianus (Caracalla)

Xiphilinus following Dio Cassius, makes express reference to Papinian in his account of the attempted murder of his father (Severus) by Bassianus. He relates that the emperor said nothing but 'going to the tribunal (at York) he performed his duties there and returned to the praetorium. Summoning his son, Papinian, and Castor, he spoke to the first of his crime, saying: "If you wish to kill me, do so here, but if you refuse or fear to do so by your own hand, here is the prefect Papinian whom you can order to slay me and who will obey you, since you are ruler.'"

Reputation of Papinian

Papinian[1] was Praetorian Prefect under Severus and under his successor Bassianus or Antoninus Caracalla. Spartian calls him 'sun,' 'sanctuary' and 'treasure house' of legal learning and the Corpus of Justinian abounds in such praises. He must have practised and taught in Britain and doubtless held first place among the senior friends appointed to assist Geta in his judicial administration. On account of their perspicuity and subtlety his writings could be undertaken only by students in their third year—'Papinianists[2]' as such students were formally called.

Roman jurists in Britain

On the other hand I do not know of any legal biography or old history recording his stay in Britain except Dio Cassius, whose 'History' leads one to think that its author took part, under Severus, in the judicial administration of this country. It is not unreasonable to assume that such distinguished jurists as Paul and Ulpian were also members of the imperial retinue in Britain. Scholars are agreed

[1] Papinian was put to death by the order of Caracalla. Costa (*op. cit.*), I, 30, gives the date as A.D. 212 and discusses the various reasons for this execution.
[2] In the law schools of the later Roman Empire, the first-year students, called 'dupondii,' studied Gaius: the second-year students, called 'edictales,' read the Praetorian Edict: in their third year they studied Papinian: in their fourth they read, on their own account, the Responses of Paul. See Flach, *De l'enseignement du droit chez les Romains* (1873).

illius Juris Caesarei heroes comitatus heic tunc imperatorii partes fuisse non ita absonum est autumare, dum scilicet ex senioribus Antonini Getae amicis (quod illo in aevo nomen dignitatis singularis[1], non tantum officii, in domo et comitatu Augastali fuisse sciunt docti) adsessores ei adsignatos advertimus, et tam Ulpianum quam Paulum, Papiniano praefecto qui plane heic aderat adsessuram[2] gessisse consideramus. Imo et rescripti illius de mancipiis bona vel mala fide possessis Ceciliae cuidam a Severo et Antonino Augg. Eboraci, consulibus Fausto et Rufo, id est anno Christi 210 dati[3] originem seu causam e lite aliqua Britannica duxisse, non est quod non admittamus. Ita floruit tunc temporis juris Caesarei heic usus uti et simul heic floruere juris ejusdem viri peritissimi illustrissimique e Romanis. Et sane firmatur diffusior in hac insulae parte quae Romanis parebat ejusmodi usus etiam ex eo quod Augustus ille animam exhalaturus Eboraci (ubi obiit[4], postquam biennio amplius sub eo regimen heic civile quale diximus viguerat) 'turbatam se,' dixit[5], 'rempublicam ubique accepisse, pacatam etiam Britannis relinquere.' Atque ex ejusmodi qualem diximus heic Juris Romani usu apud veteres occurrunt illa, 'Latia sub lege Britanni[6],' et non tam Britanniam quam Romaniam[7] dicendam citeriorem insulae partem, ut Taciti[8] testimonium de moribus Romanis in Britannos transfusis expressissimum, alia id genus praetereamus. Provinciae igitur, pagi, praefecturae, oppida hoc jure tunc regebantur; secundum quod de Londinio optime Gulielmus Camdenus ubi nec coloniae nec municipii nomine insignitam urbem illam adnotat. 'Praefecturam itaque,' inquit[9], 'ut opinor, constituerunt (Romani); sic enim vocabant oppida in quibus nundinae agebantur et jus dicebant, ita tamen ut magistratus suos non haberent, sed praefecti quotannis in ea mitterentur, qui jus dicerent, quod in publicis negotiis nempe census, tributorum, vectigalium, militiae etc....a Romano Senatu peterent.' Etiam municipia si quae fuere[10] non aliter eidem juri heic suberant atque urbes oppidaque apud nos non pauca, quibus sui sunt mores legesque singulares, Juri Anglicano quod Commune vocitamus. Jure enim illo mores illi legesque singulares et interpretationem recipiunt et saepenumero ex ejusdem autoritate coercentur, quod nemo nescit.

---

[1] Salmasius in August. pp. 47, 307 et 308.
[2] Lampridius in Alex. Severo et vide 40 lecta est D. tit. de Rebus Creditis.
[3] C. tit. de rei vendicat.   [4] Dion. lib. 76.
[5] Spartianus in Severo.
[6] Vet. Poet. Catalect. lib. 1, tit. 7.
[7] Gildas in epist. de Excid. Brit.   [8] In vita Jul. Agricolae.
[9] Britan. p. 304.   [10] Videsis Camden. Brit. pag. 572.

that the assessors, such as assigned to Geta, were high public dignitaries and not merely personal friends; we maintain that Ulpian and Paul were of their number during the prefecture of Papinian, who indubitably was here. Furthermore, the imperial rescript[1] concerning property acquired by good or bad faith, issued at York in A.D. 210, originated from a British suit.

Severus left Britain pacified

Thus there flourished here at that time both the use of the imperial law and Romans expert and eminent therein. The fact of its wider use in this part of Britain is confirmed by this, that after more than two years of this regime, Severus, just before his death at York[2], was able to say that he had found the whole empire turbulent at his accession and left even Britain satisfied.

Municipia in Roman Britain

Some ancient writers say 'The Britons are under Latin law,' others that the southern part of the island should be called Romania rather than Britannia. On this point Tacitus speaks of the transfusion of Roman customs into Britain, where provinces, cantons, prefectures and towns were administered by Roman law. Writing of London, which was not designated by the name of colonia or municipium, Camden states that 'they constituted it a prefecture, a name given to towns in which there were markets and where law was administered by prefects sent there every year for such purposes as the census, tribute, taxes and military service on instructions received from the Roman Senate.' Whatever municipia existed were subject to the same law, just as with us numerous towns and cities which possess their own laws and customs are subject to what we call the English common law. Such laws and customs derive their interpretation and often their sanction from English common law.

---

[1] C. 3. 21. 1.
[2] February 4, A.D. 211.

IV. Duravit autem Juris Caesarei quale diximus heic regimen, sed pro vario ac mutante subinde rerum statu aliter atque aliter se subinde habens, per annos trecentos ac sexaginta aut circiter, id est a Claudii Caesaris temporibus (inde enim heic merito auspicamur, non a Julio aliisve Claudium antecedentibus, qui potius Britanniam cogitarunt quam partem ejus aliquam sibi subjecerunt) usque in imperium Honorii Augusti seu tempus quo ab Alarico Gotho Roma capta est. Id est ab anno quasi 50 Christi ad annum ejusdem 410 aut circiter. Sub id scilicet tempus[1] Marco, dein Gratiano et demum Constantino regibus etiam per defectionem[2], seu Augustis heic constitutis, atque Constantino relicta insula in Gallias transeunte rebusque adversis plane oppresso sublatoque, transrhenanis item barbaris cuncta pro libito invadentibus, atque Romanorum imperio adeo in Occidente acciso ut amicis nullatenus subvenire possent, tum Celticae aliquot gentes tum Britanni nostri necessitate adigebantur τῶν Ῥωμαίων (sic Zosimus[3]) ἀρχῆς ἀποστῆναι καὶ καθ᾽ ἑαυτοὺς βιοτεύειν οὐκ ἔτι τοῖς τούτων ὑπακούοντας νόμοις 'ut ab imperio Romano et Romanorum legibus non amplius obedientes arbitratu suo viverent.' Et Celticae illae nationes Τοὺς Βρεττανοὺς μιμησάμεναι, 'imitatae Britannos' (ita idem scriptor), κατὰ τὸν ἴσον σφᾶς ἠλευθέρωσαν τρόπον. Ἐκβάλλουσαι γὰρ τοὺς Ῥωμαίους ἄρχοντας, οἰκεῖον δὲ κατ᾽ ἐξουσίαν πολίτευμα καθιστᾶσαι 'consimili modo se liberarunt. Nam ejectis praesidibus Romanis propriam quandam rempublicam ex arbitratu suo constituerunt.' Heic finis usus juris Caesarei jam dicti collocandus, qua Caesarei, seu qua autoritatem ex Caesarum imperio habentis; utcunque proculdubio e tam diutina quae per secula illa anteacta invaluerat consuetudine, non superesse, saltem aliquamdiu, non potuerint aliquot ejusdem, in regimine novo seu recenti ex arbitratu incolarum nato, reliquiae, quae nunc consensu utentium retinente temperanteve, non omnino ut ante imperantium seu Caesarum autoritate subniterentur. Atque hoc est quod ait Beda[4], 'ex eo tempore' (quo capta est a Gothis Roma) 'Romani in Britannia regnare cessarunt,' quod sane etiam Procopio[5] satis affirmatur. Apud alios finis Romani heic imperii citerius ponitur, anno scilicet Christi 434[6] aut 435 seu sub media Theodosii junioris tempora. Chrono-

---

[1] Zosimus, lib. 6. Olympiodorus apud Photium cod. 80.
[2] Procopius Vandalic. lib. 1, pag. 94 b.   [3] Histor. lib. 6.
[4] Hist. Eccles. lib. 1, cap. 11 et in epit. Hist. Anglic.
[5] Vandalic. lib. 1, pag. 94.
[6] Chronolog. Saxon. Aethelwerdus, Florilegus, etc. Vide Jacob. Armachanum de Britannicarum Eccles. Primordiis, cap. 12 et pag. 599. Guid. Panziroll. in Notit. Occidentis cap. 83, adde Camden. Brit. pag. 94.

Collapse of Roman rule

IV. This rule of the imperial law survived for about 360 years, varying from time to time with political changes[1]. Starting from Claudius, whose predecessors had aimed more at conquest than settlement, it lasted till the days of Honorius when Rome was captured by Alaric the Goth, in other words from about A.D. 50 to A.D. 410. Marcus[2], then Gratian[3], and lastly Constantine[4] succeeded, either from a national revolt or because set up here as kings. With the defeat and death of Constantine in Gaul[5] and invasions from across the Rhine, the Roman Empire in the west was so ruined as to be unable to help its allies. Then the Britons were obliged, as Zosimus records, 'to desert the Roman rule and the Roman laws, living thenceforth in their own way.' These Celtic nations, following this example, 'rejected their Roman guards' and, in the words of the same author, 'established states of their own.'

Date of termination of Roman rule

Here must be placed the termination, in Roman Britain, of this type of use of imperial law—imperial as deriving its authority from the empire of the Caesars. Considering how long this use had been in force some traces must have survived, at least for a time, in the new autonomous governments that were set up, but these survivals were modified to suit the needs of their users and could not, as before, derive any backing from the imperial sanction. Hence Bede's statement that 'from the capture of Rome by the Goths, the Romans ceased to reign in Britain,' a statement confirmed by Procopius. By some writers the date of the termination of Roman rule is put later —A.D. 434 or 435. The Anglo-Saxon Chronicle has the latter date[6],

---

[1] For an estimate of Roman-law influence on the Anglo-Saxon conception of 'boc-land' see Vinogradoff, *Romantische Einflüsse im Angelsächsischen Recht* in *Mélanges Fitting*, II (1908).
[2] A.D. 407. [3] *Ibid.*
[4] *Ibid.* For these see Gibbon, *Decline and Fall*... (ed. Bury), III, 287 ff.
[5] Constantine was executed shortly after the siege of Arles, September, A.D. 411.
[6] Really A.D. 409 in all the texts except MS. Domitian A, VIII, which gives A.D. 408.

logia vetus Anglo Saxonica[1]; 'ccccxxxv Her Gotan abraecon Rome burh. ꠋ naefre siþþan Romane ne ricsodon on Britene. Hic Gothi urbem Romanam vastarunt. Neque unquam postea Romani regnabant in Britannia.' Quod vero adjicitur ibi regnum illud ab Julio Caesare sic durasse ex veterum aliquot natum est hallucinatione, qui adventum ejus in 'quaesitos' ut ait Lucanus, 'Britannos,' pro victoris oscitanter nimis sumsere. Atque alii de Romani imperii heic fine aliter aliterque. Sed de minutioribus temporis apicibus heic non disputamus. Et quantum ad rem quam tractamus sufficere puto quae dicta sunt. Qui autem de tempore citeriore loquuntur, non tam de fine heic imperii Romani, quam de Romanis hinc discedentibus videntur capiendi.

Caput Quintum

I. Quibusnam in libris Jus illud Caesareum contineretur cujus per intervallum Romani heic imperii seu annorum quasi 360 superius memoratum, usus, qualis ante ostensus est, heic habitus.

II. De Codice Theodosiano. Editionis ejus annus verus sibi restitutus, contra tum jurisperitos tum chronologos hactenus ea in re hallucinatos.

III. Quomodo mutatum in Codice illo Jus Caesareum novaque facie tunc indutum.

IV. De Juris Caesarei a barbaris itidem novati usu in Occidente post vastatum ab illis Imperium Romanum usque in Justiniani tempora, in Italia, Hispania, Galliis; juris scilicet maxime in Theodosiano codice reliquisque Anianeis seu Alaricianis reperti.

V. Justinianei Juris, qua talis, in Oriente usus diutinus. In Occidente, per multa ab eo secula, in regimine publico, nullus. Theodosianum Corpus, cum adjunctis, Romani seu Caesarei nomine ut ante ita et post Justinianum usque in seculi duodecimi aut circiter medium, variatim in publico apud Occidentales aliquot gentes regimine receptum.

VI. Codicis Theodosiani atque adjunctorum apud scriptores et studiosos per intervallum illud usus. Et de celeberrima lege Constantiniana in, seu cum eo, vulgo obtensa, qua immanis olim et stupenda Episcopis seu generi hieratico tributa jurisdictio. Eam revera Codicis illius (cujus ad calcem reperitur) partem nunquam fuisse, sed diu ante abrogatam, a falsariis aliquot esse adjectam.

I. Per intervallum annorum 360 aut circiter jam ante ostensum, seu a Claudii Augusti tempore usque in Honorii, quo finis heic Imperii Romani, Jus, cujus in hac insulae nostrae parte usus quem diximus habitus est, Caesareum sedes habuit suas in Duodecim Tabularum reliquiis; in Senatusconsultis ac Plebiscitis priscis recentioribusque, quotquot scilicet a principibus firmata, admissa, retenta sunt; in praetorum edictis; veteribus

[1] Pag. 507.

but its statement that the Roman rule dated back to Julius Caesar is due to a misconception which confounds a conquest with what Lucan[1] described as Caesar's 'quest' of the Britons. There are other opinions about the date, but we do not dispute here of small points of time. Those who quote a later date should be understood to speak of the departure of the Romans, not of the end of Roman rule here.

Chapter V

I. In what books was comprised the imperial law as applied in this country during the 360 years of Roman occupation.

II. Of the Theodosian Code. The true date of its publication established.

III. With what changes the imperial law is found in that Code.

IV. The use, by the western barbarians in Italy, Spain and Gaul of the revived imperial law as found in the Theodosian Code and the Anianean or Alarician fragments in the period from the fall of Rome to the time of Justinian.

V. The long use of Justinian's Corpus in the east and its absence from public administration in the west. The varied reception of the Theodosian Code and its adjuncts in the governments of several western nations in the period prior to Justinian and after him up to about the middle of the twelfth century.

VI. The use of the Theodosian Code and its adjuncts by writers and scholars during this period. Concerning the famous law of Constantine attributing unheard-of power to the Clergy. This law, alleged to have been put forward in the Code or as an accompaniment to it, was never really part thereof, but formed an appendix. It had long before been abrogated and was inserted there by forgers.

Early codes

I. During the three hundred and sixty or so years of the Roman occupation, the imperial law as used in this country had its origin in (*a*) the fragments of the Twelve Tablets, (*b*) such senatus consulta and plebiscita old or new as had been confirmed or retained, (*c*) Praetorian Edicts, (*d*) old books like those of Gaius, Scaevola, Papinian, Ulpian and Paul, from which the Pandects of Justinian were after-

---

[1] Rheni gelidis quod fugit ab undis
Oceanumque vocans incerti stagna profundi
Territa quaesitis ostendit terga Britannis?
LUCAN, *Pharsalia*, II, 570–2.

illis libris, Gaii, Scaevolae, Papiniani, Ulpiani, Pauli, reliquorum id genus vetustiorum e quibus postea conflatae sunt Justiniani Pandectae, atque in Sanctionibus demum Caesarianis Theodosium juniorem antecedentibus adeoque tum in eis quae relatae fuerant in Codices Gregorianum et Hermogenianum tum in reliquis in Codice Theodosiano repertis, quotquot scilicet juxta superius dicta Romani imperii heic finem anteverterint. Gregorius juris studiosus leges principales ab Hadriano ad Valerianum usque et Gallienum in Codicem suum conjecit uti et Hermogenes in suum eas quae fuere a Claudio Gallieni successore ad Diocletianum. Ea de re consulas Cujacium in Paratitlorum in Codicem Justiniani praefatione unde sua de Codicibus hisce exscripsit Possevinus[1]. Hujus generis fuere libri Constitutionum Divorum Fratrum quos composuerat Papirius Justus[2]. Haec omnia per intervallum quod diximus in musaeis ac foro studiosis judicibusque in usu. Centum autem aut circiter ante Justinianum, cujus corpore juris nunc utimur, annis, finis illius intervalli erat seu imperii heic Romani, adeoque nullus Justinianei, qua Justinianei, tunc usus esse heic alibive quibat.

II. Jam vero haud ita diu post seu potius sub ipsum intervalli illius seu imperii Romani, juxta aliquos, heic finem, seu consule Theodosio illo quindecies et Valentiniano Augusto tertio quartum, id est anno Christi 435 Novella seu lege singulari promulgatus est et firmatus Codex sanctionum principalium Theodosianus. Ita scilicet, si impressis codicibus[3], qui heic sibi invicem consoni omnes, fides. Sed in MS. meo (ubi lex illa non cum Novellis ejus sed cum ipso Codice ut praefatio, sicut ut debet, conjungitur, quemadmodum etiam in editione Sichardiana[4]) legitur 'Theodosio Augusto sedecies consule,' id est, consule illo et Fausto seu Festo; quod ad annum Christi attinet 438. Et certe manifestum est 'quindecies' ibi male legi, impressosque codices esse heic ut in non paucis aliis depravatos. Ad hunc enim modum se habent tunc fasti consulares,

Christi, 435. Theodosius Aug. XV. Valentinianus IV.
       436. Isidorus; Senator.
      437. Aetius II. Sigesvultius.
      438. Theodosius Aug. XVI. Faustus seu Festus.
Atque emissum ad Darium praefectum praetorio Orientis edictum anno proximo ante sextumdecimum Theodosii consulatum,

---

[1] Biblioth. Sel. lib. 12, cap. 15, et vide Guid. Panzirol. de Claris Leg. Interp. lib. 1, capp. 65, 66. De Gregorio vide Fr. Baldwin. in Proleg.
[2] Cujac. Observ. lib. 1, cap. 4 Panzirol. de Clar. Leg. Interp. lib. 1, cap. 51.
[3] Novell. Theodos. tit. 1   [4] Basileae 1528.

V II SOURCES OF ROMAN LAW 57

wards compiled, (e) imperial sanctions as recorded in the Gregorian and Hermogenian Codes, and (f) such imperial sanctions to be found in the Theodosian Code as are anterior to the termination of Roman rule in this country. Gregorius[1], who was devoted to legal study, collected in his Code the chief laws from Hadrian to Valerian and Gallienus, while Hermogenes collected those from Gallienus' successor, Claudius, up to Diocletian[2]. For this subject, consult Cujas' preface to the Paratitles in Justinian's Code, a treatise utilised by Possevino[3] for his extracts from the above Codes. Similar to these were the Constitutions of the Imperial Brothers[4], compiled by Justus Papirius[5]: all of these, in the period under consideration, were utilised by students and practising lawyers. There is no question here of the use of the Corpus of Justinian since that was not compiled until about a century after the fall of the Roman Empire.

Theodosian Code: date of its promulgation

II. In A.D. 435 in the XVth consulship of Theodosius and the IVth of Valentinian III, the Theodosian Code of imperial sanctions was promulgated and confirmed by a Novel or special law. This statement is based on the printed texts, unanimous on this point. In my MS. however, where that law is not inserted as an addendum, but rightly incorporated as a preface—as in Sichard's[6] edition—there is the reading 'in the XVIth consulship of Theodosius,' *i.e.* A.D. 438. It is obvious that XVth is based on a misreading and is one of the many errors in the printed texts. The consular cycle was then as follows:

A.D. 435. Theodosius Aug. XV: Valentinian IV.
„ 436. Isidore: Senator.
„ 437. Aetius II: Sigesvultius.
„ 438. Theodosius Aug. XVI: Faustus or Festus.

The edict[7] concerning the Decurions and Silentiarii sent to Darius, Praetorian Prefect of the east in the year before the XVIth consulship of Theodosius, or A.D. 437, is to be found in the Code. It is sub-

---

[1] *Circa* A.D. 300.
[2] A.D. 296 to 324.
[3] Antonio Possevino, Italian Jesuit, explorer and writer (1534–1611). Selden refers to his *Bibliotheca Selecta*, an encyclopaedia of general knowledge. Possevino was employed by the Vatican for diplomatic visits to Russia and Transylvania: his published works include descriptions of these countries. See L. Karttunen, *A. Possevino, un diplomate pontifical au XVI siècle* (1908).
[4] Marcus Aurelius Antoninus and Lucius Commodus Verus (A.D. 161–180). They were brothers by adoption.
[5] Alternatively, Papirius Justus. He lived in the time of Severus; there is an extract from his Constitutions in D. 49. 1. 21.
[6] Sichard was born at Ingolstadt in 1499 and died in 1552. His edition of the Code was published at Basle in 1528. See Stintzing, I, 212–219.
[7] C. Theod. 6. 23. 4.

seu Christi 437, de decurionibus scilicet et silentiariis, habetur in Codice illo[1]; subscribitur nempe 'Dat. XVIII. Kal. Aprilis Constantinopoli post consulatum Isidori et Senatoris' qui anno illi respondet. Edictum igitur de autoritate Codicis illius a Theodosio et Valentiniano Augustis ad Florentium praefectum praetorio Orientis perperam plane signatur consulatu decimo quinto Theodosii, quod nemo non videt. Ad decimumsextum plane consulatum seu annum Christi 438 attinet edictum illud. Adeoque erroris chronologici non ferendi omnino convincuntur qui editionem Codicis illius triennio ante collocare solent, ut Sigonius[2], Contius[3], Freymonius[4], Baronius[5], Calvisius, chronologiae Codici Theodosiano subjunctae autor, alii. Codex hic primus erat sanctionum imperatoriarum ex autoritate principali seu Augustorum auspiciis editus, Gregorius enim, Hermogenes ac Papirius, ut privati tantum suos composuerant codices, in quibus constitutiones fuere tantum principum qui antecesserant paganorum. In Theodosianum vero receptae sunt tantummodo Christianorum principum sanctiones quae scilicet a Constantino magno et successoribus ejus ante Theodosiani natales emissae atque a Theodosio et Valentiniano tertio selectae.

III. Voluere Augusti illi in Theodosiani confirmatione, 'licentiam fore nulli ad forum et quotidianas advocationes' (ita se habet Novella seu Praefatio jam dicta) 'jus principale deferre vel litis instrumenta componere nisi ex his videlicet libris' (ipso nempe Codice Theodosiano seu ejusdem libris 16) 'qui in nostri nominis vocabulum transierunt et sacris habentur in scriniis. Quanquam nulli retro principum aeternitas sua detracta est; nullius latoris occidit nomen. Imo lucis gratia munerati' (ita e MS. legendum, pro eo quod in editis est nunc 'mutuati' nunc 'mutati') 'claritudine consultorum augusta nobiscum societate conjunguntur.' Papiniani item Pauli, Gaii, Ulpiani, Modestini, uti et aliorum quorum tractatus et sententias suis illi operibus miscuerant, veluti Scaevolae, Sabini, Juliani, Marcelli, omniumque quos illi celebrarunt scripta eodem in Codice[6] firmantur. Ubi autem diversae sententiae proferebantur, potius numerus vincebat autorum. Vel si numerus aequalis esset, ejus partis praecedebat autoritas in qua excellentis ingenii Papinianus eminebat; qui ut singulos vincebat cedebat duobus. Notas autem Pauli atque Ulpiani in Papiniani corpus factas, sicut dudum statutum est, praecipiebant infirmari. Ubi autem pares

---
[1] Lib. 6, tit. 23, 4.   [2] De Occident. Imperio, lib. 12.
[3] In Fastis Consularibus.
[4] Symphonia Juris Chronologica.
[5] Tom. 5, ann. 435, num. 23.
[6] L. unic. C. Theod. tit. de Resp. Prudent.

THE THEODOSIAN CODE

scribed as 'given on the XVIIIth Kalends of April at Constantinople after the consulship of Isidore and Senator,' which corresponds with A.D. 437. Obviously, therefore, the edict sent by Theodosius and Valentinian to Florentius, Praetorian Prefect of the east, concerning the authority of that Code, is wrongly signed 'in the XVth consulship of Theodosius,' the edict really pertaining to the XVIth consulship or A.D. 438. So those who put the publication of this Code three years earlier, including Sigonius[1], Contius[2], Freymon[3], Baronius[4] and Calvisius[5] (author of the chronology affixed to the Code) and others, are guilty of an intolerable error[6].

The Theodosian an official code

This was the first code of imperial law to be issued by government authority, for Gregorius, Hermogenes and Papirius had compiled theirs as private persons, merely embodying in them the constitutions of preceding pagan rulers. But the Theodosian Code contained a selection of the laws of Christian emperors only, *i.e.* those enacted by Constantine the Great and his successors up to the time of Theodosius and Valentinian III[7].

Sanction of the Code

III. These emperors, in confirming their Code, decreed, in the words of the Novel[8] or Preface already mentioned, that no one should be allowed to adduce an imperial law either in the central courts or in the daily pleadings, nor prepare articles of indictment except from the sixteen books of the Theodosian Code, published in their name and deposited in sacred archives[9]. 'The glory of preceding rulers is not detracted from: the fame of no lawgiver is destroyed, rather these are accorded the privilege of light and by the perspicacity of jurists are joined in august alliance with us.' The writings of Papinian, Paul, Gaius, Ulpian, Modestinus and of those others whose opinions and discussions are embodied in the works of the five above-named jurists (for instance, Scaevola, Sabinus, Julian and Marcellus) are confirmed by this Code, as also those authors who were cited with approval by these writers. Where two contrary opinions were adduced, the victory went to the opinion of the majority: where the numbers were equal, Papinian's view had precedence, being superior to any other one but yielding to two. The notes of Paul and Ulpian

---

[1] 1524-1584. See *infra*, p. 73, n. 1.
[2] French jurist, died 1586. Taught at Bourges and Orléans. Edited a Corpus Juris Civilis et Canonici.
[3] Bavarian jurist, late sixteenth century.
[4] 1538-1607. Librarian of Vatican. Engaged (1580-1607) on his *Annales Ecclesiastici* (to 1198), Rome (1589-1603).
[5] German astronomer and musician, 1566-1625.
[6] This correction was made by Gothofred in his edition of the Code (1665). See Seeck, *Regesten der Kaiser und Päpste*, I, 1-18.
[7] It included a number of laws that had ceased to be valid.
[8] Printed *in extenso* in Mommsen and Meyer's edition of the Code, p. x.
[9] Under the 'magistri scriniorum' at Ravenna and Constantinople.

eorum sententiae recitabantur, quorum par censebatur autoritas, quod sequi deberet, eligebat moderatio judicantis. Pauli quoque sententias semper (sed non sine temperamentis antedictis) valere praecipiebant[1]. Sequutae sunt Constitutiones Novellae Theodosii hujus, Valentiniani ejusdem, Martiani, Majoriani, Severi, Anthemii Augustorum. Id autem quod diximus constituerant inter alia ad Senatum Romanum missa Theodosius et Valentinianus sub annum ante Codicis illius editionem decimum seu Christi 428 id est Theodosio Aug. XII (non VII, ut mendose in impressis) et Valentiniano consulibus. Et recte numerum heic correxit Baronius[2], quem oscitanter retinuit, ubi sanctionem hanc describit, Valentinus Forsterus[3] impressorum secure nimis sequax. Idem etiam in Codicem suum retulere Augusti illi; ubi in Anianeo seu Alariciano interpretamento[4] habetur, 'Gregorianum et Hermogenianum ideo legem istam praeteriisse quia suis autoritatibus confirmabantur ex lege priore sub titulo de Constitutionibus Principum et Edictis.' Id quidem verum est, primum Codicis hujus titulum ita se habere. Sed nihil omnino in eo mihi reperitur, quo Codices illi bini alteri aut Constitutiones aliquae omnino principales temporum anteriorum firmentur. Sed vero quibusnam tunc temporis in libris haberetur jus quod obtinuit Caesareum ex jam breviter dictis satis liquet, unde partim etiam de Jure illo, qua usus heic ejusdem proxime ante erat, est dijudicandum.

IV. Haud ita post, quasi in nihilum evanuit Imperium per Occidentem Romanum (modo angustias illas Exarchatus Ravennatis excipias) ab irrumpentibus Gothis, Vandalis, aliis e Septentrione gentibus dilaceratum, variaque in regna distractum. Inde simul Juris Caesarei quod diximus Justiniano vetustioris, qua Caesarei aut ex Augustorum autoritate pendentis, usus ut evanesceret necesse etiam erat. Ita tamen, sub condentium etiam nomine, retinebatur usurpabaturque inter gentes illas victrices ut Romae ac per Italiam in regimine publico a Theodorico rege sub id tempus Ostrogotho et successoribus aliquot adhiberetur ipsorum interim novis edictis interspersum; id quod ex Cassiodori libris Variarum, manifestissimum est. Atque Alaricus secundus Wisigothorum in Hispaniis Galliaque meridionaliori rex opera Aniani e Codice Theodosiano ac diversis libris[5] leges sive species juris elegit et explanavit, nec aliud cuilibet aut de legibus aut de jure licere in disceptationem pro-

---
[1] Vide Jo. Bertrand. de Jurisperitis, lib. 1, p. 12.
[2] Annal. tom. 5, ann. 435, num. 23.
[3] In Hist. Juris Civilis, lib. 2, in Papiniano.
[4] Ad unic. C. Theod. tit. de Resp. Prud.
[5] Praefat. ad Cod. Theod. Sigon. de Occiden. Imperio, lib. 16.

on Papinian they ordered, as had already been decreed, to lose authority. Where contrary views of equal weight were quoted from these writers, choice should rest with the judge, otherwise (with the above qualifications) the opinions of Paul should prevail. Then followed the recent constitutions of Theodosius, Valentinian, Martianus, Majorian, Severus and Anthemius.

Date of this Sanction

Such were the decrees[1] of Theodosius and Valentinian about ten years before the publication of the Code, *i.e.* A.D. 428, or in the XIIth consulship of Theodosius, not, as the printed texts have it, the VIIth. Baronius[2] made this correction, but Valentine Forster[3], incautiously relying on printed texts, repeats the erroneous date. The above sanction was retained in the Theodosian Code for, in the Anianean or Alarician interpretation, it is stated that 'This law completely passed over the Gregorian and Hermogenian Codes because their sanction was confirmed by an earlier law under the title "De Constitutionibus Principum et Edictis."' As a matter of fact this is the first title of the Code itself. Yet I can find nothing in it by which either the Gregorian and Hermogenian Codes or any earlier imperial constitutions were confirmed. But it is clear in what books of that time the contemporary imperial law is to be found, from whence one may form a partial estimate of that law as it was used in this country just before that time.

The Breviarium Alaricianum

IV. Shortly afterwards, the Roman Empire in the west was almost destroyed, except for the small Exarchate of Ravenna, by invading Goths and Vandals, and was divided up into kingdoms. In consequence imperial law, in so far as enforced by imperial authority, practically disappeared. Nevertheless, under the name of its promulgators, it was appropriated by the victors and, in the government of Rome and Italy, it appears interspersed with the edicts of the Ostrogoth Theodoric and some of his successors. This may be gathered from the Miscellanies of Cassiodorus. The Wisigoth Alaric the Second, king of Spain and southern Gaul, assisted by Anianus, selected and expounded laws from the Theodosian Code and other books, decreeing that in legal disquisitions no one might advance anything not contained in this compilation. This book or

---

[1] C. Theod. 1. 1. 5 (March 26, A.D. 429).
[2] In the 1741 edition of the *Annales* (VII, 490) it is corrected in an editorial footnote, but not in the text.
[3] Born Wittenberg 1530; died 1609. Studied at Bourges. The work from which Selden quotes (*Historia Juris Civilis*) was Forster's first and best-known work (Basle, 1565).

ponere constituit praeterquam quod liber inde congestus amplecteretur. Liber seu Breviarium, tum Anianeum tum Alaricianum dicendum, ipsissimus est Codex ille Theodosianus nec tamen ipse satis integer quo nunc utimur, et reliquae cum eo conjunctae Theodosii, Valentiniani, Martiani, Majoriani, Severi, Anthemii Augustorum Novellae, uti etiam excerpta ex Codicibus Gregoriano et Hermogeniano atque interpretamenta qualiacunque Anianea a sensu Caesareo nimis interdum aliena (quod ab viris doctis saepius notatur) praeter Gaii, Pauli, Ulpiani, Papiniani seu Papiani, ut ibi dicitur, fragmenta, sed pro transcribentis libitu interdum mutata[1], atque intersertum ut puto Voluti Metiani opusculum de vocabulis ac notis partium in rebus pecuniariis. Anianus ipse[2]; 'Ex his omnibus jurisconsultoribus ex Gregoriano, Hermogeniano, Gaio, Papiniano (seu Papiano) et Paulo quae necessaria causis praesentium temporum videbantur elegimus.' Nonnulli tamen octo tantum libros priores Theodosiani in Alaricianis hisce fuisse malunt[3]. Denominata autem sunt reliqua conjuncta Theodosiana non minus atque ipse Augusti Codex, unde tum Ivo Carnotensis[4] tum Gratianus[5] Pauli Sententias aliquot leges appellat expressim Theodosianas. Hinc etiam verba Pauli et interpretatio, Aniana lex diserte antiquitus nuncupatur[6], qua de re videsis plura apud Joannem Savaronem ad Sidonium Apollinarem[7], ubi etiam rationem reddit dicti illius Sidoniani de Seronato (sub Anthemii Augusti tempora, seu paulo ante Anianum) 'leges Theodosianas calcans Theodoricianasque proponens, veteres culpas, nova tributa perquirit.' Ita scilicet ante Anianum seu Alaricum illum leges signanter discriminatae. Et de Theodoricianis heic nominisque causa vide itidem Cujacium[8] in Epistola ad Emaricum Ranconetum, Baronium[9] et Innocentium Cironium[10]. Atque observandum est quidem diu ante Alaricum hunc seu sub annum 412 consilium iniisse Ataulphum[11] Gothum Romana adeo in Gothicum nomen moresque mutandi ut Romanum

---

[1] Alciat. Parerg. lib. 2, cap. 26.
[2] Gl. ad C. Theod. unic. de Resp. Prud.
[3] Panzirol. de Clar. Leg. Interp. lib. 2, cap. 3.
[4] Pannorm. capp. 127 et 128.
[5] Caus. 2, quaest. 6, cap. 22.
[6] In Synod. Paris. sub Ludovico Pio apud Ivonem Decret. part. 14, cap. 21. Pannorm. lib. 5, cap. 124. Grat. Caus. 24, quaest. 3, cap. 1.
[7] Lib. 2, epist. 1.
[8] Praefix. Cod. Theodos.
[9] Annal. tom. 6, ann. 468, num. 12.
[10] Observat. Jur. Canon. lib. 5, cap. 1.
[11] Orosius, lib. 7, cap. 43 et vide Goldast. Imperator. Constitut. tom. 3, pag. 586.

abstract, called the Anianean or Alarician[1], is simply the Theodosian Code, but not so complete as the one we use. With it were joined (*a*) Novels of the emperors Theodosius, Valentinian, Martian, Majorian, Severus and Anthemius, (*b*) extracts from the Gregorian and Hermogenian Codes, (*c*) several of Anianus' interpretations, which, as scholars have noted, are sometimes very divergent from the imperial meaning, (*d*) fragments of Gaius, Paul, Ulpian and Papinian occasionally altered to suit the fancy of the copyist, and (*e*) (an insertion, I think,) the little work by Volutius Metianus [Maecianus] on financial sub-divisions and terminology[2]. Anianus himself stated that from these various sources he had selected what seemed essential for contemporary litigation.

Relationship between the Theodosian Code and the Breviarium

Some hold that only the first eight books in the Alarician compilation were Theodosian[3]. The remaining parts are known as Theodosian no less than the Code itself, whence Ivo of Chartres and Gratian expressly refer to some Sentences of Paul as Theodosian. Thus the words of Paul and the interpretation thereof were anciently styled Anianean law—for this point consult John Savaro's commentary[4] on Sidonius Apollinaris[5], where there will be found an explanation of the latter's remark about Seronatus[6] (time of Anthemius[7]) having 'trampled on the Theodosian laws and propounded those of Theodoric[8], raking up old offences and devising new taxes.' Thus before Anianus or Alaric the laws were clearly distinguished. For information on the Theodorician laws and the reason for the name consult Cujas' letter to Ranconet[9], also Baronius and Cironius.

The Goth Ataulphus

It should be noted that as early as 412 Ataulphus the Goth thought of obliterating the very name of Rome by changing everything into

---

[1] For the Breviarium see Conrat, *Das Breviarium Alaricianum*.

[2] Published (from a MS. in the abbey of Lorsch) by Sichard in his edition of the Code. It deals with coins, weights and measures.

[3] This appears to have been Panzirol's opinion. There are extracts from all sixteen books of the Theodosian Code in the Breviarium.

[4] The second edition of Savaro's complete *Opera* of Sidonius Apollinaris with commentary appeared in 1609. Savaro (I, 98) noted that the laws of Theodoric were really those of Euuarige or Euarig, contemporary with Anthemius.

[5] For a study of Sidonius Apollinaris in relation to Roman law studies, see L. Duval-Arnould, *Études d'histoire du droit romain d'après les lettres et les poèmes de Sidoine Apollinaire* (1888).

[6] For Seronatus, see Gibbon, *Decline and Fall...* (ed. Bury), IV, 45.

[7] Eastern emperor, 467–472.

[8] Theodoric I (420–451). Sidonius' letter (written between 469 and 471) is important as one of the few references to the legislation of this Theodoric. For the texts of early Wisigothic legislation, see the edition of Zeumer, in *Monumenta Germaniae Historica* (1902), quarto.

[9] French scholar and jurist, 1498–1559.

plane obliteraretur, sed postmodum consilio hoc gravissimas ob rationes rejecto magnopere studuisse ut 'Romanae restitutionis autor haberetur, postquam esse non poterat immutator.' Promulgatum autem est illud tam seu potius Alaricianus sic quam Theodosianus dicendus Codex, anno Christi 506. Nec dubitari potest quin apud Francos plerunque eo in saeculo retinerentur jura illa in corpore illo reliquisque jam dictis contenta. Nam expressim Agathias[1] de tempore non suo solum (vixit ille sub Justiniano) sed et pristino verba faciens, moresque Francorum enarrans, καὶ πολιτεία inquit ὡς τὰ πολλὰ χρῶνται Ῥωμαϊκῇ καὶ νόμοις τοῖς αὐτοῖς καὶ τὰ ἄλλα ὁμοίως ἀμφί τε τὰ σύμβολα καὶ γάμους καὶ τὴν τοῦ θείου θεραπείαν νομίζουσιν 'et politia plerunque utuntur Romana et legibus eisdem, eandem etiam contractuum et nuptiarum rationem et divini numinis cultum tenent.' Quae ut reliqua antedicta de tempore post Theodosium juniorem, de Codice Theodosiano aliisque illis Anianeis seu Alaricianis intelligenda. Et de Occidente usque ad Justiniani tempora, post adeo accisum ibi Romanum imperium, quantum ad Jus attinet Caesareum, sic statuendum.

V. Sub nonagesimum autem a prima Theodosiani Codicis editione atque ab Alariciana interpretatione vigesimum quartum annum seu Christi 530 partes aliquot corporis sui Justinianus in Oriente promulgare coepit, quod integrum ante annum 565, quo ille mortuus est, absolvitur. Nec Theodosiani jam aut Gregoriani aut Hermogeniani aliorumve juris codicum mansit ibi autoritas qualis ante fuerat, nec Papiniani praerogativa pristina. Alia quamplurima novata, refixa, abrogata, inducta. Militaria, forensia, leges mutavit, alias invexit Justinianus, Ὅπως ἅπαντα νεώτερά τε καὶ αὐτῷ ἐπώνυμα εἴη quod scribit Procopius[2], id est, 'ut omnia nova et de suo nomine dicerentur.' Qua de re vide apud eum plura in 'Arcana Historia' atque in Nicolai Alemanni Notis, observatu etiam ad hanc rem perquam digna. Corpus illud dein, ab jure pristino seu Theodosiano admodum diversum, tum per Orientales imperii partes tum in Exarchatu Ravennate usque ad illum ab Aistulpho rege anno Christi 752 deletum[3], et postmodum sane in Oriente usque ad captam a Turcis Constantinopolim sub annum Christi 1453 cum etiam, Mahumedis qui cepit jussu, Maximus patriarcha inter alios libros καὶ τοὺς Κώδικας τοὺς Βασιλικοὺς 'Codices Imperatorios' (quod de Juris Caesarei sive corpore Justinianeo sive Basilicorum libris sexaginta inde sumtis par est ut intelligas)

---

[1] Historiae Justiniani lib. 1.
[2] Hist. Arcan. pag. 49.
[3] Sigon. de Regno Italiae, lib. 3.

THE ALARICIAN BREVIARY

the Gothic fashion, but having, for good reason[1], abandoned this idea he aimed chiefly at being held the author of Rome's restoration, since he had failed to be the cause of its destruction.

The Franks and Roman law

This Breviary, which should be called Alarician rather than Theodosian, was promulgated in A.D. 506. Doubtless also the Franks retained these laws. Agathias, who lived in Justinian's time, referring to his own and the preceding period, says of the Franks: 'To a large extent they adopt the Roman polity and laws: the same rules for contracts and weddings and the same religious cult.' This, like what has already been said of the times after Theodosius the Younger, is to be understood of the Theodosian Code and of those other compilations of Anianus or Alaric[2].

So much may be said regarding imperial law in the west from the fall of the Roman Empire to the time of Justinian.

The Codes of Justinian and Theodosius

V. About A.D. 530 Justinian began to publish in the east some parts of his Corpus Juris, and this was completed before his death in A.D. 565. Thereafter none of the older codes retained their sanction in the east nor did the old-established authority of Papinian survive. Many others were altered, reformed or abrogated. In matters military and legal Justinian made changes and innovations in order, as Procopius said, 'that everything should be declared afresh and in his own name.' On this subject there are many apposite remarks in Procopius' *Secret History* and in the notes of Nicholas Alemannus[3]. This Corpus, then, so different from the old or Theodosian law, [prevailed] in the eastern Empire and in the Exarchate of Ravenna until the abolition of the latter by king Aistulph in A.D. 752, thereafter in the east until the capture of Constantinople by the Turks in 1453, when the Patriarch Maximus is said to have begun, by order of Mohammed, a translation of the imperial Codes into Arabic for use in the Mohammedan Empire. This is to be understood as referring to the Corpus of Justinian or to the sixty books of the

[1] Influenced perhaps by his Roman wife Placidia. See Bury, *Later Roman Empire*, 2nd ed. I, 197.
[2] Several compendiums were made of the Breviary, *e.g.* the text found by Canciani at Udine and published in his *Leges Barbarorum*, IV, 461 ff.
[3] Procopii 'Ανέκδοτα...ex bibl. Vaticana Nic. Alemannus protulit et notis illustravit. Leyden, 1623.

dicitur[1] in Arabicum transtulisse, in futurum ut videtur Mahumedici imperii usum. Et continuum Juris illic veteris Caesarei usum satis scimus ex Basilicis ipsis, eorum Synopsi, Harmenopulo, Attaliata, Photii Nomocanone, Balsamone, Zonara, Psello, aliis non paucis Graecis Juris sive Caesarei sive Pontificii cum Caesareo mixti libris passim obviis. Quod vero ad Occidentem attinet, ejus imperium, qua Caesareum, annis amplius quinquaginta ante Justinianum in nihilum ferme evanuerat. Et de ipsius Justiniani etiam tempore satis testantur Procopius et Agathias ei coaevi. Nec omnino admittendum aliter atque palam adulatorium quod Justino juniori, Justiniani successori, aliquoties tribuit Corippus Africanus ubi eum Mundi ac Orbis Dominum appellat. Alia id genus eo in saeculo perquam ridicula sunt; nisi adeo tantum dicta velis ut avita Imperatorum jura sic assererentur, non ut potestas ac imperandi facultas praesens in Occidente inde innueretur, quam quidem in cancellos angustissimos jam ante coercitam post unum et alterum saeculum aut circiter omnino desiisse, ex historiis est manifestum. Jam vero Jus Caesareum tum post barbarorum irruptiones illas ante Justinianum, tum in seculis post eum sequentibus dupliciter considerandum est; aut qua in regimine publico usurpatum est, aut qua studiosis in musaeis lectum est neglectumve seu a scriptoribus adhibitum. Atque in utraque consideratione per se Codicis Theodosiani et reliquorum quae cum illo conjuncta sunt, seu corporis Alariciani, id est juris Justinianum antevertentis seu Caesarei vetustioris, ac per se corporis Justinianei seu Caesarei Juris ita recentioris ratio est habenda singularis. In regimine publico Ostrogothorum in Italia, Wisigothorum in Hispaniis et Galliis, aliorum aliquot vicinorum ante Justinianum uti et per annos complures post eum obtinuit quidem jus Romanum vetustius quod ante Justinianum vim habuit, sed Theodoricianis, Anianeis seu Alaricianis, atque id genus aliis tum edictis novis tum interpretationibus superinductis haud parum interpolatum, nec omnino aliter admissum atque nova principum admittentium autoritate donaretur. Quod sic dictum ad corpus Justinianeum seu partem ejus aliquam non omnino attinet, sed ad Theodosianum quod diximus et reliqua cum eo conjuncta atque in usum publicum adhibita. Et hyperbole est

---

[1] Hist. Politic. Turcograec. lib. 1, num. 56.

V v   THE CORPUS JURIS OF JUSTINIAN   67

Basilica. That the use of the imperial law was continuous in the east we know from the Basilica[1] themselves, from their Synopsis[2], from Harmenopulus[3], Attaleiates[4], the *Nomocanon* of Photius[5], Balsamon[6], Zonaras[7], Psellus[8], and from several other well-known Greek books of imperial or mixed imperial and pontifical law. As regards the west, the empire, as such, had practically disappeared more than fifty years before Justinian, for whose times Procopius and Agathias, his contemporaries, are sufficient witnesses. The occasional references by Corippus Africanus[9] to Justinian's successor as 'Lord of the World' should be regarded as mere flattery: such statements must be taken to mean not that the imperial prerogative held sway in the west but that the old imperial rights were asserted. That prerogative, as we know from historians, had already, for about one or two centuries, been confined within narrow limits, or had entirely subsided.

In the period between the barbarian invasions and the rule of Justinian, as well as in the period after Justinian, the imperial law is to be considered in two ways—either as appropriated for public administration, or as read and cited (or neglected) by students and commentators. In both we have specially to consider, on the one hand, the older imperial law prior to Justinian, consisting of the Theodosian Code and its adjuncts: and, on the other, Justinian's Corpus, or the later imperial law. Of these, the former, reinforced by new edicts and interpretations of Theodoric[10] and Anianus or Alaric, and sanctioned by the authority of each prince admitting it, prevailed in the government of the Ostrogoths in Italy, of the Wisigoths in Spain and Gaul, and in the government of some of their neighbours both before Justinian and for many years after him. This applies exclusively to the Theodosian Code and its adjuncts: it does not apply to that of Justinian.

[1] Βασιλικῶν libri sexaginta, ed. C. A. Fabrot, Paris, 1647.
[2] There were two *Synopses* of the Basilica—the *Synopsis Major* (about A.D. 950) and the *Synopsis Minor* (early thirteenth century). They have both been edited by Zachariä van Lingenthal in *Jus Graeco-Romanum*, parts II and V (Leipzig, 1856–1884).
[3] 1320–1380. The Πρόχειρον Νόμων...*Epitome Juris Civilis* was published at Paris in 1540.
[4] Attaleiates was pro-consul and judge under Michael Ducas (about 1072). His Ποίημα Νομικόν was edited by Leunclavius in *Juris Graeco-Romani*... (Frankfort, 1596).
[5] Photius the Canonist (815–891) was Patriarch of Constantinople. The *Nomocanon* is in Bibliotheca Patrum, VI, 1175 *sqq*. (Paris, 1589).
[6] Balsamon, Greek canonist and Patriarch of Antioch, died in 1204. His *Exegesis Canonum* was undertaken in the years 1169–1177.
[7] Greek canonist, died 1130. His *Pandecta Canonum* were published in *Canones SS. Apostolorum et Sacrorum Conciliorum* (Paris, 1618) and at Oxford in 1672.
[8] Psellus (c. 1020–1110) assisted Constantine Monomachus in his reforms of legal education.
[9] Fl. Cresconii Corippi Africani *In laudem Justini Augusti Minoris*.
[10] The great Ostrogoth 455–526. The Edictum Theodoricianum was first published by Pierre Pithou in 1578. See *M.G.H.* (Leges), V, 145–170.

5-2

crassissima in epigrammate Graeco Florentinis praefixo; homines scilicet Asiae, Africae, Europae, quasi genus universum humanum, gentes universas, Justiniano suisque Digestis paruisse. Theodosiana plane et qualia diximus cetera fuere in Occidente jura quae obtinuere Romana. Neque alia omnino fuere Romana apud Francos jura de quibus, ut ante memoratur, loquutus est Agathias, qui dixit ὡς τὰ πολλὰ 'plerunque' politia et legibus uti eos Romanis. 'Simpliciter,' dicere non potuit tum propter immixtos ipsorum mores, tum ob mutationes perquam insignes quas, ut monitum est, invexerat Justinianus. Neque alia est praeter Italiam Theodosianam illam Lex Romana quae viguit Romae atque per Italiam, 'absque universis procellis,' ut ait sub annum Christi 850 Leo papa quartus in epistola ad Lotharium primum Augustum; qua de re consulas Gratianum[1] ac Ivonem[2]. Atque hujus vestigia in Marculphi Formulis aliisque veteribus, quemadmodum ante in Cassiodori Variis, frequentia. Nec sane Romana magis proprie tunc dicta est quam linguae provinciales illae Hispanica et Gallica ex Romana veteri per degenerationem natae Romanae nomine et Romance indigitari solent. Illae non magis a Latino abiere sermone quam leges, utcunque Romanae tunc dictae, abierant, qua in usum admissae formataeque, a primaevo corporis illius Theodosiani sensu. Nam etiam in ipso imperio utcunque translato in Occidentem, adeo capitularibus stirpis Carolinae novis auctum mutatumque est pristinum illud jus ut novam plane faciem induceret atque a veteri plane diversissimam. Quale itidem dicendum de ejusdem juris Romani vetustioris per Hispanias et Gallias usu; id quod nemo nescit qui legibus Longobardorum, Wisigothorum, reliquarum gentium in legum antiquarum codice congestis alienus non fuerit. Etiam apud Wisigothos a Cindaswintho rege sub annum Christi 650 juris Romani expressissima lege[3] usus pro-

---

[1] Dist. 10, capp. 9 et 13.
[2] Part. 4, cap. 179, et Pannorm. lib. 2, tit. de Legibus, cap. 152.
[3] Leg. Wisigoth. lib. 2, cap. 9, et observa epist. Joannis Papae 8 apud Ivonem in Decreto parte 3, cap. 98, citat. capite proximo, 1.

SURVIVAL OF THEODOSIAN CODE

The Theodosian Code not displaced by that of Justinian

Thus there is a gross exaggeration in the Greek epigram prefixed to the Florentines where it is said that all men of Asia, Africa and Europe, *i.e.* practically the whole human race, obeyed Justinian and his Digests, since it is clear that the Roman laws prevailing in the west were the Theodosian Code[1] and the other compilations connected therewith, as already described. Such also were the Roman laws accepted by the Franks, in regard to which we have just quoted[2] the qualified statement of Agathias, qualified, because of their diverse customs and because of very important changes introduced by Justinian. No other Roman law than this held sway in Rome or Italy 'free from all attack,' as Pope Leo IV described it in a letter[3] of A.D. 850 to the emperor Lothair I. For this subject consult Ivo and Gratian. There are many illustrations of this in the *Formulae* of Marculph[4] and in the *Varia* of Cassiodorus[5].

Sense in which Theodosian law was Roman

The name Roman was then as fitting for this law as the names Roman and Romance when applied to the Spanish and French languages which developed from the decayed forms of the old Roman speech. These languages differed from their prototype to no greater extent than did the so-called Roman laws of that period, in their use and substance, from the original sense of the Theodosian Code.

Roman law in Carolingian times

In the western empire revived by the Carolings, this original jurisprudence was so increased and changed by new capitularies that its appearance was completely altered. The same is seen in the use of the old Roman law in Spain and Gaul as evidenced by the laws of Lombards[6], West Goths[7] and other peoples collected into a code of ancient laws. Moreover, among the Wisigoths the use of Roman

---

[1] For this question see Patetta, *Il Breviario Alariciano in Italia* (in *Archivio Juridico*, XLVII), Pisa, 1891, and E. Besta (in *Storia del Diritto Romano* ed del Giudice, Milan, 1923). On the whole, Ficker and Brunner are opposed to the theory that the Breviary was used in Italy in the period after Charlemagne; Patetta, Flach and Salvioli argue on behalf of its use. It may be noted that while Justinian's legislation was not a dead letter, the Digests (because of their theoretical nature) were neglected. [2] *Ante*, p. 66.

[3] In Mansi, *Conciliorum Nova Collectio*, XIV, 887.

[4] Compiled about A.D. 700; it has been edited by Zeumer in *Formulae Merovingici et Carolini Aevi* (*Mon. Germaniae Hist.*—Leges); see Gubian, *Le formulaire de Marculf, est-il Lorrain?* (Paris, 1906).

[5] Cassiodorus was quaestor palatii, magister officiorum and praefectus praetorio under Theodoric, Athalric, Amalaswintha and Justinian. His *Varia* was published in Paris, 1579. See Hasenstab, *Studien zur Variensammlung des Cassiodorus* (Munich, 1883), and Besta, in *Storia del Diritto Italiano* (Milan, 1923), I, 93 ff.

[6] Known to Selden in Herold's edition of the Leges Langobardorum (1557).

[7] The Lex Wisigothorum was known to Selden in the editions of Pithou (1579) and Lindenbrog (1613).

hibetur. Et perquam variatim in regimine Occidentalium aliquot partium illud jus vetustius Romanum habitum est tractatumque per secula illa quae finem imperii Romani in Britannia seu quasi seculi quinti medium seu annum 450 interveniunt et medium aut circiter duodecimi id est 1150, quando velut ex intermortuis in Occidente nuper resurrexerat corpus ut statim ostendetur Justinianeum. Atque ea de re, quantum ad Gallias spectat, vide prae aliis opus doctissimum jampridem editum[1] ab M. Antonio Dominico J.C. 'De Praerogativa Allodiorum in provinciis Narbonensi et Aquitanica,' tum Innocentium Cironium[2] in Observationibus Juris Canonici, ubi memorat etiam Joannis Costae antecessoris Tholosani tractatum 'De origine juris in Gallia' in hanc rem proditurum. Atque heic imprimis observandum, Isidorum Hispalensem[3] cum de legibus accuratius agere instituisset, earumque enumerare autores, Gregoriani Codicis, Hermogeniani et demum Theodosiani meminisse, non tamen Justinianei utpote tunc per Occidentem non in usu. Floruit ille sub ann. 630 seu circiter 70 ab Justiniano. Quinimo in ipso imperio Romano libertas data est profitendi quo jure sive Romano (quod de Theodosiano illo cum adjunctis semper intelligendum; tunc scilicet condito quando conditores in Occidente imperabant, quale de Justinianeo, quatenus ex eo vim nactum est, dici omnino nequit) sive Gothico sive Longobardico sive alio tunc obtinente quis regeretur, quod satis scimus ex Lotharii primi Augusti ea de re lege[4]. Quam tamen sic capiendam existimo ut integrarum urbium, pagorum, territorium principibus seu praefectis simul ac incolis civiliter in universitatem coalescentibus qui professionem ejusmodi elegerint, libertas illa indulgeretur vivendi juxta hujus seu illius legis normam, non personis singulis, qua singuli solum erant, de quibus ne quidem cum ratione posse videtur intelligi. Specimen habetur effectus hujusmodi professionis apud Carolum de Tocco[5] de Romano et Longobardo, sic legum professione distinctis, invicem in foro litigantibus. Atque exemplum ejusmodi professionis visitur illustre in illis Bonifacii Tusciae Ducis ac Matildis Comitissae filiae ejus professionibus; illum scilicet Longobardicam esse professum hanc vero Salicam legem, quod

---

[1] Parisiis 1645, videsis Guil. Ranchinum var. lect. lib. 2, cap. 3.
[2] Lib. 5.
[3] Originum lib. 5.
[4] Leg. Longobard. lib. 2, tit. 57. Sigon. de Reg. Italiae, lib. 5, et videsis Hincmarum Rhem. de Coercendo Raptu, cap. 12, pag. 234, edit. Sirmondi. Ivo, Decret. part. 3, cap. 38. Goldast. Const. Imperialium, tom. 1, pag. 186.
[5] Gloss. in Leg. Longobard. lib. 2, tit. 57.

law was expressly forbidden by king Cindaswintha[1] about A.D. 650. Indeed the old Roman law was very variously received and treated by the governments of western countries in the period from about A.D. 450 to about A.D. 1150, when, as if from the dead, the Corpus of Justinian was revived. On this subject, so far as concerns France, see the recent *De Praerogativa Allodiorum...* of Dominicy[2], also the Observations of Cironius on the canon law where he cites[3], as about to appear on this subject, a dissertation by John Costa, a predecessor of his at Toulouse, on the origins of French law. And here it may be noted that when Isidore of Seville set up to make a careful survey of the laws and their authors, he recalled the Gregorian, the Hermogenian and the Theodosian Codes but not that of Justinian, as though this last was not then in use in the west. He flourished[4] about A.D. 630 or about seventy years after Justinian.

Freedom to choose one's law

Within the Roman empire itself it was permissible to profess by which law one would be governed—whether by the Roman, *i.e.* the Theodosian Code with its adjuncts, by the Gothic or Lombard or any other in force at the time. This we know from the edict of the emperor Lothair[5]. In my opinion this privilege was enjoyed not by private persons as such, but by heads or rulers of cities, cantons and territories, or by subjects united in a corporate sense[6]. An instance of the effect of such profession is seen in the account by Charles of Tocco[7] of Roman and Lombard acknowledging different laws and conducting their suits at the Bar in turns. There is also a good illustration in the declarations of Boniface, duke of Tuscany and his daughter, countess Matilda, whereby the former chose Lombard

---

[1] The aim of Cindaswintha (642–653) and his successor Reccesvinda was apparently to abolish the duality of law and to sacrifice both barbaric custom and Roman law to a uniform system. See Besta, *op. cit.* I, 52.

[2] French jurist and historian, died 1650.

[3] The reference in Cironius is to a 'tractatus de origine juris in Gallia qui lucem expectat.' It does not appear ever to have been printed. Costa died in 1637, cf. Buder, *Vitae clarissimorum iure-consultorum* (1722), 203.

[4] Isidore of Seville was born in 560 and died in 636. The fifth book of his *Ethymologiae* was considered, throughout the Middle Ages, as a manual of law and a convenient preface to the Breviarium.

[5] A.D. 824. It is in *M.G.H.* (Leges), I, 239–240. It allowed free choice only to those whose personal or national law was doubtful.

[6] Everyone had to live according to the law of his nation but there were exceptions: (*a*) illegitimate children might choose their law, (*b*) on marriage, women might choose their husband's law but revert on widowhood, (*c*) the Church always lived according to Roman law, (*d*) libertini might follow the law of their native country or that law by the rules of which they had been manumitted. Savigny discusses the subject in I, chapter III. See Pertile, *Storia del Diritto Italiano* (2nd ed.), I, 66. For the very large literature on this subject see Besta in *Storia del Diritto Italiano*, I, 226 ff.

[7] Sicilian jurist, early thirteenth century. Studied at Bologna. Compiled a glossed edition of Lombard laws.

notat ex ipsorum tabulis, quae plurimae in ecclesia Mutinensi asservantur, Carolus Sigonius[1]. Sed vero etiam hanc Langobardicam postmodum elegisse elicitur ex charta ejus donationis qua anno 1096 fundavit abbatiam Montis S. Petri in dioecesi Metensi, unde Sigonium falsi convincendum volunt nonnulli[2]. Sed nimis opinor immerito. Alterum jam annis fecit ea juvenilibus. Alterum jam senectute provectissima. Locorum item discrimen eam in rem advertendum. Atque huc palam facit Caroli Calvi Francorum regis edictum Pistense[3] quo, juxta legis Lotharianae illius mentem, toties de regionibus ac terris in quibus 'secundum legem Romanam judicia terminantur,' et de illis 'qui secundum legem Romanam vivunt,' verba fiunt. Legem autem Romanam tum in capitulis illis tum in vetustioribus Caroli et Ludovici Pii Augustorum, alibique in id genus scriptis eo in aevo memoratam intelligas semper oportet de Theodosiano illo corpore et reliquis ei conjunctis, non omnino de Justinianeo. Inde in capitularibus Caroli et Ludovici pro legibus e Theodosiano aliqua expressim[4] afferuntur. Et ubi in additionibus[5] Ludovici de poenis eorum qui venerem in alteram formam mutant lex Romana 'omnium humanarum mater legum' nuncupatur, de alia quam quae in Theodosiano habetur capi nequit. Scilicet igne criminis ejusmodi patratores cremari ex ea lege ibi dicitur. At vero ex Justinianea, id est Constantini et Constantis in Codicem ejus[6], sed non in Theodosianum recepta, gladio illi puniendi. Sed vivicomburium, Theodosii, Valentiniani et Arcadii rescriptum ad Orientium vicarium urbis Romae[7], in Codice Theodosiano repertum, praescribit, quod male typis editum ita e MS. corrigendum; 'Omnes quibus flagitii usus est, virili corpore muliebriter constitutos, alieni sexus damnare patientiam (nihil enim discretum videntur habere cum feminis) hujusmodi scelus, spectante populo, flammis vindicibus expiabunt.' Unde hodieque plerunque apud gentes exteras quibus lex illa Romana per secula in usu, retinetur mos flammis damnandi ejusmodi flagitiosos ut a jurisconsultis[8] notatur. Atque ut novata est poena illa ex lege Justinianea id est Constantiniana illa ab ipso in usum revocata, ita sane corpus integrum Theodosiani Codicis, qua autoritatem

---

[1] De Regno Italiae, lib. 8, anno 1007.
[2] Innoc. Ciron. Observat. Jur. Canon., lib. 5, cap. 5.
[3] A.D. 864. Capp. 13, 16, 20, 23, 28, 31.
[4] Capitul. lib. 6, capp. 281 et 307.   [5] Addit. Ludovici 4, c. 102.
[6] C. ad Leg. Juliam de Adulteriis 31.
[7] C. Theodos. lib. 9, tit. 7, seu ad Leg. Jul. de Adulteriis 6.
[8] Damhouderius in Prax. Crim. cap. 98, § 12. Julius Clarius, Sentent. lib. 5, § Sodomia, num. 4.

V v   THE THEODOSIAN CODE SUPERSEDED   73

law and the latter Salic law, as Sigonius[1] infers from their inscriptions, of which there are many in the church of Modena. That Matilda afterwards chose the Lombard law is proved from the charter by which she founded in 1096 the abbey of Pierremont[2] in the diocese of Metz, which has misled some into thinking that Sigonius was in error. But this is unjust, for the acts of her youth differed from those of her extreme old age, and the difference of place is also to be noticed. This is made clear by the Pistensian Edict[3] of Charles the Bald, where, in the sense of Lothair's edict, there are many references to territories where 'judgments are given according to Roman law' and to those 'which live according to Roman law.' The Roman law specified in such capitularies and in the earlier ones of the emperors Charles and Lewis is to be understood as the Theodosian Code, never as that of Justinian.

Carolingian references to the Theodosian Code

In the capitularies of Charles and Lewis[4] some things are expressly adduced from the Theodosian Code as laws and where, in that part of the Additions of Lewis which treats of penalties for unnatural offences, the Roman law is styled the mother of all human laws, this can refer only to the Theodosian Code[5]. The Theodosian penalty[6] for such offences was burning alive, whereas by the law of Justinian—that is, the law of Constantine and Constans as embodied in Justinian's Code[7], but not in that of Theodosius—the penalty was destruction by the sword[8]. The former penalty is retained to this day by some foreign peoples who at that time used the Theodosian form of Roman law. And just as the penalty of destruction by the sword was renewed by Justinian from the law of Constantine, so the authority of the whole Theodosian Corpus was practically abolished

[1] Italian archaeologist and historian (1524–1584). For an account of his career see Muratori's preface to the edition of Sigonius' works (Milan, 1732). There are several modern monographs on Sigonius—e.g. Krebs (Frankfort, 1840), Franziosi (Modena, 1872) and Hessele (Berlin, 1899).
[2] Or Standelmont, near Nancy. See A. Overmann, *Die Besitzungen der Grossgräfin Mathilde* (Berlin, 1892), 48.
[3] *M.G.H.* (Leges), I, 488–9. The name Pistensian is derived from the fact that it was promulgated at Pistae, probably Pitri or Petri in Lorraine.
[4] See *infra*, p. 75, n. 4.
[5] This view is contested by Savigny (I, 132 ff.).
[6] C. Theod. 9. 7. 6.   [7] C. 9. 9. 31.
[8] For the Theodosian rescript see Selden's text.

haberet aut in foro usurparetur, et qua tale, quasi in nihilum redactum est ex Justinianea lege (quantum scilicet inde fieri potuit) de novo Codice confirmando. Sed imperium ejus et potestas tunc solum ferme in Oriente. Utcunque vero, Theodosianum illud corpus jam plane Caesareum proprie non erat aut Caesaris autoritate fultum, sed a regibus gentibusque quas diximus Occidentis variatim ac pro libitu admissum. Atque in compluribus corpus Justinianeum ei erat uti et etiamnum est adversissimum.

VI. Quod vero attinet ad scriptores ac studiosos illius quod tractamus intervalli quibus etiam juris Pontificii sive in synodis sive in collectaneis confarcinatores accenseo; dubitari omnino nequit quin apud eos usus esset Codicis Theodosiani frequens, utpote in regimine publico adeo obtinentis. Qua de re etiam ante diximus. Certe Codicem hunc haud dubito intelligi, sed an solum nescio, ubi de Legum Romanorum studio verba fiunt[1] a Germano ut videtur anonymo, ad Bonifacium Moguntinum antistitem sub annum Christi 750. 'Neque enim parva temporum intervalla,' inquit, 'in hoc studio protelanda sunt, ei duntaxat qui solerti sagacitate legendi succensus legum Romanorum jura medullitus rimabitur et cuncta jurisconsultorum decreta ex intimis praecordiis scrutabitur,' quod de se dixit anonymus ille Poetices et Mathematices pariter atque Juris studiosus. Atque ejusmodi, seculis in illis, usus specimen duximus heic unicum illustrius prae aliis animadvertendum. Reperitur quidem in editionibus aliquot Codicis illius, scilicet Cujaciana et sequacibus, ad libri decimi sexti calcem, titulus 'de Judicio Episcopali' qui libris in aliquot dicitur 'deerrasse a corpore Theodosiano.' In eodem titulo tres habentur sanctiones Imperatoriae quarum prima est illa celeberrima qua immanis ac prodigiosa potestas ac jurisdictio episcopis a Constantino Magno per rescriptum ad Ablavium praefectum praetorio conceditur, 'ut pro sanctis scilicet semper et venerabilibus habeatur quicquid episcoporum fuerit sententia terminatum,' idque in causis omnimodis 'quae vel praetorio vel civili jure tractantur.' Eadem ipsa recipitur ut 'lex cunctis perpetua tenenda' in Capitularia Caroli et Ludovici Imperatorum ab Ansegiso abbate collecta[2], idque ex XVI Theodosii Imperatoris libro capitulo videlicet XII ut in Lindenbrogiana editione. Jam advertendum est librum 16 titulos habere undecim quos tunc capita dixere, adeoque pro duodecimo seu postremo titulo sic accipiendum hunc 'de Judicio Episcopali.' Sed vero in editione Pithoeana citatur, uti etiam apud Gratia-

---

[1] Apud Bonifac. Moguntini in epist. 68.
[2] Capitular. lib. 6, cap. 281.

(so far as that was possible) by Justinian's confirmation of the new Code. But his authority was then almost wholly confined to the east. The Theodosian Code was however not absolutely backed by imperial sanction, but was variously received at their discretion by those western nations we have mentioned. Moreover in many respects it was, and still is, absolutely contrary to that of Justinian.

Boniface of Mainz

VI. Something has already been said of the repeated use of the Theodosian Code, as still prevailing in public administration, among writers and scholars, including compilators of canon law in the period under consideration. An anonymous German correspondent[1] of Boniface, Archbishop of Mainz, writing in A.D. 750 refers as follows to the study of Roman law, and his words may be understood of the Theodosian Code, though whether this is the only one in question I do not know: 'The scholar of discrimination who would thoroughly explore the Roman laws and carefully scrutinise the decrees of jurisconsults must devote no small time to this study.' These are the words of an anonymous writer who was poet and mathematician as well as lawyer[2].

Constantine's supposed rescript to Ablavius

But the most remarkable instance of the use to which the Code was put in those times is seen at the end of Book XVI, in such editions as that of Cujas and its successors[3], where there is a title 'De Judicio Episcopali.' In some books this title is stated to have become separated from the Theodosian Code. In the title are three imperial sanctions, of which the first is that famous one contained in a rescript of Constantine to the prefect Ablavius granting tremendous power and jurisdiction to the bishops in these terms: 'whatever was the considered opinion of the bishops should always be held sacred' in all causes 'adjudicated by praetorian or civil law.' This is embodied as a law 'to be perpetually observed by all' in the capitularies of the emperors Charles and Lewis (compiled by the abbot Ansegisus[4]) and there it appears as from the twelfth title of Book XVI of the Theodosian Code, as in Lindenbrog's edition. But it should be remarked that Book XVI has eleven titles, then called chapters, and so this one 'De Judicio Episcopali' may be taken for the twelfth or last. In Pithou's edition[5] of the capitularies and in

[1] This often-quoted letter is sometimes regarded as by Boniface himself. In Wharton's *Anglia Sacra* (1691), II, 6, it is assigned (on the authority of William of Malmesbury's *Gesta Pontificum*, v, 341, in Rolls Series edition) to Aldhelm, Abbot of Malmesbury. It appears to have been written to Hedda, Bishop of the West Saxons. See Jaffé, *Bibliotheca Rerum Germanicarum*, III, 32.
[2] This Selden must have inferred from the remaining part of the letter.
[3] 1566 and 1586.
[4] Abbot of Fontenelles 823–833. His text of the Capitularies was first published in 1548. See *M.G.H.* (Leges), II, 397 ff. [5] Paris, 1571.

num[1] eam e capitularibus afferentem, e libri 16 capitulo seu titulo XI. Atque ita sane ut pars tituli 'de Religione' seu undecimi est censendus. Ceterum in codice meo MS. sparsim inseruntur, non serie continua, tres illae sanctiones titulo de Episcopis, Ecclesiis et Clericis qui libri decimi sexti secundus est. Subjicitur autem illa de episcoporum jurisdictione Concilio Valentino[2] tertio sub Lothario primo Augusto et Carolo Calvo habito anno 855, Constantini quidem nomine, sed non expressim ut ex Codice Theodosiano cujus tamen exemplaribus vetustis aliquot eam cum aliis non nullis velut appendicem fuisse liquet ex eis quae praefatus est Jacobus Sirmondus ad appendicem suam Codicis Theodosiani. Atque habetur inde haec sanctio Constantiniana tum apud Ivonem[3] et Gratianum[4] tum apud Anselmum Lucensem, ut in notis editionis Decreti Gratianei Gregorianae monetur. Et sane sive ex capitularibus Carolinis sive ex ipso Theodosii codice seu ejus appendice sumserint, plane ut Theodosianum et juris Theodosiani partem censuere. Nam in Justinianeum nunquam omnino est admissa. Collocat eam Baronius[5] in anno 314 seu Constantini 9, sensumque ejus summatim habere existimat, nec male, tum Eusebium[6] tum Sozomenum[7]. Et gratissimus erat proculdubio dilectissimusque codicis hujus usus generi hieratico ob sanctionem hanc cum eo repertam quae tam immensam episcopis suis potestatem ita tribuens summis proculdubio in deliciis eis erat. Atque inde sane exemplarium codicis illius sive veri sive interpolati usum apud studiosos ac scriptores per intervallum illud infrequentem non fuisse elici potest. Quod vero ad sanctionem ipsam heic attinet (quod obiter monere liceat) in ambiguo mihi non est eam a Theodosio in codicem suum revera nunquam omnino receptam esse, sed plane diu ante initia ejus abrogatam. Scilicet a Valente Gratiano et Valentiniano, anno 376 qui ea tantum episcopis permisere quae ad religionis[8] observantiam pertinebant; quod et firmatum est ab Honorio et Arcadio cum cancellos potestati episcopali prudenter circumscribentes[9], 'quoties de religione ageretur' constituere 'ut episcopi agitarent, caeteras vero causas quae ad ordinarios cognitores vel ad usum

---

[1] Caus. 11, quaest. 1, c. 27.
[2] Concil. Gallic. Sirmond. tom. 3, p. 106. Concil. Gen. tom. 3, part. 2, p. 394, 1618.
[3] Decret. part. 16, cap. 312. Pannorm. lib. 5, cap. 23.
[4] Caus. 11, quaest. 1, c. 35.
[5] Tom. 3, ann. 314, num. 38 et 39.
[6] De Vit. Constan. lib. 4, cap. 27.
[7] Lib. 1, cap. 9.
[8] C. Theod. tit. de Episcopis, 23.
[9] Cod. eod. tit. de Religione.

THE DONATION AN *EXTRAVAGANT*

Gratian (who cites it from the capitularies) it is quoted as from the eleventh title of Book XVI, and so it may be regarded as part of the eleventh title 'De Religione[1].'

This sanction really an appendix

In my MS.[2] the three sanctions are inserted not consecutively but separately[3] in the title 'De Episcopis, Ecclesiis et Clericis,' which is the second title of Book XVI. Added to them is the sanction concerning episcopal jurisdiction[4] decreed by the Third Council of Valence (855) in Constantine's name but not expressly from the Theodosian Code. Sirmond's Appendix to the Theodosian Code[5] shows that in some old copies this sanction, with several others, was added by way of appendix; moreover it was taken therefrom by Ivo, Gratian and Anselm of Lucca, as may be seen from the notes to the Gregorian edition[6] of Gratian's *Decretum*. But from whatever source they derived it, whether from the Caroline Capitularies or the Theodosian Code itself, or from its appendix, they obviously regarded it as an integral part of Theodosian law. It was never admitted into Justinian's legislation.

The sanction not part of the Theodosian Code

Baronius dates the sanction A.D. 314 or the ninth year of Constantine and considers Eusebius[7] and Sozomen[8] to have accurately described its purport. Because of it, this Code was doubtless very popular with the clergy, and copies, whether the true or interpolated ones, were probably in wide circulation. The sanction itself, however, was never part of the Theodosian Code. It had been abrogated as early as A.D. 376 by Valens Gratian and Valentinian, who conceded[9] to bishops merely what concerned religious observances, a measure confirmed by Honorius and Arcadius, who, wisely restricting episcopal jurisdiction, decreed[10] that bishops should decide in religious matters, but that matters within the cognizance of the public magistrates or of the established law, should be dealt with according to the

---

[1] On the general subject of the Donation of Constantine see W. Martens, *Die Falsche General-Konzession Konstantins des Grossen* (1889), and K. Zeumer, *Der Älteste Text des Constitutum Constantini* (in *Festgabe für Gneist*).
[2] The MS. collections of William of Malmesbury, presented by Selden to the Bodleian Library. Now MS. Seld. Arch. B. 16. For this MS. see *supra*, p. xxiii and *infra*, pp. 106–8.
[3] On f. 177 *b*, col. 1, f. 175 *b*, col. 1, and f. 175 *b*, col. 2 of the MS.
[4] Mansi, *Nova Collectio*, XV, 13.
[5] Paris, 1631. Jacques Sirmond (1559–1651) was a French Jesuit, a scholar and a voluminous writer.
[6] See *infra*, p. 89, n. 3.
[7] Eusebius Pamphili, bishop of Caesarea, *De vita Constantini Magni*, 1612.
[8] Hermias Sozomenes, *Ecclesiasticae Historiae libri IV*, Basle, 1549.
[9] C. Theod. 16. 2. 23.
[10] C. Theod. 16. 11. 1.

publici juris pertinent, legibus oportere audiri.' Atque haec tum in Theodosianis habentur[1] tum ab Valentiniano tertio aperte in hanc rem explicantur. Citra laicorum litigantium voluntatem interpositam causas eorum cognoscere tunc nequibant episcopi eorumve consistoria. 'Quoniam,' inquit Augustus ille, 'constat episcopos et presbyteros forum legibus non habere nec de aliis causis secundum Arcadii et Honorii divalia constituta, quae Theodosianum corpus ostendit, praeter religionem posse cognoscere.' Sic Valentinianus ille. Nec sane aliunde puto locum, veluti extravagans, in calce codicis Theodosiani habuit sanctio illa aut in MS. mei titulum 'de Episcopis' aliunde surrepsit quam ex solennibus generis hieratici fraudibus ac falaciis quibus principes et respublicas imperio suo et potestate legitima per fas et nefas emungere pro more illis in seculis, ne de aliis dicam, sedulo variatimque satagebat commodo suo scilicet ac ambitioni nervosissime religionis obtentu ut fieri amat inserviens. Nec enim in Theodosiano locum habere quibat, nisi admittas eos qui codicem illum congerebant sanctiones sibi invicem plane contrarias in re tam insignis momenti oscitanter infarsisse; quod credibile omnino non est. Sanctioni huic item adversissimum est jus Justinianeum in quod non modo nunquam receptum est sed eo plane abrogatum. Cum nihilominus etiam post Justinianeum per Occidentem, ut mox dicetur, maxime ab genere hieratico receptum, ea ipsa sanctio velut Theodosiana, simulato interim Constantini nomine, simul et ut Carolina et quasi etiamnum vim retinens, obtendatur, quod videre est apud Innocentium tertium[2] sub annum 1200 ad episcopos per Franciam constitutos. Fefellere Carolum et Ludovicum Augustos, ii qui velut Theodosiani codicis partem eam eis obtrusere. Et recte glossa in Gratianum[3]—'nota quod haec lex est abrogata; nec habet locum hodie.' Atque tametsi in codice meo veteri sub annum 1120 conscripto pars fuerit tituli 'de Episcopis' seu secundi in libro Theodosiani decimosexto atque in eum cum binis illis aliis ut diximus conjecta, vix tamen dubitandum videtur quin illud in pontificum gratiam atque ad majorem abrogatae diu ante sanctioni, quae hactenus extra vagata esset, autoritatem conciliandam, per fraudem factum sit. Nam in codicibus vetustioribus seu eis qui sub Carolo Magno seu circa annum 800 seu trecentis amplius ante MS. meum annis, in usu, ad calcem Theodosiani habebatur, atque ut in appendice; ita tamen et tunc et postmodum saepius ab agyrtis aliquot afficta ut aut pro tituli

---

[1] Valent. Novell. tit. 12.
[2] Antiq. Collect. 3, lib. 2, tit. 1, et Extr. tit. de Judiciis c. Novit. 13.
[3] C. 11, quaest. 1, c. quicunque 35.

THE DONATION ABROGATED

laws. These laws are those of the Theodosian Code, and Valentinian elucidates the matter further in these words: 'it is certain that bishops and priests have no court of justice nor can they determine of other than religious matters, as is shown in the constitutions of Arcadius and Honorius embodied in the Theodosian Code[1].' Without the consent of both parties, the Church could not at that time intervene in lay suits.

Clerical use of this sanction

In fine, this sanction, as an Extravagant, obtained its place at the end of the Theodosian Code by the usual pious frauds of the clerical order, by which in those days, not to mention others, it was busy defrauding rulers and states of their legitimate power in accordance with its custom, serving its own advantage zealously under the cloak of religion, a favourite practice. To assume that the sanction had a place in the Theodosian Code is to suppose that the compilers of that Code stuffed it with fundamental enactments contradicting each other. The sanction is inconsistent with and abrogated by the Corpus of Justinian which was received in the west mainly by the agency of the clergy themselves, when it was palmed off as Theodosian, even as Carolingian, and as still authoritative, Constantine's name having meanwhile been forged. The epistles of Innocent III to the French bishops about the year 1200 contain evidence[2] of this, and the emperors Charles and Lewis were deceived when it was foisted upon them as part of the Theodosian Code. The gloss on Gratian[3] is right—'this law is wholly abrogated and has no force to-day.'

The sanction abrogated in the Code itself

In a MS.[4] of mine written about the year 1120[5] the sanction, with the other two already mentioned, is part of the title 'De Episcopis,' *i.e.* the second in Book XVI. Nevertheless this was certainly effected by fraud for the clergy's advantage and to bolster up a sanction, previously a 'stray' and long since abrogated. For in the older MSS., such as those of about 800, the sanction is found at the end as an Appendix. But then and afterwards it was often arranged by impostors so as to seem a part of the eleventh title, which, by the way,

[1] *Liber Legum Novellarum Divi Valentiniani,* xxxv.
[2] *E.g.* 'ut illud humiliter omittamus quod Theodosius statuit et Carolus innovavit.' *Antiquae collectiones decretalium* (1609), 282.
[3] In *Decretum Gratiani...una cum Glossis* (Leyden, 1572), col. 900.
[4] See *supra,* p. 77, n. 2.
[5] Probably 1130.

undecimi (in quo interim plane continetur ut diximus ejusdem abrogatio Honoriana) parte existimaretur, aut, ab eo inciperetur novus seu alius, ut nunc 'de Episcopali Judicio' titulus. Et recte cum sociis 'deerrasse' in impressis dicitur. Locum autem qualemcunque ad calcem sic habuisse palam est ex Capitularibus ante citatis. Et fraus heic sane mihi videtur manifestissima. Nec novum est adulterinas leges[1] verarum corporibus inserere et assuere. Sed hac de sanctione alibi, Deo volente, plura et fusius. Hactenus autem de Codicis Theodosiani per intervallum de quo loquimur etiam et post initia Carolini Imperii, pro lege Romana, usu, dictis accedat quod saepius ea de re occurrit apud Hincmarum Rhemensem antistitem qui floruit sub annum 860. In epistola de coercendo raptu, 'publicas Romanorum leges' in testimonium affert, 'quibus' inquit[2] 'orbem universum vivere sub sua dominatione constituerunt.' Ipsas autem citat quae in Theodosiano[3] habentur nec in Justinianeum receptae. Gregorianum item memorat codicem[4] Hincmarus eadem in epistola[5]. Alios ex Theodosiano locos, ut juris tunc Romani promptuario receptissimo[6] affert, saepius etiam interpretationem adjiciens quae ipsissima est Aniana Theodosianis annexa. Hujus autem rei apud eum specimen est praecipuum in epistola ad Carolum Calvum pro Hincmaro Laudunensi seu episcoporum causis jam nuper a Sirmondo primum edita[7]. At quanti etiam et primarii usus esset codex ille in studiosorum aliquot doctorumque musaeis per intervallum illud, dum de jure agebant, satis insuper liquet tum ex Ivonis Carnotensis et Decreto[8] et Pannormia[9], seu si mavis Pannomia, etiam Parnomia interdum, ut in exemplari MS. pervetusto ac nitidissimo bibliothecae ad S. Jacobi Regiae dicta (quae ante Gratianum, corpus Canonum juristis supplesse nonnullis[10] dicuntur; aliis Hugonem Cathalaunensem interponentibus) ubi aliquoties veluti vigorem obtinens adhibetur, tum ex Gratiano[11] aliisque unde is sua compilavit vetustioribus, in quibus non pauca e Theodosiano etiam sub pontificum veterum aliorumque nominibus afferuntur quod adnotatum habes ad calcem codicis ejusdem editionis tum Genevensis[12] tum Parisiensis[13] uti etiam in viri praestantissimi Davidis Blondelli

---

[1] Vide Alciat. Parerg. 6, cap. 9, etc.
[2] Cap. 5, pag. 228, edit. Sirmondi tom. 2.
[3] Lib. 9, tit. 24.
[4] Tit. ad Leg. Juliam de Adulteriis.
[5] Cap. 9.
[6] Opusc. 55 capit., cap. 36, pag. 527, 545, 780, 784, 796, 801 in tom. 2, edit. Sirmond. et pag. 719, tom. 1.
[7] Tom. 2, pag. 318, Paris. 1645.
[8] Part. 16, tit. de causis laicorum saepius.
[9] Lib. 4, capp. 127, 128, et lib. 5, cap. 13.
[10] Tritemius de Scriptoribus Ecclesiasticis, Gesnerus, Possevin. etc.
[11] Caus. 2, quaest. 6, cap. 22.
[12] 1593.
[13] 1586.

contains Honorius' abrogation of the sanction, or to appear as if a new title, like this one 'Of Episcopal Jurisdiction' commenced therefrom. The printed editions rightly class this and its fellow sanctions as 'strayed.' The Capitularies already cited show that whatever place the sanction had was at the end of the Code and to my mind there is no doubt about the fraud. It is no new thing to find spurious laws inserted in or appended to codes of genuine laws. But elsewhere we hope, God willing, to treat this subject more fully and freely.

Hincmar of Rheims

Returning now to the evidences of the general use of the Theodosian Code in the west up to Carolingian times, Hincmar, Archbishop of Rheims may be mentioned. In one of his epistles[1] he cites, as evidence, 'the public laws of the Romans according to which, it was decreed, the whole world should live.' He adduces several things in the Theodosian Code not embodied in the Corpus of Justinian, quoting the former as a most widely-applied manual of Roman law, and he frequently adds Anianus' interpretation. In the same letter he mentions the Gregorian Code. Another good instance is in one of his letters, recently published by Sirmond, to Charles the Bald on behalf of Hincmar of Laon.

Ivo of Chartres and Burchard of Worms

But how great and fundamental was the use of the Theodosian Code among several scholars of this period, is seen in (*a*) the *Decretum* and *Pannormia* of Ivo of Chartres (or *Pannomia* if you will, or even *Parnomia*, as in a fine old MS.[2] of the Royal Library at St James'), compilations said by some writers to have provided a pre-Gratian code of Canons, while others interpose Hugh of Châlons[3], (*b*) Gratian and (*c*) the older writings from which Gratian compiled his Code, in all of which one finds many things derived from the Theodosian Code under the names of former popes and others. This is noted at the end of the Genevan and Parisian editions of the Theodosian Code

[1] This is in one of his letters 'communi episcoporum nomine de coercendo et exstirpando raptu viduarum' (in *Opera*, ed. Sirmond, Paris, 1645, II, 225 ff.).
[2] Royal MS. 7 B, v. MS. 11 B, XIII, has 'Parmonia.' For modern texts of the *Decretum* and *Pannormia* see *Patrologia Latina*, CLXI.
[3] Little seems to be known of this canonist except that he made a compendium of Ivo's *Decretum*. From the *Chronica Albrici Monachi Trium Fontium* (*M.G.H.* Scriptores, XXIII) it appears that he was a bishop of Châlons in the earlier part of the twelfth century. See Savigny, II, 304–5.

Prolegomenis[1] ad Pseudo-Isidorum. At vero sub posteriora intervalli quod diximus tempora seu saeculum undecimum, ex invalescentibus per aevum retro actum diversissimis aliarum gentium moribus legibusque evenit proculdubio ut etiam lex illa Romana seu Theodosiana evanescere coeperit et apud alios, utcunque juris studiosissimos, plane neglectum jacuerit. Nam advertendum, Burchardum Wormatiensem antistitem qui sub annum 1030 floruit et juris Pontificii corpus confecit, non solum in corpus illud e Theodosiano, qua tali, nihil omnino attulisse, verum etiam in lege Familiae S. Petri[2] quam condidit ipse de jure dotali, haereditatibus, contractibus, judiciis publicis, forensibus aliis, inde nihil sumsisse nec quid ejusdem ibi imitatum esse, unde vix credendum eo aevo, sicut ante, adeo frequentem in Occidente Christiano fuisse ejusdem usum.

Caput Sextum

I. Juris Justinianei, qua talis, usum per secula quae a Justiniano seu anno 560 aut circiter usque in priorem seculi duodecimi partem seu annum 1130 aut circiter effluxere, in regimine Occidentis publico fuisse nullum, licet ab ecclesiasticis tam hoc quam Theodosianum subinde adhiberetur.

II. Ejusdem sub Lothario Augusto II seu circa annum 1130 per Occidentem instauratio. Et de Irnerio qui primus ejusdem Illuminator dictus, Lucerna Juris, et Glossarum autor primus, a quo Azonum, Accursiorum, id genus reliquorum deducitur familia.

III. Sub idem tempus aliarum disciplinarum in Christianismi Occidente velut ab intermortuis resurrectio.

IV. Quanam sub ratione ita receptum in Occidente juris Justinianei usus; ut in Gallia, Hispania, Lusitania, Italia, Germania, alibi.

V. Undenam evenerit, adeo libenter tempore Lotharii secundi seu aevo ante dicto jus Justinianeum a principibus ac populis Christianis in Occidente ita esse receptum, conjectura.

I. Jam vero quod ad jus Romanum recentius seu Justinianeum attinet, qua in corpore scilicet Justinianeo visitur atque a Theodosiano illo veteri ut perquam diversum etiam et saepius adversum discriminatur; per intervallum ab ipsius natalibus (qua Justinianeum est) seu Justiniani imperio aut circiter, seu seculi sexti quasi medio (id est sub annum 560) usque in seculi duodecimi partem priorem seu tempora Lotharii secundi Augusti aut circiter, seu per annos septuaginta supra quingentos, jus illud apud Occidentales[3] in regimine publico ac civili extra Exarchatum Ravennatem seu angustias illas aliquot Orientalis in

[1] Cap. 12.   [2] Burchardi editio 1560 Colon. Agr.
[3] Vide Francis. Baldwin. in Prolegom. Jur. Civ., Alciat. Parerg. 5, cap. 25, et citata ad § heic 2.

THE CORPUS JURIS IN THE WEST

and in the noted Blondell's Prolegomena[1] to the Pseudo-Isidorian Decretals. But by the end of the period, that is by the eleventh century, with changed customs and laws, the Theodosian Code fell into decay even among the best scholars. Burchard, archbishop of Worms[2] (*c.* 1030), who compiled a code of canon law, cited there nothing from the Theodosian Code, and the same is true of his Lex Familiae S. Petri[3] which treats of dowries, inheritances, contracts, public judgments and other legal matters. Hence in western Europe the use of this Code was not so frequent as before.

Chapter VI

I. The Corpus Juris was of no force in public government throughout western Europe during the period from about A.D. 560 to 1130, though, like the Theodosian Code, it was sometimes used by the clergy.

II. Its revival in the west about 1130. Concerning Irnerius, 'the lantern of the law,' the first glossator and literary progenitor of such writers as Azo and Accursius.

III. The revival of other studies in western Europe about that time.

IV. To what extent this revived jurisprudence of Justinian was received in France, Spain, Portugal, Italy, Germany and elsewhere.

V. A suggested reason for its spontaneous and widespread reception in the time of the emperor Lothair II.

Justinian's legislation in the west, 560–1137 A.D.

I. There can be no doubt that in the period of about five hundred and seventy years from A.D. 560 to the time of the emperor Lothair II[4], the legal system of Justinian as contained in the Corpus and as distinct from, often inconsistent with that of Theodosius, had no force in the civil government of the west except in the Exarchate of Ravenna, that small enclave of the eastern empire whose connection

[1] Geneva, 1628.
[2] 965–1023. See *ante*, p. 7, n. 5.
[3] Printed by F. Walter in *Corpus Juris Germani Antiqui*, III, 775 ff. See A. M. Koeniger, *Burchard von Worms und die Deutsche Kirche seiner Zeit* (Munich, 1905).
[4] 1125–1137.

Occidente Imperii reliquas (quae sub annum 750 prorsus imperii illius esse partes etiam desiere) locum plane habuit nullum. Certe etiam scriptoribus Occidentis raro et apud paucos eorum, qui per intervallum illud vetustiores sunt, quid inde memoratur. Ab Isidoro jam ante citato, ubi de legum agit autoribus[1] et corpus Theodosianum uti et Gregorianum et Hermogenianum memorat, praetermittitur Justinianeum, veluti cujus ratio in Occidente parum omnino tunc haberetur. Floruit is post Justinianum circa annum septuagesimum. Atqui interea Gregorio primo[2] quidem citantur et Novellae aliquot Justiniani et leges nonnullae ejusdem codicis, id est paulo ante Isidorum. Et seculis etiam hujus intervalli sequentibus apud hieratici generis scriptores atque ecclesiasticos in pretio leges Justinianeas aut saltem earum aliquas fuisse singulari liquet. Forsan sane tam Justinianeae leges quam Theodosianae intelliguntur nomine Romanorum legum in epistola anonymi supra citata[3] ex Bonifacii Moguntini epistolis, quae sub annum 750 conscriptae. Et Joannes Papa octavus ut in decreto[4] Ivonis Carnotensis legitur, sub annum 870 consultus a Sineboldo Narbonensi antistite in synodo Tricassina de privilegiis ecclesiae violatis seu, ut vocabant, sacrilegio (cui in libro legis Gothicae nulla praescripta erat poena apud Gallos Hispanosve; nec juxta aliam legem ibi erat tunc judicandum). 'Nostra,' inquit, 'serenitas cum praescriptis episcopis, inspectis legibus Romanis ubi habebatur de sacrilegiis, invenimus ibi a Justiniano Imperatore legem compositionis sacrilegii constitutam, scilicet in quinque libras auri optimi.' In codice quidem ejus habetur illa lex[5], Arcadii nempe et Honorii. Sed mirum interea est severiores multo quae sunt apud Justinianum[6] in sacrilegos leges eos praeteriisse, nisi ipsis Digestorum libris tunc forte carerent. Sed vero et magis mihi mirum, legem hanc e Justiniano sic tunc in Occidente allatam esse cum eadem ipsa haberetur[7] in Codice Theodosiano qui adeo tunc in Italia, Gallia, Hispaniis etiam et Germania variatim in usu atque multo receptior fuerat. Idem ipsum de Joanne octavo habetur apud Ivonem in Pannormia[8], demto quod, ut in editis, legitur heic 'in decem libras optimi auri' pro 'quinque' qui numerus erat plane Justinianeus. Sed corrigenda est editio Pannormiae utraque tum Sebastianii Brantii tum Melchioris a Vosmediano et quinque substituendum, quod etiam constat ex

---

[1] Originum lib. 5.
[2] Lib. 11, epist. 54, ad Jo. Defens. vide caus. 11, q. 1, c. 38.
[3] Cap. 5, § 6.   [4] Part. 3, c. 98.
[5] C. tit. de Ep. et Cler. 13, si venerab.
[6] L. 2 et 6, D. tit. ad leg. Jul. Peculat.
[7] C. Theod. tit. de Ep. 34.   [8] Lib. 2, cap. 80, tit. de Sacrilegio.

VI I THE CANONISTS AND JUSTINIAN 85

with the parent empire was severed in A.D. 750[1]. In that period few western writers even refer to it. Isidore of Seville (already quoted), who flourished[2] about seventy years after Justinian, cites the Theodosian, Gregorian and Hermogenian Codes, but not that of Justinian.

Papal references to Justinian

Meanwhile, shortly before Isidore's time, several of Justinian's Novels and some laws from his Code were cited by pope Gregory the First[3]. In succeeding years, some if not all of Justinian's laws appear to have been held in singular repute by ecclesiastical writers. The title 'Roman Laws' in the already quoted anonymous letter of about A.D. 750 addressed to Boniface[4], archbishop of Mainz, may have included those of Justinian as well as of Theodosius. In Ivo's *Decretum* we read that about A.D. 870 pope John VIII was consulted at the Synod of Troyes[5] by Sinebold, archbishop of Narbonne, concerning violation of ecclesiastical privilege, or sacrilege as they called it; there being no penalty for this in the Gothic law of France or Spain, nor, at that time, might judgment be given there by any other law. 'We find,' says pope John, 'after enquiry into the Roman Law of sacrilege that there is a fine for the offence prescribed by the emperor Justinian, namely five pounds of pure gold[6].' This law of Arcadius and Honorius is certainly to be found in the Code[7], but it is remarkable that they passed over laws in Justinian[8] providing much severer penalties for sacrilege, unless perhaps they did not possess the books of the Digests. Equally remarkable is the fact that Justinian should thus be quoted at a time when the Theodosian Code was much more widely used. In the *Pannormia*[9] Ivo makes the same statement about pope John VIII, but in the printed editions by Sebastian Brant and Vosmedian the reading is 'ten pounds of pure gold' instead of 'five pounds.' The latter is the correct reading as may be seen from the MS. in the Royal Library at St James'.

[1] 752.
[2] 560–636.
[3] Cf. *Opera Omnia*, in Migne, *Patrologia Latina*, LXXVII, 515 and 1021.
[4] *Ante*, p. 75.
[5] A.D. 878. Mansi, *Nova Collectio*, XVII, 346–358.
[6] *Ibid.* 351.
[7] C. 1. 3. 13.
[8] D. 48. 13.
[9] In *Patrologia Latina*, CLXI, 1099. This text has 'decem libras.'

vetustissimo et perpulchro operis illius exemplari bibliothecae ad S. Jacobi Regiae. In Concilio itidem Parisiensi[1] tempore Ludovici pii Augusti, annis aliquot ante Joannem octavum habito, seu in priore seculi noni parte, Novella Justiniani celeberrima et cum primis animadvertenda de Excommunicatione affertur, adjecto, 'quam probat et servat Ecclesia.' Ejusdem sub id ipsum tempus est sequax Hincmarus Rhemensis antistes eandem ad hunc modum Novellam exprimens. 'Proponam' inquit[2] 'tibi legalem sententiam Justiniani Catholici Imperatoris quam probat et servat Ecclesia Catholica, qua constitutione[3] decrevit ut nemo episcopus, nemo presbyter excommunicet aliquem antequam causa probetur propter quam ecclesiastici canones hoc fieri jubent.' Alibi[4] item e Novellis Justinianeis 'quibus debitae observationis reverentiam sancta ecclesia exhibet,' ut ait ille, testimonia affert. Quinetiam eodem in seculo de Abbone patre Odonis abbatis Cluniacensis legitur, eum 'veterum historias et Justiniani Novellam memoriter retinuisse' qui, ut videtur, illud ut jurisprudentiae studiosissimus fecit. Nam subjungitur 'si quando lis quoquomodo inter parentes fuisset exorta tanta in eum censurae (inde) excreverat veritas ut undique omnes ad eum ob diffiniendi proficiscerentur gratiam.' Ita Joannes monachus Cluniacensis[5] in Odonis vita, ejus nimirum discipulus. Et sub finem hujus intervalli Ivo ille Carnotensis qui sub annum 1100 floruit de Novellis Justinianeis loquitur ut de legibus 'quas[6] Catholici reges composuerunt et ex autoritate Romanae Ecclesiae Catholicis populis servandas tradiderunt,' et 'quas[7] commendat et servat Romana Ecclesia,' et singularia inde sumit in rem quam tractat. Certe et Ivo ille aliique aliquot unde sua deprompsit Gratianus non solum e Novellis sed etiam ex reliquis corporis Justinianei partibus, Institutionibus scilicet, Digestis, Codice, non pauca hoc in intervallo habent. De Ivone res manifesta est tum ex Decreto[8] tum Pannormia[9] et Epistolis[10] ejus. Apud Gratianum etiam velut ex pristino sibi usu obviae sunt[11] e corpore Justinianeo leges. Atque hi sane aliique, idem per intervallum, interdum celato nomine Justinianei corporis ex eodem, uti etiam ex Theodosiano,

---

[1] Ivo. Decret. part. 14, cap. 21. Pannorm. lib. 5, cap. 124. Grat. caus. 24, quaest. 3, c. 1.
[2] Opusc. 55, cap. 29, pag. 509. [3] Novell. 123, cap. 11.
[4] Ibidem, cap. 51, pag. 587, et epist. de presb. criminosis, § 31, pag. 799, tom. 2, edit. Sirmond.
[5] In bibl. Clun. p. 15. [6] Ivo. Carnotensis Epist. 242.
[7] Idem, Epist. 280. [8] Part. 16, tit. de causis laic. passim.
[9] In prologo cap. 33, et lib. 2, 146, 160, lib. 3, cap. 166, lib. 5, capp. 25, 45, etc. [10] Epist. 99, 112.
[11] Caus. 2, quaest. 6, c. 28, 29, et 30. Caus. 10, quaest. 2, c. 2.

IVO OF CHARTRES

References by Hincmar of Rheims

In the Council[1] of Paris the famous Novel of Justinian concerning excommunication is produced with the observation: 'this is approved and observed by the church.' About the same time Hincmar, archbishop of Rheims, interpreting the same Novel, says: 'I shall propound to you a legal judgment of the Catholic emperor Justinian, approved and observed by the Catholic Church, by which it is decreed that no bishop or priest shall excommunicate anyone until the fact is proved for which the canons enjoin this penalty.' The same writer elsewhere quotes from Justinian's Novels 'to which,' he says, 'the Church pays the reverence of due obedience.' Moreover, it is recorded of the same period that Abbo, father of Odo of Cluny, 'had committed to memory the histories of the ancients and the Novel of Justinian,' which he must have done as a devoted student of law, for it is recorded[2] by his biographer and pupil, John of Cluny, that 'when a dispute arose among relatives his judgment was, from his study of the law, so accurate that people flocked to him from all parts, in order to obtain a decision.' Likewise Ivo of Chartres (c. 1100) speaks[3] of the Novels as 'laws compiled by Catholic kings and, by the authority of the Church, delivered to Catholic peoples for their observance' and also[4] as 'approved and observed by the Church.' This writer has several remarkable quotations from the Novels bearing on points discussed by him. Ivo and some of the writers used by Gratian drew largely from this and the other parts of the Corpus, while Gratian himself is wont to quote Justinian's laws as if these were of direct and original service to him.

The Clergy combine elements from both Codes with their Canons

In other words laws, as still having force, are cited in this period from Justinian and Theodosius (though the name of the former is

[1] A.D. 824. Mansi, *Nova Collectio*, XIV, 417.
[2] In *Vita sanctissimi patris Odonis abbatis Cluniacensis* in *Bibliotheca Cluniacensis*, 1615.
[3] In *Patrologia Latina*, CLXII, 247.
[4] *Ibid.* 281.

leges quasi vim habentes proferunt. Adeoque apud ecclesiasticos tam Theodosianae tam Justinianeae, licet invicem saepius adversarentur, parili tunc in usu quoties canonibus neutiquam refragarentur. Adeoque satyram legum mirandam ex duplici hoc genere et Canonico seu Pontificio ad laicos pro re nata ac more suo suumque in commodum fallendos, intricandos, emungendosque composuere. At vero in regimine civili seu publico locum habuisse seculis in illis jura corporis Justinianei, qua talis, nullibi comperitur.

II. Haud parum autem inclinante, sub intervalli hujus tempora posteriora, Codicis Theodosiani in Occidente autoritate ac usu qui tam diu ibi, ut ostensum est, quatenus permiserunt gentium singularum mores legesque aliae variatim obtinuerat, copiosius illud Justiniani corpus in studia a curiosioribus adhibitum, quod scimus maxime ex Ivone Carnotensi et Anselmo Lucensi, subinde in notis ad Gratianum editionis Gregorianae citato. Anselmus hic sub annum 1080 floruit. Cui Ivo coaevus, qui anno 1092 creatus est episcopus Carnotensis[1] ex praeposito S. Quintini Belvacensis qua fruebatur dignitate anno 1078, quod itidem ex Sigeberto, Tritemio aliisque cognoscitur. Migravit autem is e vita anno 1117, ut expressim Rogerius Wendoverius et Matthaei Parisius et Westmonasteriensis. Alii[2] mortem ejus annis aliquot priorem aut faciunt aut esse suspicantur. Sed de anno ipso certissimum est; quod etiam expressim firmatur ab Roberto de Torrineio in Chronico MS. seu Sigiberti continuatione. Atque etiam sub Henrico quinto Augusto seu circa annum 1120 adeo Justinianearum legum ratio in fori ecclesiastici decisionibus habebatur, ut etiam ex hieratici generis suggestione in edictum de juramento calumniae imperatorium[3] earum pars aliqua nec sine Justiniani nomine reciperetur, quemadmodum etiam in decretum ea de re Honorii[4] secundi. Et tam in edicto quam decreto illo Martiani Augusti sanctio adhibetur (in editis male Marci legitur) velut e Codice[5] Justiniani. Nam in Novellis Martiani cum Theodosiano conjunctis non habetur. Dein autem seu sub medium scilicet duodeni aut paulo ante seu sub annum 1130 aut circiter, viri docti Pandectas aliasque corporis illius partes publice, ut scilicet civilis doctrinae quantivis pretii thesaurum, Bononiae explicatum ierunt. Horum primus Pepo

---

[1] Ivo, Epist. 1.
[2] Videsis Testimon. vett. praefix. Epistolis ejus et Baron. tom. 12, ann. 1114. Calvus, 116, etc.
[3] Vide Leg. Longobard. lib. 2, tit. 47, L. 11. Antiq. Collect. 1, lib. 1, tit. 34, et Anton. Augustin. ibid.
[4] Extr. tit. de Jur. Calumniae, cap. 1. Append. ad Concil. Lateran. 3, part. 23, cap. 1.   [5] L. 25. C. tit. de episcopis et clericis.

sometimes concealed), and so both Codes, though in many respects contrary to each other, were alike used by ecclesiastics where they did not conflict with the Canons. Thus, in their usual way and for their own advantage, the clergy constructed, from this two-fold source and the Canons, that wonderful medley of laws in order, as opportunity served, to perplex and cheat the laity. But in public administration the law of Justinian had no influence in these ages.

Revived use of Justinian's laws

II. Towards the end of this period, as the Theodosian Code lost its authority in the west, that of Justinian began to be used more copiously by the better scholars, as we learn from Ivo of Chartres[1] and Anselm of Lucca[2], the latter being frequently cited in the notes to the Gregorian edition[3] of Gratian. This Anselm flourished about 1080; Ivo was a contemporary and was raised in 1092 to the bishopric of Chartres from the abbacy of St Quentin of Beauvais which he had held since 1078. This we learn from Sigebert[4], Trithemius[5] and others. According to Roger of Wendover, Matthew Paris and Matthew of Westminster he died in 1117; some writers however favour an earlier date. But 1117 is correct—it is affirmed by Robert of Torigny[6] in his MS. continuation of Sigebert.

An instance of this

In the time of the emperor Henry V, or about 1120, so great was the authority of Justinian in ecclesiastical courts that on the suggestion of the clergy some parts of his law, with due acknowledgment of their source, were embodied in the imperial edict and, later, in the decree[7] of Honorius III concerning the oath of calumny. In both edict and decree the sanction of the emperor Martian (erroneously called Marcus in the printed texts) is quoted as if from Justinian's Code. It is not to be found in the Novels of Martian annexed to the Theodosian Code.

Irnerius: Odofred's testimony

About the year 1130 scholars went to Bologna in order to expound in public the Pandects and other parts of the Corpus of Justinian as a valuable storehouse of civil law doctrine. Of these the first was Pepo, an obscure and unauthoritative expositor. Foremost in

[1] See *ante*, p. 81. For complete editions of his works, see Migne, *Patrologia Latina*, CLX–CLXIII.
[2] Anselm's *Collectio Canonum*, compiled in 1086, is in Migne, CXLIX.
[3] *Decretum emendatum et notationibus illustratum...Gregorii XIII jussu editum*, Rome, 1584.
[4] There are numerous sixteenth-century editions of Sigebert's Chronicle; see *M.G.H.* (Scriptores), VI, 268–474.
[5] *Liber de scriptoribus ecclesiasticis*, Cologne, 1546.
[6] *Roberti accessiones ad Sigebertum*, in Rolls Series, ed. Howlett, 1889, p. 100.
[7] In *Antiquae collectiones decretalium* (1609), 28.

habetur, sed nominis obscuri neque ex autoritate publica interpres. Primas igitur hac in re tulit paulo post sed coaetaneus Irnerius, Yrnerius item et Wernerius dictus, glossarum autor primus. Odofredus[1]; 'Dominus Irnerius fuit,' inquit, 'apud nos Lucerna Juris, id est primus qui docuit in civitate ista (scilicet Bononiae). Nam primo cepit studium esse in civitate ista in artibus; et cum studium esset destructum Romae, libri legales fuerunt deportati ad civitatem Ravennae et de Ravenna ad civitatem istam. Quidam dominus Pepo cepit autoritate sua legere in legibus. Tamen quicquid fuerit de scientia sua, nullius nominis fuit. Sed dominus Yrnerius dum doceret in artibus in civitate ista cum fuerunt deportati libri legales, cepit per se studere in libris nostris et studendo cepit docere in legibus. Et ipse fuit maximi nominis, et fuit primus Illuminator scientiae nostrae, et quia primus fuit qui fecit glossas in libris nostris vocamus eum Lucernam juris.' Et jurisprudentiam illam Constantinopoli ubi tunc studia ejusdem florebant didicisse dicitur[2] hic Irnerius qui etiam magister erat in artibus Bononiae antequam doceret in legibus, quod scribit idem Odofredus[3]. Adeo autem paulo post Lothario secundo Augusto Academica illa juris Justinianei instauratio Bononiensis placuit, ut 'ex uno jure civili Romano' (Justinianeo scilicet; quod jam in pristinum Theodosiani locum haud aliter ferme successit atque philosophia Aristotelica olim in Platonicae locum) 'posthac judicia fieri lege is sanxerit' quod 'constantem doctorum hominum in monumentis esse famam' ait Carolus Sigonius[4]. Atque 'ante hoc tempus,' scribit ille, 'Italici certe alii Longobardica, alii Salica, alii Romana lege utebantur (id est Theodosiana). In posterum autem omnes uni juri unique legi, reliquis abrogatis, nempe Romanae (id est Justinianeae) obtemperarunt; jusque civile publicis Italiae in gymnasiis majore celebrari studio et diligentiori coli opera coeptum.' Factum est autem hoc sub annum 1137 seu haud ita diu postquam in bello a Lothario contra Rogerium Normannum gesto, capta Amalphi urbe, repertae sunt in ejusdem spoliis Pandectae illae vetustatis autoritatisque prae aliis eximiae, quae Pisanas et literam Pisanam[5] olim (eo quod illuc eas transtulerat Lotharius) dixere jurisconsulti, ut nunc Florentinas, quia Florentiae in bibliotheca Medicaea velut cimelium ingens, asservantur. Aliae partes corporis Justinianei Ravennae etiam sub id

[1] Ad L. Jus Civile est D. tit. de Instit. et Jure.
[2] Innoc. Ciron. Observat. Jur. Can. lib. 5, cap. 5.
[3] L. ult. C. tit. de In Integ. Restit.
[4] De Regno Italiae, lib. 11, et vide lib. 7, in Ottone Magno.
[5] Ang. Politian. Epist. lib. 10. Marquardo Breisacio et mox citati.

THE BOLOGNESE REVIVAL

this science was his somewhat younger contemporary, named Irnerius[1], Yrnerius, sometimes even Warnerius, the first glossator. According to Odofred[2], 'Irnerius was our legal lantern and leader of the Bolognese teachers. Arts were first studied there and, when the school [studium] had been destroyed at Rome, the law-books were taken to Ravenna and thence to Bologna. A certain Pepo began, on his own authority, to give readings in the laws but, whatever his learning, he gained little reputation. But Irnerius, a teacher in arts, began an independent study of our law-books as they were introduced and, while studying, he began to teach. He was of great reputation, the chief expounder of our legal science and, as he was the first to make glosses on our texts, we call him the lantern of the law.' This Irnerius is said to have studied law at Constantinople[3] when law schools flourished there. Shortly afterwards the emperor Lothair II was so gratified with this academic revival of the law of Justinian as to decree[4] that thenceforth causes should be decided by one system of Roman civil law only—namely, that of Justinian, which now displaced the Theodosian as the Aristotelian philosophy had displaced the Platonic. Sigonius terms the decree 'a perpetual glory in the records of learned men' and records how previously 'some Italians used the Lombard, some the Salic, and some the Roman (*i.e.* the Theodosian) law. After that time, however, all used the same legal system exclusively, namely the Roman (*i.e.* the law of Justinian); and thereafter the civil law began to be studied much more assiduously in the learned schools of Italy.'

Discovery of the Pisan MS. of the Pandects

This took place about 1137, or shortly after Lothair started his war against Roger of Normandy. With the sack of Amalfi were unearthed those Pandects whose age and authority are so much greater than those of any others. These were formerly called the Pisans or Pisan MS. because Lothair transferred them to Pisa, just as they are now called the Florentines because preserved in the Medicean Library at Florence as a great treasure[5]. At the same time other parts of the Corpus of Justinian were discovered at

---

[1] For the name Irnerius see Ricci, *I primordii dello studio di Bologna*, Bologna, 1888. See also the account in Savigny (IV, 1–62); also Besta, *L'Opera d'Irnerio*, 1896, and F. Patetta, *L'Opere recentemente attribuite ad Irnerio* in *Bulletino dell' Istituto di diritto romano*, VII, 39 ff. Patetta contests the attribution by Fitting (in *Summa Codicis des Irnerius*) of a Summa Codicis to Irnerius written in 1084; Patetta regards this Summa as late twelfth century. [2] For Odofred see *supra*, p. 33, n. 3.

[3] Cironius (*Observat. Juris Canonici*, V, 5) appears to have been the first to maintain this. There is no evidence. According to Robert of Torigny he had studied at Pavia.

[4] Selden gives this on the authority of Sigonius. There is no evidence regarding the existence of such a decree.

[5] For the controversy to what city this MS. may be attributed see Besta, in *Storia del Diritto Italiano*, I, 102.

tempus e situ erutae, ut ex Odofredo jam citato liquet. Atque tunc florescere coeperunt in Italia maxime juris Caesarei studia. Alibi autem Sigonius, 'anno,' inquit, '1102 Irnerius philosophus Bononiae docens, Matildis rogatu, Pandectas interpretari coepit et primus glossas in eas scripsit.' Ita scilicet in argumento historiae Bononiensis. Etiam et adjicitur ad finem Conradi abbatis Urspergensis, de Matilda tantundem id est Matilda Comitissa celeberrima illa, filia Bonifacii Tusciae Ducis. Sed vero usque in annum 1190 aut circiter vixit Irnerius[1], adeoque ob aetatem haud ita commode ferri potest ut is anno 1102 hoc faceret rogatu Matildae, quae etiam mortua[2] est anno 1115, seu compluribus annis antequam Irnerium Bononiae legisse plerunque recipitur; id est sub Henrico quinto Augusto et circa decennium ante Lotharii initia. Neque sane id de Irnerio et Matilda ad Urspergensis calcem ab ipso autore sed ab alio quopiam temere assutum existimo. Nam ante in Chronici corpore habet ille quod debuit de instauratione juris Caesarei jam dicti sub Lothario. Et nescio unde in calce adjicitur Gratianum tunc scripsisse (quod attinet ad annum 1150 aut Frederici primi tempora) et tunc 'eisdem quoque temporibus dominus Wernerius libros legum qui dudum neglecti fuerant, nec quisnam in eis studuerat, ad petitionem Matildae Comitissae renovavit et secundum quod olim a divae recordationis Imperatore Justiniano compilati fuerant, paucis forte verbis alicubi interpositis....' Quae sane male invicem conjuncta chronographo. Floruit autem Urspergensis sub annum 1230. Sed vero si de juris Justinianei in Occidente plura velis, praeter jam memoratos, consulantur Tiberius Decianus[3], Franciscus Baldwinus[4], Valentinus Forsterus[5], Joannes Fichardus[6], Guidus Panzirollus[7] (qui trini posteriores vitas jurisconsultorum etiam post sic instauratum jus Justinianeum conscribunt), Wolfgangus Freymonius[8], Paulus

---

[1] Jo. Fichardius in Vitis Jurisc. Panziroll. de Clar. Leg. Interp. lib. 2, cap. 13, etc.
[2] Sigon. de Regno Italiae, lib. 10.
[3] Apologia adversus Alciat. de Jurisconsult. Resp. cap. 8, § 6, etc.
[4] In Prolegomenis de Jure Civili.   [5] In Hist. Jur. Civ.
[6] De Vitis Jurisconsultorum.
[7] De Clar. Leg. Int. lib. 2, capp. 3 et 13.
[8] In Symphonia Juris.

Ravenna, as Odofred narrates, and there then commenced the most brilliant period of civil law study in Italy.

Conrad of Ursperg's reference to Irnerius

In his history of Bologna Sigonius says 'in 1102 Irnerius began, at the request of Matilda, to interpret the Pandects and was the first to write glosses on them[1].' This Matilda is the famous countess, daughter of Boniface of Tuscany, and the above is also narrated of her at the end of Conrad of Ursperg's Chronicle[2]. But as Irnerius lived to about 1190[3] it is difficult to see how he could have complied with Matilda's request in 1102. The latter died in 1115 or several years before Irnerius is said to have commenced his teaching. My own opinion is that the statement concerning Irnerius and Matilda at the end of Ursperg's chronicle is an interpolation, Ursperg having already, in the body of his narrative, paid fitting tribute to this revival of imperial law. There are two statements at the end of this chronicle for which I cannot account—first, that Gratian wrote at about this time (this refers to 1150) and, secondly, that 'at this time, Wernerius, at the request of the countess Matilda, revived law-books that had long been neglected and restored them as they were in the time of the emperor Justinian, a few words here and there being altered.' These matters are not properly co-ordinated by the chronicler. Ursperg flourished about 1230[4].

Imperial claim to descent from Justinian

For further study of this revival, consult Tiberius Decianus[5], Francis Baudouin[6], Wolfgang Freymon[7], Paul Merula[8], Innocent

---

[1] The relations between Irnerius and Matilda are symbolised in a painting at Sassuolo in which Irnerius expounds Justinian to Matilda (Besta, *L'Opera d'Irnerio*, I, 57). In 1113 Irnerius was engaged with Matilda in the question of the donation of her property to her second husband and later (after her divorce) to the Papacy (*ibid.* 64).

[2] *Abb. Urspergensis Chronicon* (Basle, 1569), 278. The modern edition is in *M.G.H.* (Scriptores), XXIII, 333 ff.

[3] He was born 1050–1060. Fitting (in *Summa Codicis des Irnerius*, Berlin, 1894) supposes that he started teaching about 1090. He probably died in the reign of Lothair II (1125–1137).

[4] He died in 1226.

[5] Venetian scholar, 1508–1581.

[6] Born Arras, 1520; died in Paris, 1573. Was a student at Louvain and a professor at Bourges. Took an active part in politics; see J. Heveling, *De Francisco Baldvino iuris consult.* (Bonn, 1871).

[7] Born Ingoldstadt, 1546, died 1610. Was employed in the Bavarian and Imperial services. His *Symphonia Juris Chronologica* (Frankfort, 1574) is a source-book in four parallel columns, the biographies of jurists being in the third column. See Stintzing, I, 512–519.

[8] Born Dordrecht, 1558; succeeded Lipsius at Leyden, 1591.

Merula[1], Innocentius Cironius[2], alii etiam ab his citati. Sub idem autem tempus inde in tabulis Imperii Romani seu Germani publicis, Justiniani nomen[3], velut decessoris, cui ut primario successores essent jam Augusti, occurrit. Unde etiam eam in rem metrice senatores Romani ad Lotharium jam dictum:

> Rex valeat, quicquid cupit obtineat, super hostes
> Imperium teneat, Romae sedeat, regat orbem
> Princeps terrarum ceu fecit Justinianus,
> Caesaris accipiat Caesar....

Tantumdem, quantum ad Justiniani nominis usum ejusmodi, Hadrianus quartus Papa[4] ad Episcopos Germaniae. Atque paulo post Monte Pessulano in Galliis, in Hispaniis, etiam alibi propagata juris Justinianei studia usus idque in regimine publico.

III. Eodem in aevo, aut circa idem tempus, ut jurisprudentiae Justinianeae qualem diximus, instauratio eximia facta est, ita etiam (quod observatu non indignum) et Pontificiae et disciplinarum reliquarum per Occidentalem Europam. Neglectae enim nimis et ignoratae diu jacuerant extra Arabum Africanorum[5] et conterminorum Hispaniensium gymnasia, per Occidentem artes omnimodae et scientiae liberales; etiam ipsa Dialectica, quae scientiarum et modus est et gubernator, veluti 'ars cujus dogmata sophismata essent et quasi sacrae lectioni contraria' in plane execrandis[6] habebatur, ipsaque Theologia inde quasi illotis nimium tractabatur manibus. Nunc autem sub hujus id est duodecimi seculi medium, sicut ex Arabum qualibuscunque veterum Graecorum versionibus interpretamentisque Philosophia, prima, Naturalis, Moralis, Logica, Medicina, Mathematica quae ut sydera nubibus obfuscata tam diu deliteurant refulgere quasi simul coeperunt, ita etiam Jura Pontificia et Theologia ipsa; quod scimus ex Gratiani Decreto et Petri Lombardi Sententiis quae instaurationi quam diximus coaetanea. Et de Theologia heic animadvertendum illud de Roberto Pullineio Oxoniensi, 'MCXXXIII Magister Robertus Pullein' (ita Thomas Wikius[7] canonicus Osneiensis) 'scripturas divinas quae in Anglia obsoluerant apud Oxonium legere coepit. Et postea cum ex doctrina ejus ecclesia tam Anglicana quam Gallicana pluri-

---
[1] Cosmograph. part. 2, lib. 4, cap. 23.
[2] Observat. Jur. Canon. lib. 5, cap. 5.
[3] Goldast. Constit. Imp. tom. 1, pag. 261.
[4] Ibid. pag. 226.
[5] Vide Jo. Sarisbur. in Metalogico, lib. 4, cap. 6, etc.
[6] Petrus Abaelardus, Epist. 4, et Jo. Sarisbur. in Metalogico lib. 4, capp. 24 et 25.
[7] MS. in Bibliotheca Cottoniana. De eo vide plura in hanc rem ex Bostono Buriensi et Lelando, apud Balaeum, Cent. script. 80 et Jo. Pitzeum aet. 12, script. 203 atque ex I. Roffo apud Brian. Twinum in Antiq. Oxoniensib. pag. 108.

A RENAISSANCE

Cironius[1], Valentine Forster[2], John Fichard[3] and Guy Panzirol[4], the last three being biographers of jurists subsequent to this revival. About the same time we find in the public inscriptions of the Roman or German Empire the name of Justinian as that of an ancestor from whom the emperors claimed descent. This explains the invocation[5] addressed by the Roman senators to the above-mentioned Lothair, and pope Adrian IV, in a letter to the German bishops, makes similar use of Justinian's name.

Study of Justinian extends to France and Spain

Shortly afterwards the study of the Corpus of Justinian and its use in public administration spread to Montpellier, to Spain and elsewhere.

Revival of other studies

III. Almost contemporaneously there was a revival of canon law and other studies in western Europe. The liberal arts and sciences had long been neglected in the west, except in the schools of the Arabs in North Africa and the neighbouring parts of Spain, while even dialectic—the standard and regulator of the sciences—was held in complete contempt as an 'art based on sophistry and in some measure contrary to the Scriptures.' In consequence, theology itself was frequently handled by unclean hands. But about the middle of the twelfth century, from some Arab versions of ancient Greek texts, and commentaries thereon, physics, moral philosophy, logic, medicine and mathematics began almost simultaneously to shine out like stars that had long been obscured, and so likewise canon law and theology, as we know from the contemporary *Decretum* of Gratian and the *Sentences* of Peter the Lombard. As regards theology, the following reference by Thomas Wykes[6], canon of Osney, may be noted: 'In 1133 Master Robert Pullein[7] began to lecture at Oxford on those parts of Holy Scripture that had become obsolete in England. And when he had taught to the great edification of both the English and the French Church he was promoted (*c.* 1145)

---

[1] Was professor and chancellor of the University of Toulouse when Selden was writing the *Dissertatio*.
[2] Of Wittenberg, died 1620. His *Historia Juris Civilis* was published at Mainz in 1607.
[3] Born Frankfort, 1512, died 1584. A pupil of Zasius. Selden's reference is to his *Jurisconsultorum Vitae Veterum* (Basle, n.d.).
[4] Born Reggio, 1523, died 1598. Was a professor at Padua and Turin.
[5] For the invocation see Selden's text.
[6] Selden probably read Wykes' chronicle in MS. Tiberius A. IX, 6. See, for this reference, *Chronicon T. Wykes* (Rolls Series, 1869), 20.
[7] For Pullein see Oxford Historical Society, *Collectanea*, III, and the article by Hastings Rashdall in *Dictionary of National Biography*.

mum profecisset a papa Lucio secundo' (id est sub annum 1145) 'vocatus et in cancellarium sanctae Romanae Ecclesiae promotus est.' Atque ita sane eodem fere tempore disciplinarum omnium simul ab intermortuis resurrectio seu restitutio habita. Et quae sub Lotharii tempora ita coepta sunt, sub Conrado et Frederico primo Caesaribus haud parum sunt aucta.

IV. Quod vero ad jus Romanum vetustius seu Justinianeum in imperio Caesariano sic instauratum attinet; id non ita capiendum est quasi penitus ac revera abrogatis (quo vocabulo utitur Sigonius) reliquis quae ante obtinuerant juribus, purum illud quod Justinianeum est ita successisset ut aliud nullum vim dein retineret aut, ut XII Tabularum jus olim Athenis Romam allatum, vigorem per se indueret; sed ita jam receptum fuisse juris Justinianei usum, ut quoties aut interpretandi jura sive vetera sive nova sive ratio sive analogia desideraretur, aut mos aut lex expressior non reperiretur, ad jus illud Justinianeum tum veluti rationis juridicae promptuarium optimum ac ditissimum, tum ut quod legem in nondum definitis ex ratione seu analogia commode suppleret, esset recurrendum. Certe ita ferme Rhodiam recepere veteres Romani legem in rebus nauticis, ut etiam apud nos et gentes vicinas leges recipiuntur Oleronianae; cum interim nec hae nec illae ex autoritate sui, qua primo conditae sunt, vim sic obtinuerint. Atque ut academiae demum non paucae aliae per Europam Occidentalem hac in re, quoad studiorum institutionem, Bononiensem, ita etiam regna alia et respublicae Imperium Caesarianum quoad usum juris ejusdem aliquem imitatae sunt; retentis semper ac ubique moribus alias avitis legibusque sibi, pro varia regiminis cujusque formula, ante conditis, novasque condendi tum libertate tum usu. Neque ullibi pro simplici juris norma in Occidente inde usurpatum est jus illud Caesareum, sed cum temperamentis quae jam diximus; quod cuique manifestum sit tum ex morum variorum ac sanctionum quibus utuntur Galli, Hispani, Bohemi, Hungari, Poloni, Siculi, Belgae, Italiae ac Germaniae respublicae variae aliaeque, voluminibus perplurimis, tum ex decisionibus eorum innumeris atque ad ea commentariis quae passim prostant. Quinetiam cum Justinianeis in eodem ipso corpore conjungi solitae leges seu mores feudales qui Longobardici sunt, eodem etiam in aevo a Gerardo Nigro ac Oberto de Orto consulibus Mediolanensibus congesti, uti etiam Caesarum recentiorum aliquot sanctiones quae etiam extra imperii Caesarei limites non raro pariter qua rationem habent recipiuntur. Exemplum est egregium juris Caesarei modo quo diximus recipiendi in Lusitanica[1] illa ea de

[1] Ordinazones, lib. 2, tit. 5.

chancellor of the Church by Pope Lucius II.' Thus at this time there was an almost simultaneous revival of all the sciences, and what was begun in Lothair's time was considerably advanced under the emperors Conrad and Frederick I.

The sense in which Roman law was 'received'

IV. This Roman law revival is not to be understood as involving the complete abrogation (Sigonius uses this expression) of all other laws in force, nor as if the Corpus of Justinian by its acceptance excluded all others. Nor should it be thought that this revived jurisprudence derived its force from any inherent sanction such as that of the Law of the Twelve Tables. It was received only in this sense that wherever a principle or analogy was required for interpreting old or new laws, or where a tradition or express enactment was lacking, recourse might be had to it as the best and richest repository of jurisprudence and because, by deduction or analogy, it might conveniently supply a rule in matters hitherto undecided. In this manner the ancient Romans admitted the Rhodian Law in maritime affairs as we and our neighbours accept the Code of Oleron, though neither of these systems obtained its force from the authority of its original enactment.

Restrictions on the use of Justinian's legislation

As the example of Bologna was followed by several other universities in western Europe, so kingdoms and states imitated the example of the Empire in its use of the imperial law, retaining, according to their several constitutions, both old customs and laws and the right of enacting and using new ones. Nowhere was this imperial law introduced as a juristic criterion without the reservations already specified, as is clearly seen from many compilations of customs and sanctions in force among Gauls, Spaniards, Bohemians, Hungarians, Poles, Sicilians and Belgic peoples and in several states of Italy and Germany, as well as from very many decisions and commentaries based thereon. Moreover the feudal laws and customs of the Lombards, collected[1] by Gerard Niger and Obertus de Orto, consuls of Milan, together with some sanctions of the later emperors, received outside the Empire where applicable, were often joined in the same collection with Justinian. There is a good illustration of the character of this Reception in the Portuguese edict[2] prescribing

[1] For this see Besta in *Storia del Diritto Italiano*, I, 439 ff.
[2] The book from which Selden quotes (*Ordinazones*) is the only one of his books which I have been unable to find in the Bodleian.

re constitutione. Si res eveniat forensis de qua leges moresve regni nihil statuant (nec aliter) 'sendo materia que nom tragua peccado, mandamos que seia julgado po las leis Imperiaes posto que es sacros canones determinem o contrario; as quas leis imperiaes mandamos soomente guardar po la boa razam em que sam fundadas,' rebus scilicet in civilibus tunc ex jure judicandum Caesareo, nisi adversentur canones sacri. Neque sane aliter apud alias Occidentis gentes quae jus illud recepere se res nunc habuit. Quod ad Hispanos in hanc rem attinet consulas Gregorium Lopez[1] in 'Partitas' et Alphonsum de Azevedo in 'Constitutiones Regias[2].' Quod ad Gallos, 'Nos Galli,' inquit Choppinus[3], 'de Quiritum jure ita censemus, eo scilicet uti nos, quatenus ei lex Gallica non refragetur.' Ita Bodinus[4], Gulielmus Ranchinus[5], Rebuffus[6], Carolus a Grassaliis[7], alii satis obvii. Etiam interdictum postmodum juris Caesarei omnimodum in Academia Parisiensi[8] locisve vicinis studium, uti et omnimoda ejusdem in foro citata in Gallia[9] alibique. De ipso item Imperio seu Germania ac Italia res satis aperta est; aliis quampluribus legibus moribusque in judiciis ibi esse necessario utendum. De juris Longobardici tum Francorum in regno Neapolitano Siculoque, post instauratum sic in Occidente jus Justinianeum, usu, visendi Andreas de Isernia[10], Carolus Tapia[11], Andreas Molfesius[12], Marius Muta[13] praeter Bartolum[14] atque ad eum Julii Feretti Additiones Aureas. Atque in hanc rem, praeter decisiones innumeras in quibus alia praeter Justinianea jura saepenumero adhibentur, constitutionum in Imperio Germanico tum veterum tum recentiorum morumque a Justinianeis perquam ibi dissonorum collectiones obviae sunt consulendae; imprimis illa Melchioris Goldasti cum ejusdem ad eam prolegomenis. Et populi in Imperio, Regna, Urbes singulares suarum habent copiam frequentem atque prostantem.

[1] Gl. ad L. 6, tit. 4, partit. 3.
[2] Tit. 1 libri secundi et vide Oldrad. Consil. 69.
[3] De Dom. Franc. lib. 2, tit. 15, § 5.
[4] De Repub. lib. 1, cap. 8.
[5] Guil. Ranchinus, Var. Lect. lib. 2, cap. 3.
[6] Tom. 1 Constit. tit. de Constit. in proemio, gl. 5, num. 20.
[7] Regalium Franciae lib. 1, jure 2 et 12, adde Extr. tit. de Privilegiis, cap. 28. Super Specula, Compilat. 5, lib. 5, tit. 12, cap. 3, atque ibi Innocentium Cironium uti etiam Observat. Juris Canonici, lib. 5, cap. 5.
[8] Extr. tit. de Privilegiis, cap. 28.
[9] Vide Paridem de Puteo, Tract. de Syndicatu verb. Testis § fui semel num. 9 et Minsing. Cent. 5, Observat. 88.
[10] In lect. Peregrina.
[11] In Jura Regni Neapolit. lib. 1, tit. 13, § Justitiam.
[12] In Consuetud. Neapolit. part. 6, quaest. 8, num. 23, etc.
[13] In Capit. Regni Siciliae tom. 1, cap. 33, num. 203, etc.
[14] De Diff. Juris Civilis et Langobardorum.

that if a case should arise on which the laws and customs of the country are silent, then, and only then, 'we decree that it shall be judged by the imperial laws if they are not inconsistent with the sacred canons. Thus we order that the imperial laws be wisely preserved because of the right reason on which they are based[1].'

The interdict of Honorius III (1219)

The same is found to-day in other western nations receiving the Roman law. For Spain consult Gregory Lopez on the Partitas[2] and Alfonso Azevedo[3]. As regards France, Choppin[4] writes: 'we Frenchmen use the Imperial Law wherever the Gallican Law is not opposed to it.' The same view is expressed by Bodin[5], Ranchin, Rebuffy, Charles of Grassaille[6] and others. In later years the study of Roman law was absolutely forbidden in the university of Pari and surrounding schools[7], and citations therefrom were ruled out in French law-courts and elsewhere. As for the Empire itself, that is Germany and Italy, it is obvious that in law-suits recourse must have been made to several other laws and customs. For the use of French and Lombard, as well as Roman law in Naples and Sicily after the Bolognese Revival consult Andrew of Isernia, Charles Tapia, Andrew Molfesius, Marius Muta[8], as well as Bartolus[9] and the *Golden Additions* appended thereto by Ferettus[10]. Consult the numerous cases where laws other than those of Justinian are cited, and the collections of constitutions and customs, ancient and modern, of the German empire, especially that of Goldast, together with his Introduction. The peoples, kingdoms and separate cities of the Empire have a large number of such distinct laws and customs. For this consult

---

[1] An ordinance of Philip IV refers to written law as moulding custom to a better use—'legum et juris scripta dogmata perficiunt intellectum rationis ...nec non praeparant ad consuetudinum intellectum' (quoted in J. Baron, *Franz Hotmans Anti-Tribonian*, 1888, p. xi). Cf. also Leibnitz' opinion that the almost mathematical precision and logic of the classical Roman law jurists was in itself an intellectual training. (For this see Duten's edition of Leibnitz' juristic writings, IV, 92–158, and G. Hartmann, *Leibnitz als Jurist und Rechtsphilosoph* in *Festgabe Rudolph v. Ihering*.)
[2] *The Partitas of Alfonso the Wise*, first printed in 1555.
[3] See *infra*, p. 195, n. 8.
[4] See *ibid*. n. 5.
[5] See *ibid*. n. 2.
[6] Ranchin, Rebuffy and Charles of Grassaille were sixteenth-century French jurists.
[7] In 1219 by Honorius III.
[8] These four names are the names of Neapolitan and Sicilian jurists and scholars of the latter half of the sixteenth and earlier half of the seventeenth century.
[9] 1314–1357. Professor of Civil Law at Perugia. The greatest of the post-Glossators. For the political interest of his teaching see Woolf, *Bartolus of Sassoferato*.
[10] D. Julii Feretti, *Aureae Additiones in Summulam Differentiarum sive Varietatum inter Jus Civile et Langobardum D. Bartholi de Saxoferato* (Venice, 1619).

Vide item hac de re Franciscum Suarezium in libris de legibus[1]. Et tametsi etiam in Scotia usus sit juris hujus Caesarei tam forensis quam academica, is nihilominus haud alius est quam ut juris extranei rationem in se optimam disputantibus suggerentis, non autoritatem, qua talis, omnino obtinentis. Nam expressim ibi sanctionibus cavetur[2] parlamentariis non alias illic leges autoritatem habere praeter eas 'quae sunt regni et communes regni.' Sed de his satis superque.

V. Videtur autem eo libentius atque gratiori animo recepisse per Occidentem tot Christianos populosque juris Caesarei ita resuscitati qualemcunque usum quo instantius sub idem ipsum tempus eos urgeret Innocentius papa secundus, idque in manifestum et perquam odiosum civilis regiminis dispendium, ut decreta pontificia ab eo collecta veluti juris juxta quod viveretur corpus passim reciperent. Ordericus Vitalis monachus[3] de Concilio Generali a Papa illo Romae habito et de eis qui illuc confluxerant verba faciens, 'multa eis,' inquit, 'Papa de priscis codicibus propalavit, insignemque sacrorum decretorum textum congessit. Sed nimis abundans per universum orbem nequitia terrigenarum corda contra ecclesiastica scita obduravit' (ita impudentius blaterare solent sacerdotes ambitione turgentiores in eos qui artibus quibus ad eludendos emungendosque principes ac populos nefariis utuntur, honeste ac pie refragantur) 'unde remeantibus ad sua Magistris apostolica decreta passim per regna divulgata sunt. Sed nihil, ut manifeste patet, oppressis et opem desiderantibus profuerunt, quoniam a principibus et optimatibus regnorum cum subjectis plebibus parvi pensa sunt.' Certe idem ipsum forsan est Decretorum heic corpus quod statim postea ab Eugenio secundo confirmatum et Gratiani nomine editum pars est prior notissima corporis Juris Canonici. Simulac enim Bononiae legendum voluere imperatores Jus Caesareum, adeoque singularem haberi in Academia ejusdem facultatem, pontifex ille Eugenius tantundem de Jure Pontificio in corpore Gratianeo[4] contento etiam fieri jussit. Illud autem Innocentii Papae spectat ad annum 1139. Verebatur puto Papa ne invalescerent nimis jura per se Caesarea ita tunc reflorescere in Occidente incipientia. Ideo Decreta versutius obtrusit Pontificia, quae ante, pro gentium populorumque moribus variis, haud ita ut postea uniformia habita. Haec autem ne in Academicorum studiis, adeoque inde in regimine publico nimis praevalerent, ut subsidium sibi adversus astutias pontificias,

[1] Lib. 3, cap. 8.
[2] Parl. 3 Jac. I, cap. 48, et Parl. 6 Jac. I, cap. 79.
[3] Hist. Eccles. lib. 13, pag. 919.   [4] Cronic. Cronicarum.

Francis Suarez[1]. In Scotland, although use is made of the Roman law in the courts and universities, its function is that of a foreign system providing pleaders with excellent arguments but having in itself no authority. It is expressly provided in that country by parliamentary enactment that only the common laws of the realm shall be of force.

The papacy promulgates canons

V. It would appear as if this revived jurisprudence was accepted with all the more eagerness as at the same time (c. 1139) pope Innocent II, to the obvious damage of the civil power, was urging the acceptance of the papal decrees as a rule for conduct. Speaking of the General Council[2] held by Innocent in Rome, Ordericus Vitalis[3] says: 'the Pope spoke of ancient codes, and compiled a famous collection of ecclesiastical decrees. But because of the wickedness everywhere prevalent, the hearts of worldly persons were hardened against them.' (So priests, puffed with ambition, are wont to bellow against those who conscientiously resist their wicked devices for cheating rulers and subjects.) 'The council,' he continues, 'broke up: the decrees were promulgated: but obviously they could be of no avail to persons seeking redress since they were held in such slight esteem by princes, rulers and people.'

Gratian

Probably this is the collection of decrees confirmed just afterwards by Eugenius II[4]. Issued under the name of Gratian[5], this is the first and most famous part of the canon law Code. As soon as the emperors established imperial law studies at Bologna and created in the university a special faculty for this purpose, pope Eugenius ordered the same to be done for the canon law as contained in Gratian. In my opinion the pope feared that this revived Roman law would prove too powerful, and so he craftily issued his decrees as a uniform whole, whereas previously they had differed with local custom. But lest the canon law should prosper too much in the universities and so extend to public administration, several princes and peoples encouraged the civil law as a bulwark against ecclesi-

---

[1] The famous Jesuit theologian, scholar and political theorist. For a general account of his theories see Figgis, *From Gerson to Grotius*.

[2] The Second Lateran Council (1139). Mansi, *Nova Collectio...*, XXI, 523-542.

[3] Quoted by Selden from *Gesta Normannorum in Francia*, ed. Duchesne (1619), p. 919.

[4] Selden must mean Eugenius III (1145-1153). Although at once accepted by the Church, Gratian's *Decretum* was a private performance and not an official or papal code of Canons. The first official compilation was that of Pietro Collevacino da Benevento, drawn up by command of Innocent III.

[5] It appeared about 1142. See *Decretum Gratiani*, ed. Friedberg (Part I. *Corpus Juris Canonici*, Leipzig, 1879). For the large bibliography on Gratian see Besta in *Storia del Diritto Italiano*, I, 420 ff.

principes ac respublicae pleraeque Occidentis Jus item Caesareum foveri volebant atque in pretio haberi. Atque postmodum ut pontificii jus hoc ubi canones sui non adversarentur publice admitti voluere[1], ita sane principes ac respublicae canones deinceps admittere soliti sunt, quoties nec Caesareo, qua receptum est, nec moribus legibusve refragaretur.

Caput Septimum

I. Usum Juris Caesarei, sive Theodosiani sive Justinianei, in Britannia nostra a fine imperii heic Romani, usque tempus ante dictum instaurati Justinianei in Occidente, seu per annos amplius septingentos, publico in regimine fuisse nullum. Allatae in Angliam leges Caesareae sub ipsum tempus quo earum in Bononia studia instaurata, seu sub annum 1140.

II. Testimonium de allato in Angliam sub id tempus jure seu codice Theodosiano.

III. De Justinianeo jure in Angliam sub idem tempus allato, atque tum eximiis interpretationibus illustrato tum in compendium redacto heic ab jurisconsulto praecellenti, Rogerio Magistro Vacario, gente Langobardo, monacho Benedictino, priore et demum abbate Beccensi in Normannia septimo, qui primus ejusdem heic praelector extitit doctissimus. Edictum in eum ac jus illud Stephani regis. Schola disciplinarum illustris tunc coenobium Beccense.

IV. In annalibus et historicis nostris ea de re omnino siletur. Rogerii Vacarii, primi apud nos Juris Justinianei praelectoris, qualis apud jurisconsultos alibique mentio. Placentino is perquam invisus. In archiepiscopum Cantuariensem post Thomae Becketi obitum electus confirmatusque ut consentiret ipse induci omnino nequibat.

V. Conjectura seu potius suspicio de Vacarii illo in seculo nomine.

VI. Undenam illud Stephani regis edictum; quod cito aut revocatum est aut evanuit. Interdictum sub id tempus pontificium et synodicum, ne leges Civiles seu Caesareas extra coenobia sua praelegerent monachi.

VII. De Anglicanis jurisconsultis eo in saeculo et praecedentibus.

I. Ad modum supra breviter ostensum, se habuit Jus Caesareum tum Theodosianum seu vetustius, tum Justinianeum seu recentius in seculis quae a fine Romani in Britannia imperii excurrunt in duodecimi, ut dictum est, medium seu partes priores; per eas inquam Occidentis partes quas insederunt Gothi illi, Langobardi, alii quibus jus illud Theodosianum, ut narravimus, diversimode est receptum. Summa est autem, Justinianei extra musaea aut scriptorum cancellos atque pontificiorum decreta actionesque, usum per intervallum illud fuisse in Occidente

[1] Vide Extr. tit. de Novi Operis Nunt. cap. 1, et Extr. tit. de Privilegiis, cap. 28, Super Specul. Alexandri 3. Epistolam sub annum 1180 subjunctam Petro Cellensi pag. 42.

astical guile. And afterwards as popes admitted the public use of the civil law where it did not conflict with their Canons, so nations accepted the Canons, provided they clashed neither with the imperial law, in so far as received, nor with national laws and customs.

Chapter VII

I. There was no use of imperial law in the civil government of Britain during the period of more than seven centuries extending from the end of the Roman occupation to the revival at Bologna, about 1140, when the imperial laws were introduced into this country.

II. Evidence that the Theodosian Code was introduced into England about that time.

III. The introduction of Justinian's Corpus into England about the same time; the valuable comments and summary by the Benedictine monk of Lombardy, Roger Vacarius, prior, afterwards seventh abbot of Bec and our first distinguished professor of Roman Law. King Stephen's edict. Bec as a famous centre of learning.

IV. The silence of our annals on this subject. References to this Roger Vacarius by our lawyers and others. The grudge of Placentinus against him. Vacarius' election to the archbishopric of Canterbury after the death of Becket and his refusal to accept this dignity.

V. A tentative suggestion regarding the name Vacarius in that age.

VI. Reasons for king Stephen's edict, which was either revoked or fell into desuetude. The papal and synodical edict prohibiting monks from teaching civil law outside their monasteries.

VII. Concerning English lawyers in that and the preceding age.

Use of imperial law in Britain after the occupation

I. It has already been shown that, outside the Exarchate of Ravenna, no use was made of the Corpus of Justinian in western Europe during the period from the end of the Roman occupation of Britain to about the middle of the twelfth century, except by scholars in their studies and the clergy in their legal transactions. This is

(Exarchatus angustias semper excipias) nullum, adeoque nec in Britannia seu Anglia nostra, quae nec Theodosiano omnino per intervallum illud, sicut aliae gentes, usa est. Etenim cum sub finem Romani heic imperii Anglo-Saxones huc advenerant et regna inter se, ut notissimum est ex historiis nostris, distribuerant, nec, ut gentes illae septentrionales reliquae Australiora Europae invadentes, corpus Juris Caesarei Theodosianum, utpote nondum aut vix natum nedum in Britanniam tunc allatum, aliudve quid ejusmodi receperant, suis tantummodo quos secum e Germania attulerant moribus usi sunt. Atque ut apud Gothos aliosque qui Italiam, Gallias, Hispanias insederant, lex erat Gothica, Longobardica, Salica, aliis ejusmodi nominibus insignita, ita etiam apud Anglo-Saxones nostros habebatur Mercionum lex, Ostrosaxonum lex et postmodum Danorum lex variatim recepta, sed nullibi per intervallum hoc lex Romana, quemadmodum apud gentes illas exteras. Etenim in regimine publico apud majores nostros hujus quod tractamus intervalli, Caesarei alicujus juris, usus plane reperitur nullus, id est per annos amplius septingentos. Dico qua talis. Nam et studiosis aliquot heic uti et apud exteros partim saltem cognitum fuisse, haud dubito; et qua capita seu sententiae aliquot ejusdem in canones subinde pontificios conjectae fuissent, usum ejusdem aliquem in disciplina heic pontificia tunc fuisse, non est quod non credamus. Nectamen omnino in regimine publico quod civile vocitamus. Tandem vero sub idem ipsum tempus quo Lotharius Imperator proximique successores ejus usum Juris Justinianei in regiminis publici rationem ut ostensum est reduxit, id est, postquam a fine Romani heic imperii Anglo-Saxones primo, dein Dani et demum Normanni (qui omnes in unicam eandemque regnantium lineam satis involvuntur) jure sibi peculiari, sed pro vario rerum statu, ut semper fit, aliter atque aliter mutato, quod idem est quod jam Anglorum Commune vocitamus, per 740 aut praeter-propter annos sine ulla Romani aut Caesarei intermixtione fuissent usi; tunc inquam allatae sunt in Angliam leges ipsae Caesareae raro ante, si umquam, heic vulgo aut simul aut sparsim visae, eaeque tam Theodosiani corporis quam Justinianei. Atque Justinianeum tandem (utcunque primo quod statim ostendimus heic ita displicuerit ut publico edicto vetaretur) per annos complures apud jurisconsultorum nostratium aliquot in rebus forensibus adhibitum quemadmodum apud alias tunc gentes. Quatuor autem heic ad hanc rem potissimum advertenda. Primum est, tempus ipsum quo sic in Britanniam nostram primo allatum est Jus Caesareum et quinam sic afferrent, tam Theodosianum quam Justinianeum.

VIII ROMAN LAW IN MEDIAEVAL ENGLAND 105

specially true of Britain in this interval as not even the Theodosian Code was used. The Anglo-Saxon invaders of England used neither this nor any similar code, but only their native Germanic customs, differing in this respect from the other northern invaders who penetrated farther south. And just as among the Goths who invaded Italy, Gaul and Spain, their laws were called Gothic, Lombard, Salic and other names, so among our Anglo-Saxons there were the laws of the Mercians, of the East Saxons and later of the Danes, but at no time was the Roman law admitted. In our public administration, there are no traces of its use during this period of more than 700 years, though doubtless it must have been known, at least in part, to some English and foreign scholars. Doubtless also it was utilised by the canon law wherever additions had to be made to ecclesiastical jurisprudence. But it was never of any authority in our civil government.

Roman law re-introduced into Britain in the twelfth century

About the time when Lothair and his successors introduced the law of Justinian into public government, or just after the Anglo-Saxons, the Danes and the Normans had in succession, during a period of about 740 years, used their own laws (*i.e.* our English common law) without any Roman admixture, then the imperial law, in the form of the Codes of Theodosius and Justinian, was brought into England where previously they had been almost completely unknown. This law, though at first so disliked as to be prohibited by a public edict, was eventually used for several years by some of our jurists in legal matters, as it was among other nations.

Four things are here to be chiefly considered:

(*a*) When, and by whom Roman law was first introduced into this country.

(*b*) The admission, progress and use of the law of Justinian in law schools and in the English common law courts.

Secundum, Justinianei admissio, progressus ususque in studiis ac tribunalibus etiam quae Jure Anglicano utebantur regiis. Tertium, quandonam in desuetudinem abierit usus ejusmodi vetustior atque in angustias quibus per secula aliquot retroacta finitur coerceturque fuerit redactus. Et quartum denique, undenam fieret ut in desuetudinem ejusmodi abierit, seu a majoribus nostris ita cancellis arctaretur. De hisce singulis, et eorum appendicibus aliquot, in sequentibus agetur.

II. Quod ad primum spectat, tam de Theodosiano quam Justinianeo Jure huc allato testimonia sunt satis luculenta. Theodosianum sub tempus antedictum a seculi doctoribus in studia heic receptum videtur ex eo quod Gulielmus monachus Malmesburiensis prae aliis plerisque aevi sui eruditus politusque scriptor, postquam Haymonis Floriacensis Imperatorum ab Justinianeo usque in Carolum Magnum, gesta in epitomen seu abbreviationem, ut vocat ipse, redegerat, insequentiumque Caesarum usque ad Henrici quinti qui Lotharium secundum proxime praecedit exitum seu sua tempora (inde enim floruit, id est ab anno 1125 aut circiter usque in annum 1142 quo[1] mortuus est sub Stephano scilicet rege) successionem ostenderat, statim, ut habetur in codice MS. penes me pervetusto nec Gulielmo ipso opinor recentiori, subjungit, 'Nunc quicquid de principibus Italiae et Romae potuimus invenire, curavimus non omittere. Congruum videtur leges Romanorum apponere. Non eas quas Justinianus fecit. Esset enim hoc ingentis operis et laboris. Sed eas quas Theodosius minor filius Archadii a temporibus Custantini usque sub titulo uniuscujusque imperatoris collegit. Ponantur ergo XVI libri ab eo collecti, quorum sententiae plures explanantur. Quaedam explanatione non egent. Divi Theodosii ejusdem Novellarum liber 1, Divi Valentiniani filii Placidiae liber 1, Divi Martiani Orientis liber 1, Divi Anthonii et Leonis liber 1, Divi Majoriani liber 1.' Nec quid de Gregoriano aut Hermogeniano codice loquitur quorum Theodosianis editis fragmenta quaedam junguntur. 'Sed' inquit 'quoniam quaedam sunt in legibus Imperatorum obscura, ad plenum intellectum apposuimus libros Institutionum Gaii et Pauli jurisconsultorum.' Praefixa dein Novella Theodosii prima quam epistolam Theodosii minoris vocat de confirmatione legum antiquarum, libros quidem exhibet ipsos. Sed adeo mutilos ut integro libro subinde unicus sufficiat titulus, et leges plerisque titulis desint non paucae, etiam et non raro tituli ipsi. Quinetiam primus in impressis liber omnino deest. Secundus vocatur heic primus et reliqui pariter deinceps. Atque licet XVI

[1] Balaeus, Cent. 2, script. 73. Pitsaeus, Aet. 12, script. 201.

(c) When this older use fell into decay and was reduced to the narrow limits in which it has for some time been confined.
(d) Why it was thus neglected or restricted.
Each of these points, together with some supplementary matter, will now be dealt with in turn.

The Theodosian Code in England: William of Malmesbury's MS.

II. The evidence with regard to the first point is clear. That the Theodosian Code was accepted by scholars in this country, just after the above-mentioned period, may be inferred from the following statement, to be found in one of my MSS.[1], probably contemporary with its writer (William of Malmesbury). The statement is appended to his epitome of Haymo of Fleury's Lives of the Emperors (continued down to the emperor Henry V, predecessor of Lothair II) by William of Malmesbury, one of the most learned and cultivated writers of his age, who flourished c. 1125–1142: 'We have taken care to omit nothing regarding the rulers of Italy and Rome. It is now thought fit to add the Roman laws—not those of Justinian which would be too great a labour, but those of Theodosius the Younger, son of Arcadius, who collected them in sixteen books, from the time of Constantine, under the name of each emperor. Several of the decisions are explained, others require no comment. Of this emperor Theodosius there is one book of Novels and one each of the Emperors Valentinian, Martian (eastern emperor), Anthony [Anthemius] and Leo, and Majorian[2].' He takes no notice of the Gregorian or Hermogenian Codes, fragments of which are added in the printed editions of the Theodosian Code. 'But,' he adds, 'as some things in the imperial laws are obscure we have, for their better understanding, added the Institutes of Gaius and Paul.'

Lacunae in this MS.

Having prefixed the first Novel of Theodosius which he refers to as 'the epistle of the younger Theodosius for the confirmation of old laws' William of Malmesbury then gives the books themselves. These are so imperfect that frequently for one whole book a single title suffices; in many titles a large number of laws are missing, and whole titles are sometimes lacking. The book called the first (in the printed copies) is here entirely wanting; the second is called the first and so on. Thus, though there is here mention of sixteen books,

---

[1] Now MS. Bodley Seld. Arch. B. 16. For this important MS. see K. Witte, *De Gulielmi Malmesburiensis Codice Dissertatio* (Breslau, 1831); G. Haenel, *Novellae Constitutiones...* (Bonn, 1844, XII–XIV); Mommsen, *Theodosiani Libri XVI* (Berlin, 1905), I, LXV–LXVII; W. Stubbs, *Malmesburiensis Gesta Regum* in Rolls Series, 1887, I, CXXXI–CXLIII; Madan and Craster, *Summary Catalogue of Western Manuscripts in the Bodleian Library, Seventeenth Century*, I, No. 3362. The MS. appears to have been written about 1130 and is believed to be in the handwriting of William of Malmesbury. See *ante*, p. 77, n. 2, and p. xxiii.   [2] f. 140 of the MS.

memoret ipse, habentur heic tantum quindecim, sed ut dictum est mutili. Ejusmodi nihilominus sunt uti et Novellae Imperatorum sequentium atque Gaii et Pauli Institutiones ab eo traditae, ut ex eis haud pauca quae depravatissime in editis leguntur sibi possent commodissime restitui. Dum autem ita exhiberi vult monachus Malmesburiensis Theodosiana cum congeneribus jam dictis, de Justinianeis plane loquitur velut sibi suisque tunc non ita ignotis, ut ex verbis ejus jam citatis liquet. Veri autem videtur mihi simillimum eosdem ipsos qui Justinianeum corpus tunc huc attulere etiam et Theodosium illud quo sic usus est Malmesburiensis, simul attulisse, ut ita Juris Romani quod Latine extaret promptuaria haberentur apud nos integra, qua comparari potuerint.

III. De Justinianeo autem corpore legibusve Romanis aut Italiae huc publice allatis (quibus nominibus etiam Theodosianum continetur) Joannis Sarisburiensis, qui episcopus erat Carnotensis et Malmesburiensi monacho aliquanto recentior (anno utpote 1182 seu sub Henrico secundo mortuus) testimonium habetur expressissimum. Sub rege scilicet Stephano, qui regnare coepit anno 1136 atque obiit 1154 eas huc allatas, id est sub idem tempus quo Bononiae publice eas legendas instituerat Lotharius Caesar et veluti per Occidentalem Europam exemplo suo disseminarat. Saresburiensis[1] verba sunt 'Alios vidi qui libros legis deputant igni nec scindere verentur, si in manus eorum Jura pervenirent aut Canones. Tempore regis Stephani a regno jussae sunt leges Romanae quas in Britanniam domus venerabilis patris Theobaldi, Britanniarum primatis, asciverat. Ne quis etiam libros retineret edicto regio prohibitum est et Vacario nostro indictum silentium; sed deo faciente, eo magis virtus legis invaluit quo eam amplius nitebatur impietas infirmare.' Theobaldus hic antistes Cantuariensis, qui primo legati nati[2] titulo ad successores dein transmisso, ab Innocentio secundo donatus dicitur, consecratus est anno 1139 circa triennium ante Malmesburiensis obitum. Ex abbate Beccensi fiebat Archiepiscopus atque Roma pallium petiit ubi atque Rhemis synodis aliquoties intererat. Domum ejus leges Romanas in Britanniam ascivisse, intelligendum videtur de asseclis ejus quos in comitatu seu itinere ac redux secum habuerat. Anglos carere legibus tunc apud exteros ita reflorescentibus noluere illi, adeoque exemplaria earum huc transvehenda curarunt, quae regi ita displicuisse ait Saresburiensis ut publico edicto eas vetaret; qua de re statim plura. At quid illud est? 'Et Vacario nostro

---

[1] Policrat. lib. 8, cap. 12.
[2] Joscelin. Antiq. Eccles. Brit. pag. 127, edit. Hanoviae.

we find only fifteen and many of these imperfect[1]. Nevertheless both the Novels of later emperors and the Institutes of Gaius and Paul are handed down by him in such a way that with their help many errors in the printed editions may be rectified[2].

Both Codes introduced into England together

The above quotation also indicates that the Corpus of Justinian was not unknown to William of Malmesbury or his contemporaries. It seems to me probable that the two Codes were introduced into England together in order that the most complete manuals of the Roman law extant in Latin might be available.

John of Salisbury's evidence

III. Concerning the introduction into Britain of the Corpus of Justinian or Roman law brought from Italy, including the Theodosian Code, there is express evidence provided by John of Salisbury, bishop of Chartres (who died about the year 1182), that these laws were imported in Stephen's reign, *i.e.* about the same time as the emperor Lothair established the public teaching of civil law at Bologna and by his example disseminated it throughout western Europe. These are John of Salisbury's words[3]: 'I have seen some who, if the law books fell into their hands, would not hesitate to burn or destroy them. In the time of king Stephen the imperial laws, brought hither by the household of Theobald, primate of Britain, were proscribed, and even the owning of books of such laws was forbidden. Silence was imposed on our Vacarius, but by God's grace the strength of the law increased in proportion as the forces of iniquity threatened it.'

Archbishop Theobald

This Theobald was the first archbishop of Canterbury to receive the title of Legatus Natus[4] (conferred by Innocent II), a title transmitted to his successors. From the abbacy of Bec he was consecrated archbishop in 1139; he received his pallium in Rome and sometimes attended synods both there and at Rheims. By his household is to be understood his attendants who accompanied him when travelling. This bodyguard was unwilling that England should lack the jurisprudence then creating such a stir abroad, and so were at pains to bring back transcripts which, as John of Salisbury says, were proscribed by Stephen's edict. Of this more anon.

[1] Selden did not realise that the transcription was from the Alarician Breviary, not the Theodosian Code.
[2] This has been done by Haenel.
[3] *Joannis Saresberiensis Policraticus*, ed. C. C. J. Webb, Oxon. 1909, II, 399.
[4] This title was transferred from Henry of Winchester to Theobald in 1146. It was the mission sent to Pope Celestine for this object which induced Vacarius to come to England (see Oxford Historical Society's *Collectanea*, II, 169).

indictum silentium.' Ita enim plane legendum. Binae sunt Policratici, in quo haec occurrunt editiones veteres. Altera Constantini Fradini, altera Bertholdi Rembolti. Utraque autem anno eodem signatur eodemque mense, anno scilicet 1513 ac Maio. In Rembolti legitur 'Et Vicario nostro...,' in Fradini, 'Et Vacario....' Ceterum in tribus quae sunt reliquis (quarum binae[1] sunt Lugdunobatavicae et tertia in Bibliotheca Patrum[2] reperitur) recte retinetur 'Et Vacario,' adjecto nihilominus in margine 'al. Vicario,' quasi lectio satis esset dubia et forte de vicario Theobaldi aliquo leges Romanas seu Caesareas legente atque de silentio ei indicto res capienda foret. Sed palam est Vacarii nomen heic retinendum eoque intelligi Rogerium Magistrum Vacarium, etiam Wacarium dictum, gente Langobardum, qui Lethardo abbate Beccensi seu coenobii S. Mariae de Becco Herluini, dioecesis Rothomagensis in Normannia (quae tunc Anglo suberat, uti et diu postea) sexto[3], et Theobaldi successore proximo, demortuo, in ejus locum suffectus est, atque tempore Stephani adeoque Theobaldi cui proculdubio charus erat, in Anglia discipulos perquam multos jura Caesarea e corpore Justinianeo docebat. Ita scilicet expressim Chronicorum Normanniae ab anno 1139 in annum 1238, e bibliotheca S. Victoris Parisiensis pridem editorum autor[4], in anno 1148. Sed res spectat ad annum sequentem seu 1149. Nam 'obiit,' inquit ille, 'Bechardus (legendum plane Lethardus) VI abbas Becci cui successit Rogerius Magister Wacarius gente Langobardus, vir honestus et jurisperitus, cum leges Romanas anno ab incarnatione Domini MCXLIX in Anglia discipulos doceret et multi tam divites quam pauperes ad eum causa discendi confluerent.' In margine ibi conjectura infelici ac frustranea adnotatur 'forte Baccalarius.' Sed Wacarium legendum, seu Vacarium ex Sarisburiensis allatis plane confirmatur. Neque solum publice docuit ille sed etiam rogatu pauperum quorum sacculi non tantos faciebant sumtus ut corpus Justinianeum commode nancisci quirent, uti et eorum quibus compendiosior juris tractatio magis placeret, Pandectas et Codicem (quemadmodum itidem in pauperum usum postea Summam suam Juris Canonici composuit Raimundus, quod ait ipse) in novem conjecit libros qui studiosis promptuarii juris ditissimi vicem suppleret. Idem de eo autor jam dictus, 'suggestione pauperum,' statim post allata inquit, 'de Codice et Digesto exceptos IX libros composuit qui sufficiunt ad omnes

[1] 1595 et 1639.
[2] Edit. Colon. 1622, tom. 15, pag. 338.
[3] Videsis Claud. Robert. in Gallia Christiana, pag. 503.
[4] In Scriptoribus Normann. pag. 983.

John of Salisbury's reference to Vacarius

But what of the words 'Silence was imposed on our Vacarius[1]'? There are two old editions of the *Polycraticus* from which these words are taken—one by Fradinus, the other by Rembolt, both dated May, 1513. In the former, the reading is 'Vicarius': in the latter 'Vacarius.' In the three other editions, two of which were printed at Leyden and the third in the series *Bibliotheca Patrum*, the correct reading 'Vacarius' is given, but a marginal note 'alternatively Vicarius' shows that there is still some doubt, as if the reference might be to some vicar of Theobald's. But clearly by this name is to be understood Master Roger Vacarius or Wacarius, a Lombard, who, on the death of Lethard, sixth abbot and immediate successor of Theobald, succeeded to the abbacy of Bec[2], or Herluin's monastery of Mary of Bec in the diocese of Rouen in Normandy, a province then and for some time later under English rule. This Vacarius taught[3] the imperial law in England from the Corpus to numerous students in Stephen's reign and had doubtless commended himself to Theobald.

Vacarius becomes abbot of Bec

Such is the information given for the year 1148 by the Norman Chronicles[4] (1139-1238) from the library of St Victor in Paris. But the information really relates to the year 1149, for that is the year assigned to Lethard's death, and the succession of Vacarius, 'a man of integrity and legal learning, who, in the year 1149, was teaching Roman law in England to a great concourse of rich and poor. In the margin there is the unfortunate and frustraneous conjecture 'perhaps Baccalarius,' but John of Salisbury's evidence plainly proves that Wacarius or Vacarius is to be read.

His teaching

He did not confine himself to public teaching, but, at the request of poor students who could not afford a complete Justinian and of those who preferred a compendium of the law, he abridged[5] the Pandects and Code into nine books—as Raymond[6] afterwards did for the Canon Law on behalf of poor students. John of Salisbury also

[1] For the political element in Vacarius' teaching see Liebermann in *English Historical Review*, XI (1896), 305 ff.

[2] It is at this point that Selden, misinterpreting a passage of Robert of Torigny's chronicle, confuses Vacarius with Roger of Bec.

[3] By collating the evidence of Robert of Torigny and Gervase of Canterbury, Liebermann concludes that Vacarius lectured at Oxford 'not later than about 1148' (*English Historical Review*, XI, 310).

[4] In *Hist. Normannorum scriptores antiqui*, ed. A. Duchesne, 1619. For this confusion of Roger with Vacarius see *ante*, p. xxvii.

[5] Parts were printed from the Bruges MS. of Vacarius' *Summa* by Stölzel, *Die Lehre von der Operis Novi Nunciatio* (1865), 592. There is a transcript of portions of this MS. in Lincoln's Inn Library (Stewart Papers, B. 2. 5). See the account of the Avranches MS. by Prof. Zulueta in *E.H.R.*, Oct. 1921.

[6] Raymond of Peñaforte, born 1175: studied at Barcelona and Bologna. The reference is to his *Summa de Poenitentia et Matrimonio*. See *ante*, p. 7, n. 4.

legum lites quae in scholis frequentari solent decidendas, si quis eas perfecte noverit.' Docuerat igitur publice heic Jus Justinianeum Rogerius Vacarius sub Stephano rege, cujus anno 14, id est 1149, Lethardo abbati Beccensi datus est is successor. Et palam videtur, per aliquot ante annos eum sic docuisse, etiam ex eo quod expressim dictum sit in Chronicis jam memoratis, eum tunc successisse 'cum doceret' heic et multi tam pauperes quam divites ad eum eo nomine confluerent. Verisimilius est etiam libros ejus heic ante compositos quam Abbas factus est; id est dum Prior Beccensis erat. Priorem enim ante fuisse liquet ex Roberto de Torrineio abbate etiam Beccensi MS.[1] Nec sane postquam Abbas factus est, heic docuisse eum, facile ex Roberto illo est eliciendum. 'In anno 1149,' ait ille, 'obiit sanctae recordationis dominus Letardus VI Abbas Beccensis Ecclesiae; vitae suae cursum virgo senex finivit VI Nonas Julii, Sabbato, infra octavas apostolorum Petri et Pauli.' Festum illud ad Junii diem 29 spectat, adeoque obiit ille 2 Julii. 'Huic sancto viro' paulo post inquit idem, 'successit dominus Rogerius Prior secundus (scilicet primus fuerat Lanfrancus ille postea Cantuariensis antistes), in utroque testamento apprime eruditus, nec non clericali et seculari scientia decenter ornatus et ab omni communiter congregatione electus in ipsis octavis videlicet apostolorum Petri et Pauli (id est die Mercurii qui Julii sextus erat) qui benedictus apud Sanctum Wandregisilum in die festivitatis Sancti Jacobi apostoli (seu Julii 25) a venerabili Hugone Rothomagensi archiepiscopo, ab eodem coram conventu Beccensi in sede sua collocatus est, ex tunc super gregem sibi commissum pro posse suo die ac nocte decenter invigilans.' Erat igitur in Anglia Rogerius ubi jus praelegebat, cum electus est a monachis Beccensibus. Inde in Normanniam transiit, ubi abbas est consecratus. Atque 'die ac nocte ex tunc super gregem suum decenter invigilasse' dicitur; unde satis sequi videtur, eum postea haud a regimine illo sacro ad Juris Civilis praelectiones terris in exteris divertisse. Sed sane liquet, heic ante, per annos aliquot ab allato jure Justinianeo, eum illud publice ut dictum est legisse. Atque observandum est omnigena disciplinarum studia perquam eminenter in coenobio Beccensi, illis in seculis viguisse, indeque Rogerium hunc inter studiosos ita demum praecelluisse. Robertus ille de Torrineio, in anno 1117, 'mortuus est etiam,' inquit, 'hoc anno vir religiosus et magnae literaturae Ivo Carnotensis episcopus. Hic dum esset juvenis audivit Lanfrancum Priorem Becci de secularibus et divinis literis tractantem in illa famosa

---

[1] In Bibliotheca v. Cl. Simonidis d'Ewes. Vide Balaeum, Cent. 13, script. 13.

records that his summary of Code and Digest was sufficient, if completely assimilated, for deciding any question that might arise in the law schools. The statement in the above-mentioned chronicles that he succeeded to the abbacy of Bec in the same year (1149) as he was teaching in England, taken in conjunction with the information that his lectures were thronged by rich and poor, may be held to indicate that he had been teaching for some years. It is also probable that he compiled his books here before becoming abbot or when prior of Bec, for that he was prior before abbot is clear from the MS.[1] of Robert of Torigny, also an abbot[2] of Bec. It cannot be inferred from this MS. whether he ever taught here after becoming abbot, but it records that Lethard died on the 29th of June 1149, and 'was succeeded by Roger, the second prior (archbishop Lanfranc having been the first), learned in the Old and New Testament, distinguished in sacred and secular studies. He was unanimously elected by the whole congregation (on 6th July)...and after being installed in the abbacy watched diligently over his flock, day and night[3].'

His activities at Bec

Thus Roger was in England lecturing on law when he was elected by the monks of Bec. He went over to Normandy to be consecrated and, from the words 'he watched over his flock day and night,' it may be assumed that he did not desert his sacred duties there for law teaching. But that he had taught law in England for some years after the introduction of Justinian's Corpus may be taken for established fact.

The fame of Bec

It is worthy of notice that at this time the abbey of Bec was famous for all kinds of learning and this was how Roger eventually attained his distinguished position among scholars. Robert of Torigny, recording[4] the death of Ivo of Chartres in 1117, notes that 'when young Ivo had studied sacred and secular subjects under prior Lanfranc in the famous abbey school at Bec, frequented by many well-born and virtuous persons, and by many who afterwards

---

[1] Harleian MS. 651. Robert of Torigny's Chronicle is in the Rolls Series (ed. Howlett, 1889).
[2] Robert was prior of Bec in 1149, but was never abbot. He was elected abbot of Mont St Michael in 1154.
[3] Translation slightly abridged at this point.
[4] pp. 100-1 in Rolls Series edition.

schola quam Becci tenuit, in qua multi et nobilitate seculari et honestate morum convenerunt; viri praedicti et qui postea ad summum apicem ecclesiasticae dignitatis attigerunt.' Etiam dum Rogerius hic noster coenobio illo praefuit duodecim abbates ad regimen ecclesiarum inde assumti sunt[1]. Et seminarium erat semper feracissimum coenobium illud unde[2] quamplurimi in praefecturas apud Anglos sacras adsciti. Praefuit coenobio Beccensi Rogerius hic Vacarius annis triginta aut circiter. Mortuus est anno 1180 seu sub posteriora Henrici regis secundi tempora, postquam scilicet summa cum laude dignitate illa jugiter functus fuisset. 'Nullus praedecessorum suorum excepto sancto Herluino primo abbate tanta fecit in Becco monasterio quanta ipse' ut verba sunt Roberti Montensis qui ea quae feliciter praestitit sigillatim enumerat. Successit ei Osbernus prior Bellimontis, monachus ejusdem loci. Utrum vero Oxoniae, Cantabrigiae, Londini aut Theobaldi antistitis Cantuariensis in aedibus aliisve id genus sive secularium sive regularium, professus fuerit praelegeritque heic Rogerius ille, non omnino liquet. Nec an certo aliquo loco; quod tamen veri est multo similius.

IV. Sed vero neque temporis legum Caesarearum in Britanniam nostram sic allatarum, nec Rogerii, sic praelegentis mentio mihi hactenus occurrit omnino ulla in annalibus aut historiis nostris. Certe Ranulphus Higdenus ubi in praefatione historicos aliquot scriptores nominatim enumerat unde Polychronicon congessit, non solum diserte Joannem Saresburiensem sed et librum ejus Policraticum dictum in eis memorat, in quo nimirum de legibus illis huc allatis et Rogerio hoc Vacario, ut ante ostensum est, expressimum habetur et praecipuum testimonium. Attamen ea de re, cui sane in Policratico toto res alia historica ad Angliam pertinens minime est aequiparanda, omnimodo silet Ranulphus ille. Atqui alibi Rogerii illius non obscura mentio. Neque enim dubitandum est quin abbas hic Beccensis septimus, qui dum Prior ibi fuerat, primus in Anglia post[3] instauratum in Occidente uti diximus jus Caesareum, illud publice prelegit (quemadmodum Placentinus annis aliquot post primus ejusdem juris professionem in Galliis ad Montem Pessulanum propagare coepit) ipse fuerit Rogerius qui 'veteris glossatoris' interdum atque 'Summae juris primae, Paratitlorum primi autoris,' etiam 'antiqui ac immortalis memoriae doctoris' nomine scriptoribus aliquot atque editionibus memoratur. Ab Wolfgango Freymo-

---

[1] Robert. Montens. in Append. ad Sigibert. anno 1180.
[2] Vide Balaeum, Cent. 13, script. 23.
[3] Valentin. Forster in Placentino, Jo. Fichardus, etc.

attained the highest dignities in the Church.' Even while Roger was abbot, twelve were taken from Bec to be abbots elsewhere, and many of its alumni were promoted to high posts in England.

Was Roger professor at Oxford, Cambridge or London?

Roger ruled over Bec for about thirty years and died in 1180, having acquitted himself honourably of his duties. 'None of his predecessors did so much for Bec as he, except St Herluin, its first abbot,' says Robert of the Mount[1], who narrates in detail the successes of Roger's administration[2]. 'He was succeeded by Osbern, prior of Beaumont, a monk of the same place.' But whether Roger was professor or prelector at Oxford[3], Cambridge or London, or in archbishop Theobald's household, or in any other place secular or ecclesiastical, is not certain. It is not even certain that he taught in a definite place, though this much at least is very probable.

Further references to Roger: his writings

IV. I can find in our annals no reference[4] either to Roger's teaching nor the time when the imperial laws were introduced into this country. In the preface to his *Polychronicon*[5], where he enumerates the historical and other sources of his work, Ralph Higden mentions John of Salisbury and his *Polycraticus*, in which, as already mentioned[6], there is explicit and important reference to Vacarius and the introduction of Roman law into England. But Ralph makes no reference to the subject, though it is of more historical importance than anything else treated in the *Polycraticus*. Elsewhere, however, there is clear evidence about Roger. There can be no doubt that this seventh abbot of Bec and first teacher of imperial law in England (as Placentinus, a few years later was the first teacher of the subject in France) was identical[7] with the Roger who is referred to as, 'the old glossator,' 'the author of the first epitome of the law and of the Paratitles,' and 'a doctor of old and immortal memory.' Freymon[8]

---

[1] *I.e.* Robert of Torigny (Rolls Series), 286.
[2] See *ibid.* Roger appears to have done much for the amenities of Bec.
[3] It is certain that Vacarius lectured at Oxford. See *ante*, p. 111, n. 3.
[4] It is not surprising that Selden could find no reference to Roger's teaching in England. For that matter, there are few references to Vacarius, except those quoted by Selden. It may be noted that two opinions of Vacarius are quoted in the MS. commentary by Bulgarus on the title De Regulis Juris (Royal MS., IIB, xv, f. 89 b).
[5] R. Higden, *Polychronicon* (Rolls Series, 1865), I, 23.
[6] See *ante*, p. 111.
[7] Here Selden confuses the abbot Roger with the jurist Roger. Duck (*De Usu et Autoritate Juris Civilis*, ed. 1653, p. 139) was guilty of a similar confusion.
[8] See *ante*, p. 59, n. 3.

nio, primus jurisconsultorum fit qui ab anno 1200 ad 1300 floruere. Sed certissimum est ex ante dictis, eum annis viginti ante ducentesimum supra millesimum obiisse, atque coaevum fuisse Irnerio, Martino, Bulgaro, Jacobo, Bandino, Hugolino, Pyleo, Ottoni, Placentino reliquisque juris in Occidente Caesarei quiqui fuere instauratoribus primaevis, id est, ad Frederici Aenobarbi Caesaris seu Stephani ac Henrici secundi regum nostrorum tempora seu seculi duodecimi medium et annos aliquot inde sequentes attinuere. Catellianus Cotta[1]; 'Rogerius Odofredi Beneventani praeceptor, qui primus Paratitla conscripsit, id est rerum summas titulatim appositas quod a Justiniano[2] permissum fuerat.' Sed tempora vix omnino ferre videntur ut Odofredo esset Rogerius noster Vacarius praeceptor. Nam mortuus est Odofredus anno 1265[3], cum certum fit anno 1180 adeoque annis 85 ante mortem Odofredi obiisse Rogerium. Et praeceptorem suum seu dominum millies agnoscit alium Odofredus; scilicet Jacobum Baldwini (a quo tamen plerunque dissentit) nullibi quantum observavi Rogerium, quem interdum sed raro satis citat. Joannis et Azonis Summae erant in ore Odofredo frequentissimae, subinde etiam Placentini. Rogerium autem nostrum antiquorum nomine complectitur. Ita enim appellare est ei solenne eos qui Azonem et Joannem anteverterant, ut reliquos modernos. Ad 'L. Eam quam C. tit. de Fideicommissis' aliquoties occurrit apud eum 'Ro' pro Rogerio nostro, alibique[4] ait 'in illis tribus quaestionibus fuit opinio domini Mar. (Martini), Pla. (Placentini), Rog. (Rogerii) et Fregerii et domini Alberici antiqui doctoris.' Sed suspicor sane 'Frogerii' legendum neque nomine hoc alium a Rogerio innui; et sive e librarii sive e lectoris alicujus notis, ut Rogerio synonymum, illud irrepsisse. Neque enim Fregerii alius jurisconsulti veteris mentio puto alibi. Et tam Frogerium quam Rogerium nostrum hunc dictum, certum est. Ita enim diserte nuncupatur Placentino[5]. Atque Odofredus ipse eodem alibi pro eo utitur nomine. De eo quod est transigi posse super praesenti vel futura lite, verba faciens ille, 'Estne istud verum (inquit) sive moveatur lis juste sive injuste? dixerunt quidam quod sic. Et pro eis videtur C. e. 11. Dominus Frogerius in articulo isto contradixit. Et ita invenietis scriptum in Summa sua quam fecit super C. et fuit prima summa quaecunque fuerit facta. Et tenet forte per

[1] In lib. de Jurisperitis.
[2] L. 1, § ult. C. de Vet. Jure Enucleando.
[3] Jo. Fichard. Vit. recent. Jurisconsult. in Othofredo. G. Panzirol. De Clar. Leg. Interp. lib. 2, cap. 35.
[4] Ad L. quod tempore C. tit. de Restitutionibus Militum.
[5] In Summae Initio.

classes him as the first of the thirteenth-century jurists, but it is clear from the above that he died twenty years before the beginning of the thirteenth century, and was coeval with Irnerius, Martinus, Bulgarus, Jacobus, Bandinus, Hugolinus, Pyleus, Otto, Placentinus and other restorers of imperial jurisprudence in Europe.

Various names of Roger

According to Catellianus Cotta[1], Roger was the tutor of Odofred of Benevento[2] and the first to draw up the Paratitles, *i.e.* summaries arranged under their respective titles as authorised by Justinian. But chronology hardly permits of this, since Odofred lived till 1265, while Roger must have died in 1180. Odofred frequently refers to another as his tutor, namely Jacobus Balduinus[3], from whom he sometimes differs, and he nowhere, so far as I have noticed, refers to Roger as his tutor, though he occasionally quotes from him. He frequently cites the *Summae* of John, Azo and Placentinus: he includes Roger among the 'ancients'—this is his way of referring to those who preceded Azo and John, the others being styled 'moderns.' In his comments on the title in the Code concerning Trusts (C. 6. 42. 14), 'Ro' sometimes appears for Roger, and elsewhere Odofred cites 'Mar' (Martinus), 'Pla' (Placentinus) and 'Fregerius.' In reference to the last name I conjecture that 'Frogerius[4]' should be read and that by this name is meant none other than our Roger—it may have crept in as a synonym through an editorial emendation. I do not know of any other reference to an old jurist called Fregerius, but I know that Roger was often called Froger—as he clearly is by both Placentinus and Odofred himself. The latter speaks of "Frogerius' *Summa* of the Code—the first ever produced, consisting of

---

[1] Sixteenth-century Italian jurist, pupil of Alciati. His *De Jurisperitis* is a series of short biographies of jurists.

[2] By some writers (*e.g.* Panzirol, *De Claris Legum Interpretibus*, II, xxxv) Odofred is associated with Benevento and with the family of Roffred.

[3] Jacobus Balduinus was Podesta of Genoa in 1229. See Savigny, v, 91–105.

[4] It is generally held that 'Roger' and 'Froger' are the same person. But Tamassia (in *Odofredo*, 102) conjectures that there may have been two jurists, Roger and Froger. Tradition associates Roger with Italy and Bologna, but Fitting (in *Summa Codicis des Irnerius*, XXIV) conjectures that he lived and taught in southern France. Fitting also supposes that Roger's Summa was based on that attributed to Irnerius (the *Summa Trecensis*).

xx cartas. Post eum fecit Dominus Placentinus suam. Post eum dominus Joannes Basianus fecit suam quae incipit Quicunque vult. Et est nulla; et postea Dominus Azo fecit optimam summam qua hodie utimur[1].' Sic ille. Summistarum igitur primus Rogerius hic, ut Glossatorum primus Irnerius. Certe et summa Juris Canonici Rogerio puto huic tribuitur apud Antonium Augustinum[2]. Atque inter Pandectarum etiam interpretes pauculos insigniores expressim recensetur Rogerius hic a Fulvio Mariotello[3] uti in Summistis veteribus a Justino Goblero[4]. Raro satis ab Jurisconsultorum biographis alibive memoratur ejus nomen. Subinde tamen in commentariis occurrit; unde etiam in Modo veteri Legendi Abbreviaturas habetur 'Rog. id est Rogerius legista' pro eodem. Sed vero Guidus Panzirolus[5] fusius de eo atque expressius quam alii. 'Martini' inquit ille 'et Bulgari aetate clarescere Rogerius coepit qui primus in eam Pandectarum partem quam Infortiatum vocant' (id est librum 24 et reliquos qui usque ad finem 38 sequuntur; iis qui praecedunt Digesti veteris, qui supersunt Digesti Novi nomine appellari solitis) 'glossas emisit[6]. Cum enim publico stipendio non nisi Digestum vetus et Codicem antiqui professores interpretari tenerentur, reliquas legum partes negligentius tractabant, nec nisi privatim soluta stipe explicabant, et ob id extraordinarias eas lectiones vocabant. Sed Rogerius, ne haec quoque legum pars obscura permaneret, in eam suas lucubrationes edidit. Primus etiam juris compendium (quod 'summam' vocant) viginti chartarum numerum non excedens composuit[7]. Hunc aemulatus Placentinus aliam longe luculentiorem summam emisit; tertiam sed inanem Joannes (Basianus scilicet, Azonis praeceptor Cremonensis) fecit[8]. Postremo vero ceteris locupletiore condita omnes ante se Azo superavit. Rogerium alii corrupte Frigerium (lege Frogerium) nonnulli etiam Fredericum nominant[9]. Idem de diversis praescriptionibus forma dialogi scripsit, in quo se cum Jurisprudentia loquentem inducit. Nulla ejus mortis aut sepulchri memoria habetur.' Hactenus de Rogerio nostro Panzirolus. Sed mortem ejus ante ostendimus nos. Dialogus quem memorat de Praescriptionibus habetur in tomo 17 Tractatuum Illustrium Juris-

[1] Ad l. 1 D. tit. de Transactionibus.
[2] In Praefat. de Quinque vet. Collectionibus.
[3] In Neopaedia, pag. 164.
[4] In Praefat. ad Summam Othonis.
[5] De Clar. Leg. Interp. lib. 2, cap. 18.
[6] Odofred. in L. 1 ff. sol. Matrimonio et in L. Divortio in princ. eod.
[7] Idem in L. 1 ff. tit. de Transactionibus.
[8] In Summa Azonis in princ. trium lib. Cod.
[9] Gl. et Odofred. in dict. L. 1 ff. de Trans.

ROGER AND PLACENTINUS

about twenty quires. Afterwards Placentinus, John Bassianus and Azo made their *Summae*, that of the second being of no value, while the third is the best and is the one now in use."

Eulogies of Roger

So Roger is the first epitomiser as Irnerius the first glossator. Antonius Augustinus[1] credits this Roger, I think, with a canon law *Summa*: Fulvius Mariotellus[2] ranks him with the few more famous interpreters of the Pandects, and Justin Gobler[3] includes him with the old epitomisers. Otherwise his name is seldom mentioned in the biographies of jurists, though it occurs in commentaries, whence, in old 'Key[4] to Legal Abbreviations,' there occurs 'Rog. *i.e.* Roger the legist.'

Panzirol's reference to Roger

Panzirol speaks more fully of him as follows: 'In the time of Martin and Bulgar, Roger rose to eminence as the first to write glosses on that part of the Pandects called the Infortiatus' (*i.e.* chapters 24–38[5], as distinct from the preceding chapters called the Old Digest and the succeeding chapters called the New Digest). 'Formerly the professors of law were obliged, for their public salary, to interpret only the Old Digest and the Code, and treated the other parts of the law more scantily, expounding them as extra subjects and only for a private fee. But that this part of the law might not remain obscure, Roger published his elucidations of it: he was moreover the first to compose a compendium or summary of the law and this did not exceed twenty quires. Placentinus[6] followed in his footsteps with a much better *Summa*: a third, but useless one, was produced by John Bassianus of Cremona, preceptor of Azo. Azo however excelled all his predecessors in the completeness of his *Summa*. This Roger is sometimes wrongly called Frigerius (read Frogerius) and sometimes even Fredericus. He wrote, in the form of a dialogue, a treatise on the various prescriptions in which he introduces himself as conversing with Jurisprudence. There is no record of his death or burial-place.'

Tracts by Roger

Thus Panzirol on Roger. We have already spoken of his death. The dialogue referred to may be found in vol. XVII of the Treatises of Illustrious Jurists, where there is another tract on the same

---

[1] See *ante*, p. 37, n. 5.
[2] Scholar of Perugia, sixteenth–seventeenth centuries. His *Neopaedia* is an encyclopaedia.
[3] German jurist, 1496–1567.
[4] *Modus legendi abbreviaturas in utroque jure* (1510? by Ferettus?).
[5] Really 25–38 inclusive.
[6] For Placentinus see Savigny, IV, 210–240, and Tourtoulon, *Placentin, sa vie, ses œuvres* (Paris, 1896).

consultorum, ubi etiam alius de eadem re tractatulus ejusdem reperitur hoc sub titulo 'Rogerii antiqui Glossatoris de diversis praescriptionibus.' Libelli illi bini etiam eduntur[1] cum Azone, Dino, aliis aliquot de praescriptionibus, ubi nuncupatur ille 'antiquus et immortalis memoriae Doctor Rogerius.' Breviter memoratur Gesnero in bibliotheca, 'Rogerii jurisperiti liber de Praescriptionibus impressus,' qui ipsissimus est Magister Vacarius noster. Hic igitur is erat cui indictum est apud Joannem Sarisburiensem silentium, ne scilicet heic jus Caesareum publice ut ceperat amplius praelegeret. Atque factum est hoc a Stephano rege sub annum ejus 14 qui Christo 1149 respondet, quo legisse eum atque docuisse publice in Anglia ex jam ostensis est manifestum. Atque ut Irnerius Bononiae seu in Italia, ita Rogerius Vacarius in Anglia Juris Caesarei in Occidente instaurati expositor primus; quemadmodum etiam in Gallia, Monte Pessulano erat Placentinus, annis nimirum post Rogerii nostri obitum 16, aut circiter, id est sub annum 1196 quo tempore is Monte Pessulano coepit, 'Rogerii nominis abolendi cupidus[2], eique tenebras offusurum jactans.' Certe summam, ut dictum est, Codicis composuit ille. Atque ea, neglecta tandem Rogerii Summa quae nullibi puto jam reperitur, apud studiosos, ante Azonis editam, primario obtinuit. Etiam tres posteriores libri Summae quam dicimus Azonis, Placentini sunt. Et Rogerianam potius inchoatam quam absolutam innuit Placentinus qui famae ejus sane haud parum invidebat. Memoratur quidem etiam in rescripto[3] Alexandri tertii Papae de causa in dioecesi Eboracensi nuptiali, Magister Vacarius ad quem simul cum Abbate de Fontibus, mittitur rescriptum, quod Rogerio plane coaevum est; sed ille per annos complures ante Alexandrum illum factus est Abbas Beccensis, ut ostensum est. Adeoque non credendum videtur eum voluisse tunc Papam M. Vacarium tantum nominare nec ut abbati alteri dignitatis nomen tribuere. Forte sane Magister ille Vacarius successor erat Rogerio in Jure Caesareo heic praelegendo. Tribuuntur autem aliquot in Juris etiam Canonici libros, veluti in summam Bernardi Compostellani, glossae seu interpretationes Rogerio[4] ut videtur huic nostro. Sed error est manifestus ex inscitia ejusdem obitus natus. Diu enim ante, seu anno, ut ostendimus 1180 mortuus est. Singularis autem viri existimatio ac dignitas etiam inde ediscitur, quod tum in Thomae Archiepiscopi Cantuariensis

---

[1] Lugduni 1466.
[2] Vide Guid. Panzirol. de Clar. Leg. Interp. lib. 2, cap. 20.
[3] Append. ad Concil. Lateran. sub Alex. 3, part. 5, tit. de Sponsal. cap. 13.
[4] Videsis Guid. Panzirol. de Clar. Leg. Interp. lib. 3, cap. 8.

subject by 'Roger the Old Glossator.' These two tracts were published, together with the works of Azo, Dinus and others on Prescriptions, and there he is styled 'Roger, the Doctor of immortal memory.' Gesner[1] mentions a printed book on Prescriptions by 'the jurist Roger.' This is our Master Vacarius who, according to John of Salisbury, was silenced, lest he might continue his public teaching,of imperial law in this country, this prohibition having been imposed, as we have seen, by king Stephen in 1149. What Irnerius did for the revived imperial jurisprudence at Bologna, Roger did for England and Placentinus for France. About the year 1196 Placentinus set up at Montpellier 'to wipe out the name of Roger and drown him in obscurity,' and Placentinus' *Summa* held first place until the appearance of Azo's, Roger's *Summa*[2] (which I believe is nowhere to be found) having meanwhile fallen into neglect. The three last books of Azo's *Summa* are really by Placentinus, who, somewhat envious of his predecessor, hinted that Roger's *Summa* was only a tentative beginning, not a finished work.

The real Vacarius in a papal rescript

Vacarius[3] is also mentioned in a rescript of pope Alexander III addressed[4] to him and the abbot of Fountains concerning a matrimonial suit in the diocese of York, but as Vacarius was appointed abbot of Bec many years before Alexander's pontificate, it seems incredible that he should be addressed simply as Master and not as Abbot. Possibly this Master Vacarius succeeded to Roger as expounder of imperial jurisprudence in this country.

Glosses wrongly attributed to Roger

Some Glosses on canon law books, such as those on the *Summa* of Bernard of Compostella are attributed to our Roger, but this error is due to ignorance of the date of his death, he having died in 1180[5].

Roger [of Bec] elected to succeed Thomas à Becket

The remarkable esteem in which he was held is shown by this, that, in preference to other notable men, he was elected by the prior and chapter at Lambeth successor to Thomas, archbishop of

---

[1] C. Gesner, born Zürich 1516, died 1565. A distinguished researcher in medicine and botany. The book from which Selden quotes (the *Bibliotheca Universalis*), compiled 1545–9, was a universal bibliography, perhaps the first of its kind.

[2] Roger's *Summa* beginning ' Incipit Summa Frogerii Iurisperiti' has been printed, from the Tübingen MS., by A. Gaudentius in *Bibliotheca Juridica Medii Aevi* (1892), I, 10–174. Selden's reference presumably is to the *Summa Pauperum* of Vacarius of which there are several MSS. in existence, *e.g.* those at Worcester, Avranches, Bruges and Prague. For Wenck's MS. (now lost) see C. Wenck, *Magister Vacarius* (1820). For the Avranches MS. see Prof. Zulueta's article in *English Historical Review* (October, 1921). See also *ante*, p. 111, n. 5.   [3] Here Selden stumbles across the real Vacarius.

[4] *Antiq. Coll. Decretorum* (Paris, 1609), I, vii, 2.

[5] *I.e.* Roger of Bec. Roger the jurist died about 1170.

successorem non solum ab Odone Priore et Conventu, prae aliis magni etiam nominis viris tunc candidatis, Lambethae electus fuerit, verum etiam ab Henrice secundo rege, nec sine suffraganeorum assensu, confirmatus, tum nullo modo induci potuerit ipse ut tantum subiret munus, tametsi instantissime eam in rem urgeretur. Gervasius Doroberniensis in Chronico[1] narrat tria, velut candidatorum, fuisse proposita nomina (quod etiam ex Jure Caesareo[2] faciendum) in quibus Rogerius hic, et tunc Prior, inquit, 'cum quibusdam monachis affuit, et tandem Rogerium Abbatem Beccensem solenniter elegit, consentientibus utcunque episcopis (scilicet Richardus de Luci summus tunc Angliae Justitiarius, ut de electione hac consulerent, Londinum episcopos Angliae congregarat) et assensu regio electione confirmata, singuli ad sua recesserunt. Et Prior Cantuariensis rediens ut suum electum adduceret in proximo transfretavit. Sed ipse spe sua fraudatus est, quia praedictus electus nullius instantia induci potuit ad consentiendum. Institit autem Prior acrius per regem et legatos (Pontificis Romani; Albertum et Theodinum) qui adhuc erant cum rege in Normannia vim electo inferre gestiens ut consentiret. Sed frustra. Nam cum instarent Rex et Legati simul cum Priore nec praevalerent, apud Sanctam Barbaram (in episcopatu Lexoviensi) in Coena Domini ab electione est absolutus.' Florilegus item; 'Anno MCLXXIII Rogerius Abbas Beccensis electus est in archiepiscopum Cantuariensem. Sed Abbas nimis religiosus penitus contradixit.' Sed Robertus Montensis[3], 'ille vero praetendens infirmitatem suam noluit acquiescere electioni eorum.' Radulphus item de Diceto[4]; 'VI Non. Martii (anno 1173) suffraganei Cantuariensis Ecclesiae ut de Archiepiscopi electione tractarent sub edicto vocati venerunt Lamehedam et quoniam Lanfrancus, Anselmus, Theobaldus in ea sede tam late floruerant, id idem fortunae loci quodam modo deputantes, in Rogerum Beccensem Abbatem (nam trini illi etiam fuerant Beccenses) si non unanimiter saltem voce tenus concorditer convenerunt. Orta est tunc prima controversia, quis electionem pronuntiaret in publico. Suffraganeis hoc ad jus episcopi Londinensis ab antiquo pertinere dicentibus (nimirum episcopus Londinensis, antistiti Cantuariensi in collegio suo episcoporum seu suffraganeorum corpore, erat, ex veteri apud nos jure, Decanus, ut Wintoniensis, Cancellarius, Lincolniensis, Vice-Cancellarius,

---

[1] MS. ann. 1173 in Bibliotheca Cottoniana.
[2] Novell. 123, cap. 1 et 137, cap. 2.
[3] Anno 1174.
[4] MS. in Bibliotheca Cottoniana.

Canterbury, an election assented to by the suffragans and confirmed by Henry II. But although urgently pressed, he could not be induced to accept this great responsibility. Gervase of Dover[1] says that three names were proposed as of candidates (this was the civil law practice) of whom Roger was one. 'The prior,' he writes, 'being present with some of the monks, eventually Roger, abbot of Bec, was duly elected with the consent of the bishops (specially summoned to London by the justiciar Richard de Lucy), and the election received royal confirmation. Next day the prior went over seas in order to escort back the archbishop-elect, but his mission was fruitless, because the latter could not be induced to accept. The prior became more insistent, invoking the name of the king and the papal legates Albert and Theodinus, who were then in Normandy, but threats were useless, and the abbot was eventually absolved from his election in the church of St Barbara (Lisieux).'

The election

Also Florilegus[2] records that in 1173 Roger, abbot of Bec, was elected archbishop of Canterbury, but being too scrupulous declined the dignity. Robert of the Mount[3] says that the refusal was on the ground of pretended illness. Ralph de Diceto[4], recording the election, says: 'As Lanfranc, Anselm and Theobald, all of the abbey of Bec, had so recently adorned this dignity, and as this was attributed in part to the good fortune of the place, their choice—unanimous in expression, if not in sentiment—fell on Roger. A dispute then arose as to who should publish the decision. The monks of Canterbury declared that the duty devolved on their prior, while the suffragans maintained that it belonged to the bishop of London, who, by an ancient rule, was dean to the archbishop in his College of Bishops, as the bishop of Winchester was his chancellor, the bishop of Lincoln vice-chancellor, the bishop of Salisbury precentor, the bishop of

[1] MS. Vespasian B. IX, 4. *Opera Historica* (Rolls Series), I, 241.
[2] *Flores Historiarum* (Rolls Series, 1890), II, 85.
[3] *I.e.* Robert of Torigny (Rolls Series, 1889), 256.
[4] Selden used MS. Vespasian A. XXII, 37. See edition in Rolls Series (1876), I, 354.

Sarisburiensis, Precentor, Wigornensis, Capellanus, Roffensis Cruciferarius[1]) Cantuariensibus e contrario monachis asserentibus Priorem suum hac in re potius praeferendum. Pro bono itaque pacis, ne quid in absentia regis oriretur discidii, salvo jure partium Ricardus Pictavensis Archidiaconus in omnium adjutorio recitavit. Abbas electus hoc intelligens in Normannia coram rege in praesentia cardinalium Alberti et Theodoni, electioni factae sicut diximus, penitus contradixit. Hoc eum fecisse religionis obtentu suspicabantur nonnulli. Ab aliis dicabatur quod spiritus pusillanimitate contractus se imparem oneri tanto protestatus sit.' Alii; 'electioni factae penitus contradixit utrum pusillanimitatis intuitu an religionis incertum est' ut Rogerius Wendoverius et Matthaeus Parisius. Sed horum in editis Robertus depravate nominatur, uti etiam apud Archiepiscorum biographos.

V. At curnam ac unde dictus sive hic sive ille alter Vacarius? Ita enim non Wacarius, ut in chronicis ante citatis, nedum Vicarius apud Sarisburiensem, est plane legendum. Certe si familiae cognomen fuisset, aut locum cognominis ejusmodi occupasset, haud ita commode dictus fuisset Rogerius Magister Vacarius sed aut Rogerius Vacarius Magister aut Magister Rogerius Vacarius. Sed fateor locutiones hujusmodi seculis maxime in illis fuisse ut hodieque satis incertas. At suspicio sane mihi est, Vacarium esse heic, uti etiam in rescripto illo Alexandri tertii ad Abbatem de Fontibus et M. Vacarium, nomen appellativum quo designaretur singulare munus susceptum juris nempe lectioni heic vacandi adeoque profitendi. Quo nomine forsan et alii illo in aevo dicti. Ut armis, choreis, philosophiae, postulationibus vacare usurpatum veteribus pro eo quod est, his enixius prae aliis operam dare, ita 'lectioni vacare' ac professioni, idque in seculo, de quo nunc loquimur. Joannes Januensis in Catholico; 'Vaco, esse vel fieri vacuum. Et licet videtur ad alias significationes transferri tamen omnes redolent illam. Dicitur etiam vaco lectioni et operam do. Et vaco a lectione, id est deficio a lectione. Vaco nummis, id est careo. Sed istae omnes significationes redolent primam. Cum vero dico vaco lectioni, idem est acsi diceretur, vaco ab aliis rebus et insisto lectioni, unde vacat impersonale, id est esse vacuum, vel licitum esse vel opportunum. Unde vacat mihi legere, opportunitatem legendi habeo et non impedior ab alio negotio.' Totidem ferme verba habet etiam in opere 'De Derivationibus' Hugo Pisanus[3]. Certe ut ab aquari, arbitrari, parare (sensu quo

---

[1] Lindwood. ad Constit. Provinc. tit. de Poenis C. Eternae, verb. tanquam.
[2] f. auditorio.
[3] MS. in Bibliotheca Lambethana.

Worcester chaplain, and the bishop of Rochester cross-bearer. Without prejudice, and to prevent a dispute in the king's absence, Richard, archdeacon of Poitiers, was authorised to make public the election. The abbot however...absolutely declined. Some attributed this to pretended piety, others to pusillanimity[1].'

Roger wrongly called Robert

Roger of Wendover[2] and Matthew Paris[3] are doubtful why he refused. In the printed works of these writers and in the biographies of the archbishops he is wrongly called Robert[4].

Suggestion regarding the name Vacarius

V. But why were both these persons called Vacarius?—taking this, and not Wacarius or Vicarius, as the correct form of the name? If this had been a surname or a substitute for it, he would not fittingly have been called Roger Master Vacarius but either Roger Vacarius Master or Master Roger Vacarius. But these forms of address were as ill-defined then as they are now[5]. In my opinion the name, as it appears in the above rescript of pope Alexander III, must here be taken as an appellation to indicate a particular duty which he had accepted—namely, to devote himself to the teaching of law in this country. Others were perhaps called by the same name in those days. As the ancients were wont to speak of 'having leisure to devote to ("vacare") such things as arms, dancing, philosophy or litigation, so in this period men might speak of "devoting oneself to reading and teaching."'

Its possible derivation

In his *Catholicon*[6], John of Janua defines 'vacare' as 'being vacant.' 'Though there are other meanings, they are all secondary to this, e.g. "vaco lectioni"—I have time for reading and devote myself thereto.' Hence the impersonal 'vacat' meaning 'disengagement from' implies also 'freedom or fitness to apply oneself to some object.' Hugh of Pisa in his work on Derivations[7] uses almost identical terms. Just as the words 'aquarius,' 'arbitrarius' and 'pararius'

---

[1] Translation abridged here as the same information is already given *ante*, p. 123.

[2] *Flores Historiarum* (Rolls Series, 1886), I, 91.

[3] *Chronica Majora* (Rolls Series, 1874), II, 286.

[4] One MS. of Roger of Wendover has 'Roger.'

[5] The difference in social status between 'Magister Petrus' and 'Petrus Magister' is thus defined by Placentinus (*Summa Codicis*, 1, 2, 3): 'Si dicimus, hic est Magister Petrus, literatorie scientic preceptorem designamus. Si dicimus, hic est Petrus Magister, aliquando cerdonem, aliquando locorum turpium purgatorem significamus' (quoted Tourtoulon, *Placentin, sa vie, ses œuvres*, 93).

[6] The *Catholicon* of John Balbus of Janua appears to have been first printed at Strasburg in 1470 and went through numerous editions.

[7] Selden's note refers to a MS. of this work in the Lambeth Library. I cannot trace it in M. R. James' *Catalogue of the Lambeth MSS.* (Cambridge, 1900).

parare et comparare usurpatur[1] pro 'inter se convenire') aquarius, arbitrarius, pararius, alia ejusmodi priscis rite facta sunt, ita forsan in sensum quem diximus barbara recentiorum audacia nec interim sine ceterum exemplis atque analogia formavit Vacarius a Vaco ad eum qui prae ceteris lectionibus diligentius vacaret, ut sane Rogerius noster fecit, designandum. Certe minus inique ita fit Vacarius a Vaco quam Accursius ab accurro. Jam vero Accursius ipse[2], advocatorum idolum illud ut a non nemine vocatur, ad Gaii verba de nominis ferendi conditione haeredis institutioni adjecta, quae de honestis non famosis aut turpibus nominibus est admittenda, 'ut,' inquit, 'instituo te haeredem si imponas tibi nomen meum scilicet Accursium, quod est honestum nomen dictum, quia accurrit et succurrit contra tenebras juris civilis. Secus si dixi si imponas tibi nomen Vespillo quod est turpe nomen.' Et non ita mirum est ejusmodi eis in seculis nominum compositiones seu derivationes factas esse, cum etiam non deessent qui[3] dubitarent an Justinianus ipse a Justitia sic dictus fuisset, an ex eo quod Justini esset filius, cui revera ex sorore nepos erat, sed et filius adoptatus. Atque nugacibus hujusmodi conceptionibus adhibent illud Justiniani[4], 'consequentia nomina rebus esse studentes...' unde etiam perquam ridicule Flavum illum aiunt nuncupatum (pro Flavium) 'quia talis erat coloris.' Sed vero in Novellis[5] Theodosianis impressis vox ferme cum Vacario eadem occurrit; scilicet Vecarii. 'Et apud inlustrissimas praefecturas (sic ibi) et apud Vecariis Rectores Provinciarum de quolibet negotio pulsari...' Sed mendum est crassissimum, qualia sunt in impressis illis perplurima. Legendum, apud viros clarissimos (seu vi. clariss. unde Vecariis ibi perperam factum) Rectores...,' quod e MS. meo codice ante citato, seu Gulielmi Malmesburiensis collectaneis juridicis palam liquet.

VI. Haud vero est adeo mirum, Stephanum regem edicto vetuisse leges Romanas earundemque libros ita a Theobaldi Cantuariensis antistitis domo seu adseclis et proculdubio ejusdem auspiciis in Angliam allatos, cum scilicet ei sub id ipsum tempus insensissimus rex, utpote qui cum eo quod ad Concilium Rhemense injussu regio se contulerat[6] proscripsit, ut vicissim interdicti sentenia antistes regnum percussit. Henricum etiam episcopum tunc Wintoniensem gratia apud regem insigniter pollentem atque summo conamine Theobaldo rebusque

---

[1] Vide Annot. in Festi Pappi....
[2] Gl. ad L. 63, D. tit. Ad Senatuscons. Trebellianum § Si in danda lit.
[3] Odofred. in praef. Codicis. Alia ejusmodi in tit. de Emendat. Cod.
[4] § Est et aliud Inst. tit. de Donationibus.
[5] Novell. Theodos. tit. 14, L. 4.   [6] Joscelin. in Vita Theobaldi, etc.

are derived by the ancients from 'aquari,' 'arbitrari' and 'parare,' so a modern licence—not without classical precedent—has formed Vacarius from 'vaco,' as designating one who, like this Roger, devoted himself specially to readings (*lectiones*).

Derivation of name 'Accursius

This derivation is at least as likely as that which derives Accursius from 'accurro.' Accursius himself—styled the 'idol of lawyers'—comments as follows on the passage in Gaius concerning the conditions in which an heir might assume another's name, provided it were reputable—'Suppose I appoint you my heir on condition that you adopt my name "Accursius." That is a good name, because [its bearer] runs [accurrit] to give succour in the obscure passages of the civil law. It would be otherwise if I gave you a bad one, such as Vespillo [corpse-carrier].' Such derivations were not infrequent in those days, some even conjecturing that the name Justinian may be derived from Justitia, rather than from the fact that the emperor was nephew and adopted son of Justinus. Justinian's phrase, 'anxious that names should fit things,' is quoted in order to advance these fanciful theories, some actually holding that the emperor was called Flavus, and not Flavius, 'because his hair was yellow.'

A misprint

In the printed copies of the Theodosian Novels the word 'Vecarius' occurs. But this is a bad mistake—and there are many in the printed texts. It ought to be read 'viros clarissimos' or 'vi. clariss.' whence the mistaken 'Vecariis.' This is clear from my already cited MS. containing the legal compilations of William of Malmesbury[1].

King Stephen's prohibitory edict

VI. It is not surprising that Stephen should have proscribed the Roman law and treatises thereon as, at the time of their introduction into England, he was enraged against Theobald and had exiled him for attending the Council of Rheims against his orders, while Theobald, in turn, put the kingdom under interdict. There can be little doubt but that Henry of Winchester, a great favourite of the king's and an enemy of Theobald, had a hand in the affair. Stephen's

---

[1] See *ante*, p. 107.

ejus adversari solitum in causa simul vix ambigendum est fuisse,
ut legum praelectiones ac libri Justinianei quorum domus Theobaldiana ita ut dictum est heic autores fuere ac splendidius
inde clarescere coeperunt, improbarentur atque ut eorum vetaretur usus. Edicti illius prohibitorii meminit etiam Rogerius
Baconius[1] celeberrimus ille philosophus et mathematicus, sectae
Franciscanae, qui sub Edwardo primo scripsit. 'Rex quidem,'
inquit, 'Stephanus allatis legibus Italiae in Angliam publico
edicto prohibuit ne ab aliquo retinerentur.' Postmodum autem
in gratiam regiam redeunte Theobaldo, atque, ut fieri amat,
secundis de legibus illis cogitationibus habitis, effectu caruit
edictum illud aut revocatum aut evanescens. Adeoque eo non
obstante, libri retenti, lectiones, professio habita. Id quod expressim testatur coaevus ille Joannes Sarisburiensis ubi indictum Rogerio illi Vacario primo heic legum Caesarearum
lectori publico silentium memorat. Statim enim subjungit[2];
'sed Deo faciente, eo magis virtus legis invaluit quo eam amplius
nitebatur impietas infirmare.'

VII. Ante haec tempora, viri, alias etiam bonis literis imbuti,
legibus moribusque vetustis Anglicanis qui ad regimen attinuere
publicum et civile, serio incubuere; atque ex eis in foro advocati,
judicesque selecti. In monasteriis, academiis, antistitum clariorum familiis, collegiis, alibique pro educationis, qualitatis,
dignitatis, opportunitatis discrimine ii degebant. Nullus autem
eis sive Justiniani sive Theodosiani juris usus erat heic publicus.
Sed moribus majorum tantum patrioque utebantur illi jure quod
et ante et ad nostra usque tempora Angliae Commune vocatur,
quemadmodum temporibus Anglo-Saxonicis þeoda riht seu
jus seculare seu mundanum, ut distinctum a Godes riht seu jure
divino; quod obvium est in legibus Anglo-Saxonum. Scilicet
decisiones praeeuntes, quales in juris quibus nunc utimur
annalibus, earum rationem mutuamque analogiam praeter leges
e re nata variatim novatas mutatasque tum in musaeis tum in
foro tantum adhibere solebant illi. Hujus generis fuere terni illi
jurisconsulti Anglicani diu ante allatas huc leges Romanas seu
sub Gulielmi primi tempora, id est annum Christi 1070, Sacolus
et Godricus monachi et Alfwinus rector ecclesiae Suttunensis,
quos legibus patriae optime institutos esse testatur tabularium
vetus[3] coenobii Abindoniensis, ubi item legitur 'eis tantam
secularium facundiam et praeteritorum memoriam eventorum
(id est plane, ut nunc, annalium juridicorum peritiam) 'infuisse
ut ceteri circumquaque facile eorum sententiam ratam fuisse,

---

[1] In Compend. Theolog. seu Opere Minori MS. in Bibliotheca Cottoniana.
[2] Policratic. lib. 8, cap. 22.   [3] MS. in Bibliotheca Cottoniana, fol. 121.

prohibitory Edict is described in the following terms by the famous Franciscan Roger Bacon[1], writing in the time of Edward I: 'King Stephen by edict forbade the maintenance of the laws brought from Italy to England.' But afterwards when Theobald was restored to favour and when, as commonly happens, the question of these laws was re-considered, the Edict was either revoked or became obsolete. John of Salisbury[2] affirms as much.

The learned monks of Abingdon

VII. In earlier times men, otherwise skilled in good learning, applied themselves to the study of old English customs and laws as affecting public administration, and from their number were selected advocates and judges. These men, according to their education, rank and opportunities, lived in monasteries, academies, households of famous bishops, colleges or elsewhere. They made no public use of the law of Justinian or Theodosius, but used those ancestral customs and native jurisprudence then, as now, called English common law, *i.e.* the secular law of the Anglo-Saxons, as contrasted with the divine law. In other words, they used, in their studies and in the courts, decided cases as precedents, like those we have in our Year Books, relying on such common principles and analogies as could be deduced therefrom, as well as on laws renewed or changed as occasion required. Examples of this are the two monks Sacolus and Godricus, and Alfwinus, rector of Sutton, who flourished in the time of William the Conqueror (that is, long before the introduction of Roman law into England) and who, as we are assured by an old Abingdon register[3], were 'expert in the laws of their country.' The same register tells us that these men 'had such eloquence in secular matters and such a knowledge of the past (*i.e.* of Year Books, as we would say now) that their opinions were generally accepted.' There

---

[1] *Compendium Studii*, cap. IV (Rolls Series ed. p. 420).
[2] *Policraticus*, ed. Webb, II, 399. See *supra*, p. 109.
[3] MS. Claudius C. IX, f. 134.

quum edicerent, approbarent.' Sed et alii plures de Anglis causidici per id tempus in abbatia ista (sic ibi legitur) habebantur quorum collationi nemo sapiens refragabatur, quibus rem ecclesiae publicam tuentibus, ejus oblocutores elingues fiebant. Et Guilielmus primus dicitur[1] Londinum anno suo quarto convocasse omnes a provinciis suis universis 'Anglos nobiles sapientes et lege sua eruditos, ut eorum et jura et consuetudines ab ipsis audiret.' Atque ut ante ita post usque in tempora quibus ita in studia ac forum qualitercunque receptum est heic Jus Caesareum, jurisperiti ac causidici nostrates nullo alio jure omnino praeter patrium (nisi forsan Pontificii aliquot capita quae in usu quotidiano excipias) ex instituto imbuti sunt. Ex eo genere fuit Ranulphus ille 'invictus causidicus[2]' Guilielmo secundo regi procurator primarius; quo tempore qui ex clericali fuere ordine etiam Juris Anglicani, cui serio incumbebant, peritorum locum maxime supplebant, quod plane etiam innuit Gulielmus Malmesburiensis dum inquit, 'nullus clericus nisi causidicus,' sub Gulielmo scilicet rege illo. Et sub idem ipsum tempus quo primo ita coepit Jus Caesareum heic alibique recipi, eminentissimus erat pristini plane communis juris sine ulla Caesarei intermixtione peritus atque exercitatissimus apud nos Albericus de Ver, Comes Guinarum qui procuratoris primarii munus Stephano regi gessit. Is ipse est qui Guilielmo Malmesburiensi nuncupatur[3] 'quidam Albericus de Ver homo causarum varietatibus exercitatus' quod itidem de eo dicitur a Rogerio Wendoverio ac Matthaeis Parisio et Westmonasteriensi, qui insuper, ut res ipsa erat, 'Comitem Albericum de Ver' nominant. Scilicet Comes ille Guinarum in Normannia erat. Hujus Londini in tumultu seditioso trucidati filius Albericus de Ver primus fiebat tum a Mathilda Augusta tum a filio ejus Henrico rege secundo Comes Oxoniensis, unde eodem per lineam masculam retento nomine eadem gaudet jam nunc dignitate Albericus de Ver Roberti filius, vigesimus Oxoniae comes, juvenis nobilissimus. Quemadmodum autem Rogerius monachus ac prior Beccensis, heic, ut ostensum est, praelegebat, ita alii etiam monachi juri tum Caesareo tum Anglicano, tam in foro ac scholis extra coenobia sua quam intra, tunc incumbere soliti. Atque mos ille quidem et seculis ante Rogerium actis et aliquantulum post ejus heic professionem, haud parum obtinuit. At vero circa quatuordecim a tempore quo ipse heic praelec-

---

[1] Roger de Hoveden part. post fol. 347, edit. Lond. Francofurt. 601 et seqq. in 608. Idem ipsum in codice Lichfeldensi MS. in Biblioth. Cottoniana.
[2] Guil. Malmesbur. de Gest. Regum, lib. 4, pag. 123, edit. Francof.
[3] Hist. Novell. lib. 2, an. 1139.

were several other English lawyers in the same abbey whose opinions were not lightly disputed, and who silenced detractors of the Church.

Ralph Flambard and Aubrey de Vere

William the Conqueror is said to have summoned to London in 1069 from the provinces 'all the English nobility who were learned in their law in order that he might understand their rules and customs at first hand.' Prior to the introduction of Roman law into England our lawyers were trained only in this native jurisprudence, except that some parts of the canon law were in daily use. Of such lawyers a good example was Ralph (Flambard), 'the unbeaten lawyer[1],' William II's justiciar who lived at a time when such clergy as were well-versed in the law filled the places of lawyers. This is the point of William of Malmesbury's remark: 'No priest who is not a lawyer[2].' About the same time as the imperial laws were introduced, Aubrey de Vere, earl of Guisnes, king Stephen's justiciar[3], was very skilled in the old common law, free from any Roman admixture. He is referred to by William of Malmesbury as 'a man well versed in divers legal causes': Matthew Paris[4] and Matthew of Westminster[5] speak of him in similar terms. He was killed[6] in a London riot and his son was made earl of Oxford first by Matilda and then by Henry II. The title is now enjoyed (the same name being retained) by the noble youth Aubrey de Vere, twentieth earl, descended in the male line[7]. In the same way that Roger, prior of Bec, lectured in this country, so other monks, both inside and outside their monasteries, devoted themselves to Roman and English law in the courts and in the schools—a usage which prevailed before Roger's public teaching and for some time thereafter. The practice ceased however, or by canonical

---

[1] William of Malmesbury, *Gesta Regum* (Rolls Series, 1889), 369.
[2] *Ibid.*
[3] He was Great Chamberlain (Madox, *Baronia Anglica*, 158) and was advocate for Stephen when the latter was criticised by the Council for the arrest of several bishops. The statement *that he was Justiciar* rests on an assertion by his son William in a tract De Miraculis S. Osythae (Round, *Geoffrey de Mandeville*, 390).
[4] *Chronica Majora* (Rolls Series), II, 371.
[5] *Flores Historiarum* (Rolls Series), II, 61.
[6] In 1141; see *Dictionary of National Biography*.
[7] In 1625 when, for the second time, the direct male line came to an end, the earldom was claimed by Lord Willoughby de Eresby, whose mother was an aunt of the last (eighteenth) earl. The House of Lords referred the case to the Judges who adjudged the earldom to the heir male. In 1621 Selden had been examined, with Sandys and the eighteenth earl of Oxford, by the Privy Council for his part in the Commons' Protestation of that year.

tionem finivit annos, aut plane, quantum ad praelectionem extra coenobia attinet, desiisse aut desinere ex Jure Pontificio debuisse morem illum pariter est concedendum. Scilicet anno 1164 in synodo Turonensi constituit Alexander papa tertius 'ut nullus omnino[1] post votum religionis, post factam in loco aliquo professionem, ad Physicam, Legesve mundanas legendas permittatur exire. Si vero exierit et ad claustrum suum infra spatium duorum mensium non redierit, sicut excommunicatus ab omnibus evitetur et in nulla causa, si patrocinium praestare voluerit, audiatur. Reversus autem in choro, capitula, mensa et ceteris, ultimus fratrum existat et (nisi forte ex misericordia apostolicae sedis) totius promotionis spem amittat. Episcopi vero, abbates priores, tantae enormitati consentientes et non corrigentes spolientur propriis honoribus et ab ecclesiae liminibus arceantur.' Postmodum itidem confirmatur tantumdem ab Honorio tertio[2]. Ipseque synodi Turonensis canon in Gregorianum Decretalium corpus[3] recipitur. Atque hinc plane eliciendum, morem antea nec quidem infrequentem obtinuisse ut monachi alii, quemadmodum et Rogerius noster monachus Beccensis, tam extra quam intra coenobia sua jura Caesarea aliaque publice praelegerent docerentque, etiam et postmodum intra coenobia sua.

Caput Octavum

I. De usu apud majores nostros Juris Justinianei a tempore Stephani regis (quo primum huc allatum est) per Henrici, Richardi primi et Joannis regum tempora.

II. Usus ejusdem heic qualiscunque vestigia sub Henrico tertio et Edwardo primo, qui Franciscum Accursium in Angliam ad praelegendum invitavit.

III. De tempore Edwardi secundi et legibus aliquot ex Pandectis, locis ipsarum, more solenni ab jurisconsultis nostratibus in tribunalibus regiis laudatis.

IV. Juris Justinianei seu Caesarei usus tum in consistoriis pontificiis tum in tribunalibus binis regiis (quorum alteri rerum militarium, alteri nauticarum cognitio propria est) uti etiam in academiis nostris usque in nostra duravit tempora.

V. Usus ejusdem juris qualiscunque is olim fuerit tum in tribunalibus ceteris regiis tum in jurisperitorum nostratium studiis scriptisque, qua talium, evanuit sub Edwardi tertii initia.

I. Ex eo quod diximus ita primo allatarum praelectarumque in Anglia legum Justinianearum tempore, publicus tum in studi-

---

[1] Apud Guil. Nubrigens. lib. 2, cap. 15 et in Concil. tom. 3, par. 2, p. 534, edit. 1618. Antiq. Collect. 1, lib. 3, tit. 37, cap. 2. Append. ad Conc. Lateran. 3, part. 27, cap. 2.   [2] Compilat. Decretal. lib. 5, tit. 27.
[3] Extr. tit. Ne clerici vel monachi secularibus negotiis..., cap. 3.

rule should have ceased about 1163[1], at least so far as concerned extra-mural teaching, for in 1164 [1163] pope Alexander III decreed in the Synod of Tours, that 'no one who had taken the vows should be allowed to leave his monastery in order to read physics or secular laws. Should such a person leave his monastery and not return within two months, he is to be held excommunicated and is not to be heard in any suit should he offer a defence. On his return he is to be treated as lowest in chapter, refectory and elsewhere and (except with papal permission) is to lose all hope of preferment. Bishops, abbots and priors conniving at such misdeeds are to be deprived of their functions and expelled from the Church.'

Effect of this prohibition

This was afterwards confirmed by pope Honorius III[2] and the decree is embodied in the Gregorian Decretals. From this it may be deduced that up till that time it was fairly common for monks like Roger of Bec to give public teaching in Roman and other law outside their monasteries as well as within, and, even after the decree, within the monastic walls.

Chapter VIII

I. Of the use of the Corpus in the reigns of Henry II, Richard I and John.

II. Traces of this use, such as it was, in the reigns of Henry III and Edward I. The latter's invitation to Francis Accursius to lecture in England.

III. The time of Edward II. Some laws from the Pandects cited, with references, by English lawyers in royal courts.

IV. The use up to our own times of the imperial law in (*a*) Church courts, (*b*) the two royal courts which take cognizance of military and maritime matters and (*c*) the Universities.

V. The cessation of this use, about the beginning of Edward III's reign, in the other royal courts and in the studies and writings of our jurists.

Roman law references by John of Salisbury

I. From the time of its first introduction into England there was some public use of the civil law in academic curricula, in legal practice

---

[1] Mansi, *Nova Collectio*, XXI, 1179.

[2] *Super Speculam*, 1219. This bull forbade the study of Roman law in Paris, even by laymen. In 1235 the clergy were forbidden to frequent the law-school of Orléans. These restrictions were renewed by Innocent IV in the bull *Dolentes*, of which the authenticity has been contested. The prohibition did not extend to Italy and may have been intended to protect the monopoly of the law-schools in Rome. See Caillemer, *Le Pape Honorius III et le droit civil* (1881); Tardif, *A propos de la bulle Super Speculam* (*Nouvelle Revue de droit français*, 1881) and De Marléon, *L'Église et le droit romain* (1887).

orum ratione tum in forensi praxi responsisque ac consiliis dandis, earum invalebat heic qualiscunque usus. Nec, ut ante e Sarisburiensi notatum est, obstitit Stephani edictum. Quo paulo post mortuo, adeo indulsit Theobaldo antistiti ejusque adseclis Henricus rex secundus, ut etiam leges illae heic tutius colerentur ac majori, ab aliquibus saltem, inde haberentur in pretio. Ejusce rei specimina habentur clarissima tum apud Joannem illum Sarisburiensem Theobaldo, cujus domus sic adsciverat leges Caesareas in Angliam, charissimum adeoque domus illius partem non exiguam, tum apud discipulum ejusdem Joannis, Petrum Blesensem, archidiaconum Bathoniensem et Cantuariensem cancellarium. Apud Joannem illum, in locis Policratici compluribus[1], ubi e corpore Justinianeo in rem suam testimonia non pauca adfert, eaque velut vim heic obtinentia aut obtinere sibi credita, atque ipsam etiam Legem Regiam (de qua supra egimus) quasi tunc in ore hominum nostratium non infrequentem. Idem in epistola ad anonymum[2], sed manifestum est ad prelatum aliquem Anglicanum adeoque de rebus Anglicanis (quod ex Lincolniensis ecclesiae ibi mentione etiam liquet) 'ea cautela,' inquit, 'diligentiae versare in talibus (in jurisdictione exercenda) ut videri non possis sitire pecuniam delinquentium, sed quod pastorem decet, quaerere salutem animarum. Nosti siquidem quod et seculi leges eos acerbissime puniunt lege Julia Repetundarum, qui in faciendis ex officio[3] et non faciendis sordidum sectantur lucrum.' Loquitur heic, uti etiam in Policratico[4], de Lege Julia Repetundarum, cujus est tum in Digestis tum in Codice titulus singularis, velut ea quam inter leges seculares seu Anglis tunc qualitercunque receptas recensendam admitteret. Alibi item liberos ex damnato coitu genitos nec Jura Civilia nec Leges agnoscere ait ubi[5] reddit Alexandro tertio papae rationem causae quae tum coram se ut judice heic delegato, tum in foro regio inter Richardum de Anestia nepotem ex sorore Guilielmo de Saccavilla et Mabiliam de Franchevilla ejusdem filiam, de successione in Guilielmi defuncti bona ventilata fuisset. De natalibus Mabiliae quaestio fiebat, spuriane an legitima illa. Res, ut fieri solet, ad ecclesiasticum examen refertur a tribunalis regii praefectis, sed in ipso examine et discussione inita Legum Principum et Civilium pariter atque Canonum usus fit. Et autoritas legum et Canonum simul affertur, ubi plane Jus intelligitur Caesareum. Mabiliae etiam ibi

[1] Lib. 4, cap. 1, 2 et 6; lib. 5, cap. 13, 14, 15, 16; lib. 7, cap. 20.
[2] Epist. 68.
[3] L. 48. D. tit. de Lege Julia Repetundarum.
[4] Lib. 5, cap. 16.
[5] Epist. 80.

and in the giving of opinion by counsel. Stephen's edict, as we know from John of Salisbury, did not prove a permanent obstacle, while his successor Henry II so favoured Theobald and his household that these laws could be studied more safely and so, at least in some quarters, brought into higher esteem[1]. Good instances of this are to be found in the writings of John of Salisbury—an eminent and cherished member of Theobald's household, and of his pupil Peter of Blois, archdeacon of Bath and chancellor of Canterbury. Frequently in the *Polycraticus* illustrations are drawn from the Corpus Juris as if still in force or believed to be in force, and even the Lex Regia is treated as something in every-day parlance. John of Salisbury in a letter[2], probably addressed to an English prelate, writes, referring presumably to English conditions: 'You must proceed with such caution as not to appear covetous of the bribes of offenders, but, as becomes a pastor, you must seek rather the salvation of their souls. For those who, by omission or commission, strive after filthy lucre are severely punished by the Lex Julia Repetundarum.' Here, as in the *Polycraticus*, the Julian law of bribery, a separate title in Code[3] and Digest[4], is spoken of as a law admitted to some extent in contemporary English practice.

Roman law cited in a law-suit

Elsewhere[5] the same writer declares that neither civil nor national laws recognise those born out of wedlock, and gives an account to pope Alexander III of a case argued before him as judge delegated for the purpose, and also in the royal court, between Richard of Anesty, nephew on the sister's side of William of Sackville, and Mabel of Francheville, William's daughter, concerning succession to the deceased William's estate. The question was whether Mabel had been born in wedlock and, as was customary, the matter was referred to an ecclesiastical court; but in the examination and discussion of the case, use was made of the civil law and the laws of princes, as well as of the canon law. The authority of the 'laws and canons' was asserted, by which obviously the imperial law was meant. Mabel's

[1] The *Ordo Judiciarius Bambergensis* was composed about 1181–5 by John, archbishop of Dublin (published by Schulte, 1872). For an account of the Anglo-Norman jurists of this time see Caillemer, *Le droit civil dans les provinces anglo-normandes*.
[2] In *Patrologia Latina*, CLXIX, 55.
[3] C. 9. 27. 3.
[4] D. 48. 11.
[5] *Patrologia Latina*, CLXIX, 75.

advocatus dum subveniendum vult ei ex parentum juris ignorantia ac temporis conjugii diuturnitate, rescriptum Divorum Fratrum affert de matrimonio Flaviae Tertullae incesto sed ex ignorantia juris contracto et per plurimos annos sine controversia durante, velut id quod in re tunc in judicium deducta autoritatem sortiretur. Sed rescriptum illud nec in Justinianeis nec alibi hactenus reperio. Ex Codicis Gregoriani exemplari aliquo eis quibus utimur fragmentis ampliori forsan hausit hoc ille, aut forte ex Justi Papirii Codice[1], qui puto prorsus jam periit; Divorum scilicet Fratrum Constitutionum. Verba rescripti sunt; 'Movemur et temporis diuturnitate quo ignorantia juris in matrimonio avunculi tui fuisti, et quod ab avia tua collocata es, et numero liberorum. Idcircoque, cum haec omnia in unum concurrant, confirmamus statum liberorum vestrorum in eo matrimonio quae vesitorum (lege 'quaesitorum') quod ante annos XL concitatum est, proinde atque si legitime concepti essent.' Et certe in Policratico ejus occurrunt veterum alia aliquot haud alibi nunc lecta. Petrus autem archidiaconus Bathoniensis seu Blesensis ille se Juri Caesareo heic diligentius incubuisse ostendit[2] uti et complures alios in familia Thomae Antistitis Cantuariensis sub Henrico secundo rege convictores. Postmodum quidem ad Theologiam is transit. Sed interea qualis juris ejusdem jurisperitorum Caesareorum usus heic tunc fuerit, intelligendum videtur ex eis quae de se suisque, dum juris studiis incubuit, similibus in antistitis Cantuariensis familia degentibus memoravit. 'In domo domini mei,' inquit, 'Cantuariensis archiepiscopi, viri literatissimi sunt, apud quos invenitur omnis rectitudo justitiae, omnis cautela providentiae, omnis forma doctrinae. Isti post orationem et ante comestionem, in lectione, in disputatione, in causarum decisione jugiter se exercent. Omnes quaestiones regni nodosae referuntur ad nos, quae cum inter socios nostros in commune auditorium deducuntur, unusquisque secundum ordinem suum sine lite et obtrectatione ad bene dicendum mentem suam acuit et quod ei consiliosius videtur et sanius, de vena subtiliore producit. Quod si Deus minori quae potiora sunt revelaverit, ejus sententiae sine omni invidia et depravatione universitas acquiescit.' Haud ita diu post Sylvester Giraldus Cambrensis[3] vixit, seu sub Richardo et Joanne regibus. Is in Distinctionibus de Principis Institutione, Justinianeas Institutiones citat Elementorum nomine, quasi jam pro primariis juris simpliciter atque absolute dictis rudimentisque heic re-

---

[1] Cujac. Observ. lib. 1, cap. 1. Freymon. in Symphonia Juris.
[2] Epist. 6, 8, 26, 71, 140 et in Opusc. pag. 497.
[3] Dist. 1, cap. 10. MS. in Biblioth. Cottoniana.

advocate, arguing the case from her parents' ignorance of the law and the long period of their union, cites, as an authoritative analogy, a rescript of the Imperial Brothers regarding the incestuous marriage of Flavia Tertulla—an alliance originally contracted in ignorance and for many years unchallenged—by which the children of that marriage were declared legitimate. This rescript I have been unable to find either in Justinian or elsewhere[1]. Perhaps it was taken from a copy of the Gregorian Code more complete than the existing fragments, or from Justus Papirius' Codex of the Constitutions of the Imperial Brothers[2], which is now lost[3]. It may be remarked that in the *Polycraticus* are to be found fragments of old writers not to be traced elsewhere[4].

Reference by Peter of Blois

Peter of Blois[5], archdeacon of Bath, was also devoted to the study of imperial law, as were other members of archbishop Thomas' household. This is my inference from Peter's own words: 'In the household of my lord archbishop of Canterbury are to be found many cultured men, noted for justice, learning and shrewdness. After prayers and before refection, they generally occupy themselves in reading, debate and the deciding of causes. All the thorny questions of the kingdom are referred to us. These are first mooted by our fellows in the common hall where each one, in order of seniority, without strife or personalities, endeavours his best to suggest the wisest solution. If God should reveal the most cogent opinion to a junior, it is accepted without envy by all.'

Shortly after this, Giraldus Cambrensis, who lived in the reigns of Richard and John, refers in his *Distinctiones de Principis Institutione*[6] to the Institutes of Justinian as 'elements,' *i.e.* first principles of jurisprudence accepted in this country. 'You will find it written,'

---

[1] It is in D. 23. 2. 57 (from Institutes of Marcian). See Selden's text.
[2] See *ante*, p. 57, n. 4.
[3] For fragments of Papirius Justus see O. Lenel, *Palingenesia Juris Civilis*, I, 947.
[4] See Prolegomena, par. 5 to *Ioannis Saresburiensis Policraticus*, ed. C. C. J. Webb.
[5] Born about 1135; studied at Bologna 1160; became archdeacon of Bath in 1175. His Epistolae and Opuscula will be found in *Patrologia Latina*, CCVII. Selden's quotation is from letter VI (1155).
[6] Read by Selden in MS. Tiberius B. XIII, 1. See the Rolls Series edition (1891), VIII, 32.

ceptas. 'In Elementorum libro scriptum,' inquit, 'in capite reperies Imperatoriam majestatem non solum armis decoratam sed et legibus decet esse ornatam.' Quae frontis Institutionum Justinianearum verba sunt. Sed verum quidem est Elementorum etiam nomine emitti ex codicibus vetustis Institutiones illas ut videre est in Cujaciana editione aliisque sequacibus. Atque ipse Justinianus in prooemio sic eas nuncupat. Gervasius item Tilburiensis in Otiis Imperialibus[1] ad Ottonem Augustum quartum, de Britannia sua ejusque longitudine ac latitudine verba faciens, mensurae rationem ex Digestis velut heic receptissimis sumit. Floruit ille sub Joanne rege. 'Haec,' inquit, 'insula omnium uberrima in longum tenditur octingentis miliaribus (scilicet Bedam heic sequitur) in latum ducentis. Vicenis itaque millibus passuum pro dietis (itineribus diurnis) computandis ut ff. Si quis cautionibus l. 1. protenditur in longum quadraginta dietis et in latum decem.' Citatis nempe titulo et lege Gaius habet, 'vicena millia passuum in singulos dies dinumerari praetor jubet.' Quod etiam apud jurisconsultos nostros olim receptum est in eo quod Journees Accomptes seu dietas computatas nuncupant. Et quam ferax etiam illis in seculis esset jurisprudentiae Caesareae studiorum Anglia, satis ostendit visio illa decantatissima monachi Eveshamiensis quae ficta est anno 1196, seu sub Richardo primo. Collocatur scilicet ibi[2] in tertio Purgatorii loco poenali clericus ante monacho bene cognitus. 'Atque hic,' inquit monachus, 'suo tempore eorum quos Legistas et Decretistas appellant peritissimus habebatur, unde in redditibus' (ita in Matthaeo Parisio; sed legendum ex visione illa quam habeo per se antiquitus manuscriptam, 'earum etiam facultatum auditores in scholis quamplurimos instituerat et subinde magnatum familiaritatem sibi conciliarat. Hinc redditibus') 'Ecclesiarum ampliatus....' De legista aliquo et decretista aut gentis nostrae aut apud nos degente legenteque loqui eum palam est. Tunc igitur seu sub quadragesimum a prima Rogerii Vacarii praelectione, Legistae heic id est Juris Caesarei periti fuere et Decretistae id est Pontificii professores qui a Caesareo auspicari solebant. Atque hi in scholis etiam tunc aliis jura praelegebant, nec quidem paucis. Plurimos hunc unum instituisse ait monachus heic atque eorum qui sic dicti peritissimum esse habitum; unde sane etiam a Rogerii tempore aut circiter institutionis ejusmodi, etiam in jure utroque, usum heic fuisse perpetuum merito sentias, qualis item duravit heic usque in tempora quibus Pontificis apud nos Romani autoritas sanctione Parlamentaria

---
[1] MS. in Biblioth. Cottoniana.
[2] Apud Matth. Paris. an. 1196. Roger. Wendover. MS.

A LAWYER IN PURGATORY

he says, 'in the beginning of the book of Elements that the imperial majesty should be illustrious in laws as in arms.' These are the opening words in Justinian's Institutes and, as may be seen from the Cujacian and later editions, these Institutes were issued under the name of some old compilations called the Elements, Justinian himself using that name in his preface.

Gervase of Tilbury

Gervase of Tilbury, who flourished in John's reign, in his *De Otiis Imperialibus*[1] addressed to the emperor Otto IV, speaks of the length and breadth of Britain, and takes his standard of measurement —20,000 paces for a day's journey—from the Digests[2], as if these last were widely received here. Among our old lawyers this was the standard for 'journées accomptés' or day's marches.

Vision of the monk of Evesham [Eynsham]

How fruitful in civil law studies was England of those days is sufficiently attested by the famous Vision of the Monk of Evesham[3] (1196). Placed in the third circle of Purgatory is a clerk, formerly well-known to the monk, who 'was considered in his time the most skilled among legists and decretists, and was received with favour by the great, after he had trained up many students in the schools of the Faculty. Having become rich by ecclesiastical revenues...' etc. The legist or decretist here referred to may have been native-born or here only for teaching purposes. It appears that about forty years after Vacarius' first teaching here, there were in this country legists or experts in civil law, and decretists or experts in canon law, the latter generally commencing with civil law studies. Such decretists taught law in other schools, of which there were not a few, and it may be assumed that from about the time of Roger, teaching in canon and civil law was an established institution among us until the power of the pope in England was abolished by parlia-

---

[1] MS. Vespasian E. IV, 1. Portions of Gervase's work have been published in *Script. Rer. Brunsvicensium* (ed. Leibnitz, I, 884–1004).
[2] D. 2. 11. 1.
[3] *Visio Monachi Eyneshamensis*. Now in Bodleian (MS. Selden, supra, 66). The reference is on f. 20. Selden's mistake of Evesham for Eynsham appears also in Matthew Paris, *Chronica Majora*, II, 423 (Rolls Series).

abolita est. Etenim exinde Juris Caesarei non Pontificii in academiis nostris praelectiones, professio, dignitates. Dictis vero jam seculis 'legum etiam mundanarum periti[1]' vocabantur heic quotquot legibus Patriis Caesareisque simul operam navarent. Neque apertum semper Juris Caesarei heic et Anglicani professorum tunc temporis discrimen apud scriptores occurrere comperio. Civilis nomine, qua utriusque heic sed admodum diversus erat in foro, saltem nonnullis, usus, utrunque venisse videtur. Ad haec autem tempora Henrici secundi, Richardi primi et Joannis regum spectat illud Gualteri Mapezii ministri tunc aulici non incelebris de Goliae (hoc sibi nomen fingit) 'praedicatione ad terrorem omnium' et de extremo judicii die:

> Cogitate, Divites, qui vel quales estis
> Quid in hoc judicio facere potestis.
> Tunc non erit aliquis locus hic Digestis.
> Idem erit Deus hic Judex, Autor, Testis,
> Judicabit judices Judex generalis.
> Nil ibi proderit dignitas regalis....

Digesta heic memorat ille dum de omnimodis apud nos judiciis loquitur, quasi in usum passim forensem admissa existimasset. Atque de Caesareo Jure in Jus Pontificium qua heic illud exercebatur seculis in illis admisso, testimonia sunt non infrequentia nec obscura tum in appendice illa Concilii Lateranensis tertii sub Alexandro tertio, tum in Collectionibus seu Compilationibus vetustioribus, uti etiam in Decretalibus Gregorianis, ubi in rescriptis pontificiis innumera occurrunt de litibus in Anglia tunc forensibus tum ex Jure Caesareo quam Pontificio (sed quidem in consistoriis pontificiis) institutis quarum ratio ex Jure Caesareo seu Justinianeo etiam discussa. Et scimus sub Richardo rege Justitiarii Angliae[2] munus obiisse Hubertum Walteri archiepiscopum Cantuariensem Ranulpho de Glanvilla discipulum[3], qui in causa proculdubio non esse nequibat ut Juris Caesarei sic generi maxime suo heic nuper admissi ratio in studiis foroque haberetur singularis. Quale itidem dicendum de Cancellariis Angliae aliisque in summas aliquot publici regiminis praefecturas e genere hieratico tunc adscisci solitis[4]. Atque interdum et Cancellarius simul et Justitiarius Angliae erat episcopus, ut Willielmus Eliensis sub Richardo jam dicto. Sed vero et legum terrae peritorum mentio etiam illis in seculis signantius habetur apud historicos obvia. Et dubitari nequit,

---

[1] Vide visionem Thurcilli Purgatorii in Mat. Paris anno 1206.
[2] Mat. Paris in Richardo rege anno 1198.
[3] Joscelin in vita Huberti.
[4] Vide Henric. Spelman in Glossar. verb. Cancellarius.

ment. Thereafter it was for civil law alone, not canon law, that teaching and rewards were available in our universities. Those who, in this period, studied national laws as well as the civil law, were styled 'skilled in secular laws,' and among the writers of these times I do not find a clear distinction between the exponents of civil law and of English law. In some writers, both systems seem to have shared the name 'civil' in so far as used in court, though used differently.

Walter Mapes

Walter Mapes[1], a famous courtier of this period, puts the following words concerning the last judgment into the mouth of one of his characters:

> Consider, rich men, whatever your degree
> In the day of judgment where will you be?
> In vain your quotations from the Digests;
> God accuses, judges and attests, etc.

The digests are here referred to as if they were current in our legal practice.

Ecclesiastical exponents of Roman law

Concerning the admission of civil law into canon law practice there is a good deal of clear evidence in the appendix to the proceedings of the third Lateran Council[2]; in the old compilations, and in the Gregorian Decretals. In papal rescripts to be found there, many instances occur of English law suits, based on civil or canon law, in which the fundamental principles are adduced from Roman law or the Corpus of Justinian. We know that in the reign of Richard I Hubert Walter, archbishop of Canterbury (a pupil of Glanvil), discharged the office of justiciar of England, and it was doubtless due to him that the principles of the civil law were held in special esteem both in teaching and practice, his own order being responsible for the recent introduction into England of this jurisprudence. The same is true of the chancellors of England and other high public dignitaries generally recruited from the clergy. Sometimes a bishop appears as both chancellor and justiciar, *e.g.* William of Ely under Richard I.

Lex Terrae

Historians of those times frequently refer to persons notably skilled in the laws of the land[3] ('leges terrae'). Doubtless many

---

[1] Selden probably read Walter Mapes in MS. Titus A. xx. The modern edition is that by T. Wright (Camden Society, xvi).

[2] 1215. See Mansi, *Nova Collectio*, xxii, 213-458.

[3] This had not always been Selden's interpretation of 'lex terrae.' In 1627, when counsel for Hampden, he had defined 'lex terrae' not as 'law of the land' (since it distinguishes freeman from villein), but as 'due process of law,' *i.e.* indictment or impeachment (see Selden's argument in *Opera*, ed. Wilkins, III, pt. II, 1932).

quin quamplurimi legibus terrae seu patriis etiam tunc ita incumberent, ut Caesareas neutiquam commistas vellent.

II. De Henrici regis tertii tempore hac in re testimonia habentur amplissima apud Bractonium, de quibus etiam superius est dictum. Atque huc puto attinet quod in tabulis publicis habetur de 'scholas regentibus de legibus in civitate Londini' sub eodem rege. Verba sunt[1]; 'Mandatum est Majori et Vicecomitibus London. quod clamari faciant et firmiter prohiberi ne aliquis scholas regens de legibus in eadem civitate de cetero ibidem leges doceat. Et si aliquis ibidem fuerit hujusmodi scholas regens ipsum sine dilatione cessare faciant. Teste R. apud Basing XI die Decembris.' Credibile non videtur de legibus Anglicanis earumve praelectione mandatum hoc fieri. Et certe Londini antiquitus, idque diu ante Collegium Greshamium institutum, publica aliarum in scholis erat disciplinarum, praeter Grammaticam, professio ac disputationes[2]. In Registro MS. veteri consuetudinum ecclesiae S. Pauli, inter officia Magistri scholarum Grammaticae, quae olim ibi institutae, recensetur etiam et hoc, 'item quod more solito deputationes (lege disputationes) Dialecticae et Philosophiae teneat apud S. Bartholomaeum in festo ejusdem, et disputata apud S. Trinitatem.' Occurrit etiam in tabulis Henrici tertii publicis non raro Joannes de Lexinton seu Lessinton, tribunalibus praefectus celebris, qui in annalibus coenobii Burtonensis[3], senescallus regis vocatur et 'vir providus et discretus et in utroque jure, Canonico scilicet et Civili peritus.' Et notissimum est ex historiis nostris archivisque, praesules et antistites sacros qui tam Caesareo quam Pontificio juri etiam incubuerant uti et simul Anglicano, regiis tribunalibus illis in seculis saepius esse praefectos judiciaque exercuisse sane heic omnimoda. Advocatos autem id genus imbutos studiis, ex genere etiam sacerdotali, forum tunc omnimodum heic frequentasse res ipsa palam satis facit, quod et manifestum fit ex constitutionibus Ottonis et Ottoboni legatinis tum de advocationis officio tum de judiciis secularibus hujusmodi generi hieratico heic inhibendis. Quod ad Edwardi primi tempora seu sequentia spectat, faciunt huc quae ex Thorntonio et Fleta itidem ante observavimus. Quo item pertinet id quod in archivis de Francisco Accursii filio, legum doctore, compertum est; eum scilicet cum familia sua ab Edwardo primo in Angliam accersitum, ut proculdubio leges Oxoniis praelegeret

---

[1] Rot. Claus. 19 Hen. III, membrana 16 seu anno 1234.
[2] Vide Stephanidem De Urbe Londin. et Jo. Stowaeum in Notit. Lond. p. 118.
[3] MS. in Bib. Cottoniana anno 1255.

VIII 11   ROMAN LAW IN HENRY III's REIGN   143

applied themselves even then to the laws of the land, or national laws, without desiring any admixture of civil law.

Teaching of Civil Law in London

II. The evidence for Henry III's reign is abundant in Bracton, of whom something has already been said. Apposite to this subject is the reference in our public records to licensed law teachers of London in the following mandate[1]: 'The Mayor and Sheriffs of London are to proclaim that for the future no licensed law teacher is to give legal instruction in the city, and anyone found doing so is to be compelled to desist.' It is very unlikely that this could refer to the English laws or to English law teaching; moreover in London, long before the days of Gresham's College there was public teaching and debate of subjects other than Grammar. In an old register[2] of the Customs of St Paul's there is recorded among the duties of the Master of the Grammar School, that 'of holding, in the accustomed manner, debates of Dialectic and Philosophy at St Bartholomew's on his feast day and at Holy Trinity.'

John of Lexington

Also, in the public records of this reign, there is frequent reference to John of Lexington[3] or Lessington, a famous judge, who, in the Annals of Burton Abbey[4], is styled 'the royal steward, a man of great prudence, skilled in both laws, *i.e.* the civil and the canon.' Moreover it is well known from our histories and archives that in those days archbishops and bishops who had studied civil and canon law as well as English law were frequently appointed His Majesty's judges and exercised full jurisdiction. Lawyers, qualified in such studies, even if clerics, were practising in every kind of court, as is clear from two legatine constitutions[5] of Otto and Ottoboni, one on the subject of accepting briefs, the other prohibiting the exercise by the clergy of such secular functions in a court of justice.

Francis Accursius in England

As for the period of Edward I, our remarks on *Fleta* and Thornton may be recalled. To these may be added the invitation, found in our archives, extended to Doctor Francis Accursius and his family to come to England, doubtless in order to teach civil law at Oxford.

---

[1] Close Rolls, Henry III, 1234–7, p. 26.
[2] Not identified.
[3] Lexington occasionally held the Seals in Henry III's reign; he took a prominent part in proceedings against the Jews after the murder of the boy Hugh of Lincoln (1255).
[4] MS. Vespasian, E. IV, 1. *Annales de Burton* (Rolls Series, 1857), p. 345.
[5] Selden's MS. of these Constitutions is in the Bodleian—(MS. Selden, supra, 43), ff. 9 and 17.

Caesareas, ipsumque Franciscum advenire sibi saltem statuisse, si re vera non advenerit. Neque sane advenisse existimandum videtur ex eis quae mox ostendimus. Accersitum autem satis ostendit mandatum hoc[1] ejusdem regis Vicecomiti Oxoniae, de eo ibidem accommode excipiendo.

'Rex Vicecomiti Oxoniae salutem. Praecipimus tibi quod Francisco Accursii doctori legum vel ejus mandato has literas nostras deferenti, liberes manerium (aedes tunc regias ibi seu castrum) Oxoniense ad inhabitandum una cum uxore sua et familia quamdiu nobis placuerit. Nolumus tamen quod tu propter hoc impediaris quin diebus statutis in aula ipsius manerii tenere valeas Comitatum. In cujus rei testimonium... Teste rege apud Windesore septimo die Decembris.' Franciscus hic filius erat Accursii Florentini illius celeberrimi glossatoris. Atque ut Accursii patris nomen millies glossis subjicitur, ita non raro, maxime ad illud quod Digestum Novum dicitur, Franciscus et Franciscus Accursii qui hic ipse est ita in Angliam accersitus, glossis subjungitur ejusdem singularibus. Institutiones item habemus cum ejusdem glossis adjectis. Jurisconsultorum biographi de adventu ejus in Angliam haud omnino loquuntur. At vero et pactum iniisse aiunt cum rege Angliae (qui plane Edwardus noster primus) ut Bononia in Galliam se transferret ad docendum Jus Caesareum in territoriis ibi Anglo subjectis, atque demum discessisse, sed adeo invitis civibus suis ut bonorum ideo eum mulctarent publicatione, quae, eo postea reduce, est rescissa. Guidus Panzirolus[2]; 'Is a rege Angliae in Galliam, ut ibi doceret, deducendus erat, quod cum Bononienses praesensissent, poena publicationis bonorum indicta, praeceperunt ne recederet. Ipse vero cives eludens, omnibus amico venditis, discessit, sed bona nihilominus sunt publicata, unde redire coactus, ubi reversus est, eorum restitutionem[3] impetravit. Interea Tolosae Jus Civile aliquamdiu docuit.' Hinc sane eum in Angliam non venisse eliciendum est, uti et causa ob quam non venerit juxta pactum cum eo regium. Et Bononiae mortuus est, ubi Patris ejusque sepulchrum habetur cum hac inscriptione brevi[4], 'Sepulchrum Accursii Glossatoris legum et Francisci ejus filii.' Sed patri, quem mortuum esse aiunt anno 1229, superstitem fuisse Franciscum hunc usque in annum saltem 1276 liquet ex regio mandato supra ostenso quod ad hunc scilicet spectat annum. De usu item tempore hujus regis frequenti heic

---

[1] Rot. Pat. 4, Ed. I, membran. 35.
[2] De Claris Legum Interpret. lib. 2, cap. 29.
[3] Vide Alberic. in l. 17, hi qui C. tit. de Rescindenda Venditione.
[4] Jo. Fichard. in Vit. Jurisc. Valentin. Forst. etc.

VIII ii ROMAN LAW IN EDWARD I'S REIGN 145

It is certain, at least, that Francis intended to come, even if he did not actually do so[1]. The mandate from Edward I to the Sheriff of Oxford concerning the provision there of suitable accommodation for Accursius is proof that he was asked to come.

Treatment of Accursius by the Bolognese

This Francis was the son of the famous Florentine glossator whose name is so often found appended to glosses. In many cases (especially in copies of the New Digest) we find glosses over the name of Francis and Francis Accursius, who is no other than the person invited to England, and we still possess his glosses on the Institutes. The legal biographers are silent on the subject of the son's visit to England, but they record how he arranged with Edward I to leave Bologna to teach civil law in those parts of France subject to England, and that his migration so displeased the Bolognese as to induce them to confiscate his goods—a measure revoked on his return. Panzirol affirms that the Bolognese ordered him, on pain of confiscation of his property, not to accept the English king's invitation to visit France, but he managed to elude the vigilance of the citizens, sold his property to a friend and left the city. His goods were nevertheless impounded[2], whereupon he returned and received them back, having meanwhile taught civil law for some time at Toulouse[3]. From this it may be gathered that he did not come to England, and why he failed to keep his pact with the king. He died at Bologna, the inscription on the grave of father and son being:

> The tomb of Accursius, Glossator
> of the Laws, and of Francis his son.

The date of the above royal mandate is 1276. The father is said to have died in 1229[4]; the son must have survived until at least the former date[5].

---

[1] It is said that Francis Accursius was invited to come to England by Edward I when the latter was passing through Bologna in 1273 on his way from the Holy Land. In 1275 Accursius was sent as one of Edward's proxies to a Parlement held by Philip Augustus (*Patent Rolls*, Edward I, 1272–81, p. 94); in the course of 1276 he appears to have been in England and in Oxford, for he was appointed to conduct enquiries regarding injuries inflicted on the King's Jews in Oxford (*Calendar of Close Rolls*, 1272–9, p. 289) and he is styled a king's councillor (*ibid.* 1272–9, pp. 237, 296, 388); in 1280 he is shown as king's secretary (*ibid.* 1279–88, p. 5). In the same year he was appointed to the custody of the manor and castle of Dunster (*Patent Rolls*, 1272–81, p. 374). In 1278 he had gone to Rome on royal business (*ibid.* p. 278). In 1281 he was given a grant for life of 40 marks yearly, in consideration 'of past and future services' (*ibid.* p. 460). He appears to have left England in 1281. There does not appear to be any record of his teaching at Oxford. For the mandate to the Sheriff of Oxford, see Selden's text.
[2] In 1274 when the Lambertazzi family, to which Accursius belonged, was suppressed (see Savigny, v, 279–282).
[3] There is no evidence of this.
[4] He died in 1260.
[5] The son died in 1293.

Juris Caesarei maxime inter sacerdotalis generis homines, seu clericos qui ut ante sic et nunc (quicquid in contrarium statuerint canones eorum sacri) dignitatibus heic juridicis etiam in tribunalibus regiis omnimodis saepe nimis fruebantur, testatur Rogerius ille Baconus coaevus[1]. 'Omne regnum,' inquit, 'habet sua jura quibus laici reguntur; ut jura Angliae et Franciae. Et ita fit justitia in aliis regnis per constitutiones quas habent, sicut in Italia per suas. Quapropter cum jura Angliae non competant statui clericorum, nec Franciae, nec Hispaniae, nec Alemanniae, similiter nec jura Italiae ullomodo. Quod si debeant clerici uti legibus patriae, tunc est minus inconveniens ut clerici Angliae utantur legibus Angliae, et clerici Franciae utantur legibus Franciae; quapropter maxima confusio clericorum est quod hujusmodi constitutionibus laicalibus subdantur colla. Rex quidem Angliae Stephanus allatis legibus Italiae in Angliam publico edicto prohibuit ne ab aliquo retinerentur; si igitur laicus princeps laici principis alterius leges respueret, multo magis omnis clericus deberet respuere leges laicorum. Addo etiam quod magis concordant jura Franciae cum Angliae et e converso, propter vicinitatem regnorum et communicationem majorem gentium istarum, quam Italiae et illarum. Quare deberent magis clerici Angliae subjicere se legibus Franciae et e converso, quam legibus Italiae.' Sic ille. Tametsi de clericis tantum loquatur Baconus, nihilominus, cum certum sit illo in aevo genus apud nos sacerdotale etiam in tribunalibus regiis partes egisse primarias, dubitare nequit quin ex ejusmodi clericorum juris hujus usu, illud etiam in tribunalibus illis subinde invaluisset, et plane, qua tale, inter discutiendum esset adhibitum. Atque consulendus Joannis de Acton (Athona vulgo vocitamus) commentarius in constitutiones legatinas unde receptum tunc temporis ut ante etiam usum Juris Caesarei heic apud pontificios fuisse manifestum fit. Quibus accedat etiam formula solennis qua illis in seculis antistites Cantuarienses libertatem Juris Caesarei professoribus in Academiis legendi indulgebant, illis scilicet qui alias a beneficiis suis sacris abesse licite nequibant. Scilicet in Formulario Ecclesiastico penes me MS. temporis Edwardi primi seu Joannis Peckhami antistitis Cantuariensis legitur:

'Joannes...dilecto filio magistro R. de B. rectori ecclesiae parochialis de W. talis dioecesis, Juris Civilis professori, salutem. ...Fructum in Dei Ecclesia, quae ad sui juris regimen literatis permaxime noscitur indigere per te legendo et proficiendo in

---

[1] In Compend. Theolog. seu Operi Minori MS.

Roger Bacon

Regarding the frequent use of the civil law in Edward I's reign, especially among the clergy (who then, as before, in spite of canonical prohibitions occupied the highest secular judicial posts) Roger Bacon[1] writes as follows: 'Every kingdom has its own laws by which laymen are governed, as the laws of England and France. In other kingdoms justice is administered in accordance with the constitutions in force, *e.g.* in Italy. As the laws of England are not adapted to the clerical estate, neither are those of France, Spain, Germany or Italy. If the clergy ought to live by the laws of their country, then English clerics would naturally use English laws and French clerics French laws, but this subjection of the clergy to lay jurisdiction results in great confusion. King Stephen prohibited by edict the reception in England of laws brought from Italy. If therefore a lay prince can repudiate the laws of another prince, much more ought the clergy to repudiate the laws of the laity. Moreover the laws of France and England, owing to vicinity and intercourse, have more in common with each other than they have with the laws of Italy, so English clerics should rather submit to French law and *vice versa* than that either should submit to Italian law.'

A 'dispensation for study'

Although Bacon speaks only of clerics, it is clear that since the clergy exercised essential functions even in the royal courts, clerical use of this law must consequently have been admitted into these tribunals and must have been cited in the adjudication of cases. The Commentary of John of Acton (or Athon) on the Legatine Constitutions[2] shows that the imperial law was then, as before, used by the English clergy, and there is further corroboration in the formal patent by which the archbishops of Canterbury licensed students of civil law in our universities. Without such license these persons would have had to betake themselves to their spiritual duties. There is an example in a MS. Ecclesiastical[3] Formulary in my possession of the time of archbishop John Peckham:

'John...to our beloved son R. de B., Rector of the Parish Church of W., student of the civil law, Greeting. In the hope that your study and proficiency will accrue to the benefit of the Church, which is known to need men of learning for its judicial administra-

---

[1] *Compendium Studii* (Rolls Series, 419-420).
[2] There are numerous MSS. of John of Acton's *Commentary*. It was printed in 1496 in William of Lyndwood's *Provinciale*.
[3] This MS. cannot be traced.

scientia literarum, afferri sperantes, ut per biennium a datu praesentium numerandum, in Universitate Oxoniensi insistere valeas studio literarum et promoveri interim minime tenearis, nisi ad ordinem subdiaconatus duntaxat infra annum recipiendum a tempore tibi commissi regiminis in ecclesia supradicta, tecum ratione juris etc. juxta formam constitutionis Bonifacii[1], "Cum ex eo," in ea parte editae, libere dispensamus, ita tamen quod eidem ecclesiae interim deserviatur laudabiliter in divinis et animarum cura diligenter exerceatur in ea. Proviso etiam quod procuratorem idoneum ibi constituas, qui medio tempore ordinariis respondeat vice tua, quodque absentiae tuae damnum recompensetur eleemosynarum largitione nostro arbitrio facienda. Dat....' Titulus autem in margine est 'Dispensatio ad Legendum,' qualis tunc temporis in usu ut hinc videtur non infrequenti.

III. Quae diximus eo de seculo firmantur etiam ex eo quod occurrit in annalibus juridicis[2] Edwardi regis secundi, e Richardi de Winchedon coaevi, ac primi ut videtur eorundem confarcinatoris codice perpulchre descriptis, et a Joanne Bakero Equite Aurato et sub Philippum et Mariam reges Fisci Cancellario, bibliothecae Interioris Templi cujus socius erat, donatis. Etenim ibi non solum ipsissima Juris Caesarei[3] ejusque regularum verba, locis interea ubi sedes habent ipsa, non expressim indicatis in forensi litium apud judices regios disceptatione aliquoties generatim adferuntur (qui mos etiam hodieque apud jurisconsultos nostros interim reperitur), verum etiam interdum tum ex Juris Civilis seu Caesarei vi rem pendere admittitur, tum ipsi ejusdem juris textus juxta tralatitium citandi morem designantur. De Juris Caesarei vi seu ratione tunc adhibita, veluti juxta quam

---

[1] C. unic. lib. 6, tit. de Excessib. Praelatorum.
[2] MSS. in bibliotheca Interioris Templi. Vide ibi 1 Ed. II, fol. 2.
[3] Et M. 12 Ed. II, fol. 151 *a*.

tion, we hereby license you to apply yourself to the study of letters in the University of Oxford for two years from this grant, in which period you will have to proceed no further than sub-deacon, and this within a year of presentation to the above living. We hereby dispense with you 'ratione juris[1]'...in accordance with the constitution of Boniface 'Cum ex eo[2]' on these conditions—that the above church be properly served in spiritual matters, that you appoint a proxy to answer, in the interval, to the Ordinaries and that the loss due to your absence be made up by such alms as we shall judge proper[3].'

The title in the margin is 'Dispensation for Study' and, as the above example shows, it must have been in fairly frequent use.

The Year Books of Edward II

III. Further confirmation is supplied by the Year Books of Edward II[4], beautifully transcribed from the MS. of Richard of Winchedon[5], who it would appear was their original compiler, and presented to the Library of the Inner Temple by a member, Sir John Baker, Chancellor of the Exchequer under Philip and Mary. There one finds not only the very words and maxims of the civil law as cited in pleadings before the king's judges (though without express references to their sources—a custom occasionally found to-day among our lawyers), but sometimes one also finds there that a question hangs on the interpretation of the civil law, and the original texts themselves are indicated in the manner traditional among lawyers.

Civil law citation in the record of an English law suit

Of the authority of the imperial law and its function in providing the principle (or what was thought to be the principle) by which a

[1] Unfortunately Selden abridges, or seems to abridge, his extract at this point; the original from which he was copying may have been 'ratione juris ex,' *i.e.* 'ratione juris exigentiae,' the usual form being 'juxta juris exigentiam.'

[2] Boniface, *Liber Sextus Decretalium*, v, 6. This was a rule framed in order to prevent the scandals consequent on the unlicensed migration of priests into towns.

[3] It is probable that Selden has misunderstood the purpose of this license and it is not unlikely that it is wrongly transcribed. The license was probably to enable a priest, already qualified in civil law, to complete his studies at Oxford in canon law in order that he might thus have the full qualification Doctor Utriusque Juris. There is nothing whatever to support Selden's contention that a license was required by priests for the study of civil law. The mediaeval university was not a place for research by graduates, but for the utilitarian purpose of obtaining degrees qualifying for definite posts.

[4] An edition of the Year Books for this reign was published from Maynard's MS. in 1678 (*Les Reports des cases argue et adjudge in le temps del roy Edouard le Second*). This edition is very incomplete and badly edited. The Year Books for Edward II's reign are being edited and published by the Selden Society.

[5] No trace of this MS. has been found. See *supra*, p. xxiv.

decisum est aut saltem decidendum tunc fuisse est existimatum, egregium habes ibi exemplum. Statutum habetur[1], 'si depredationes vel rapinae fiant Abbatibus, Prioribus etc. et ipsi jus suum de hujusmodi depredationibus prosequentes morte praeveniantur antequam judicium inde fuerint assecuti, successores eorum habeant actiones ad bona ecclesiae suae de manibus hujusmodi transgressorum repetenda.' Titium priorem Walingfordiae bonis spoliaverat Seius. Dignitate privatur Titius suffecto in ejus locum Sempronio qui actione[2] hoc nomine utitur in Seium. Excipit ille, Titium adhuc esse superstitem, adeoque nec morte praeventum juxta statutum jam dictum, quo actio nitebatur. Sed decisum est (uti et tam tempore Edwardi primi[3] quam biennio ante in causa prioris Lantoniensis[4] itidem fuerat decisum) frustraneam esse exceptionem illam; ratione quidem heic adjecta sed ab eo qui primo scripsit aliquantulo discussa ex Jure Civili seu Caesareo atque improbata et demum ab eo qui descripsit ex eodem jure asserta. 'Quia duplex est' (in codice MS. verba se habent) 'mors, et naturalis et civilis, et in hoc casu mortuus est prior quia dignitate privatur.' Sed clericus qui librum istum scripsit videlicet Richardus de Winchedon dicit quod salva pace seniorum suorum, et salvo meliore judicio, minus bene dicunt, quia quamvis quis dignitate privatur, morte civili non est affectus. Hactenus Winchedonius ille. At vero qui codicem descripsit etiam suam adjicit sententiam. 'Sed hujusmodi privatio' inquit 'dignitatis vocatur, prout memoriae meae occurrit in Jure Civili, media capitis diminutio. Sed hic mortuus est civiliter qui efficitur servus poenae, licet nondum mortuus; sicut etiam qui deportatur in insulam, id est exulat, velut is cui aqua et ignis sunt interdicti, ut utlegatus.' Eadem decisio memoratur in annalium ejusdem regis juridicorum MSS. in bibliotheca Hospitii Lincolniensis, ratione ad hunc modum tantum adjecta, 'quia duplex est mors, scilicet civilis et naturalis, et in hoc casu Prior fuit mortuus, quia dignitate privatur, Jure Civili.' Dignitatis igitur privationem pro media capitis diminutione sumtam, etiam mortem civilem (quam non minus atque naturalem in statuto jam dicto intelligi volebant illius seculi judices) intulisse existimabant, idque ex Juris Caesarei[5] interpretatione. Qua etiam ipsa de re inter jurisconsultos qui tunc floruerant controversia est habita; quod ex Odofredo[6]

---

[1] Stat. Marlebrig. cap. 30, 52. Hen. III.   [2] Mich. 12 Ed. II, fol. 151 a.
[3] Temp. Ed. I. Fitzherb. tit. Trespas. 242.
[4] Pasch. 10 Ed. II, fol. 133 b.
[5] D. tit. de Capitis Diminutione l. 11. Instit. eod. tit.
[6] Ad l. 2, D. tit. de Capitis Diminut. et vide ibi DD. et ad l. 3, D. tit. de Senatoribus.

VIII III   ROMAN LAW IN THE YEAR BOOKS   151

decision was come to, the following is a good example[1]. It was enacted by a statute that 'if abbots or priors were despoiled and prevented by death from securing redress, their successors should have actions for demanding the restoration of ecclesiastical property from such transgressors.' Seius had despoiled Titius, prior of Wallingford. Titius is deprived and Sempronius substituted. The latter sues Seius on this account. Defendant [Seius the despoiler] excepts that Titius [the deprived prior] is still living, and therefore not prevented [from suing] by death, as required by the statute on which the action depended: but (as already in Edward I's reign and two years earlier in the case of the prior of Llanthony) it was here decided that the plea [exception] was invalid. The justification for this was rejected by the original recorder of the case [Richard of Winchedon?] but approved by the copyist, both adducing arguments from the civil law: for, according to the MS., 'Death may be natural or civil, and deprivation brings the prior within the second category.' But the clerk who wrote this MS., that is to say Richard of Winchedon, says that this opinion, with all due deference, is wrong, because though a man may be deprived, he is not therefore civilly dead. But the copyist[2] adds his view as follows: 'Deprivation of this kind is called, so far as my recollection of civil law[3] serves me, Media Capitis Diminutio. A slave by punishment [*servus poenae*], an exile and an outlaw are civilly though not yet naturally dead.'

The same decision is recorded in another MS.[4] of the Year Books of this reign in the Library of Lincoln's Inn, the only reason given being—'because death is two-fold, civil and natural, and in this case the prior was dead in civil law because deprived.' Deprivation was therefore assumed to mean Media Capitis Diminutio and hence civil law death, both assumptions being adduced from the civil law. Odofred, the eminent lawyer who flourished in Edward I's reign[5], shows that there was a controversy on this subject among con-

---

[1] There is a summary account of this interesting case on p. 351 of Maynard's edition of the Year Books. The case has been traced by Mr Turner to the De Banco Roll 225 r. 18 Berks.

[2] Notice the change from the third to the first person. Maitland in his preface to the third volume of the Selden Society Year Books concluded that Richard of Winchedon and the copyist may have been the same person.

[3] Inst. 1. 16. 5. and D. 5. 1. For a criticism of the copyist's Roman law see Selden Society Year Books, III, p. xx.

[4] Lincoln's Inn MS. CXXXIX.

[5] Probably a slip for 'Henry III's reign.' See *ante*, p. 33, n. 3.

jurisconsulto clarissimo, qui tempore Edwardi primi floruit, satis scimus. 'Quaere,' inquit, 'quid si aliquis in dignitate constitutus eam perdit, ut quia princeps, vel episcopus, nunquid dicitur capite minui? Dicunt quidam quod sic, quia prior status mutatur....' Bis item citatas in codice illo annalium juridicorum Interioris Templi MS. Pandectas olim observabam, indicatis etiam ut assolet titulis legibusque. Locus alter est in anno ejusdem quinto[1], ubi agitur ex conventione qua promiserat reus actricem in uxorem se accepturum atque interea alimenta ei suppleturum. Quaestio sit utrum obligaretur reus simulac promiserat, praestare statim promissum; ubi Hervaeus actricis advocatus, 'si ieo me oblige a vous en M. li. et en l'escript il ny ad pas jour de paie nest pas la dette due maintenant apres la fesance del escript? Certes cy est.' Rationem ex Jure Caesareo sic reddit, 'in omnibus obligationibus quibus dies non ponitur, praesenti die debetur ff. de Regulis Juris l. in omnibus,' quae sunt Pomponii verba l. 14 eodem titulo, unde huc ita expressim sunt allata. Sed in codice Lincolniensis Hospitii ne litis quidem hujus mentionem reperi. Alter est locus in ejusdem regis anno duodecimo ubi actionem de bonis aliquot sublatis instituit[2] Seius in Abbatem Abindoniensem. Excipit Abbas, consuetudinem in Abindonia perpetuo obtinuisse, ut quisquis ibi cervisiam confecerit et vendiderit, denarium unicum (Colcestre peny dictum) Abbati persolvere deberet, quo non soluto abbatibus ex eadem consuetudine jus semper fuisse pignus e bonis solventis capiendi; Seium cervisiam et confecisse et vendidisse nec solvisse, ideoque bona illa se in pignus sustulisse. Ad haec Devonius advocatus heic Seii, consuetudinem ait hanc sine ratione atque ex injuria in alios natum, nec inde jure Abbatem in actorem frui posse aliquo, 'quia quod non ratione introductum est, sed errore primo, deinde consuetudine obtentum, in aliis similibus non obtinet ff. de legibus, lege, non obtinet.' Ipsissima sunt Celsi ibi verba l. 39 quae ita inde in foro a Devonio heic judicibus citantur regiis, ut lex illa altera e titulo Diversis Regulis ante ab Hervaeo. Atque in margine adjicitur heic charactere antiquo 'Nota loye, Nota.' Ceterum in codice Lincolniensi quem diximus licet causa ipsa totidem ferme verbis inseratur, citatio ejusmodi habetur nulla. Sed rarissimae sunt ejusmodi in seculo apud nostros citationes, quod scimus ex annalibus juridicis Edwardorum tum primi tum secundi. Neque in primi annalibus quid ejusmodi mihi occurrit.

---

[1] Pasch. 5 Ed. II, fol. 73 b.
[2] Hill, 12 Ed. II, fol. 156 a MS.

VIII III ROMAN LAW IN THE YEAR BOOKS 153

temporary lawyers. 'If it be asked,' he says, 'whether anyone, such as a bishop or prince, can be held to suffer Capitis Diminutio through loss of office, some say Yes, because his original status is altered.'

Another Year Book reference

I noted that the Pandects are twice cited in the Inner Temple MS. of the Year Books, the titles and laws being referred to in the usual way. The first case[1] is in the fifth year of the reign and concerns a pact whereby defendant had undertaken to marry plaintiff, in the meantime providing her with maintenance. To the question whether defendant was bound to implement this promise immediately after making it, Hervey[2], counsel for the plaintiff, replied in the affirmative, basing his conclusion on the civil law doctrine to be found in the Regulae Juris that 'in contracts where the date is not specified, performance is due on the day of contract.' The words of this maxim, thus expressly cited, are taken originally from Pomponius[3]. In the Lincoln's Inn MS. I have been able to find no record of this case.

A Civil law maxim cited

The other case is in 12 Edward II when Seius sues the abbot of Abingdon for taking away some of his goods. The abbot pleads a custom, immemorial in Abingdon, that whoever brewed and sold beer therein should pay to the abbot one penny, called Colchester[4] penny, otherwise the abbot had the right to take a distress from the goods of the person liable. Seius, having brewed and sold beer, had not paid; hence the distress on his goods. Devonius [Denom], counsel for Seius, arguing that this custom had grown up without justification and to the detriment of others, pleads that 'whatever is introduced irrationally and by an initial error, though it may become a custom, does not avail in similar cases.' These are the very words of Celsus[5], thus quoted in court, as in the other case Hervey had quoted from the title De Diversis Regulis Juris. At this point there is added a marginal note in an old hand, 'Nota loye, nota.' In the Lincoln's Inn MS., though the case is given in almost identical words, there is no such citation. But such references are very rare in our Year Books of that period. For Edward I's reign, I do not know a single instance.

---

[1] For this case see Selden Society Year Books, 5 Edward II (1311–1312), p. 217 and xxxvii. Defendant had not promised to marry plaintiff but to procure for her a suitable husband; the lady's taste was exacting and she claimed a preposterous sum for damages.

[2] Hervey of Stanton or 'Hervey le Hastif' from his hasty temper.

[3] D. 50. 17. 4.

[4] Maitland (in preface to third volume of Selden Society edition of the Year Books) explains this term as a corruption of 'toll sester,' *i.e.* one penny paid by toll on each sester of malt.

[5] D. 1. 3. 39.

IV. Cum vero ex ante ostensis satis liqueat, duplicem fuisse apud majores nostros in seculis illis vetustioribus Juris Caesarei usum, alterum in consistoriis episcopalibus adeoque in delegatorum ad quos ab illis appellatum est foro, eorumque qui sive judicum sive advocatorum procuratorumve munera illic obirent studiis, alterum in tribunalibus etiam saltem aliquot regiis, qua eo nomine suique natura ab istis distingui solita sunt, atque in eorum studiis qui in tribunalium ejusmodi actionibus judiciisque se exercerent; usus quidem prior ejusdem heic juris, qua scilicet cum Pontificio (velut fere angues invicem caducei Mercurialis) complicatur atque ita ab eo temperatur ut quoties non adversarentur canones sacri[1], vim in consistoriis illis obtineret, usque in nostra tempora inde duravit. In causis nempe testamentariis, successionis in bona mobilia ab intestato, institutionum ac substitutionum in ejusmodi bona, aliorum aliquot singularium quorum cognitio consistoriis illis a legibus Anglicanis permissa. Atque ejusmodi usus heic luculenter cernitur tum in commentariis Joannis de Acton in constitutiones legatinas, qui ad Edwardi primi tempora spectant, tum in eis quos Guilielmus Lindwodus sub Henricum quintum adjecit constitutionibus provinciae Cantuariensis. Episcopalibus istis quantum ad hancce rem accessere alia non pauca eorum plane instar fora, velut abbatum complurium aliorumque generis hieratici quibus jurisdictionis episcopalis privilegium indultum, uti etiam consistoria utriusque Academiae. Nam et in hisce usus Juris Caesarei etiam invaluit atque in nostra duravit tempora. Quod vero ad tribunalia regia, qua vulgo ab his distingui solent, attinet, bina quidem id genus sunt in quibus ejusdem juris usus etiamnum ab antiquis seculis retinetur. In maritimo scilicet, seu Curia Admiralitatis, et Militari seu Curia Constabularii et Marescalli Angliae, adeoque in delegatorum ad quos ab his appellandum est foro, uti etiam in cognitionibus tum maritimis, quae civiles sunt, tum militaribus extraordinariis. Praesunt postulantque in his juris illius professores. Sed vero etiam in his Jus Justinianeum temperatum est auctumque. In curia militari monomachia seu certamen litigantium singulare in probationibus admittitur quod Juri Justinianeo[2] adversum. In Admiralitatis Curia, quae in titulis 'ad legem Rhodiam' de jactu, de nautico foenore, de usuris nauticis, de exercitoria actione occurrunt, alia ad rem nauticam attinentia e Jure Justinianeo adhiberi solent atque ex corpore atque interpretibus ejus expressim depromi. Sed ita ut etiam

---

[1] Videsis citata supra pagg. 100–102. Alderan Mascard. Conclus. de Statut. Interp. 2, § 254, etc.
[2] C. tit. de Gladiatoribus l. unic.

VIII IV   COMMENTARIES OF JOHN OF ACTON   155

Commentaries of John of Acton and William of Lyndwood

IV. It thus appears that in those times there was a two-fold use of the civil law, one in Diocesan courts, in the Delegates' Court of Appeal and in the studies of those who acted therein as judges, advocates or proctors; the other in some of His Majesty's courts, distinguished in name and function from the above, and in the studies of those officiating in such courts. The former use, as intertwined with canon law (like the snakes on Mercury's staff) and tempered thereby, was practised in those courts so long as not inconsistent with the Canons, and this has lasted to our own day in such matters as testamentary cases, succession to goods of intestates, dispositions and transfers of such property, etc. This is exemplified both in the commentaries of John of Acton on the Legatine Constitutions[1] (relating to Edward I's time) and in those of William of Lyndwood[2], in Henry V's time, on the Constitutions of the province of Canterbury. There were several other courts, for matters of this kind, on the model of the Church courts, for instance, the courts of several abbots and other ecclesiastics having episcopal jurisdiction, also the [Vice-Chancellor's] courts of the two universities, in which the use of civil law prevails down to our day.

The Admiralty and Marshal's Courts

As regards royal courts, in distinction from church courts, there are two in which the use of this law still survives—the Maritime or Admiralty court[3] and the Court of Chivalry, or Court of the Constable and Marshal of England[4], consequently also in the Court of Delegates[5] to which appeal lies, and also in certain maritime and military cases of civil nature[6]. In such courts the judges and advocates are civil lawyers, but even there the law of Justinian is modified and reinforced. For instance in the Court of Chivalry trial by combat is allowed, though it is contrary to the law of Justinian. In the Admiralty Court, while certain matters are directly dealt with from the Corpus of Justinian[7], nevertheless this is done in such a manner that the maritime customs, styled the Laws of Oleron, are

---

[1] See *supra*, p. 147, n. 2.
[2] For William of Lyndwood see Maitland, *Canon Law in the Church of England*.
[3] See the two volumes of *Select Cases in the Court of Admiralty* (ed. Marsden) in Selden Society publications.
[4] This court was abolished in 1640. The criminal jurisdiction of the Constable ceased in 1514 when Buckingham was discharged from his office; thereafter, Lord High Constables were created only for special occasions.
[5] Erected by 25 Henry VIII, c. 19, as a court of appeal in ecclesiastical matters. Its powers were transferred to the Privy Council in 1832.
[6] For instances see E. Nys, *Le droit romain, le droit des gens et le Collège des docteurs en droit civil* (1910) and W. Senior, *Doctors' Commons and the old court of Admiralty* (1922). The best contemporary account of these courts is in Duck, *De Usu et Autoritate Juris Civilis*.
[7] D. 14. 2 and D. 22. 2; also C. 4. 33 and C. 4. 25.

leges Oleronianae seu consuetudines marinae sic dictae, uti etiam alias apud gentes, commisceantur, et primariam obtineant autoritatem. Adeoque falluntur nimirum viri inter exteros docti[1] qui Anglis 'Romani Juris nullum esse usum' temere scripserunt. Tantundem de usu juris apud nos Caesarei ejusque interpretum in foederibus pactisque cum principibus exteris ineundis explicandisque ac legationum ratione dicendum. Atque ideo proculdubio in binis illis jam dictis tribunalibus et congeneribus extraordinariis uti et in delegatorum ad quos inde appellatur foro, juris ejusdem usus admissus retentusque, quoniam adeo frequenter in rerum tum marinarum tum militarium actionibus partes sustinent tam exteri, juri huic assuetiores, quam indigenae. Atque ratio obscura non est cur in academiarum consistoriis adhibeatur, cum scilicet et studium ejusdem ibi floruerit et ad exteros etiam studiis ibi incumbentes pariter atque indigenas lites ibi ut spectent necesse sit.

V. At vero qualiscunque ille in tribunalibus regiis reliquis aliisve jure Anglicano quod Commune dicitur et consuetudinarium utentibus, aut in jurisperitorum nostratium studiis, olim esset per intervallum ante memoratum Juris Caesarei ut dictum est usus, is sane cito postmodum evanuit, circa initia, ni fallor nimium, Edwardi tertii plane neglectus rejectusque. Neque enim post Edwardum secundum vestigium usus ejusmodi in annalibus nostris occurrit, nisi ex regula aliqua juris tam ejusdem quam Pontificii interdum sed perraro quidem Latine allata[2], nec interim ut ex alterius libris depromta, usum ejusmodi quis adstructum iret. Quod sane haud cum majore faceret ratione quam si quis Litletonum jure eodem ideo usum fuisse in elementis suis feudalibus conscribendis, quoniam illud etiam eis qui Jus Caesareum omnino negligunt ignorantque, 'partus sequitur ventrem[3]' quod Juris Caesarei effatum est celebre suis interseruerit, aut Plowdenum, Dierum, Coquum, tantundem in suis fecisse, quoniam et ipsi subinde regulas ejusmodi latine non ut ex Jure Caesareo petitas sed velut in Anglicano natas obiter usurpant. Sub Edwardi autem tertii initia inter jurisconsultos nostrates publice prorsus evanuisse, et sane sub Edwardo secundo ab eorum paucis culta esse Juris heic Caesarei studia, eliciendum mihi videtur ex causa Abbatis Torrensis sub Edwardi tertii media in foro regio agitata; scilicet sub annum 1347, ubi manifestum est, advocatum ex jurisperitis nostratibus

---

[1] Renat. Choppin. de Dominio Franciae, lib. 2, tit. 15, 5 et videsis Francisc. Baldwin. in Proleg. de Jure Civili.

[2] Videsis 41 Ed. III, tit. Laborers 28. Mowbray Extr. tit. de Reg. Juris 72. D. eod. tit. l. 108.

[3] DD. ad l. 7, Partum C. tit. de Rei Vendicatione.

VIII v ROMAN LAW SURVIVALS IN ENGLAND 157

mingled therewith and have chief place, as we find in other nations. Those foreign scholars who have denied that there was any use of Roman law in England are therefore wrong.

Civil law in Diplomacy

The like may be said of our employment of the civil law in such matters as embassies and the negotiating and interpreting of treaties with foreign powers[1].

Reasons for this exceptional use of Civil law

Doubtless the reason why civil law was received and retained in the two above-mentioned courts, as well as in extraordinary courts of this kind and in the appellate Court of Delegates, was that in military and maritime matters, foreigners, more accustomed than us to the civil law, were as frequently involved as natives. The reason why it is utilised in the University Courts is also clear, because it is necessary that litigation in such courts should have regard to foreigners studying there as well as to native students, and also because the study of civil law flourished there.

Disappearance of Civil law from English Courts

V. But whatever may have been the use of the civil law in English common law courts, it soon disappeared and about the beginning of Edward III's reign it fell into neglect. After Edward III's reign we find no trace of it on our annals though sometimes, but rarely, a maxim of civil or canon law is quoted in Latin without reference to its source. To regard this as a use of the civil law would be as absurd as to suppose that in his *Tenures* Littleton used that jurisprudence because he quotes the well-known civil law maxim[2] 'Partus sequitur ventrem' or that Plowden, Dyer and Coke did likewise because they quote Latin maxims. These they adduce as if derived from English rather than from civil law.

The case of the abbot of Torre

That the imperial law was cultivated by a few of our lawyers under Edward II and that it disappeared about the beginning of Edward III's reign seems to me to be proved from the case of the abbot of Torre. This was heard before the King's Bench about

[1] Some account of this will be found in the already mentioned (p. 155, n. 6) books by E. Nys and W. Senior. See also Harleian MS. 168, f. 114-115, for the opinion of two doctors of civil law, Valentine Dale and David Lewis, consulted by Walsingham in June, 1577, for their views regarding the act of those who buy goods from pirates, knowing them to be pirates. Such persons, in the opinion of the two civilians, 'are bound to restore full value and may be proceeded against as evil doers.'

[2] This maxim is neither one of the Regulae Juris nor a general rule in Roman law. The nearest approach to it was the Roman law rule that illegitimate children followed the status of the mother—C. 3. 32. 7 and D. 1. 5. 24. The mediaeval church regarded the son of a servile father by a free mother as a servus: Die Kinder folgen der Ärgeren Hand. In modern law the children follow the status of the father.

satis celebrem, Skipwithum nomine, se ea plane tunc ignorasse
vocabula ejusdem juris professum esse quae cuiquam qui Juri
Caesareo omnino incubuisset ignota esse nullo modo quirent.
Nimirum in jus tunc vocatus est Abbas Torrensis[1], actione regio
nomine in foro instituta, eo quod in causa fuisset ut prior quidam
in judicium evocaretur Avenionem pontificium de oratorio ex-
tructo 'contra inhibitionem novi operis,' nec ab agendo reces-
sisset tametsi rescriptum regis ea de re prohibitorium accepisset.
Ad hunc modum autem Skipwithus advocatus, seu 'serviens ad
legem,' id est Juris Anglicani doctor, 'in ceux parolx, "contra
inhibitionem novi operis," ny ad pas entendement,' unde petit
ut reus absolvatur. Cui Shardus judex, 'ceo nest que un restitution en lour ley, per que a ce n'avoumus regard; mes respondes
si vous avez suy countre la prohibition.' Ad alias igitur transit
advocatus exceptiones. Id quidem verum est, in corpore Juris
Canonici[2] (quod verbis illis 'lour ley' heic innui dubitari nequit)
titulum haberi 'de Novi Operis Nuntiatione,' qua intelligitur
denuntiatio prohibitoria seu inhibitio sive judicis sive ejus cujus
interest, ne quis viciniae injuriam inferat opus novum extruendo.
Sed vero palam est, titulum illum, ut alios aliquot, ex Jure
Caesareo seu Justinianeo esse illuc adscitum, ejusdemque juris
studiosis seu eis qui libros Justinianeos evolvissent incognitum
esse non potuisse. Tam in Codice[3] quam in Digestis[4] habetur.
Atque in eum seu de eo commentarios ante ediderant celeberrimi
jurisconsulti, Joannes, Azo, Accursius, Hostiensis[5], Durandus[6],
Odofredus, alii. Et de titulo illo Odofredus[7], eaque de re lege,
'lex,' inquit, 'est utilis (mortuus est ille sub exitum Henrici
tertii nostri seu anno 1265) et multum sibi vendicat locum in
civitate ista (Bononia) et ubique terrarum et in foro seculari et
ecclesiastico et materia hujus legis multum quotidiana est.' Jam
vero si pristinus seu qualis apud Bractonium, Thorntonium,
Fletae autorem atque in Edwardi secundi annalibus juridicis
reperitur Juris Caesarei in tribunalibus regiis seu apud jurisconsultos nostrates usus in tempora Edwardi tertii jam dicta
durasset, proculdubio Skipwithus heic advocatus, Juris Anglicani sane consultissimus, singularis, integri et notissimi ejusdem
juris tituli 'de operis novi nuntiatione' (quod idipsum est cum
inhibitione novi operis, nec quidem in Anglicano Jure quid

---

[1] M. 22 Ed. III, fol. 14, plac.
[2] Extra. lib. 5, tit. 32.
[3] Lib. 8, tit. 11.
[4] Lib. 39, tit. 1.
[5] Summ. lib. 5, eod. tit.
[6] Sepul. lib. 4, eod tit.
[7] Ad rubric. C. tit. de Operis Novi Nuntiatione.

VIII v DECLINE OF ROMAN LAW INFLUENCE   159

1347 when Skipwith, one of our well-known lawyers, confessed his complete ignorance of certain Roman law terms that could not possibly have been unknown to anyone who had applied himself to civil law studies. The case was this: the abbot of Torre was proceeded against by royal writ because he had caused a certain prior to be summoned before the papal court at Avignon for building an oratory despite an 'inhibitio novi operis,' and had persisted in his action against the prior though he [the abbot] had received a writ of prohibition. In the opinion of Skipwith, who was an attorney, or sergeant, that is, doctor of English law, 'there was no meaning in the words "contra inhibitionem novi operis",' whereupon he prayed that defendant be discharged. To defendant, Justice Shareshull said: 'It is simply a restitution in their law, hence no regard is here paid to it, but answer if you have acted against the prohibition,' and therefore the sergeant took up another line of defence[1].

English ignorance of a well-known Civil law inhibition

Now in the canon law (indubitably Shareshull's 'their law') there is a title 'De Novi Operis Nuntiatione' which is a prohibition or inhibition, whether of a judge or of him whose concern it is, whereby another is restrained from damaging the complainant's surroundings by constructing a new building. It is clear however that this title, as well as others, must have been transferred there from the imperial law and must therefore have been known to civil law students since it is found both in Code[2] and Digest[3]. Commentaries on it had already been compiled by such well-known lawyers as John, Azo, Accursius, Hostiensis, Durand, Odofred and others. Odofred[4] (who died in 1265) says of it: 'This law is a useful one and should be carefully guarded here (Bologna) and everywhere else, in ecclesiastica and civil courts. Every day sees occasion for its use.'

Proof that Civil law was no longer known in Common law courts

Now if the original use of the civil law, such as we have seen it in Bracton, Thornton and the author of *Fleta* and in the Year Books of Edward II, had remained till the time of Edward III, in the practice of courts and the studies of lawyers, then doubtless Sergeant Skipwith, who was very learned in English law, would not have publicly professed ignorance of that distinct and well-known title 'De Operis Novi Nuntiatione,' which is the same thing as the 'In-

---

[1] See the 1561 edition of the Year Books, Mich. 22 Edward III, f. 14.
[2] C. 8. 11.   [3] D. 39. 1.
[4] See *supra*, p. 33, n. 3.

habet analogum) adeo se nescium publice ac in foro ita profiteri noluisset seu inhibitionem novi operis verba esse quae sensu carerent tam fidenter asserere. Certe nec Shardus ipse qui judicio illi praefuit, se verborum illorum satis scientem exhibet dum Restitutionem Jure Pontificio in quod e Caesareo adsciscuntur, eis innui dicit. Neque enim Inhibitio est Restitutio. Sed interea verum est, ex interdicto illo seu denuntiatione ita restituendum in integrum cujus interest, ut quod contra inhibitionem extructum fuerit, sit destruendum, quod tum ex Pandectis[1] liquet, tum ex Jure Pontificio[2]. Atque ex his demum par est ut conjectemus Juris Caesarei usum illum, qualiscunque fuisset, apud Juris Anglicani peritos atque in tribunalibus heic regiis pristinum sub Edwardi tertii initia seu circa tempus quo Skipwithus ille ipsique coaevi nomina Juris Anglicani studiis primo dedere, in desuetudinem prorsus abiisse.

Caput Nonum

    I. Effectus usus qualiscunque Juris Caesarei, per intervallum ante ostensum, apud Anglos qualisnam esset. In regimine publico quod civile dicitur, nullus iis admissus.

    II. Eorum tunc Juris Caesarei in regimine publico usus Improbatio.

    III. Singularis eorum Juris Patrii seu Communis, ita vulgo dicti, aestimatio atque in eo adhaesio, in regimine publico, pertinax; Caesareo interim cancellorum aliquot velut angustiis permissis. Obiter de Clerici, Clericatus et Clergie nominibus.

I. Quali vero sensu Bractonius, Thorntonius, Fletaeque autor Juris Caesarei locos, more solenni indicatos, adhibuerint, jam ante[3] diximus. Neque alio sane reliqui, quorum sub Edwardo secundo testimonia allata; quod itidem dicendum de jurisconsultis nostratibus aliis, quiqui fuerint, eo jure, sive in studiis, sive in discussionibus scriptisve, sive in judiciorum ratione utentibus per intervallum illud, a Stephani nempe regis medio aut circiter seu ab jure illo primitus huc allato usque in Edwardi tertii initia, seu per annos quasi ducentos. Quod autem ad usus ejusmodi heic tunc effectum attinet; quicquid sane vellent cuperentve jurisconsultorum nostratium illi quibus ita utcunque adhibitum est jus illud, id certum est, in regimine publico quod civile vocitamus nihil omnino inde (de tribunalibus regiis reliquisque non pontificiis, exceptis tantummodo binis ante memoratis maritimo et militari, loquor) consecutum est mutationis,

---

[1] Tit. de Operis Novi Nunt. l. 20. Praetor.
[2] Extr. tit. de Novi Operis Nunt. c. 1.
[3] Cap. 3, § 5.

IX I ENGLISH IGNORANCE OF ROMAN LAW 161

hibitio Novi Operis' and is quite unknown to English law. Nor did Shareshull show himself fully cognizant of its meaning when he said that in canon law (which adopted it from civil law) it means a restitution. An inhibition is not a restitution. It is obvious nevertheless from both Pandects and canon law that by the interdict the aggrieved party was entitled to complete restitution, *i.e.* the demolition of whatever was put up contrary to the inhibition.

This apparent by Edward III's reign

Hence we may conclude that the original use of civil law, whatever it was, fell into complete desuetude, among exponents of English law, about the beginning of Edward III's reign.

Chapter IX

I. The result of this use of civil law in England. It was never admitted into public government.

II. English aversion to its use in matters of government.

III. The remarkable respect among the English for their common law and their constant adherence thereto, some part being allowed to civil law though within narrow bounds. Incidentally, of the names Cleric and Clergy.

Civil law of no force in English government

I. We have already indicated the sense in which Bracton, Thornton and the author of *Fleta* used their civil law borrowings, and the same may be applied to all other English lawyers who utilised this jurisprudence in the period from Stephen to Edward III, whether in their studies, writings and debates, or as a canon in their decisions. As regards the effect of this use, whatever may have been the desires of our lawyers, it is certain that it produced no change in our civil or public government—we are speaking of royal and non-ecclesiastical courts and excepting the already mentioned Courts of the Marshal and of the Admiralty. The votaries of the civil law, whether

neque usus ejusmodi effectum revera fuisse alium quam ut ii qui sic uterentur, ejusdem aut peritos aut sciolos aut amantiores se inde exhiberent aut, ut illud simul cum Anglicano in praxi forensi, accedente autoritate publica, admitteretur, cupientiores, non omnino ut in regiminis civilis partes velut vim obtinens revera reciperetur. Et gens ipsa tunc Anglicana ac qui judiciis in ea praeerant tribunalium jam dictorum (in quibus etiam ipse Bractonius et Thorntonius et forte etiam Fletae autor) morum patriorum, id est, Juris Communis Angliae semper etiam per intervallum illud tenacissimi fuere; adeoque ut neque locutionis, scriptionis aut agendi formulam aliquam in tabulas publicas ex Caesareo, quantum observaverim, desumi admittive vellent. Tabulas scilicet publicas actionum, exceptionum, transactionum, judiciorum, aliarumque rerum civilium et quotidianarum in tribunalibus illis gestarum per intervallum illud ferme integrum etiamnum in archivis habemus, in quibus haud Juris Caesarei ullatenus tunc admissi vestigia occurrunt magis atque in tabulis id genus publicis aevi sequentis nostrique, in quibus nihil omnino Caesareum redolet, utpote ab ejusdem et lingua et sensu passim discrepantibus, atque vetustatem styli forensis Anglicani qualis etiam fuit ea ante Stephani regis seu Juris Caesarei huc allati tempora, prae se ubique satis ferentibus. Adeoque non e scriptis Bractonianis, Thorntonianis aut Fletae autoris (in quibus usus heic ejus modi Juris qualis ante ostensus est reperitur) aut e laudatis more solenni locis Pandectarum in annalibus illis Edwardi secundi juridicis, de effectu usus heic ejusdem qualiscunque est dijudicandum, sed plane ex tabulis jam dictis illius intervalli publicis seu archivis, quibus adjungas etiam innumeras decisiones atque agendi heic per idem intervallum formulas, partim typis editas et passim prostantes, partim manuscriptas, uti et rescriptorum promptuarium quod Registrum Brevium vocitamus, quae ex intima Anglis vetustate ad posteros transmissa vix vocabulum habent ex Jure Caesareo sibi admixtum; cum interim in consistorium pontificiorum ac tribunalium maritimi et militaris (in quae receptum jus illud) agendi formulis innumera inde desumta comperiantur. Nec sane citationes illae pauculae in scriptoribus illis nostratibus, illaeve forenses quae in juridicis Edwardi secundi annalibus occurrunt, majori videntur mihi argumento esse, Jus Caesareum in regimen heic publicum tunc receptum esse, velut quod vim revera atque ex autoritate publica aliquam obtineret (quicquid sentirent illi qui illud sic adhiberent) quam Platonis, Aristotelis, Demosthenis, Ciceronis, Senecae, Plutarchi, id genus aliorum loca obiter atque saepenumero apud jurisperitos Gallicanos adhiberi (quod ex

EFFECTS OF ROMAN LAW INFLUENCE

expert or amateur or smatterers, may have wished that by public authority it would be merged in English legal practice, but they did not desire that it should have any force in public administration. The English nation and its judges (with whom may be numbered Bracton, Thornton and perhaps the author of *Fleta*) were so tenacious of their common law that, so far as I can find, they allowed no civil law formula—whether of speech, writing or pleading—to enter their public records. In our archives we still preserve, for almost the whole of that period, the official records of actions, pleadings, agreements and judgments, together with other civil and everyday matters transacted in this country, but there one finds hardly any more evidence of civil law, as then accepted, than is to be found in the same records of the succeeding age or of our own day, which, so far from savouring of Roman law, in language or meaning, recall rather the archaic style of English law as it was before Stephen's time.

The 'Register of Writs' shows no Roman law influence

Our estimate of the effect of this use of civil law cannot be gathered from the writings of Bracton, Thornton or *Fleta*, nor from the passages in the Pandects quoted in the Year Books of Edward II, but must be inferred from the already-mentioned public records and the many judgments and formulae of proceedings in that period (some printed, and easily purchasable by anyone, some still in MS.). To this must be added the Register of Writs[1], dating from a remote past, which contains scarcely one civil law expression.

Roman law influence in certain exceptional jurisdictions

On the other hand in the canon law courts and in those of the Marshal and Admiralty, the forms of procedure have innumerable such expressions[2].

Civilians and Canonists sometimes act in a consultative capacity

But these few citations by English writers and the civil law analogies quoted in Edward II's Year Books no more prove that civil law was admitted into our public administration than do numerous quotations by French lawyers from Plato, Aristotle, Demosthenes, etc., prove that such classics have a judicial authority

[1] Printed in 1531. Fitzherbert's compendium—the *Natura Brevium*—was first published in 1534.
[2] See Holdsworth, *History of English Law* (3rd ed.) v, 3–154, 'Developments outside the sphere of the Common Law.'

editis eorum actionibus judiciisque numerosis scimus) solita argumento sunt eorum effatis aut sententiis vim inesse apud Gallos judiciariam. Id tamen praetereundum non est tum seculis de quibus locuti sumus tum insequentibus[1] adhiberi solitos audirique etiam in tribunalibus Jure Anglicano alias utentibus, jurisconsultos Caesareos Pontificiosque quoties in actionum ex Jure Anglicano institutarum discussione orta fuerit incideritque quaestio ex Jure sive Caesareo sive Pontificio terminanda, veluti matrimonialis, testamentaria, aliave ex sua natura ad fora seu consistoria quibus jura illa in paucis permissa sunt pertinens. Sed vero ejusmodi usus jurisconsultorum illorum seu juris quod profitentur in tribunalibus jam dictis haud alius est quam ut Grammaticorum, Medicorum, aliorum ejusmodi quoties quaestio ex horum arte decidenda inter litigandum forte fuerit suborta.

II. Causa unde haud major aliusve atque jam ostensus est Juris Caesarei heic qualitercunque admisti adhibitique effectus haberetur per intervallum illud quo sic eo usi sunt etiam publice jurisconsulti nostrates, ex ratione pendet duplici. Altera est, Juris Caesarei apud majores tunc nostros (qua regimen publicum illud omnino spectaret) aperta ac publica Improbatio. Altera Juris Anglicani quod Commune vocitamus ejusdemque principiorum, qua gentis hujus genio ab intima antiquitate adaptata sunt, singularis aestimatio, atque inde nec immerito, in eodem adhaesio constans et sane pertinax. Quod ad improbationem ejusmodi attinet, exhibet ejus quidem non exiguum specimen Stephani regis edictum ante memoratum in leges Caesareas earumque praelectorem heic primum Rogerium Vacarium, uti etiam in Henrici tertii[2] scholarum Londini legum earundem inhibitione ante ostensa. Accedat etiam, sub idem tempus, in comitiis scilicet ordinum Mertonensibus, responsum publice datum esse quo satis innui videtur Ordines tunc timuisse ne Jura Caesarea ejusque capita aliqua sive per se sive per Canones Pontificios, quibus, etiam ut hodieque, involuta erant, obtrusa, Juri Anglicano moribusque patriis ac majorum multorum seculorum ratione subnixis indeque receptissimis fraudi forent. In causa nimirum illa singulari[3] qua episcopi rogarunt ut liberi in concubinatu nati per subsequens matrimonium fierent legitimi (quod non admittit Jus Anglicanum) responderunt 'nolle se leges Angliae mutare quae hucusque usitatae sunt ac approbatae,' quasi sane Caesareas designassent in regiminis haereditatum et

---

[1] 7 Hen. VI, fol. 116, etc.
[2] Rot. Claus. 19 Hen. III, membr. 16, seu anno 1234.
[3] Stat. Merton. cap. 9, 20 Hen. III, seu 1235. Vide Bracton. lib. 5, cap. 19 et Fletam, lib. 1, cap. 15, §3, et lib. 6, cap. 39.

among French jurists. It should not be forgotten however that in this and the succeeding period both civil and canon lawyers were sometimes summoned to and occasionally heard in cases which, though instituted according to English law, gave rise to a point that had to be referred either to civil or canon law, *e.g.* a question of marriage or a testamentary matter or in fact anything pertaining to those courts admitting civil or canon law in some respects. Such a service is no different from that rendered by grammarians or physicians or such like whenever in a lawsuit a question arises that must be referred to their professional opinion.

English aversion from Civil law principles in government

II. There are two reasons why civil law, however mixed with our own and quoted with it, had no greater effect in this period of its public use by our lawyers. One is the unconcealed aversion which our ancestors had to it, so far as it concerns principles of government. The other is the remarkable esteem in which the English or common law was held, and our constant faithfulness to it as something immemorially fitted to the genius of the nation.

As regards the first point, Stephen's edict against Vacarius and the teaching of civil law is a good instance; other illustrations are Henry III's already mentioned ban on the London Law Schools and the public reply given by the parliament of Merton—'we will not change the laws of England which hitherto have been used and approved'—to the request of the bishops that children born out of wedlock should (contrary to English law) be legitimated by the subsequent marriage of their parents. By this the Estates obviously showed their dread lest the imperial law, or any of its enactments, whether introduced directly or through the Papal Canons (with which, then, as now, the imperial law was entangled), should do injury to English law and native customs that were supported by many centuries of reasoned use and were therefore most fully admitted. The Estates also implied that the civil law had no validity in the public regulation of matters of inheritance and succession.

successionum publici rationem non omnino admittendas. Id quidem fatendum, episcopos rogationis suae rationem velut e Jure depromsisse Pontificio; 'quia Ecclesia habet tales pro legitimis'; quod quidem ante etiam in Jure Pontificio se sic habuisse scimus ex rescripto Alexandri tertii[1] compluribus ante annis in Angliam ad episcopum Exoniensem misso aliisque. At vero sententiam illam de subsequentis matrimonii vi, primo ex Jure Caesareo seu Justinianeo[2] desumtam in Pontificium esse palam erat; adeoque ne tam insignis fieret in Anglia legum, circa successiones in defunctorum bona, mutatio, qualem voluere episcopi ecclesiae jura heic sed ex corpore plane Caesareo mutuata obtendentes, ac ne ab exemplo hujusmodi aliae, ut fieri amat, facilius introducerentur mutationes, unde etiam potestatem aliquam Caesaream in Anglos agnosci forte existimaretur, rejectum est quod ita est obtrusum, quasi dixissent 'Legum Caesarearum nec caput hoc nec alia heic admittenda volumus,' aut 'nolumus mutare leges Anglicanas legibus Caesareis,' seu, quod idem est, Pontificiis canonibus inde desumtis. Nam simpliciter se nolle Angliae leges seu earum capita aliqua mutare in animo non habuere. Ipsis enim eisdem comitiis leges Anglicanas novarunt adeoque variatim mutarunt; in re scilicet Dotali, Pupillari, Usuraria, Praescriptionibus, aliis, ut in comitiorum capitulis reliquis cuique est videre. Sub idem autem ipsum, comitiorum nempe Mertonensium tempus, gravissima (ut obiter id adnotem) de Jure illo Anglicano quo pro legitimis non admissi sunt sic ante matrimonium nati, querela habetur Roberti Capitonis (Grossetest) episcopi Lincolniensis qui abrogari illud debere, probare[3] ex Jure Canonico, Naturali, Divino ac Caesareo operose conatur; in literis scilicet ad Walterum de Ralegh tribunalis regii praesidem quem enixe hortatus est ut in causa, quantum posset, ipse esset ut jus illud heic mutaretur. Etiam audisse se, ait, antiquum apud Anglos morem obtinuisse ut ejusmodi liberi pro legitimis haberentur, signumque ejusce rei seu symbolum fuisse positionem eorum sub pallio seu stragulo in ipsis matrimonii solennibus super parentem utrunque extento, unde tunc extracti illi velut denuo, adeoque ex conjugatis, nati haberentur. Verba sunt, 'et ut seniorum relatione didici, consuetudo etiam in hoc regno antiquitus obtenta et adprobata tales legitimos habuit et haeredes, unde in signum legitimationis nati ante matrimonium consuerunt poni sub pallio super parentes eorum extento in matrimonii solemnizatione,' id est

---

[1] Append. ad Concil. Lateran. 1181, part 33, cap. 1, et cap. 6, tanta est. Extr. tit. qui filii sint legitimi.
[2] L. 5, Divi Constant. C. tit. de Naturalibus Liberis.   [3] Epist. 23 MS.

PARLIAMENT AND CIVIL LAW

The bishops based their request on what appeared to be a canon law principle, the Church regarding such children as legitimate, and we know from pope Alexander III's rescript to the bishop of Exeter, as well as from other sources, that this was the canon law rule, but the principle came originally from Justinian, *i.e.* from the civil law[1]. Lest such a great change should be made in the law of succession as was recommended by the bishops, who were using a civil law doctrine in canon law dress, and lest such a change should open the door to others, whereby imperial law might be accepted as having force in England, the suggestion was rejected as if the Estates had said 'we will admit neither this nor that principle of civil law.' It is plain that the objection was not simply to changing English laws, for in the same parliament several innovations were made in matters of dower, wardship, usury, prescriptions and other things, as can be seen in the other chapters of the acts of this parliament[2].

Grosseteste and legitimation 'per subsequens matrimonium'

About the same time a vigorous protest was made by Robert Capito or Grosseteste, bishop of Lincoln, because in English law children born before marriage cannot be legitimated. In a letter[3] to chief justice Walter of Raleigh[4], he earnestly exhorted him to do something to change this law and supported his elaborate arguments from canon, natural, divine and civil law. He describes his recollection of an ancient English custom: 'I have heard from old persons that there existed an ancient and approved custom whereby such children were held legitimate and could become heirs. As a symbol of this, it was customary in the marriage ceremony to put the children under a cloak extended also over the parents[5].' But that Raleigh

[1] C. 5. 27.
[2] Statutes of the Realm (1810), I, 1–4.
[3] R. Grosseteste, *Epistolae* (Rolls Series, 1861), 76 ff.
[4] A famous judge, afterwards bishop of Norwich and later of Winchester.
[5] There are numerous references to this in continental literature; see F. Philipp, *Disputatio Juridica de legitimatione per subsequens matrimonium* (Leipzig, 1693) and J. Lochner, *Exercitatio academica de antiquo ritu legitimandi liberos per pallium* (Altdorf, 1697). This procedure was said to have been devised by Constantine; there is mention of the 'velamen' in Gratian and in Ambrose. In his *De Uxore Hebraica* (II, 27) Selden refers to a description of the ritual in an old Salisbury manual. In Germany the children so legitimated were called 'Die Mantel kinder.'

dum nuptiis copulabantur. Sed hoc ut nihil rejecit Raleghius, ut liquet ex epistola ad eum Roberti proxima[1] eadem de re. 'Praeterea,' inquit, 'ad confirmandam hanc legem quod bastardus sub pallio supra parentes nubentes extento positus surgit bastardus, induxisti testimonium Richardi de Lucy' (celeberrimi sub Henrico secundo Justitiarii Angliae) 'cujus testimonium quantam et qualem habeat comparationem ad testimonia Divinae Scripturae et Canonicae contrarium testificantia lippis patet et tonsoribus.' Certe consuetudinem ejusmodi in nuptiarum solennibus unquam apud majores nostros obtinuisse nondum didici, nedum inde natalium aliquam consecutam esse restitutionem. Ceterum ritum eundem ipsum, sub Richardo secundo, quando autoritate Parlamentaria[2] legitimi facti sunt liberi Joannis Gandavensis Ducis Lancastriae e Catharina uxore tertia ante matrimonium suscepti, idque in ipsis comitiis adhibitum, alicubi legisse me memini. Accedat ad jam dicta de legum Caesarearum heic in illo de quo loquimur intervallo improbatione publica, gravissimam in illustrissimo illo de successione in regnum Scotiae, sub Edwardo primo, judicio Norhamiae[3], in provincia Dunelmensi habito ortam esse quaestionem de juris genere secundum quod res decidenda esset. Utrum Anglicano scilicet, an Scoticano, an Caesareo veluti Gentium, cum a rege Angliae ut superiori tunc domino Scotiae, pro tribunali competitores essent audiendi. Et demum Caesarei in eo usum non omnino admittendum, unanimes qui intererant pronuntiarunt, ne inde majestatis Anglicanae juri fieret detrimentum. Tantundem inter alia olim excerpsi e tractatu veteri MS. cui titulus, 'Quomodo Edwardus Rex Angliae constituit Joannem de Balliolo Regem Scotiae.' Tunc enim regio nomine Rogerus de Brabanzon loco jam dicto secundum illud judicium tulit. Atque huc sane aliquatenus spectat illud Edwardi secundi edictum quo notariis publicis sive a Caesare sive a comitibus ejus Palatinis creatis autoritas heic denegabatur, 'eo quod regnum Angliae ab omni subjectione Imperiali sit liberrimum' ut in publicis legitur tabulis[4]. Adeoque non est quod non sentiamus etiam illo in

---

[1] Epist. 24.
[2] Rot. Par. 20 Rich. II, num. 28.
[3] Anno 19 Ed. I, seu 1292.
[4] Dors. Claus. 13 Ed. II, membran. 6, in schedula.

rejected this argument may be gathered from the bishop's next letter[1] to him on the same subject: 'In confirmation of the law that a bastard, placed under a pall covering his parents at their wedding ceremony, emerges still a bastard, you have quoted the opinion of Richard de Lucy [a famous justiciar of Henry II]. What comparison his evidence bears to Sacred and Canonical Scripture which testifies to the contrary, is evident even to gossip-mongers.'

Performance of a rite in Parliament

I have myself never found evidence of the authenticity of such a custom at our ancestors' weddings, still less of any legitimacy so acquired, but I remember reading somewhere of the performance of this rite in parliament, in Richard II's reign, when the children of John of Gaunt born of his third wife Catherine before her marriage were legitimated by parliamentary authority[2].

Edward I and the Scottish succession

Another instance of this public aversion from civil law is to be found in the question arising from Edward I's famous decision at Norham regulating the Scottish succession. The question was: by what law, English, Scottish or Civil (as the Law of Nations) the matter should be determined, the claimants appearing before the English king as suzerain of Scotland. It was unanimously decided that the civil law should not be used lest anything prejudicial to the English prerogative should thereby ensue. In accordance with this Roger of Brabazon gave judgment in the king's name. These, with other things, I have gathered from an old MS.[3]: 'How Edward, king of England, constituted John Balliol king of Scotland.'

Edward II's edict

Witness also Edward II's edict[4] denying authority in this country to public notaries[5] appointed by the emperor or his counts palatine 'because England is completely free from every kind of subjection to the emperor'—these are the words in the public records, and there

[1] Grosseteste, *Epistolae* (Rolls Series), 96.
[2] The legitimation of the Beauforts, *Rotuli Parliamentorum*, III, 343 (20 Richard II). The account of the ceremony here referred to cannot be traced.
[3] MS. Claudius, D. VI, 6.
[4] Calendar of Close Rolls, Edward II, 1318–1323, p. 186.
[5] The functions of the public notaries were similar to those of the *tabelliones*; they were at first appointed by pope or emperor, but lords having seignorial jurisdiction, bishops and communes acquired the right of making appointments. In Edward II's reign there are numerous complaints of the number of persons claiming to be public notaries 'imperiali auctoritate' (*Registrum Palatinum Dunelmense* in Rolls Series, I, 253). An example of a patent licensing English notaries 'per pennam, calamarium et chartam' will be found in Selden's *Titles of Honour* (in *Opera*, ed. Wilkins, III, 466–7). After Edward II's inhibition we hear only of apostolic notaries in England. For the institution in Scotland, see J. M. Thomson, *The Public Records of Scotland*, 87–8 and 97.

intervallo, eos qui summae rerum heic praeerant, idem ipsum sensisse quod Richardus secundus rex ac proceres in Comitiis. Et eorum scilicet jussu, in tabulis dicitur publicis[1] 'que le royalme d'Engleterre ne estoit devant ces heures ne a l'entent du roy nostre dit seignior et seigniors du parlament unques ne serra rule ne governe per la ley Civil.' Necdum sane didici quanam ex ratione scripserit Joannes Fortiscutius[2], Capitalis sub Henrico Sexto Justitiarius, quosdam Angliae reges legibus suis minime delectatos sategisse proinde 'leges Civiles ad Angliae regimen inducere et patrias leges repudiare fuisse conatos.' Regum nostrorum quempiam id fecisse nullibi lego. Rationem quidem reddit ille, curnam id fecerint, Legis scilicet Regiae (de qua ante diximus) gratia. Sed illud interim omnino fecisse eorum aliquem ubinam compertum? Quod vero legitur apud Joannem Sarisburiensem[3], 'nullas leges credidisse aliquos civilibus praeferendas,' inque eis inprimis illud de absoluta Principis potestate, quae in Lege habetur Regia, observandum, de assentatoribus illius seculi ex genere hieratico aliquot dictum est, non de gente Anglicana aut de aliis qui judiciis heic tunc praefuere. Atque praetereundum non est, leges criminales a Richardo primo (qui et Oleronianarum autor habetur) etiam navium suarum classi praescriptas fuisse a Caesareis diversissimas, nec quid in praefectorum ejus codicillis quorum exemplar legitur apud Rogerium Hovedenum[4] et Matthaeum Parisium[5] de legibus hisce omnino contineri. Adeo ut nondum in causis maritimis apud nos earum quidem tunc fuerit admissio.

III. Quod ad singularem per intervallum illud Juris Anglicani seu Patrii quod Commune vocamus aestimationem inque illo adhesionem spectat; cernitur quidem illa satis in ipsis Articulis Coronae et Placitis idque genus aliis quorum sub Henrico secundo et Richardo primo habemus specimina apud Hovedenum et Parisium, atque etiam in jurisconsultis nostratibus qui per idem intervallum scripsere, maxime autem in tabulis omnimodis ejusdem intervalli publicis. Parile eliciendum ex juramento ipso

---

[1] Rot. Parlam. 11 Rich. II et videsis Not. in Fortisc. pag. 41, adde Plac. coram rege Mich. 8 Hen. IV, rot. 72, cas. Pedington et Otterworth.
[2] De Laud. Leg. Angliae, cap. 33 et 34.
[3] Policratic. lib. 7, cap. 20.
[4] Annal. part 2, pag. 666, edit. Franc.
[5] Anno 1190.

is abundant reason also for assuming that, in this period, those who directed public affairs shared the sentiments of Richard II and his Lords of Parliament, thus expressed in the Rolls: 'that the kingdom of England has never been governed by the civil law and, by resolve of the king and the lords of parliament, it never would[1].'

Fortescue's remarkable statement

I could never discover the authority for Sir John Fortescue's statement that some English kings, not satisfied with native laws, attempted to introduce the civil laws into the government and repudiate English laws[2]. The reason assigned is that it was done for the sake of the Lex Regia, but where is the evidence of this? As for John of Salisbury's statement[3] that 'some believed no laws could be better than the civil laws,' this has reference to the absolutist element in the Lex Regia and was said about some priestly flatterers who were neither of the English nation nor of the English bench.

Richard I's maritime laws

Nor should it be forgotten that the criminal laws prescribed for his navy by Richard I (the reputed author of the Code of Oleron)[4] were very different from the civil law. Of the latter there is no trace to be found in the instructions of his commanders—as seen in the copy reproduced by Roger Hoveden[5] and Matthew Paris[6]. So the civil law was not then used even in our maritime laws.

English devotion to Common law

III. The singular devotion to the English common law in this period may be inferred from such documents as the Articles and Pleas of the Crown (there are specimens for the reigns of Henry II and Richard I in Hoveden and Matthew Paris), the writings of contemporary lawyers, and, best of all, the public records. It may be

---

[1] *Rot. Parl.* III, 236 and 244. This principle was laid down in the matter of the appeal of the Lords Appellant in 1388; cf. also, *ibid.* III, 170, where, when Richard proposes conditions of peace with France, the Commons complain that they do not understand civil law terms.

[2] *De Laudibus Legum Angliae*, ch. XXXIII. Fortescue may have been thinking of Richard II, the twenty-seventh accusation against whom was that he had allowed the Court of the Constable and Marshal to oppress persons accused of sedition. Coke (*Inst.* III, 35) refers to attempts to introduce civil law principles into the government of Henry VI. Selden is probably right in saying that there is no evidence to support Fortescue's statement. It was one of the articles of indictment against Wolsey that he had tried to subvert common law in favour of civil law (for a disproof of this accusation see Holdsworth, *History of English Law*, 3rd ed., V, 222).

[3] *Policraticus*, ed. Webb, II, 186.

[4] The *Fasciculus de Superioritate Maris* (1339) contains a document stating that Richard I promulgated the Code of Oleron while on passage from the Holy Land; see *Select Pleas in the Court of Admiralty* (ed. Marsden), I, XXXII.

[5] *Chronica Rogeri de Hoveden* (Rolls Series, 1870), III, 36.

[6] *Chronica Majora* (Rolls Series), II, 362.

solenni quo obstringi etiam tunc soliti illi qui judiciis praeficiebantur. Joannes ille Sarisburiensis[1] de tempore Henrici secundi; 'et quidem judices sacramento legibus alligantur jurati, quia omnimodo judicium cum veritate et legum observatione disponent.' Quod sane utcunque velut ex Justiniani[2] verbis sumatur, nihilominus ab Anglo et in Anglia dictum, de legibus patriis seu Jure nostro consuetudinario id est 'legibus Angliae et consuetudinibus rectis,' quae illius seculi[3] phrasis erat, intelligendum. De quibus etiam alibi ille[4], 'sed et leges ipsae et consuetudines quibus nunc vivitur, insidiae sunt et laquei calumniantium. Verborum tendiculae proponuntur, et aucupationes syllabarum; vae simplici qui syllabizare non novit.' Atque in formula juramenti quod subibant illis in seculis judices in regimen publicum constituti tam ex genere hieratico quam alii, expressim continebatur 'se judicaturos secundum legem et consuetudinem regni' ut liquet ex juramento a judicibus sub Henrico tertio in regimen publicum constitutis ad morem solennem praestito. Verba inter alia sunt[5] 'bona fide procurabunt quod magnus sicut parvus judicabitur secundum legem et consuetudinem regni.' Quod puto ideo signantius adjectum, ne ex Jure Caesareo nuper advecto et a nonnullis, maxime ex genere hieratico, proculdubio perquam adamato atque prae Anglicano in pretio habito, judicia omnino ab illis exercerentur. Inde etiam inolevit locutionis formula illa Lex Terrae, qua, uti etiam legis et consuetudinis regni nomine, disertius designaretur lex juxta quam vivendum judicandumque, sic ab Lege Caesarea, Civili vulgo nobis et tunc simpliciter dicta, omnino distincta disterminataque. Inde Legis Terrae in hanc rem mentio in Magna Charta[6] alibique singularis et legum antiquarum et consuetudinum Angliae in summis illis inter Joannem[7] regem et proceres dissidiis. Alia ejusmodi vocabula frequentius apud majores nostros adhibita, ut legem aliarum adeoque Caesarearum quae Anglicanis tunc velut imminebant, in regimine publico usus praecluderetur. Verba etiam tantundem significantia in juramentis a regibus nostris illius intervalli (uti et temporis insequentis) in eorum coronatione praestitis legibusque ab eis latis expressim occurrunt, unde negata est Caesareo heic Juri in regimine publico, utcunque subinde adhibito, tunc vis omnimoda. Atque ex hisce certe minus mirum est ejusdem qualemcunque usum

[1] Policratic. lib. 5, cap. 12.
[2] L. 14, C. tit. de Judiciis.
[3] Matth. Paris. circa initium Richardi primi.
[4] Policratic. lib. 5, cap. 16.
[5] Anno 1257 seu 41 Hen. III in Annalibus Burtonensibus MS.
[6] Cap. 29. [7] Matth. Paris. ann. 1217.

inferred from the solemn oath by which judges were then bound. Writing of Henry II's time, John of Salisbury[1] says: 'The judges are bound to the laws by an oath so that they must always give judgment in accordance with truth and with obedience to the law.' Spoken by an Englishman in England, these words, though taken from Justinian, must have meant 'the laws and admitted customs of England,' as the phrase then was. Elsewhere[2] the same author writes: 'the laws and customs which we now use are snares set by legal tricksters. Little verbal catches and quibbles are propounded: woe to the simple one who cannot spell.'

Lex Terrae

The form of oath taken by the judges, whether cleric or lay, contained—as appears from the undertaking exacted of those officials in Henry III's reign—these words, that 'in good faith they would judge high and low according to the law and custom of the country.' In my opinion these words were expressly inserted in order to prevent their giving any judgment based on the principles of the civil law which, as a recent introduction, was doubtless much esteemed, and preferred to English law, especially by the clergy. Hence the phrase 'Lex Terrae' became established and this, with the expression 'Laws and Customs of the Realm,' came to mean the law by which we are to live and be judged in contrast to and distinction from the imperial law. So too the phrase 'Lex Terrae[3]' in Magna Carta; and elsewhere, in the contests between John and his barons, the expression 'ancient laws and customs of England' is met with. Such words are frequently found in the past as indicating our ancestors' exclusion of the civil law from public administration lest it might threaten the supremacy of English law. There are similar phrases both in their laws and in the coronation oaths of our sovereigns in this and the succeeding period, whence it may be inferred that, whatever reference was made to it, civil law had then no public sanction in this country.

[1] *Policraticus*, ed. Webb, I, 334.   [2] *Ibid.* I, 350–1.
[3] See *ante*, p. 141, n. 3.

sic ut ante ostendimus in tribunalibus Jure Anglicano utentibus tandem prorsus evanuisse. Id vero ex eo etiam facilius evenit, quod sub idem tempus quo sic evanuit ejusmodi juris usus, mos alius pariter apud nos desiit, judices scilicet regios ex genere hieratico, veluti episcopis, abbatibus, decanis id genus aliis constituendi. Dein etiam, vix aut ne vix quidem eorum quisquam ex illo genere, cujus pars eminentior in Academiis Juri tam Caesareo quam Pontificio plerunque incubuit, tribunalium jam dictorum (excepta tantum cancellaria Angliae) judiciis praefectus est, utcunque ministri illis ipsis tribunalibus inservientes aliique in regimine publico conspicui ex illo genere etiam tunc et diu postea desumi[1] solerent, unde eorundem ministri, qui per secula aliquot ex illo genere non omnino fuere, uti et id genus alii, etiamnum Clerici forte nuncupati. Sed vero licet priscis in seculis Christianis[2], etiam et scriptoribus ecclesiasticis, Clerici et Clericatus nomen ad eos tantum qui divino cultu ministeria religionis impendunt denotandos eorumque innuendam dignitatem adhibeatur, quo sensu etiam vulgo hodieque retinetur[3], nihilominus apud Gallos Anglosque tam veteres quam recentiores usurpatum est de eis etiam qui quocunque doctrinae seu scientiae genere pollent; veluti Philosophis, Mathematicis, Historicis, Jurisprudentibus, Formulariis, id genus aliis, nec solum de Theologis seu qui ex genere sunt hieratico. Unde vox illa 'Clergie' pro ipsa scientia seu doctrina generatim sumta, et Clericus pro sciente ac docto. Hoc sensu Grandclerc, Beauclerc, Mauclerc Gallis[4] adhibitum, uti et Clergie et Grand Clergie pro summa doctrina. Et fragmentum[5] habetur pervetusti libri rhythmis Gallicanis conscripti qui dicitur 'il livre de Clergie en Romaunz, ki est appellez le ymage del munde,' cui praeter aliqua de creatione praelibata nihil inerat nisi quae ad Astronomiam, Geographiam, artes alias liberales attinet. Et capitis sexti libri primi titulus est, 'de trois manieres de genz ke li philosophie poserent au mounde, e coment Clergie vient en Fraunce.' Id est, quomodo doctrina et scientiae liberales in Franciam venerint. Et postea,

> Ki bien veult entendre cest livre
> E savoir coment il doit vivre
> E apprendre tiel Clergie
> Dunt meuz naudra tut sa vie.

[1] Vide Henric. Spelman. in Epist. Dedicator. ad Concilia Eccles. Brit.
[2] L. 2. Cod. Theod. tit. de Episcopis et Clericis. Justin. Novell. 123. Isidor. Orig. lib. 7.
[3] Vide Lindwood ad tit. de Temp. Ordinand. C. quia quidam, verb. Clericum.
[4] Pasquier, Des Recherchez de la France, lib. 8, ch. 13.
[5] MS. in Bibl. Cottoniana.

The names 'Cleric' and 'Clergy'

Its eventual disappearance from our common law courts was partly due to the change whereby judges ceased to be chosen exclusively from the clergy. The more distinguished of the latter generally studied civil and canon law at the universities but, after this period, scarcely any of their number presided in these courts, except Chancery, although then and for long after the hierarchy continued to supply officials for such tribunals as well as statesmen for the realm. Hence the application even now of the term 'clerks' to officials and functionaries who for ages have been chosen mainly from laymen. Although in early Christian times and among ecclesiastical writers, the names Cleric and Clergy were used to distinguish those exercising the sacred office of religion—in this sense it is commonly used to-day—yet the name has been applied in ancient and modern times, both in England and France, to persons eminent in some study or science, such as philosophy, mathematics, history, etc., and has not always been confined to theology nor to priests. Hence the word 'Clergie' is often used for the science or doctrine and 'Cleric' for the expert or scholar. In this sense the French use the words Grandclerc, Beauclerc, Mauclerc and the words 'clergie' and 'grand clergie' for erudition. There exists a fragment of an old Norman-French verse composition[1] entitled 'Il livre de Clergie en Romaunz, ki est appellez le ymage del munde,' which, except for a few remarks on the Creation, is concerned solely with astronomy, geography and other liberal arts. This identification between 'Clergie' and the arts and sciences[2] is definitely implied in the title of the sixth book and elsewhere.

---

[1] It is by Gautier de Metz. Selden's copy is in the Bodleian (MS. Selden, supra, 74).
[2] For the use of 'chierico' in old Italian to indicate a man of learning, see Giovanni Gentile, *I problemi della scolastica e il pensiero italiano* (Bari, 1913), p. 17. In eighteenth-century Scotland the word 'deacon' was sometimes used in a similar sense; the hero of John Galt's *The Provost* confessed that he was 'nae deacon in the deid languages.'

Hinc Henricus rex noster primus, Belloclericus seu Beauclerc dictus. Et Galfridus Chaucerus Philosophos Graecorum veterum Clericos appellat.

> Sometime in Greece that noble region
> There were eight Clerks of full great science,
> Philosophers of notable discretion....

Alibi tantundem facit, nec raro. Cum igitur in tribunalibus ac consistoriis omnimodis, praeter judices, ministri sint, atque horum alii Scribarum, Actuariorum et qui id genus alia subeant munera quae sine doctrina qualicunque praestari nequeunt, nomine veniant, alii Ostiarii, Lictores, Praecones sint, jussis tantum citra artem exsequendis inservientes; clericorum nomen non his sed illis ob doctrinam seu scientiam seu artem illam qualemcunque atque etiam amanuensibus et ab epistolis aliis tribui est solitum; uti item Ephesiorum $\gamma\rho\alpha\mu\mu\alpha\tau\epsilon\hat{\iota}$ in Actis Apostolorum[1] seu Scribae, quem Town Clerk in versione dicimus Anglicana, translatione proculdubio facta ab hieratico genere cui primo proprium erat et in quo numerosiores semper fuere, quam in alio aliquo, qui scientia qualicunque ejusve obtentu claruere. Sic Chaldaei, Auguris, Aruspicis nomina, sic alia nec ita pauca translata ad eos qui revera ipsis, si originem spectes, non omnino continentur. Sed demum ex ante ostensis satis liquet undenam in cancellos quibus est juxta superius dicta coarctatum, jus illud apud nos fuerit redactum. Et de his satis superque.

Caput Decimum

   I. De tempore autoris. Nec sub Edwardo tertio, nec Secundo scripsisse.
  II. Sub Edwardo rege primo Commentarium hunc scriptum.
 III. Fletae nominis ratio.
  IV. De provisione omnium regum Christianorum circa regum alienationes, in Commentario hoc memorata.

Ad Fletam ipsum redimus. Restat ut de tempore quo compositus seu ab autore absolutus est commentarius hic et de nominis ratione videamus. Quibus etiam non illibenter adjicimus monitum de loco perinsigni quo 'provisio quaedam omnium regum Christianorum' de Donationibus seu Alienationibus regiis hactenus puto aliunde inaudita in eo memoratur. Ex praefatione expressim liquet sub Edwardo rege scripsisse autorem. 'Quam in subditis tractandis aequalis jugiter appareat, quam eleganter...Edwardus,' inquit ibi, 'rex noster hostilitatis tempore....' An vero sub Primo, Secundo an Tertio, non inde

---
[1] Act. Apost. XIX, 35.

XI   'CLERK' AND 'CLERGY'   177

Henry I called 'Belloclericus'

Our King Henry I was called Belloclericus or Beauclerc and Chaucer calls the ancient Greek philosophers 'clerks.'

Functions of Clerks

In all law courts, there are, in addition to the judges, two classes of officials, the first consisting of scribes, registrars and functionaries for whose duties some degree of learning is essential, the second class comprising ushers, beadles and summoners, engaged in menial functions not requiring education. The first class, on account of whatever learning or skill they possessed, were called clerics and the name was used of amanuenses and secretaries, *e.g.* the scribe of the Ephesians, mentioned in the Acts of the Apostles, is called Town Clerk in the English Version. This translation was doubtless made by the clergy, to whom the office was peculiar and who, more than any other class of men, were distinguished for some kind of learning or the reputation thereof. Hence the names of Chaldean, Augur, Soothsayer, etc., were applied to persons who, if their origin be investigated, were not really comprised in such categories.

But from what has been said it is plain how the civil law was restricted to its present narrow limits and of this enough—and more—has been said.

Chapter X

  I. The period of the author of *Fleta*. It was not written under Edward II nor Edward III.
 II. It was written under Edward I.
III. Reason for the name *Fleta*.
 IV. Of the enactment of Christian monarchs concerning royal alienations, mentioned in *Fleta*.

Fleta

I. To return to *Fleta*. It remains to consider when this commentary was composed and to assign some reason for the name. An observation may be added on the remarkable passage containing the probably unique reference to 'a certain provision of all Christian princes' concerning royal donations or alienations.

Written under one of the Edwards

From the preface it is clear that the treatise was written under one of the Edwards, but whether First, Second or Third is not

constat. Sed ex Edwardis hisce regem illum fuisse dubitari nequit. Primum autem haud fuisse Edwardum illum sub quo absolutus saltem est commentarius hic argumento quidem esse videtur haud infirmo locus ille in Capitulis Coronae et Itineris, ubi mentio Edwardi patris regis. Verba sunt[1], 'qui receperint debita regis vel partem debiti et debita illa non acquietaverint tam de tempore regis E.' (neque enim in MS. Edwardi nomen aliter designatur) 'patris regis quam de tempore praesenti.' Idem enim ipse articulus tempore Edwardi primi etiam ad hunc modum concipiebatur[2], 'Qui ceperint debita regis vel partem debitorum et debitores illos inde non acquietaverint tam de tempore domini regis Henrici quam de tempore domini regis nunc.' Ergo, si ita scripsit autor ipse, Edwardus Rex Primus non erat is sub quo scripsit. Sed aut Secundus aut Tertius quorum utrique pater Edwardus. Sed de loco illo mox plura. Anne igitur sub Tertio scripsit? Nequaquam omnino si quid video. Satis scilicet diligenter de Naufragiis, Actione Dotali aliisque ea affert quae in constitutionibus habentur parlamentariis Edwardi primi uti et non pauca ex legibus Henrici tertii. Nullibi autem constitutionem aliquam Edwardi tertii memorat, quod ut non fecisset credibile non est si sub eo omnino scripsisset. Etenim exempli causa, in ipsis Edwardi tertii initiis[3] lex lata est de Convictionibus (sic actiones nostras perjurii forenses quas Attaints vocitamus appellant veteres illi) qua jus de eis pristinum adeo est immutatum ut sane immutationem illam tradere voluisse scriptorem hunc ubi de Convictionibus fusius[4] quidem et diligentius agit si post eam latam scripsisset, non est quod ambigamus. De eis enim non semel loquitur qua ex jure tunc pristino ac sanctione parlamentaria Edwardi primi[5] tantum pendent, cujus sensum esse vult ejusmodi ut non nisi ex duodecim virorum perjurio in actionibus de fundo aut rebus fundi congeneribus jureque perpetuo possessis quas liberum tenementum idiomate forensi nuncupamus, admittendae essent, neque sic sane citra gratiam ac arbitrium regium. Etiam sanctionis ipsius affert versionem qua legitur, 'concedit rex convictiones quotiescunque sibi videbitur expedire' pro eo quod est in comitiorum, quibus lex illa lata est, lingua 'Le roy de son office desormes donera attaints...quant il semblera que besoign soit.' De jure illius aevi ipso locus non est hic disserendi. Con-

---

[1] Lib. 1, cap. 20, § 59.
[2] Capitul. Itineris in vet. statut. impress. Londini, 12 Jun. 1556, part. 1, fol. 156b.
[3] Stat. 11 Ed. III, cap. 6.
[4] Lib. 5, cap. 22, vide 8 et 16.
[5] 3 Ed. I, Westm. 1, cap. 38.

XI   WHEN WAS *FLETA* COMPILED?   179

indicated, the reference being to 'Edward our King.' The words 'Edward, Father of the King' occurring in the Articles of the Eyre and the Crown[1] seem to provide an argument that at least the work was not finished in the reign of the first Edward and that its author wrote under either Edward II or Edward III, each of these kings having had an Edward for father. But of this passage, more anon.

Did he write under Edward III? In my opinion No, because he cites statutes of Edward I on shipwreck, dower and other things and frequently quotes laws of Henry III, whereas he mentions no statute of Edward III's reign. This would not have been so had he lived in the reign of the third Edward. For example, at the beginning of Edward III's reign a law was passed regarding Convictions (the name then given to accusations of perjury in court, now called Attaints) by which the original law on the subject was so changed that, had he survived this statute, our author would doubtless have given an account of it, his treatment of this matter being otherwise exhaustive. More than once he treats of Convictions under the old law and under the Statute of Edward I, concluding therefrom that Convictions could be admitted only in actions concerning freehold tenements, when the royal consent had been obtained and there had been perjury on the part of the twelve men. He thus renders the sanction itself: 'The king grants convictions as often as seems expedient to him,' which compares with the language of the parliament which passed the law: 'The king will henceforth grant attaints when he shall deem it necessary.' But this is not the place for a dissertation on this point[2]. It is sufficient to note that the author of *Fleta* takes no notice of the important change effected in this law early in

---

[1] See Selden's text for the full quotation from the Articles of the Crown.
[2] Selden (p. 180, n. 1) gives references to Bracton, *Britton*, Andrew Horn and Coke for the study of the law of convictions in the reigns of Henry III and Edward I.

sulat qui velit scriptores illud copiosius tractantes[1]. Hoc solum heic animadvertimus, Fletae autorem non omnino memorare jus ea de re insigniter in ipsis Edwardi tertii initiis sive mutatum sive explicatum, ut scilicet ex ejusmodi perjurio etiam in injuriarum actionibus idque ex Cancellarii Angliae autoritate legitima seu officio locum haberent Convictiones. Hoc praetermittere voluisse qui sub Edwardo tertio scripsisset existimandum non est. Initium Comitiorum quibus lex ea lata est in ipso erat regis hujus coronationis die, scilicet festi B. virginis crastino, id est Februarii tertio, cum decem nec amplius dies regni sui cujus primus erat Januarii 25 praeterierant. Adeoque nec ante legem illam latam sub Edwardo tertio scriptioni tempus erat. Certe nec in accuratiori illo de Convictionibus tractatu sanctionem parlamentariam anno Edwardi secundi decimo tertio latam, quae de Attinctis dicitur, omnino memorat, unde nec autumandum est eum post annum illum seu Christi 1320 scripsisse. Nec sane quidquam eorum quae temporis sunt Edwardi Secundi alicubi exhibet. Atque illinc sane, si aliud non obstat, nec sub Secundo Edwardo scripsisse sed ante, censendum est. Neque sane quid obstat omnino praeter locum superius de 'E. patre regis' allatum, qui mihi quidem tanti non est ut non satis interea credam Edwardum regem in praefatione memoratum adeoque ipsum sub quo scripsit fuisse primum. Exemplar illud vetustum unde editio fit et quod puto unicum est, Edwardi Secundi aut forsan Tertii tempore videtur exaratum. Nam autographum esse aut ab autore ipso fuisse recognitum negant plane tum menda non infrequentia, tum lacuna una et altera seu inter scribendum hiatus, quasi librarius aut legere aut intellegere dum describebat ibi nequisset. Adeoque probabile satis est librarium sub Edwardo secundo, aut 'E. patris regis' pro 'H. patris regis' (id est Henrici tertii patris Edwardi primi) oscitanter seu negligentius substituisse, aut Articulos illos Coronae praxi sui temporis forensi etiam in ipso autore imprudentius adaptasse. Certe quisquis statutum anno Edwardi Regis Primi tertio[2] de debitis suis simul ac patris editum cum articulo illo ac cum autoris nostri[3] statutum illud recitantis verbis contulerit, haud aegre forsan id concesserit. Maxime cum etiam alia sint quae Edwardum Primum regem fuisse sub quo commentarius hic scriptus est non obscure evincunt. Ejusmodi etiam habetur, ut id obiter adnotem, aut lapsus aut glossema

---

[1] Vide Bracton, lib. 4, de assisa utrum, cap. 4. Britton, cap. 97 et 98. Andr. Horn. cap. 4, sect. 19; cap. 5, sect. 1, 77 et sect. 4, pag. 324 et Coke Instit. part. 2, fol. 237, etc.
[2] Stat. Westm. 1, cap. 19.
[3] Lib. 2, cap. 33.

Edward III's reign whereby attaints should lie for such perjury in actions of trespass also and that on the lawful authority of the chancellor[1]. The session in which this act was passed began not more than ten days after the commencement of the reign so there was no time in Edward III's reign to write the book before the passing of that law.

Written not later than 1320

Similarly it may be argued that he did not write it later than the year 1320, since, in his exhaustive treatment of Convictions, he makes no mention of the Act passed 13 Edward II which concerns Attaints, nor does he at any time quote from any of the Acts of Edward II's day. In the absence of contrary proof, therefore, it may be assumed that he wrote before Edward II's reign.

A difficulty

The sole objection to this is the passage already quoted about 'Edward, Father of the King.' This however is not of sufficient weight to prevent me believing that the Edward mentioned in the preface and the monarch under whom he wrote are identical—namely, Edward I. The MS. from which the printed edition was made —probably the sole MS.[2]—seems to date from the time of Edward II or possibly of Edward III. That it was neither an autograph copy nor revised by the author appears from the frequent errors and gaps as if, in some cases, the copyist was unable to read or understand the original. It is not unlikely that the copyist, writing in Edward II's reign, either carelessly inserted 'E. patris regis' for 'H. patris regis' (*i.e.* Henry III) or thoughtlessly altered those 'Articles of the Crown' in order to conform with the legal terminology of his own day. This will be conceded by anyone comparing the Statute of 3 Edward I concerning his own and his father's debts with that article of the crown and with our author's account of the statute[3].

Fleta *written in the reign of Edward I*

There are other things which demonstrate that this commentary was written in Edward I's reign. An analogy is provided by a slip or interpolation in Thornton's MS.—a MS. contemporary with its author.

---

[1] For this see Holdsworth, *History of English Law* (3rd ed.), I, 340.
[2] See *supra*, p. 3, n. 1.
[3] *Statutes of the Realm* (1810), I, 32. Selden's argument is that in *Fleta*'s account of the statute 3 Edward I there is no mention of 'E. patris regis,' but simply 'de debitis Regis vel patris eius,' and in the statute itself the reference is to 'le rey Henri piere le rey que ore est.' Taken together these two help to show that the reference to 'E. patris regis' in the Article of the Crown (*Fleta*, I, 20, § 59) is an error on the part of the scribe.

in Gilberti Thorntonii quem ante diximus exemplari veteri de autoris tempore. Legitur ibi[1], 'dari non poterunt aliter' (quam ut possideantur, velut ab usufructuario, non a domino) 'singulari personae res quae sunt spiritualibus annexa sicut corrodia ex abbatibus et domibus religiosis percipienda et hujusmodi in quibus nullus vendicare sibi poterit liberum tenementum, temporibus retroactis. Sed hodie per statutum regis Edwardi Secundi fiat breve de Corrodio subtracto sicut de libero tenemento.' Ita citatur statutum Edwardi Secundi, cum manifestum sit Thorntonium, ut ostensum superius est, sub Edwardo Primo scripsisse, etiam et obiisse. Adeoque ita scribere ille nequibat. Certe dicere potuerat ille 'per statutum regis Edwardi Westmonasterii secundi[2],' quo lex illa de Corrodio, anno scilicet ejusdem regis 13, lata. Sed videtur potius librarii esse glossema, nec illorum verborum quid post 'poterit' Thorntonium ipsum scripsisse. Eo usque sunt Bractonii[3] quem in Summam redegit ille verba. Nec consonum omnino est 'poterit' τῷ temporibus retroactis. Nec sui temporis leges inserere solet Thorntonius, Bractonii personam passim induens. Quod vero ad Fletae autorem attinet; certe si simpliciter tum egregias tum immensas Edwardi in praefatione laudes spectes, vix est ut eas ad Edwardum Secundum pertinere potuisse omnino admittas. Et de Tertio quaestio ultra non fit. Atque ita de alio quam Primo haud sumendus ille laudum cumulus forsan videatur. Sed interim de praefatione autoris hujus hoc advertendum, eam ita esse a capite ferme ad calcem compositam ut potius ex formula veteri aliisque regibus ab aliis ante nec semel tributa sumi videatur, quam de ipso qui ibi nominatur Rege revera dici sive singulariter aptari. Id quod haud aegre concedet quisquis praefationem hanc cum illa quae et Scoticarum legum codici Regiam Majestatem dicto et Ranulpho de Glanvilla praefigitur contulerit. Eadem enim ipsa ferme verba in altera Henrico nostro Secundo, in altera Davidi Scotorum Regi Primo attribuuntur quae in Fletae autoris praefatione Edwardo suo. Adeoque laudes illae qualescunque fuerint non ita in argumentum heic trahendae.

II. Atqui alibi in ipso opere expressissima sunt temporis quo conscriptum est vestigia unde Edwardum in praefatione memoratum seu eum sub quo scripsit autor Primum fuisse palam satis constat. Primo[4], de Templariorum privilegiis, qua lex sub Edwardo Primo de crucibus erigendis lata ea spectat, loquitur[5]

[1] Gilb. Thornton MS., lib. 1, cap. 19. [2] Westm. 2, cap. 29.
[3] Lib. 2 de Acq. Rerum Dom. cap. 5, §7.
[4] West. 2, cap. 37. [5] Lib. 2, cap. 50, §16.

XII *FLETA* WRITTEN IN EDWARD I's REIGN

The words are: 'Things annexed to spiritualities, such as corrodies exacted from abbots and religious houses, will not be granted to individuals' (except as regards the usufruct) 'since in these things no one will be able to claim a freehold in times past. But now, by a statute of Edward II a writ lies for a corrody withheld as for a freehold.' Here a statute of Edward II is cited, when it is certain that Thornton wrote and died in Edward I's reign. Hence he could not have written thus. He could have quoted the Statute of Westminster 11 (13 Edward I) in regard to corrodies, but he could not have written what follows after 'will be able' (*poterit*). What follows that word must be an interpolation: what precedes it was taken from Bracton, whom Thornton was summarising. Nor is 'will be able' consistent with 'in times past.' Thornton does not generally insert laws of his own time, but speaks throughout in the person of Bracton.

Moreover it could hardly be maintained that the striking and enthusiastic eulogy of Edward, found in the preface, could apply to Edward II, and there is no longer any question of Edward III. Thus the laudatory preface can be applied to no other than Edward the First. But it may be noted of this preface that throughout it is composed as if on some old model, and as if it had already served the same purpose for earlier kings. This will be admitted by anyone comparing it with the preface to the collection of Scottish laws called *Regiam Majestatem* or with the preface to Glanvil. Almost the same words in the one are addressed to David I, king of Scots as are addressed in the other to our Henry II and these in turn agree with those dedicated to Edward in *Fleta's* preface. Therefore little can be deduced from such eulogies.

Evidence that it was written in Edward I's reign

11. Elsewhere in the treatise there are clear indications that it was written in Edward I's reign[1]. Thus in speaking of the privileges of the Templars he refers to them, equally with the Knights Hospitallers, as flourishing in his time, whereas only those quite ignorant

---

[1] F. M. Nicholls in his edition of *Britton* (1865) notes (I, xxv) that the author of *Fleta* cites Quia Emptores as if he had only heard of its proposed terms and did not understand it; from this it might be conjectured that the book was being written in 1290. This receives further confirmation from the fact that the great judicial inquisition into the conduct of the judiciary took place in 1288 and the author of *Fleta* may have been one of the functionaries sentenced to imprisonment.

velut eorum qui dum scribebat ipse pariter ac Hospitalarii florerent. At sub ipsis Edwardi Secundi initiis Templarios plane desiisse nescit nemo nisi qui et juris nostri et historiarum sit omnino nescius. Secundo ubi formulam habet[1] rescripti regii 'Moderata Misericordia' dicti quod lege subnititur in Magna Charta lata[2], verba tempori adaptans ad hunc modum nomine regio concipit, 'contra tenorem Magnae Chartae Regis H. patris nostri in qua continetur quod nullus liber homo amercietur....' Heic ut ipse Edwardus Primus innuatur necesse est, cui pater Henricus tertius. Tertio, 'Dominus Rex,' inquit[3], 'nuper in Parliamento suo apud Acton Burnell habito....' Parliamentum illud ad annum Edwardi Primi undecimum spectat. Et formula illa 'Dominus Rex' regem designare solet superstitem. Quarto etiam, capite citato, 'per formam[4],' inquit, 'statuti regis anno regni regis' (praetermisso ex librarii incuria decimo tertio) 'editi apud Westmonasterium,' statutum Edwardi primi de Mercatoribus dictum plane innuens. Quinto, Henricum Regem Secundum proavum expressim nuncupat regis sub quo scripsit. Et Edwardo Primo eum fuisse proavum, id est patrem Johannis regis, patris Henrici tertii, patris Edwardi Primi, nemo ignorat. Scilicet ubi[5] in Henrici Tertii Magna Charta capitulum habetur de 'Scutagio[6] capiendo sicut capi consuevit tempore Henrici regis avi nostri,' quo nomine plane Henricus designatur Secundus, noster legem illam suis recitans verbis, 'inhibetur,' ait, 'quod nullus destringatur pro scutagio, sed capiatur sicut capi consuevit tempore H. regis proavi regis nunc.' Sensum ipsissimum legis Henricianae retinet qua Henricum Secundum Henrici illius avum spectat; proavum interim eundem ipsum regis sui, id est Edwardi Primi recte vocans. Scio quidem viros aliquot nominis magni[7] aliter sentire atque e nonnullis quos adhibuimus locis perperam intellectis sub Edwardo Secundo et Tertio Fletae autorem vixisse existimare. Sed abunde satis mihi ex ante allatis probatur regnante Edwardo Primo opus ipsum conscriptum fuisse; adeoque ex eis esse quae jussu Edwardi Primi, sicut et Thorntonii Summa, et Compendium Britton dictum, a jurisconsultis celebrioribus[8] componebantur.

III. Quod ad nomen libri attinet, reperitur quidem in scriptoribus Britanniae[9] autor Guilielmus Flete seu Fleta dictus, exteris plerunque Anglus seu Anglicus. Sed is Theologus et

---

[1] Lib. 2, cap. 66, § 26. [2] Cap. 14. [3] Lib. 2, cap. 64, § 1.
[4] § 6. [5] Lib. 2, cap. 66, § 16. [6] Cap. 37.
[7] Coke in pref. ad part. 8. Relat. alibi Cowell in Interprete.
[8] 35 Hen. VI, pl. 42 a.
[9] Bal. Cent. 6, scrip. 41. Pitz. aet. 14, script. 648, anno 1380.

of our law and history are unaware of the fact that by Edward II's reign the Templars had completely disappeared from England. Secondly, in defining the writ Moderata Misericordia[1], based on a clause in Magna Carta[2], he frames the words to suit his time, speaking in the royal name of 'the import of Magna Carta of King Henry our Father...,' obviously Henry III, father of Edward I. Thirdly, he writes 'Our lord the king lately in his parliament of Acton Burnell.' This parliament was held 11 Edward I and the words 'Our lord the king' were commonly used of the reigning monarch. Fourthly, he explicitly refers to Statutes passed in the thirteenth year of the king's reign—by this Edward I's 'Statute of Merchants' is obviously meant. Lastly, he speaks of Henry II as the great-grandfather of the king under whom he wrote, and everyone knows that Edward I was the great-grandson of Henry II. This reference occurs in his enunciation of the clause in Henry III's edition of Magna Carta regarding the levying of scutage—he retains the sense of the passage so far as it relates to the time of Henry II, grandfather of Henry III, rightly referring to the former as great-grandfather of his king, *i.e.* Edward I.

Rival theories

I know that some men of considerable reputation have thought differently and by a wrong interpretation of several of the passages already quoted have concluded that the author of *Fleta* lived under Edward II[3] and Edward III. But it seems to me amply proved that the book was written in Edward I's reign and, like the *Summa* of Thornton and the compendium called *Britton*, was one of those books compiled by eminent lawyers at the command of the king.

Reason for the name

III. As regards the name of the book, there is to be found among British writers an author named William Flete or Fleta, often styled by foreigners 'the Englishman,' but he was an Austinian monk of

---

[1] This writ lay against the lord or his bailiff if a man was unreasonably amerced in a court not of record, such as a Court Baron.
[2] Cap. xx, 'Liber homo non amercietur....'
[3] Selden (p. 184, n. 7) quotes Coke and Cowell in this connection. There is a seventeenth century MS. copy of *Fleta* (Lincoln's Inn MS. CXC) having an illumination at the beginning showing the arms of Edward II.

Theologica tantum scripsit, e secta Heremitarum Augustinianorum. Et scripto hoc plane recentior est utpote qui sub Richardo Secundo floruit. Nominis autem ratio apud autorem in praefatione manifesta est. 'Tractatus iste,' inquit, 'qui merito Fleta poterit appellari, quia in Fleta de Jure Anglicano conscriptus est, in tres partes dividitur principales.' Fleta vero heic notissimus est apud nos carcer the Fleet dictus et e praeterlabente fluviolo sic nuncupatus. Fluvius etiam Fluctus seu Aestuarium 'Flete' Anglis dictum. Unde per metonymiam, ut Hispanis naulum 'Flete' dicitur a fluvio seu fluctu quo navis vehitur (ita volunt aliqui[1]) sic illis dicto, e quo habent item Fletador et Fletamiento; ita et nobis carcer ille uti et navium pariter classis, ac vicus insuper fluviolo illi adjacens. Certe si Cicero 'Quaestiones Tusculanas' 'Tusculum' nominaverat, eadem ipsa qua noster usus fuisset in libro denominando ratione. Sic Ovidii de Ponto libri nominantur. Atque apud majores nostros usus erat non infrequens et tempore quo floruit Fletae autor et superiori, scripta et acta publica a loco in quo transigerentur ea quae in eis continerentur nuncupari. Sic Clarendonenses Recognitiones, sic Magna Charta Johannis Regis, Charta de Runningmede, sic statuta aliquot sub Edwardo Primo Westmonasterium primum, secundum, tertium (quod et pueri sciunt) etiam et quartum, ut Glocestriae ac Exoniae statuta sic dicta, praetermittam. Quisnam autem in Fleta autor commentarii hujus fuerit nullibi quantum scio aperitur. Sed e carcerariis seu custodiae traditis eum fuisse non est quod dubitemus. Certe scimus quamplurimos eorum qui judiciis sub Edwardo Primo praefuere, viros quidem maximos et aevo in illo jurisconsultos celeberrimos, repetundarum et quod lites suas fecerant aliosque praeter ministros forenses aliquot merito damnatos, mulctis, exilio ac carcere punitos esse, e quibus veri satis est simile autorem hunc fuisse. In annalium nostrorum confarcinatoribus[2] obvia sunt damnatorum nomina. Et vetus quem habeo annalium scriptor MS. in anno 1288 'Incarceratio Justitiariorum domini regis scilicet Thomas de Weylond, Johannis de Lovetot, Willielmi de Brampton et Adae de Stratton de quo dominus rex habuit quadriginta mille marcas et amplius praeter vasa argentea et aurea.' Et de his aliisque Petri de Langtoft MS. vetus Chronographus rhythmicus.

>Quant le Roy Edward avoit demoré
>Troiz annez de la mer Dieu l'ad remené
>A son repoir trova par pleinte presenté
>Ses Justices et ses Clerks attaintz de fauseté.

[1] Sebastian. de Covarruvia in Thesauro Ling. Castellanae.
[2] Vide ex vett. MSS. Holinshed. et J. Stowaeum, anno 1289.

Richard II's time and wrote only on theology. The reason for the name is given in the preface: 'This treatise on English law may well be called *Fleta* because it was written in the Fleet: it is divided into three principal parts.' This is the famous Fleet prison, so called from the stream running by it. In English we use the word 'Fleet' of a river, a tide-way or an estuary. In Spanish the word for 'freight' ('flete') is derived from the 'flood' on which ships sail, and so also are the words 'fletador' and 'fletamiento.' In English by a similar metonymy we use the same word for a particular prison, a muster of ships and the particular district adjacent to that stream. If Cicero had called his Tusculan Disputations *Tusculum* he would have been employing a similar principle in naming his book—a principle which explains the *Pontine Books* of Ovid. In the age of our author and earlier it was customary to name public writings and acts from the places where such matters were transacted—*e.g.* the Constitutions of Clarendon, the Charter of Runnymede and several Statutes of Edward I, *e.g.* those of Westminster, Gloucester and Exeter.

The Judicial Inquisition of 1288

Who the author of *Fleta* was I cannot find from any source, but there can be no doubt that he was a prisoner[1]. It is well known that several of Edward I's judges—men of note and the most eminent lawyers of their day—were fined, banished or imprisoned for bribery and corruption and of this number our author may have been one. The names of those so condemned are on record. I have an old MS. chronicle[2] where, under the year 1288, the writer records: 'Imprisonment of the king's justices Thomas Weyland, John Lovetot, William Brampton and Adam Stratton, from the last of whom the king extracted more than 40,000 marks, besides gold and silver plate.' Of these and others the following details are given in the MS. of Peter of Langtoft's[3] rhyming chronicle:

'On Edward's return, after three years overseas, he found his judges and his clerks convicted of malpractices. Some, for bribes,

---

[1] For a list of those who were fined and imprisoned see Tout and Johnstone, *Select Trials of the reign of Edward I* (1906), Appendix III. See *ante*, p. xxiii.
[2] I have not been able to identify this MS.
[3] Harleian MS. 202. See *Chronicle of Pierre de Langtoft* (Rolls Series, 1868), II, 184–6.

Les uns avoient, par douns, les leys destourné,
Les autres la coroune avoient violé;
Thomas de Weylaunde en banc primes nomé
Par agard du court le reigne ad forjuré.
En la terre de France sans repoir est alé,
Ses compaignons, ses clerks sunt pris e mené
A la toure de Londres, deliveres par mené;
E sur ceo chescun de office est pryvé.
Elys de Begyngham nest pas entechelé
Et Johan de Metingham le chef est demoré.
Sire Rauf de Hengham ad taunt disputé
Ke du baunc le roy perdu ad le sée.
Sire Adam de Stratton est dur demené,
Jeo cray ke sauns deserte nest il pas blamé
Or, argent, sans nombre au roy ad il doné,
Avoir chaunta pur luy placebo dominé,
Dilexi quoniam fraude et fauseté.

In numerosa autem illa jurisconsultorum damnatorum turba vix dubitandum est quin fuerint aliqui carceri Fletae, utpote supremis apud nos tribunalibus prae carceribus aliis idque ex jure vetustissimo inservienti, traditi. E quibus si negaveris nostrum fuisse, non omnino contendam.

IV. Locus autem ille quem diximus apud autorem hunc perinsignis, qui et satis prodigiosus mihi videtur, ad hunc modum se habet, ubi de Donationibus agit[1]. 'Res quidem Coronae sunt antiqua maneria regis, homagia, libertates et hujusmodi, quae cum alienentur, tenetur rex ea revocare secundum provisionem omnium regum Christianorum apud Montem Pessoloniam, anno regni regis Edwardi filii regis Henrici quarto habitam.' Alia apud eum[2] habentur, de alienatione regia, consona. Sed vero itane? Omnium regum Christianorum de patrimonii regum alienatione revocanda, provisio habitane est tunc temporis apud Montem Pessulanam, urbem scilicet Languedokii inclytam quam nunc Mompellier dicimus? Neque enim puto alio de loco Mons heic Pessolonia intelligendus est. Nam et urbs ipsa etiam Mons Pullerius et Mons Pisciculanus aliterque nonnullis pro libitu dictus est. Annus ille quartus Edwardi Primi quo asseritur heic hujusmodi ibi provisionem habitam partem habet annorum Christi 1275 et 1276. Incepit nempe Edwardus ille die 16 Novembris 1272 adeoque inter diem 16 Novembris anni 1275 atque eundem in anno 1276 diem Conventus habebatur aut regum ibi omnium Christianorum, aut legatorum qui vicaria hac in re potestate fungerentur. Reges Christiani tunc erant Michael Palaeologus Imperator Orientis, Rodulphus Primus Occidentis seu Germaniae, Galliae Philippus

[1] Lib. 3, cap. 6, § 3.
[2] Lib. 1, cap. 8 in init. et cap. 17 et vide Cowell. Instit. lib. 2, tit. 8 in prin.

THE IMPRISONED JUDGES 189

had misapplied the law, others had violated the authority of the crown. Thomas of Weyland, Chief Justice of the Bench, fled from justice to France, while his accomplices and subordinates were imprisoned in the Tower, fined, and deprived of their offices. Elys of Begyngham was not of the guilty ones nor John of Metingham, who remained. Sir Ralph Hengham lost his seat in the King's Bench and though Sir Adam Stratton was severely treated, I fear that he was justly blamed. He surrendered untold wealth to the King for having sung "*Placebo Domine, Dilexi Quoniam* cheating and dishonesty."'

Author of Fleta *a prisoner*

Of the large band of lawyers thus condemned, it cannot be doubted but that some were imprisoned in the Fleet—a prison which, by old tradition, was specially utilised by our supreme courts. If it be doubted whether our author was of this number, I shall not dispute the point.

Passage in Fleta *concerning royal alienations*

IV. The remarkable and, to me, astounding passage in this author to which reference has already been made, occurs in his discussion of Donations: 'The royal possessions consist of the ancient royal manors, homages, liberties and such like which, were they to be alienated, the king would have to redeem in accordance with the decree made by all the Christian princes at Montpellier in the fourth year of king Edward, son of Henry.' There are other similar passages on royal alienations in this author.

Monarchs contemporary with Edward I

But was any decree regarding such redemption of alienated royal patrimony made at that time by an assembly of this kind meeting at Montpellier? The reference can be to no other place, its Latinised name having several variations. The fourth year of Edward I is the year 1275–6, and as Edward began his reign on 16th November, 1272, this convention of all the Christian rulers or their delegates must have met between the 16th of November, 1275, and the 16th of November, 1276. The Christian monarchs at that time were Michael Palaeologus, emperor of the East, Rudolph I, emperor of

Audax, Castellae et Leonis Alfonsus decimus, summus ille Astronomus et 'Partitarum' autor, Scotiae Alexander tertius, Daniae Ericus Octavus, Poloniae Boleslaus, Hungariae Vladislaus quartus, Aragoniae Jacobus, Boemiae Ottocarus, Carolus Siciliae, Hugo Hierosolymorum, atque alii fuere minoris nominis qui regum Christianorum vocamine tunc fruebantur. Atqui in Annalibus Historiisve alibive, extra hunc autoris nostri locum, non omnino opinor reperiri aut volam aut vestigium horum eorumve aliquorum ibi conventus ejusmodi, aut missos illuc legatos qui de ejusmodi re aliqua transigerent. Certe sub idem tempus, atque ut aliqui volunt, anno ipso 1275[1], concessit Rodolphus primus Caesar Gregorio Papae decimo Bononiam et latifundia circumquaque amplissima quae ante Imperii Romani pars insignis. Sed de anno ipso non consentiunt scriptores. At sub idem tempus factum certo certius est. Tantundem item tam a successoribus subinde quam a decessoribus factum, nec omnino revocatum. De re ipsa sane seu de patrimonii regii alienatione revocanda occurrunt quaedam apud veteres pluribus annis quartum Edwardi primi antevertentia. Illustre est rescriptum[2] Honorii Papae tertii de Andreae secundi Hungariae regis alienationibus sub annum Christi 1220 ad archiepiscopum Collocensem. Azonis item jurisconsulti illius summi vetustique, sed diu ante quartum Edwardi primi annum, demortui, eadem de re sententia nec adeo provisioni huic dissimilis citatur ex ejusdem disputationibus[3]. Et quae huc spectant leguntur in Alphonsinis[4] circa annos 25 ante quartum Edwardi nostri editis, uti etiam in Gregorianorum Decretalium[5] corpore annis triginta sex aut circiter ante hunc Edwardi edito ut qui ad illud ante conscripsere praeteream. Bractonius[6] item noster de Donationibus regiis non ita dissimiliter monet. Adde Matthaeum Parisium, Guilielmum Nubrigensem alios in initiis Henrici Secundi. Sed vero post illum annum seu tempus provisioni jam dictae tributum eadem ipsa de re perquam diligenter disputarunt docueruntque jurisconsulti non pauci, quorum nemini provisionis ejusdem mentio puto omnino aliqua. In compendio juris nostri illo Britton[7]

---

[1] Vide Aventin. Annal. Boiorum, lib. 7. Gordon. Chronic. an. 1275. Paul Langium Chronic. 1273. Durand. Specul. tit. de Rescript. Praesent. §9, num. 18.
[2] Extr. tit. de Jurejurando, c. 33, intellecto et videsis Quintam Comp. Decret. lib. 2, tit. 15, cap. 3 et ibi Innocent. Cironium.
[3] Disp. cujus initium An dominus Rex apud R. Choppin. lib. 2, tit. 1, § 6.
[4] Partit. 2, tit. 1, l. 8 et partit. 3, tit. 18, l. 29.
[5] Tit. de Jurejurando, c. 33.
[6] Lib. 2 de Acquir. Rerum Dom. cap. 5, § 7, fol. 14 *a* et 37 *a* et vide cap. 24, §2.
[7] Cap. 34, Des Dones, fol. 87 *b*.

the West, Philip III (le Hardi), king of France, Alfonso X, famous astrologer and author of the *Partidas*, king of Castille and Leon, Alexander III of Scotland, Eric VIII of Denmark, Boleslas of Poland, Ladislas IV of Hungary, James of Aragon, Ottokar of Bohemia, Charles of Sicily, Hugh of Jerusalem as well as minor potentates.

No other reference to decree mentioned by Fleta

In my opinion there is, apart from the above passage, no reference in our chronicles, annals or other sources to such a meeting at that place, nor of any sending of delegates thereto. Some scholars assign the date 1275 to the grant by the emperor Rudolph to pope Gregory X whereby Bologna and considerable surrounding territories—formerly an important part of the Roman empire—were ceded. But there is disagreement about the date, though the cession was afterwards confirmed and never revoked.

Previous references to royal alienations

Among writers prior to Edward I's time there are to be found references to this question of revocation of royal alienations—*e.g.* the famous rescript of pope Honorius III to the archbishop of Cologne about the year 1220 concerning the alienations of Andrew II, king of Hungary[1]. The opinion of that famous lawyer Azo, as cited in his Disputations, is not very different from the terms of the already mentioned decree. There are remarks also on this point in the *Alphonsines*[2], about 25 years before 4 Edward I, as also in the Gregorian Decretals[3], not to mention earlier writers. Bracton voices a similar opinion in regard to royal donations, also William of Newburgh, Matthew Paris and others early in Henry II's reign.

Fleta's *decree not mentioned in* Britton *nor* Thornton

But although in the period after 4 Edward I the subject was debated and expounded by many lawyers, yet in none of them is there any reference to such a decree. It is mentioned neither in *Britton*

---

[1] For this see Decretals of Gregory IX, II, 33 (in Friedberg's edition of the *Corpus Juris Canonici*, II, 374). The rescript is 'Archiepiscopo Collossensi' not 'Collocensi,' *i.e.* Klausenberg (Hungary) not Cologne.

[2] The reference is to the *Siete Partidas* of Alfonso the Wise. Editions appeared in 1555 and 1587.

[3] Compiled 1230-4. See *ante*, p. 7, n. 4.

dicto et non ita diu post annum illum conscripto, expressa habetur doctrina de donationibus regiis, uti etiam apud Thorntonium[1] qui intra annos sexdecim a quarto illo summam suam edidit. Neque tamen aut in hoc aut illo provisionis ejusmodi mentio aliqua. In Thorntonio, fateor, utpote Bractonii epitomatore, illo recentiora me non reperire. At in compendio illo altero occurrit non semel quod ad annos quartum illum proxime insequentes attinet. Adeoque si provisio ejusmodi revera extitisset, mirum est eam ibi neutiquam memorari. Neque sane in librorum nostrorum juridicorum in quibus versamur reliquorum aliquo provisionis hujusmodi vestigium habetur ullum, ne quidem in Johanne Fortiscutio[2] qui sub Henrico Sexto de regiis donationibus revocandis disertius loquitur. Sed interim argumenta in libris illis nostris reperimus satis luculenta, quae ejusmodi fuisse plane nullam evincunt, ut statim dicemus. Atque imponi sibi passus est proculdubio carcerarius heic noster, seu Fletae autor dum sive a peregrinatione reduces aliqui homines leviores ac ut fieri amat locutuleii (forte a Concilio Generali paulo ante Lugduni habito) sive literae libellive de provisione hujusmodi in eorum quorum intererat utcunque rem sparsi, offucias illi aliisque forsan obtrusere. Hallucinationes id genus apud nimis credulos haud ita rarae. Et sane prodigiosarum rerum exterarum narrationum usus nunquam infrequens. Exterorum quidem viri perinsignes de re ipsa seu alienatione principum supremorum sive stabilienda sive rescindenda plurima conscripsere, in intervallo nimirum quod ab anno Edwardi Primi quarto cui tribuitur haec provisio, huc usque excurrit. Veterum sententias, Caesarum, Regum sanctiones, placita forensia alia ea de re diligentissime corrogant; provisionis, quam diximus aliusve congeneris planissime ignari. Id palam docebunt tum Doctores in 'Extr. tit. de Jurejurando c. intellecto 33,' tum Bartolus[3] et Baldus[4] reliquique fere ad titulum 'quis dare feudum possit.' Quibus inter vetustiores adde Speculatorem seu Durandum[5]. E recentioribus autem qui huc faciant complures satis sunt in singularibus suis commentariis obvii. De imperio Germanico aliisque regnis quantum ad hanc rem Petrus Belluga[6], Restaurus Castaldus[7], Arnulphus Ruzaeus[8], Reginerus Sixtinus[9], Henricus Bocerus[10], Horatius Montanus[11], id genus alii

---

[1] Lib. 1, c. 19.   [2] In tract. De Domin. Regal. et Politic. MS.
[3] Ad l. perhibere § plane D. quod vi aut clam.
[4] Inc. unico praeterea duc. tit. de Prohib. Feud. Alien.
[5] In tit. de Instrum. editione § 11, num. 11.
[6] Specul. Princ. rubric 8, 2.   [7] De Imperatore quaest. 104.
[8] De Jure Regal. Priv. 42, n. 4.   [9] De Regalibus, lib. 1.
[10] De Regalibus, cap. 4, § 36, etc.   [11] De Regalibus in praelud. § 28, 29.

THE AUTHOR OF *FLETA* DECEIVED

nor in Thornton's *Summa* (c. 1291), both of which discuss the subject of royal donations, the former containing a good deal of material subsequent to 4 Edward I. Had such a decree ever been promulgated, it is extraordinary that nowhere is it mentioned—not even by John Fortescue[1], who learnedly discusses the question of revocation of royal donations.

Evidence that there was no such decree

On the contrary there is ample evidence in our books that there never was any such decree at all. Our prisoner, the author of *Fleta*, was doubtless imposed upon, either by some irresponsible babblers returned from abroad (perhaps from the General Council recently held at Lyons[2]), or by pamphlets recording such a decree and scattered abroad by interested parties. Such hallucinations are not uncommon among the credulous, and accounts of foreign wonders are always popular.

Foreign writers on the subject

Several distinguished foreigners have since treated of this subject, *i.e.* the ratifying or rescinding of royal alienations, but though they have carefully collected the opinions of old authorities and the laws of emperors and kings, they none of them show any knowledge of this decree nor of anything like it. This will be seen from the doctors on the title De Jurejurando in the Extravagants[3], as well as from Bartolus[4], Baldus[5], Speculator or Durand[6] and almost all who have commented on the title Who can grant a fee. Of modern authorities consult, for the question in relation to the German and other empires, Peter Belluga[7], Restaurus Castaldus[8], Arnoul Ruzé[9], Regner Sixtinus[10], Henry Bocer[11] and Horace Montanus[12]. Of the writers who

---

[1] Fortescue, *De Dominio Regali et Politico*, XI, XIV and XIX.
[2] In 1274.
[3] Selden probably means the title in the Decretals of Gregory IX (II, 33). See *supra*, p. 191, n. 1.
[4] See *ante*, p. 99, n. 9.
[5] 1340–1400; pupil and rival of Bartolus.
[6] A native of Provence; died 1270. Called Speculator from the title of his book, *Speculum Juris*, dedicated to Adrian IV.
[7] Spanish jurist, fifteenth century.
[8] Died 1564; was professor of civil law at Bologna.
[9] French jurist; 1485–1550 (*circa*).
[10] Born Leeuwarden 1543; died 1617. See Stintzing, I, 707–8.
[11] Professor at Tübingen late in the sixteenth century.
[12] A Neapolitan law-teacher in the early seventeenth century.

de regalibus scribentes, et qui Donationem tractant Constantini, Franciscus Hotomannus[1], Johannes Bodinus[2], Codex Henrici Quarti Juris Gallici et Romani[3], Petrus Tholosanus[4], Renatus Choppinus[5], Gregorius Lopez in Partitas[6], Bartholomaeus de las Casas[7], Alfonsus Azevedo[8], Georgius Cabedo, Hugo Gròtius[9], ut quos hi obiter memorant praetermittamus aliosque satis numerosos. Disputant scilicet hi quandoque etiam indagine diffusiore ac diligentissima utentes, de regum largitionibus donationibusque ac alienatione regaliumque usucapione. Nec quid ad eam rem alicubi sive apud veteres sive recentiores attinens omittere volunt eorum plerique. In iis Itali, Germani, Batavi, Galli, Hispani, iique celeberrimi atque historiarum jurisque peritissimi; cum interim provisionem illam omnium regum Christianorum, qualis proculdubio eos latere non quibat, omnino ignorent. Quid quod etiam ex ipsius anni Edwardi primi quarti, cui tribuitur haec provisio, Comitiis Parlamentariis palam constat donationes seu alienationes apud nos regias tum praeteritas tum futuras pro legitimis satisque validis nec eo nomine omnino infirmandis censeri. Habebantur Comitia illa post festum S. Michaelis. Jam vero quarti illius anni finis erat dies Novembris 16 proxime insequens. Ante autem Comitia illa provisionem hujusmodi factam satis negat eorundem de donationibus alienationibusque regiis omnino admittendis sanctio quod Statutum de Bigamis[10] vocitamus. Et perexiguum post illa Comitia relinquitur quarti illius anni tempus, per quod uti et secula quae sunt huc usque insecuta ita obtinuere tum sanctiones parlamentariae[11] tum regni mores, ut provisioni ejusmodi locus nunquam apud nos agnosceretur ullus. Et donationes latifundiorum quae sacri patrimonii pars, regiae frequentissimae et pro libitu regio semper olim apud nos majoresque nostros factae fuere, firmaeque, si recte alias factae, mansere, modo excipias eas quas aut infirmarunt sanctiones aliquae parlamentariae, quibus largitionibus regum aliquorum prodigentiorum et procaciori aulicorum importunitati frenum temporarium subinde est injectum, a t autoritas eadem pro re nata, cum ampliores multo quam par erat viderentur, revocavit

---

[1] Illust. Quaest. 1. [2] De Repub. lib. 1, cap. 10.
[3] Lib. 7, tit. 2. [4] Syntagm. Juris Univers. lib. 6, cap. 6, § 16.
[5] De Dom. Franc. 2, tit. 1. [6] Lib. 2, tit. 1.
[7] In quaest. utrum reges vel principes alienare. Tübing. 1625.
[8] Ad constit. reg. lib. 5, tit. 10. Part. 2, Decis. Lusitan. 40, n. 6.
[9] De Jure Pacis et Belli, lib. 2, cap. 6, § 3 et cap. 14, § 12.
[10] Cap. 1 et 2.
[11] Rot. Parl. 11 Rich. II. Pet. com. num. 23 et 24, 11 Hen. IV, Pet. Com. num. 25, etc. et vide Stat. de Resumpt. 28 Hen. VI in Archivis Parlamentariis.

XIV PARLIAMENT AND ROYAL ALIENATIONS 195

treat also of Constantine's Donation, the following may be mentioned: Francis Hotman[1], John Bodin[2], Henry IV's Code[3] of French and Roman Law, Peter Gregory of Toulouse[4], René Choppin[5], Gregory Lopez on the *Partidas*[6], Bartholomew de las Casas[7], Alfonso Azevedo[8], George Cabedo[9] and Hugo Grotius[10]. These writers discuss with care and learning the subjects of royal bounties and donations, alienation and usucaption of regalia, and little of importance seems to be omitted by them. But though they include Italians, Germans, Dutch, French and Spaniards, many of them eminent historians and lawyers, yet they all seem quite unaware of this edict of all the Christian princes, which, had it existed, must have been known to them.

Parliamentary enactment concerning royal alienations

But in the parliament of this very year 4 Edward I royal donations and alienations, both past and future, were confirmed and made valid. That before the meeting of this parliament there existed no decree of the kind referred to is proved by the Statute of Bigamy, passed by this parliament, whereby royal donations and alienations are freely allowed. In the years after this date parliamentary and national institutions so prevailed that there could have been no room for an edict of this kind. Donations of royal estates, part of the sacred patrimony, were formerly very common in this country and, if otherwise legal, were held valid, though parliament sometimes nullified or modified such grants, in order to restrain the prodigality of kings and the importunity of courtiers.

[1] See *ante*, p. 37, n. 4.
[2] 1530–1596; the great French jurist and publicist; a leading member of the Politique party and in some respects a predecessor of Montesquieu.
[3] Compiled by T. Cormerius in 1602. It had no legislative force.
[4] Sixteenth-century French jurist, author of a *Syntagma Juris Universi*.
[5] 1537–1606; a councillor of the Paris Parlement and of great reputation as lawyer and antiquarian.
[6] His editions of the *Partidas* first appeared in 1555.
[7] 1474–1566. Was governor of San Domingo and in his writings attacked the cruelty of Spanish colonial administration.
[8] Spanish jurist, died 1598.
[9] Portuguese jurist, sixteenth century.
[10] 1583–1646; the great Dutch scholar, statesman and diplomatist.

resciditque. Alia autem omnino est ratio ipsius regni majoribus nostris habita. Nam cum sub Edwardo tertio in Ordinum consessu quaestio habebatur de donatione illa decantatissima Johannis regis facta Innocentio Papae[1] tertio et successoribus ejus unde Urbanus quintus tum annuum inde natum mille marcarum, Angliae et Hiberniae simul nomine, censum sibi tunc solvi petebat, tum regnum utrunque jure tantum beneficiario atque ut Sedis Romanae feudum a regibus nostris contendebat possideri; Ordines universi, idque tam generis hieratici (quod mirere) quam proceres seu Senatus Populusque in Comitiis illis[2], solenni inita deliberatione, responderunt unanimes irritam plane fuisse Johannis donationem illam, utpote tam sine Ordinum assensu quam juramento ejus inaugurali adversam. 'Et outer ceo' (sic loquuntur archiva) 'les Ducs, Countes, Barons, Grandes et Commens accorderent et granterent que en cas que le Pape se afforceroit ou rien attempteroit per proces ou en autre manere de fait de constreindre le roy ou ses subgitts de perfaire ce que est dit q'il voet claimer celle partie, q'ils resisterent et contresteront ove toute leur peussance.' Ita in sententia ipsa pronuncianda socii erant genus hieraticum; licet, ut vides, non in professione viribus omnimodis etiam repellendi vim artesque si quae usurparentur ad extorquendum heic pontificias. Si qua autem provisio de alienationibus regiis revocandis ejusmodi qualem memorat noster antecessisset, omnium regum Christianorum consensu munita, fierine potuisse existimandum, ut eam etiam in illustri hac decisione aut adhibendam noluissent aut omnino ignorassent? Nec minus, ut a nostro memoratur, ad alienationes praeteritas rescindendas quam futuras spectare videtur. Nec certe aliud sic censuere ordines illi sub Edwardo tertio, quam quale rex ipse Edwardus Primus in literis suis[3] ad Gregorium decimum eadem de re anno proximo ante illum cui tribuitur haec provisio conscriptis. Quale etiam eadem ipsa de re uti et de aliis ejusmodi in tam insignem Imperii diminutionem alienationibus citra Ordinum assensum factis, pronunciarunt Philippus Augustus Galliarum rex, ejusque proceres, cum Waloni legato pontificio Johannianam donationem illam frivolam nequitia pontificia extortam intra biennium a tempore quo facta est procacius obtendenti responsum[4] darent. Sed de his hactenus.

FINIS

[1] Matth. Paris anno 1214.   [2] Rot. Par. 40 Ed. III, num. 8.
[3] Rot. Claus. 3 Ed. I, mem. 9, in schedula. Et vide Coke Instit. part. 4, ol. 13.
[4] Matth. Paris ann. 1216 et videsis Arnisaeum de Donat. Constant. cap. 6.

King John's donation to the Papacy

But a contrary practice is also found among our ancestors. Thus in one of Edward III's parliaments a question arose about the famous donation by king John to Innocent III and his successors, whereby Urban V now demanded an annate of 1000 marks, on behalf of England and Ireland, claiming that both countries were held by our kings as fiefs of the Holy See. To this demand, all the Estates, including (marvellous to relate) the clergy, after mature deliberation, unanimously replied that John's donation was quite invalid as given without consent of parliament and contrary to his Coronation Oath. 'And moreover,' as we read in the public records, 'the dukes, earls, barons, grandees and commons resolve that, should the pope attempt by process or other method to force the king or his subjects to grant what he says is due from this country, then they will resist it with all their might.'

Clergy would not resist extortion

Thus the clergy, while concurring in the above decision, did not participate in the undertaking to repel by force the papal arts and machinations for extorting money from this country.

Repudiation of Donations

If, however, there had already been in existence any provision concerning the revocation of royal alienations, past and future, confirmed by the consent of all the Christian princes—such as our author asserts—is it conceivable that in making such a famous pronouncement as the one just given, parliament should not have cited it or should have been unaware of its existence? The decree, as our author notes, refers as much to the rescinding of past as of future alienations. Obviously on this point the parliament of Edward III was of the same mind as Edward I himself, as recorded in a letter[1] to pope Gregory X a year before the date to which the decree is assigned. As regards the harm done to the kingdom by alienations without the consent of the Estates, Philip Augustus king of France and his barons voiced the same opinion in their reply to the legate Walo[2] when the latter impudently produced, two years after making it, that iniquitous donation of John, obtained by papal trickery. So much for these matters.

THE END

---

[1] Calendar of Close Rolls, Edward I (1272–9), p. 197–8. In this Edward I asserts that 'he is bound by the oath taken at his coronation to preserve uninjured the rights of his realm and not to do anything touching the crown of the realm without consulting the Estates.'

[2] Guala Bicchieri. According to Matthew Paris (*Chronica Majora*, Rolls Series, II, 651), when Walo went to France in order to prevent a French invasion of England (on the ground that it was a papal fief), Philip asserted: 'Angliae patrimonium Petri numquam fuit, nec est, nec erit...item nullus rex vel princeps potest dare regnum suum sine assensu baronum suorum.'

INDEX

(*The references are to the pages of the Introduction and Translation*)

Abingdon, the learned monks of, 129
Accursius, 31, 33 and n. 1, 127, 159
Accursius, Francis, in England, 143–5 and 145 n. 1
Acton, John of, 147, 155
Admiralty, court of, 155, 163 and n. 2, lviii n. 1
Adrian IV, pope, 95
Agathias, 65
Aistulf, 65
Alaric the Wisigoth (484–507), 61–63; see also under *Breviary*
Alciati, Andrea (1492–1550), xxv
Alexander III, pope, 121, 133, 135, 167
Alemannus, Nicolas, 65
Alphonsines, the, 191 and n. 2
Alfwinus of Sutton, 129
Alienations, royal, 189–197
Amalfi, sack of, 91
Amaya, Francis, 37
Andrew II, king of Hungary, 191 and n. 1
Anesty, Richard of, 135
Anianus, 61, 65
Ansegisus, abbot of Fontenelles, 75 and n. 4
Anselm of Lucca, 77, 89 and n. 2
Anselm, saint and archbishop, 123
Ataulphus, 63
Attaints, in English law, 179–181
Attaleiates, 67 and n. 4
Augustinus, Antonius, 7, 37 and n. 4
Azevedo, Alfonso de, 99, 195 and n. 8
Azo, 33 and n. 4, 117, 119, 121, 159, 191, xxvi

Bacon, Francis, Lord Verulam, li
Bacon, Roger, Franciscan, 129, 147
Baker, Sir John, 149
Balbus, John, see Janua, John of
Balduinus, Jacobus, 117
Baldus, glossator, 193 and n. 5
Balliol, John, 169
Balsamon, Greek jurist, 67 and n. 6
Bandinus, jurist, 117
Baronius, 59 and n. 4
Bartolus, 99 and n. 9, 193
Bassianus, see Caracalla
Bassianus, John, jurist, 117, 119, 159
Baudouin, Francis, 93 and n. 6, xxv
Beauforts, legitimation of the, 169

Bec, Thomas, archdeacon of Dorset, 11
Bec, abbey of, 109, 111, 113–115, xxviii
Bec, Roger of, see Roger of Bec
Bede, 53
Begyngham, Elys of, 189
Belluga, Peter, 193 and n. 7
Bernard of Compostella, 121
Bernard of Pavia, xxxviii
Blois, Peter of, 135, 137
Bocer, Henry, 193 and n. 11
Bodewell, Dr, Dean of Arches, lviii
Bodin, John, 99, 195 and n. 2
Bologna, legal revival at, 89–95, xxx–xxxvi; cession of, 191; see also under Irnerius
Boniface, archbishop of Mainz, 75 and n. 1, 85
Boniface, duke of Tuscany, 71
Boniface VIII, pope, see *Liber Sext*.
Bracton, Henry of, 5; variations in his name, 11; relationship to *Britton*, 11; arrangements of chapters, 17; on Donations, 21–23, xxxvi–xxxvii; and the Lex Regia, 25–29, xxxvii; and Oxford, 31; and the English constitution, 31, 39; and royal donations, 191; and canon law, xxxviii; and customary law, xxxix; and villeinage, xl; and Vacarius, xli
Brampton, William, English judge, 187
Bretoun, John, bishop of Hereford, 13
Breviary of Alaric, 61–65
Brisson, Barnabé, 37 and n. 4
Britton, relationship to Bracton, 11; supposed authorship of, 13; suggested derivation of name, 15; compiled by royal command, 19
Brothers, the Imperial, 57 and n. 4, 137
Bucer, Martin, xlix
Bulgarus, 33 and n. 5
Burchard, bishop of Worms, 7 and n. 5, 83

Cabedo, George, 195 and n. 9
Caesar, Julius, 45, 55 and n. 1
Caesar, Sir Julius, lvii

INDEX

Calvisius, German astronomer, 59 and n. 5
Canon law, see Law, Canon
Caracalla, emperor, 49
Carpzovius, Benedict, 41 and n. 1
Casas, Bartholomew de las, 195 and n. 7
Cassiodorus, 61, 69 and n. 5, xxxi
Cassius, Dio, 15, 37, 49
Castaldus, Restaurus, 193 and n. 8
Cecil, Robert, xxxvii
Châlons, Hugh of, canonist, 81 and n. 3
Chancery, and foreign jurisdictions, l–li
Charisius, Arcadius, 37 and n. 3
Charlemagne, xxxi
Charondas, Louis, 37 and n. 4
Chartres, Ivo of, see Ivo
Chivalry, court of, 155 and n. 4, 163 and n. 2, lviii n. 2
Chronicle, the Anglo-Saxon, 53–55
Choppin, René, 99, 195 and n. 5
Cicero, 187
Cindaswintha, 71 and n. 1
Cironius, Innocent, 7, 63, 95 and n. 1
Civil law, see Law, Civil
Cleric and *clergy*, the names, 175–7
Clerks, functions of, 177
Coke, 157, xliii, liv
Colchester, Roman settlement, 45
'Colchester penny,' 153 and n. 4
Collevacino, Pietro, canonist, 101 n. 4
Common law, English, see Law, Common
Conant, Francis, 37 and n. 4
Conrad of Ursperg, references to Irnerius, 93
Conrat (Cohn), Max, xxxv n. 2
Constable, court of, see Chivalry, court of
Constantine, emperor, 35; Donation of, 75–79; clerical use of the Donation, 79–81; authorities on, 195; Selden's account of, xxx; see also Malmesbury, William of
Contius, French jurist, 59 and n. 2
Coras, John, French jurist, 37 and n. 4
Corippus (Africanus), 67 and n. 9
Cormerius, Thomas, French jurist, 195 n. 3
Cosin, Richard, liv–lv
Costa, John, French jurist, 71 and n. 3
Cotta, Catellianus, Italian jurist, 117 and n. 1
Cotton, Sir Robert, xxx
Cowell, John, lx–lxi

Cromwell, Thomas, xxxvii
Cujas, Jacques, 39, 47, 57, 63, xxv

Damiani, Peter, xxxii
Decianus, Tiberius, Venetian scholar, 93 and n. 5
Decretals, Gregorian, 7 and n. 4, 191 and n. 1
Delegates, court of, 155 and n. 5
Devonius (Denom), 153
D'Ewes, Sir Symonds, xxi
Diceto, Ralph de, 123
Digests, transcription of, in mediaeval England, 29; the Florentine edition of, 23, 25 and n. 1
Dinus, 121
Dio Cassius, see Cassius
Dionysius of Halicarnassus, 37 and n. 1
Diplomacy, in relation to civil law, 157 and n. 1, lxiii
'Dispensation for Study,' example of, 147–9 and 149 n. 3
Dominicy, Mark Antony, 71 and n. 2
Donations in English Law, 21–23, xxxvi–xxxvii
Donations, royal, see Alienations
Duchesne, his edition of the *Gesta Normannorum*, xxviii
Durand, French jurist, 159, 193 and n. 6
Dyer, Sir James (1512–1582), 157

Edward I, and official law books, 17–19; and Francis Accursius, 143–5 and 145 n. 1; and the Scottish Succession, 169; his judicial inquisition of 1288, 187; and royal donations or alienations, 195
Edward II, see under Year Books and Notaries
Edward III, decline of Roman Law influence in reign of, 157–161; and English independence, 197
Ellesmere, Lord Chancellor, li
Epochs, conception of, 9 and n. 1
Equity and the common law, l–li; and canon law, l n. 6
Ethelwerd, 43
Eugenius II, pope, 101 and n. 4
Eugenius III, pope, 101 n. 4
Eusebius, bishop of Caesarea, 77
Eynsham, vision of the monk of, 139 and n. 3

Fabrot, Annibale, French jurist, 7
Ferettus, Julius, 99 and n. 10
Fet Assavoir, 3 and n. 3
Fichard, John, 95 and n. 3

INDEX

Fitting, Hermann, xxxii, xxxiv
Flach, E., xxxiv
Flambard, Ralph, 131
Fleet prison, 187, xxiii
Fleta, faults of the 1647 edition, 3; relationship to Bracton and Thornton, 9; on Donations, 21; date of compilation and authorship, chapter x *passim*, and xxiii; on Convictions or Attaints, 179; on royal alienations, 189–195; see also Editor's Preface for list of the printed editions
Flete, William, 185
Fleury, Haymo of, 107
Florilegus (Matthew of Westminster), 13 and n. 3, 15 and n. 4, 123, 131
Florus, 15 and n. 3
Fortescue, Sir John, 171 and n. 2, 193
Forster, Valentine, 61, 95 n. 2
Fradinus, Constantine, 111
Francheville, Mabel of, 135
Freymon, Wolfgang, 59 and n. 3, 93 n. 7, 115

Gaius, 7, 49 n. 2, 55, 63
Gaunt, John of, legitimation of his children, 169 and n. 2
Gentili, Alberic, lx
Gervase of Dover, 123
Gervase of Tilbury, 139
Gesner, Conrad, 121 and n. 1
Geta, son of emperor Severus, 47, 49
Giraldus Cambrensis, 137
Glanvil, Ranulph de, 5, 141, 183, xlv
Glosses, mediaeval, xxxiii
Gobler, Justin, 119 and n. 3
Goldast, Melchior, 99, xxvi
Goudy, Prof. H., xxxix
Grassaille, Charles of, 99 and n. 6
Gratian, 7, 63, 77, 81, 101 and nn. 4, 5
Gregorian Code, 57
Gregorian Decretals, see Decretals
Gregory, Peter, of Toulouse, 37, 195 and n. 4
Gregory X, Pope, 191, 197
Grosseteste, bishop of Lincoln, 167–9
Grotius, Hugo, 195 and n. 10
Gruter, Janus, 37 and n. 4

Harmenopulus, 67 and n. 3
Hengham, Ranulph de, 5 and n. 4, 189, xxiii
Henley, Walter of, 5 n. 7, xxiii
Henry IV of France, Code of, 195 and n. 3

Henry V, emperor, 89
Henry VIII of England and Roman Law, xlvii–lx
Herluin, St, founder of Bec, 115
Hermogenian Code, 57, 59, 61, 71
Hervey of Stanton, 153
Higden, Ralph, 115
High Commission, court of, liii–lv
Hincmar of Rheims, 81 and n. 1, 87
Honorius III, pope, 89; interdict of, 99, 133 and n. 2, 191
Horn, Andrew, 5, xxvi
Horne, Robert (1519–1580), bishop of Winchester, xlviii
Hostiensis (Henry of Susa), 31, 33 and n. 2, 159
Hotman, Francis, 36 and n. 4, 195
Hugh of Châlons, see Châlons
Hugolinus, 117

Ignoramus, xlviii
Innocent II, pope, 101
Irnerius, 89–95, 117, xxxi–xxxiii
Isernia, Andrew of, 99 and n. 8
Isidore of Seville, 71 and n. 4, 85
Ivo of Chartres, 7 and n. 6, 63, 77; his *Pannormia*, 81 and n. 2, 85, 87, 89; his studies at Bec, 113

Jacobus, Bolognese jurist, 117
James I of England and the Common Lawyers, xlviii
Janua, John Balbus of, 125 and n. 6
John, king, his Donation to the Papacy, 197
John VIII, pope, 85
John Bassianus, see Bassianus
Judges, oath of, 173
Julian (the Apostate), 59
Justinian, the Corpus Juris, 7; its promulgation, 65–67; its force in the West, 69 and n. 1, 83–85; introduced into England, 109; supposed derivation of the name, 127
Justinus, 15 and n. 2
Justus, Papirius, 57 and n. 5, 137 and n. 3

Klausenberg, archbishop of, 191 n. 1

Lanfranc, archbishop, 123, xxxii
Langtoft, Peter of, 187–9
Law, historical importance of change in, 7–9
Law, Canon, 81–83, 85–87, 101–3; influence of, on Bracton, xxxviii; its influence on legal maxims, xlv–xlvi; and English equity, l n. 6; see also under Gratian and Papacy

202 INDEX

Law, Civil, in Bracton, Thornton and *Fleta*, 25–35; sense in which England 'received' the civil law, 39 and n. 1; revival of, at Bologna, 89–95; in mediaeval England, 105–117; cited in an English suit, 135–7; teaching of, in England, 139–141; in the Year Books, 149–153; cessation of its influence, 157–161; of no force in English government, 161–3; English aversion from, 163–171; influence of, on Bracton, § II of Introduction; influence of, on English constitutional history, § III of Introduction

Law, Common, English reverence for, 163–9, 171–3; and equity, l–li

Law, Feudal, revival of, in Tudor times, l and n. 2

Law, Maritime, 155, 171 and n. 4

Law, Roman, in Roman Britain, see chapter IV *passim*

Legitimation, 'per subsequens matrimonium,' 165–9, 167 n. 5

Leibnitz and Roman Law, 99 n. 1, lxiii

Leo IV, pope, 69

Lethard, abbot of Bec, 143

Lex Hortensia, 31–33

Lex Regia, in English law, 25–29; confusion of, with Lex Hortensia, 31–33; correct interpretation of, 35; formulated for Vespasian, 37; not applicable to English constitution, 39; must be interpreted strictly, 41; supposed use of, by English kings, 171 and n. 2; as applied by Henry VIII, lix; in Sweden and Denmark, lxiii

Lex Remnia, 37

Lex Terrae, 141, 173

Liber Sext., of Boniface VIII, xlv

Lilburne, John, lxi n. 4

Lincoln's Inn Library and Selden's MSS., xxii, xxiii

Lindenbrog, 75, xxv

Littleton (Sir Thomas, 1402–1481), 157

Livy, 15, 35

London, teaching of civil law in, 143

Longchamp, William of, xl

Lopez, Gregory, 99, 195 and n. 6

Lothair I, emperor, 69, 71 and n. 5

Lothair II, emperor, 91 and n. 4, 95

Lovetot, John, 187

Lucan, 55

Lucius II, pope, 97

Lucy, Richard de, 169

Lyndwood, William of, 155

Lyons, General Council at (1274), 193

Maecianus, Volutius, 63 and n. 2

'Magister,' use of, in mediaeval Latin, 125 and n. 5

Magna Carta, 173, 185

Maine, Sir Henry, xxvi

Maitland, Frederick William, xxiv, xxvi, xlvi, xlix; see also under Year Books

Malmesbury, William of, his MS. of the *Breviary*, 77 and n. 2, 107–109, xxiii–xxiv

Manilius, 3

Manuscripts, used by Selden, xxi–xxiv and xxii n. 4

Mapes, Walter, 141

Marcellus, emperor, 59

Marches, council of the, lv–lvi

Marculph, 69 and n. 4

Mariotellus, Fulvius, 119 and n. 2

Maritime law, see Law, Maritime

Martinus, 31, 33 and n. 5, 117

Matilda, countess of Tuscany, 71, 73 and n. 2, 93

Matilda, empress, 131

Matthew Paris, 125, 131, 139 n. 3, 171, 197 n. 2

Matthew of Westminster, see Florilegus

Maxims, legal, in the Year Books, 153, xlii; importance of, in English law, xliii–xlvi

Melanchthon, Philip, xlix

Merton, parliament of, 165–7

Merula, Paul, 93 and n. 8

Metianus, see Maecianus

Metingham, John of, 189

Metz, Gautier de, 175 and n. 1

Milton, John, and Bracton, xxxvii

Modestinus, 59

Molfesius, Andrew, 99 and n. 8

Montanus, Horace, 193 and n. 12

Montpellier, Roman law at, 95, 121; supposed conference of Christian princes at, 189–191

Muretus (Marc Antoine Muret, 1526–1585), xxv

Muta, Marius, 99 and n. 8

Niger, Gerard, 97

Non Obstante clause, lix

Notaries, appointed by the emperor, 169 and n. 5

Noy, Edward, xliii, l

Odo of Cluny, 87

INDEX

Odofred, 31, 33 and n. 3; his evidence regarding Irnerius, 89–91, xxxi–xxxv; 117 and n. 2, 151, 159
Oleron, maritime laws of, 43 and n. 3, 97, 155, 171 and n. 4
Orléans, teaching of Roman law at, 133 n. 2, xxv, xxxiii–xxxiv
Orto, Obertus de, 97
Otto IV, emperor, 139
Otto, jurist, 117
Otto and Ottoboni, constitutions of, 143 and n. 5
Owen, George of Henllys, lvi
Oxford, earldom of, 131 and n. 7; teaching of civil law at, 111 n. 3, 115; a dispensation for study at, 149 and n. 3

Panzirol, Guy, 95 and n. 4, 119, 145, xxv, xxxi
Papacy, and canon law, 85, 101–3; and civil law, 99–101, 132–3 and 133 n. 2
Papinian, 47, 49, 55, 59
Papinianists, 49 and n. 2
Papirius Justus, see Justus, Papirius
Paratitles, 117 and n. 5
Paris, teaching of Roman law at, 133 n. 2, xxv
Partidas of Alfonso the Wise, 99 and n. 2
Peckham, archbishop, 147
Pepo, 89–91, xxxii
Peter the Lombard, 95
Philip Augustus, 197
Philipps, Fabian, xxxvii n. 6, lxiv–lxv
Photius, 67 and n. 5
Pisa, Hugh of, 125 and n. 7
Pisan MS., 91 and n. 5, xxx
Pistensian Edict of Charles the Bald, 73 and n. 3
Pithou, Peter and Francis, xxv
Placentinus, 115, 117, 119, 121
Plowden, Edmund (1518–1585), 157
Pole, cardinal, xlvii
Pompeius, Trogus, 15
Possevino, Antonio, 57 and n. 3
'Princeps legibus solutus,' the maxim, lxi n. 3
Procopius, 53, 65
Prynne, William, xxxvii and n. 6, lix n. 4
Psellus, 67 and n. 8
Pullein, Robert, 95 and n. 7
Pyleus, 117

Raleigh, Walter of, 167
Ranchin, William, 99 and n. 6
Rançonet, Eymeric, 63 and n. 9

Ravenna, law teaching at, xxxi–xxxiii
Raymond of Peñaforte, 111 and n. 6
Rebuffy, Jacques, 99 and n. 6, xxv
'Reception' of Roman law in England, definition of term, 39 and n. 1; in 12th century Europe, 97–9; see also Introduction, § III
Regiam Majestatem, 183
Rembolt, Berthold, 111
Requests, court of, lvi–lvii
Rhodes, maritime laws of, 43, 97
Richard I and maritime law, 171 and n. 4
Richard II and civil law, 171 and nn. 1, 2
Roger of Bec (confused by Selden with Vacarius), 111; his activities at Bec, 113, xxviii–xxix; elected archbishop of Canterbury, 121–5; see also xxvii
Roger the jurist (confused by Selden with Vacarius), 115–121; his *Summa*, 121 n. 2; see also xxvii–xxviii
Roger of Wendover, 125
Rome, law teaching at, xxxi
Ruzé, Arnoul, 193

Sachenspiegel, xl
Sackville, William of, 135
Salisbury, John of, 109, 111, 133–5, 171, 173
Savaro, John, 63 and n. 4
Savigny, xxxv
Scaevola, 55, 59
Scotland, Roman law in, 101; the succession question and John Balliol, 169
Selden, John, his share in the 1647 edition of *Fleta*, 3; his reason for undertaking the *Dissertatio*, 3; his main purpose in writing the *Dissertatio*, 41; his hope of writing more fully on the Donation of Constantine, 81; the contents of the *Dissertatio*, xix–xx; his MS. sources, xxi–xxiv; his MSS. that cannot be traced, xxii and n. 4; his printed sources, xxiv–xxvi; his injustice to Bracton, xxvi; his mistakes in regard to Vacarius, xxvii–xxix; his faults of style, xxix; his excellencies, xxix–xxx; general correctness of his treatment of the Bolognese revival, xxxv; his superficial treatment of Bracton, xxxvi–xxxvii; contrast with F. W. Maitland, xlvi; his supposed attitude to the skit *Ignoramus*, xlviii; justification for his closing his account

INDEX

of Roman law influence at the reign of Edward III, lxv; his protest in parliament against civil law analogies, lxv–lxvi; the *Dissertatio* not merely academic, lxvi
Seronatus, 63
Severus, emperor, 47–51
Shareshull, chief justice, 159
Sichard, John, 57 and n. 6, xxv
Sidonius Apollinaris, 63 and n. 5
Sigonius, Carolus, 59 and n. 1, 73 and n. 1, 91, 93, 97, xxxi
Sirmond, Jacques, 77 and n. 5, 81
Sixtinus, Regner, 193 and n. 10
Skipwith, sergeant, 159
Sozomen, Hermias, 77
Spartian, 49
Speculator, see Durand
Star Chamber, court of, li–liii
Starkey, Thomas (1499–1538), xlvii
Stephen, king, and Roman law, 109, 111, 127–9, 135
Strafford, Henry Lord, lx
Stratton, Adam, 187
Suarez, Francis, 101 and n. 1
Super Speculam, the bull, 133 n. 2
Susa, Henry of, see Hostiensis

Tacitus, 45, 51
Tapia, Charles, 99 and n. 8
Templars, 183
Temple, Inner, and Selden's MSS., xxii; see also Year Books
Tertulla, Flavia, 137
Theobald, archbishop, 109, 127
Theodoric the Ostrogoth (455–526), 61, 67 and n. 10
Theodoric the Wisigoth (420–451), 63 and n. 8
Theodosian Code, 7; date of its promulgation, 57; its contents and sanction, 59; and the *Breviary*, 61–63; its use in western Europe, 67; not displaced by that of Justinian, 69; use of, in Carolingian times, 73–75; and the Donation of Constantine, 75–79; cited by the clergy, 87–9
Thornton, Gilbert, 5; his *Summa*, 9, 15–19; civil law references, 21; and the Lex Regia, 29, 39; the MS. of, xxii–xxiii
Tillet, Jean du, xxv
Tocco, Charles, 71 and n. 7

Torelli brothers, 25 n. 1, xxv
Torigny, Robert of, his references to Roger of Bec, 113 and n. 1, 123, xxviii
Torre, case of the abbot of, 157–161
Tribonian, 7
Tudors and Roman law, li–lx

Ulpian, 7, 27, 35, 39, 41, 49, 51, 59, 63, xxv
Universities, Roman law at, see under Bologna, Montpellier, Orléans, Oxford, Paris
University courts, 157
Ursinus, Fulvius, 37 and n. 4
Ursperg, see Conrad of Ursperg

Vacarius, John of Salisbury's reference, 109, 111; confused with Roger of Bec, 111–113; confused with Roger the Jurist, 115–121; mentioned in a papal rescript, 121; his *Summa*, 121 n. 2; suggested derivation of his name, 125; see also xxvii–xxviii, xli
Valentinian, emperor, 77, 79
Vere, Aubrey de, 131
Vespasian and the Lex Regia, 37
Vico, xxxiv, lxiii
Viglius of Zuichem, xxv
Vitalis, Ordericus, 101

Walo, legate, 197
Walter, Hubert, 141
Wendover, Roger of, see Roger of Wendover
Weyland, Thomas, 187
Winchedon, Richard of, 149, 151, xxiv
Winchester, Henry of, 109 n. 4, 127
Wiseman, Sir Robert, lxii
Withernams 17
Wykes, Thomas, 95 and n. 6

Xiphilinus, 15 and n. 1

Year Books of Edward I, 9, 153, xlii; of Edward II, 149–155, 163, xlii; Inner Temple MS. of, 149, xxii–xxiv; Lincoln's Inn MS., 151

Zonaras, 67 n. 7
Zosimus, 53
Zouche, lxiii